Prophets and Kings

Ellen G. White

Edition Copyright © 2022 by 118 Publishing

All rights reserved.

No portion of this book may be reproduced in any form without written permission from the publisher or author, except as permitted by U.S. copyright law.

Contents

1. Solomon — 1
2. The Temple and Its Dedication — 6
3. Pride of Prosperity — 13
4. Results of Transgression — 18
5. Solomon's Repentance — 25
6. The Rending of the Kingdom — 31
7. Jeroboam — 37
8. National Apostasy — 41
9. Elijah the Tishbite — 45
10. The Voice of Stern Rebuke — 49
11. Carmel — 56
12. From Jezreel to Horeb — 61
13. "What Doest Thou Here?" — 66
14. "In the Spirit and Power of Elias" — 71
15. Jehoshaphat — 77
16. The Fall of the House of Ahab — 83
17. The Call of Elisha — 89
18. The Healing of the Waters — 95
19. A Prophet of Peace — 98
20. Naaman — 102

21.	Elisha's Closing Ministry	106
22.	"Nineveh, That Great City"	111
23.	The Assyrian Captivity	118
24.	"Destroyed for Lack of Knowledge"	124
25.	The Call of Isaiah	128
26.	"Behold Your God!"	132
27.	Ahaz	137
28.	Hezekiah	141
29.	The Ambassadors From Babylon	145
30.	Deliverance From Assyria	149
31.	Hope for the Heathen	157
32.	Manasseh and Josiah	163
33.	The Book of the Law	168
34.	Jeremiah	174
35.	Approaching Doom	181
36.	The Last King of Judah	189
37.	Carried Captive Into Babylon	195
38.	Light Through Darkness	201
39.	In the Court of Babylon	207
40.	Nebuchadnezzar's Dream	213
41.	The Fiery Furnace	218
42.	True Greatness	223
43.	The Unseen Watcher	227
44.	In the Lions' Den	234
45.	The Return of the Exiles	239
46.	"The Prophets of God Helping Them"	246
47.	Joshua and the Angel	253

48.	"Not by Might, nor by Power"	258
49.	In the Days of Queen Esther	261
50.	Ezra, the Priest and Scribe	265
51.	A Spiritual Revival	270
52.	A Man of Opportunity	275
53.	The Builders on the Wall	278
54.	A Rebuke Against Extortion	283
55.	Heathen Plots	287
56.	Instructed in the Law of God	291
57.	Reformation	294
58.	The Coming of a Deliverer	299
59.	"The House of Israel"	309
60.	Visions of Future Glory	318

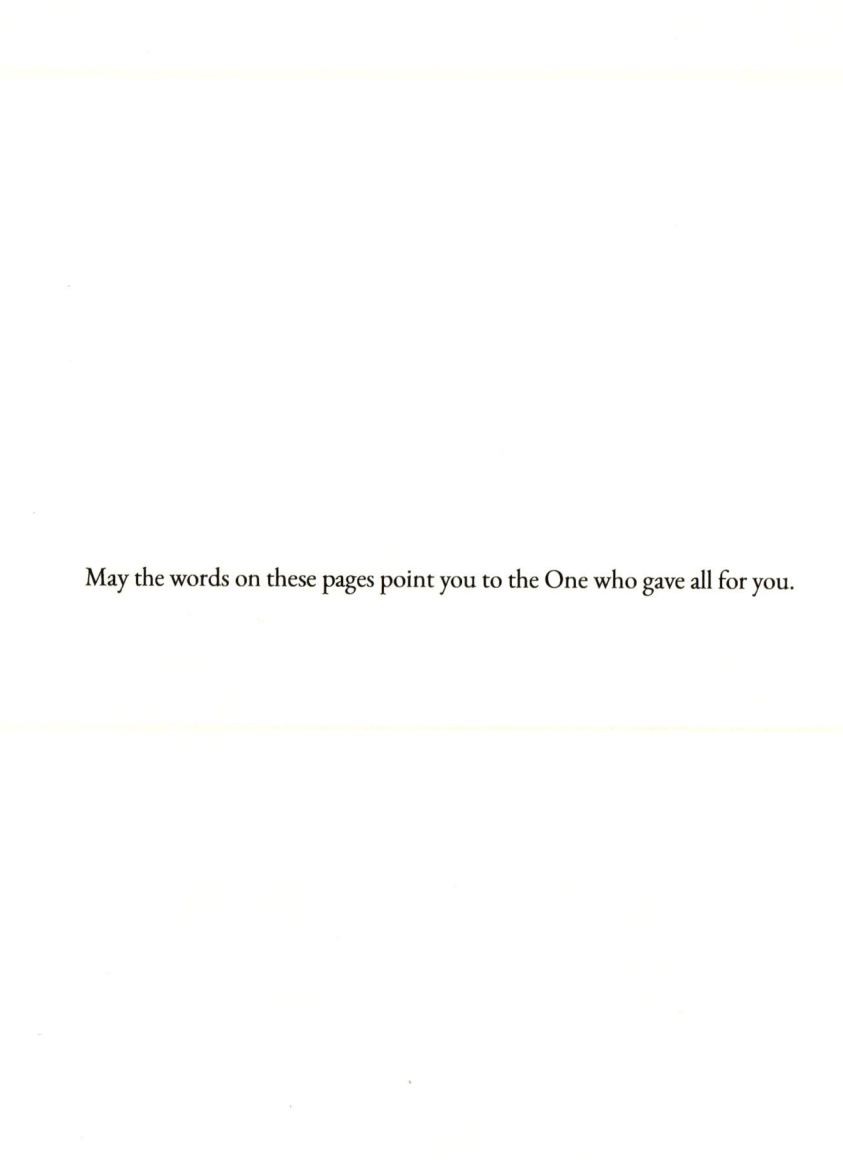

May the words on these pages point you to the One who gave all for you.

[x] indicates the page number of the original publication

Chapter 1

Solomon

Beginning of Section 1 — From Strength to Weakness

In the reign of David and Solomon, Israel became strong among the nations and had many opportunities to wield a mighty influence in behalf of truth and the right. The name of Jehovah was exalted and held in honor, and the purpose for which the Israelites had been established in the Land of Promise bade fair of meeting with fulfillment. Barriers were broken down, and seekers after truth from the lands of the heathen were not turned away unsatisfied. Conversions took place, and the church of God on earth was enlarged and prospered.

Solomon was anointed and proclaimed king in the closing years of his father David, who abdicated in his favor. His early life was bright with promise, and it was God's purpose that he should go on from strength to strength, from glory to glory, ever approaching nearer the similitude of the character of God, and thus inspiring His people to fulfill their sacred trust as the depositaries of divine truth. [26]

David knew that God's high purpose for Israel could be met only as rulers and people should seek with unceasing vigilance to attain to the standard placed before them. He knew that in order for his son Solomon to fulfill the trust with which God was pleased to honor him, the youthful ruler must be not merely a warrior, a statesman, and a sovereign, but a strong, good man, a teacher of righteousness, an example of fidelity.

With tender earnestness David entreated Solomon to be manly and noble, to show mercy and loving-kindness to his subjects, and in all his dealings with the nations of earth to honor and glorify the name of God and to make manifest the beauty of holiness. The many trying and remarkable experiences through which David had passed during his lifetime had taught him the value of the nobler virtues and led him to declare in his dying charge to Solomon: "He that ruleth over men must be just, ruling in the fear of God. And he shall be as the light of the morning, when the sun riseth, even a morning without clouds; as the tender grass springing out of the earth by clear shining after rain." 2 Samuel 23:3, 4.

Oh, what an opportunity was Solomon's! Should he follow the divinely inspired instruction of his father, his reign would be a reign of righteousness, like that described in the seventy-second psalm:

"Give the king Thy judgments, O God, And Thy righteousness unto the king's son. He shall judge Thy people with righteousness, And Thy poor with judgment.... He shall come down like rain upon the mown grass: As showers that water the earth. [27]

In his days shall the righteous flourish; And abundance of peace so long as the moon endureth. He shall have dominion also from sea to sea, And from the river unto the ends of the earth.... The kings of Tarshish and of the isles shall bring presents: The kings of Sheba and Seba shall offer gifts. Yea, all kings shall fall down before him: All nations shall serve him. For he shall deliver the needy when he crieth; The poor also, and him that hath no helper.... Prayer also shall be made for him continually; And daily shall he be praised.... His name shall endure forever: His name shall be continued as long as the sun: And men shall be blessed in him: All nations shall call him blessed.

"Blessed be the Lord God, the God of Israel, Who only doeth wondrous things. And blessed be His glorious name forever: And let the whole earth be filled with His glory; Amen, and Amen."

In his youth Solomon made David's choice his own, and for many years he walked uprightly, his life marked with strict obedience to God's commands. Early in his reign he went with his counselors of state to Gibeon, where the tabernacle that had been built in the wilderness still was, and there he united with his chosen advisers, "the captains of thousands and of hundreds," "the judges," and "every governor in all Israel, the chief of the fathers," in offering sacrifices to God and in consecrating themselves fully to the Lord's service. 2 Chronicles 1:2. Comprehending something of the magnitude of the duties connected with the kingly office, Solomon knew that those bearing heavy burdens must [28] seek the Source of Wisdom for guidance, if they would fulfill their responsibilities acceptably. This led him to encourage his counselors to unite with him heartily in making sure of their acceptance with God.

Above every earthly good, the king desired wisdom and understanding for the accomplishment of the work God had given him to do. He longed for quickness of mind, for largeness of heart, for tenderness of spirit. That night the Lord appeared to Solomon in a dream and said, "Ask what I shall give thee." In his answer the young and inexperienced ruler gave utterance to his feeling of helplessness and his desire for aid. "Thou hast showed unto Thy servant David my father great mercy," he said, "according as he walked before Thee in truth, and in righteousness, and in uprightness of heart with Thee; and Thou hast kept for him this great kindness, that Thou hast given him a son to sit on his throne, as it is this day.

"And now, O Lord my God, Thou hast made Thy servant king instead of David my father: and I am but a little child: I know not how to go out or come in. And Thy servant is in the midst of Thy people which Thou hast chosen, a great people, that cannot be numbered nor counted for multitude. Give therefore Thy servant an understanding heart to judge Thy people, that I may discern between good and bad: for who is able to judge this Thy so great a people?

"And the speech pleased the Lord, that Solomon had asked this thing."

"Because this was in thine heart," God said to Solomon, "and thou hast not asked riches, wealth, or honor, nor the life of thine enemies, neither yet hast asked long life; but hast asked wisdom and knowledge for thyself, that thou mayest [29] judge My people," "behold, I have done according to thy words: lo, I have given thee a wise and an understanding heart; so that there was none like thee before thee, neither after thee shall any arise like unto thee. And I have also given thee that which thou hast not asked, both riches, and honor," "such as none of the kings have had that have been before thee, neither shall there any after thee have the like."

"And if thou wilt walk in My ways, to keep My statutes and My commandments, as thy father David did walk, then I will lengthen thy days." 1 Kings 3:5-14; 2 Chronicles 1:7-12. [30]

God promised that as He had been with David, so He would be with Solomon. If the king would walk before the Lord in uprightness, if he would do what God had commanded him, his throne would be established and his reign would be the means of exalting Israel as "a wise and understanding people," the light of the surrounding nations. Deuteronomy 4:6.

The language used by Solomon while praying to God before the ancient altar at Gibeon reveals his humility and his strong desire to honor God. He realized that without divine aid he was as helpless as a little child to fulfill the responsibilities resting on him. He knew that he lacked discernment, and it was a sense of his great need that led him to seek God for wisdom. In his heart there was no selfish aspirations for a knowledge that would exalt him above others. He desired to discharge faithfully the duties devolving upon him, and he chose the gift that would be the means of causing his reign to bring glory to God. Solomon was never so rich or so wise or so truly great as when he confessed, "I am but a little child: I know not how to go out or come in."

Those who today occupy positions of trust should seek to learn the lesson taught by Solomon's prayer. The higher the position a man occupies, the greater the responsibility that he has to bear, the wider will be the influence that he exerts and the greater his need of dependence on God. Ever should he remember that with the call to work comes the call to walk circumspectly before his fellow men. He is to stand before God in the attitude of a learner. Position does not give holiness of character. It is by honoring God and [31] obeying His commands that a man is made truly great.

The God whom we serve is no respecter of persons. He who gave to Solomon the spirit of wise discernment is willing to impart the same blessing to His children today. "If any of you lack wisdom," His word declares, "let him ask of God, that giveth to all men liberally, and upbraideth not; and it shall be given him." James 1:5. When a burden bearer desires wisdom more than he desires wealth, power, or fame, he will not be disappointed. Such a one will learn from the Great Teacher not only what to do, but how to do it in a way that will meet with the divine approval.

So long as he remains consecrated, the man whom God has endowed with discernment and ability will not manifest an eagerness for high position, neither will he seek to rule or control. Of necessity men must bear responsibilities; but instead of striving for the supremacy, he who is a true leader will pray for an understanding heart, to discern between good and evil.

The path of men who are placed as leaders is not an easy one. But they are to see in every difficulty a call to prayer. Never are they to fail of consulting the great Source of all wisdom. Strengthened and enlightened by the Master Worker, they will be enabled to stand firm against unholy influences and to discern right from wrong, good from evil. They will approve that which God approves, and will strive earnestly against the introduction of wrong principles into His cause.

The wisdom that Solomon desired above riches, honor, or long life, God gave him. His petition for a quick mind, a large heart, and a tender spirit was granted. "God gave [32] Solomon wisdom and understanding exceeding much, and largeness of heart, even as the sand that is on the seashore. And Solomon's wisdom excelled the wisdom of all the children of the east country, and all the wisdom of Egypt. For he was wiser than all men; ... and his fame was in all nations round about." 1 Kings 4:29-31.

"And all Israel ... feared the king: for they saw that the wisdom of God was in him, to do judgment." 1 Kings 3:28. The hearts of the people were turned toward Solomon, as they had been toward David, and they obeyed him in all things. "Solomon ... was strengthened in his kingdom, and the Lord his God was with him, and magnified him exceedingly." 2 Chronicles 1:1.

For many years Solomon's life was marked with devotion to God, with uprightness and firm principle, and with strict obedience to God's commands. He directed in every important enterprise and managed wisely the business matters connected with the kingdom. His wealth and wisdom, the magnificent buildings and public works that he constructed during the early years of his reign, the energy, piety, justice, and magnanimity that he revealed in word and deed, won the loyalty of his subjects and the admiration and homage of the rulers of many lands.

The name of Jehovah was greatly honored during the first part of Solomon's reign. The wisdom and righteousness revealed by the king bore witness to all nations of the excellency of the attributes of the God whom he served. For a time Israel was as the light of the world, showing forth the greatness of Jehovah. Not in the surpassing wisdom, the fabulous riches, the far-reaching power and fame that were [33] his, lay the real glory of Solomon's early reign; but in the honor that he brought to the name of the God of Israel through a wise use of the gifts of Heaven.

As the years went by and Solomon's fame increased, he sought to honor God by adding to his mental and spiritual strength, and by continuing to impart to others the blessings he received. None understood better than he that it was through the favor of Jehovah that he had come into possession of power and wisdom and understanding, and that these gifts were bestowed that he might give to the world a knowledge of the King of kings.

Solomon took an especial interest in natural history, but his researches were not confined to any one branch of learning. Through a diligent study of all created things, both animate and inanimate, he gained a clear conception of the Creator. In the forces of nature, in the mineral and the animal world, and in every tree and shrub and flower, he saw a revelation of God's wisdom; and as he sought to learn more and more, his knowledge of God and his love for Him constantly increased.

Solomon's divinely inspired wisdom found expression in songs of praise and in many proverbs. "He spake three thousand proverbs: and his songs were a thousand and five. And he spake of trees, from the cedar tree that is in Lebanon even unto the hyssop that springeth out of the wall: he spake also of beasts, and of fowl, and of creeping things, and of fishes." 1 Kings 4:32, 33.

In the proverbs of Solomon are outlined principles of holy living and high endeavor, principles that are heaven-born and that lead to godliness, principles that should govern [34] every act of life. It was the wide dissemination of these principles, and the recognition of God as the One to whom all praise and honor belong, that made Solomon's early reign a time of moral uplift as well as of material prosperity.

"Happy is the man that findeth wisdom," he wrote, "and the man that getteth understanding. For the merchandise of it is better than the merchandise of silver, and the gain thereof than fine gold. She is more precious than rubies: and all things thou canst desire are not to be compared unto her. Length of days is in her right hand; and in her left hand riches and honor. Her ways are ways of pleasantness, and all her paths are peace. She is a tree of life to them that lay hold upon her: and happy is every one that retaineth her." Proverbs 3:13-18.

"Wisdom is the principal thing; therefore get wisdom: and with all thy getting get understanding." Proverbs 4:7. "The fear of the Lord is the beginning of wisdom." Psalm 111:10. "The fear of the Lord is to hate evil: pride, and arrogancy, and the evil way, and the froward mouth, do I hate." Proverbs 8:13.

O that in later years Solomon had heeded these wonderful words of wisdom! O that he who had declared, "The lips of the wise disperse knowledge" (Proverbs 15:7), and who had himself taught the kings of the earth to render to the King of kings the praise they desired to give to an earthly ruler, had never with a "froward mouth," in "pride and arrogancy," taken to himself the glory due to God alone! [35]

Chapter 2

The Temple and Its Dedication

The long-cherished plan of David to erect a temple to the Lord, Solomon wisely carried out. For seven years Jerusalem was filled with busy workers engaged in leveling the chosen site, in building vast retaining walls, in laying broad foundations,—"great stones, costly stones, and hewed stones,"—in shaping the heavy timbers brought from the Lebanon forests, and in erecting the magnificent sanctuary. 1 Kings 5:17.

Simultaneously with the preparation of wood and stone, to which task many thousands were bending their energies, the manufacture of the furnishings for the temple was steadily progressing under the leadership of Hiram of Tyre, "a cunning man, endued with understanding, ... skillful to work in gold, and in silver, in brass, in iron, in stone, and in timber, in purple, in blue, and in fine linen, and in crimson." 2 Chronicles 2:13, 14.

Thus as the building on Mount Moriah was noiselessly [36] upreared with "stone made ready before it was brought thither: so that there was neither hammer nor ax nor any tool of iron heard in the house, while it was in building," the beautiful fittings were perfected according to the patterns committed by David to his son, "all the vessels that were for the house of God." 1 Kings 6:7; 2 Chronicles 4:19. These included the altar of incense, the table of shewbread, the candlestick and lamps, with the vessels and instruments connected with the ministrations of the priests in the holy place, all "of gold, and that perfect gold." 2 Chronicles 4:21. The brazen furniture,—the altar of burnt offering, the great laver supported by twelve oxen, the lavers of smaller size, with many other vessels,—"in the plain of Jordan did the king cast them, in the clay ground between Succoth and Zeredathah." 2 Chronicles 4:17. These furnishings were provided in abundance, that there should be no lack.

Of surpassing beauty and unrivaled splendor was the palatial building which Solomon and his associates erected for God and His worship. Garnished with precious stones, surrounded by spacious courts with magnificent approaches, and lined with carved cedar and burnished gold, the temple structure, with its broidered hangings and rich furnishings, was a fit emblem of the living church of God on earth, which through the ages has been building in accordance with the divine pattern, with materials that have been likened to "gold, silver, precious stones," "polished after the similitude of a palace." 1 Corinthians 3:12; Psalm

144:12. Of this spiritual temple Christ is "the chief Cornerstone; in whom all the building fitly framed together groweth unto an holy temple in the Lord." Ephesians 2:20, 21. [37]

At last the temple planned by King David, and built by Solomon his son, was completed. "All that came into Solomon's heart to make in the house of the Lord," he had "prosperously effected." 2 Chronicles 7:11. And now, in order that the palace crowning the heights of Mount Moriah might indeed be, as David had so much desired, a dwelling place "not for man, but for the Lord God" (1 Chronicles 29:1), there remained the solemn ceremony of formally dedicating it to Jehovah and His worship.

The spot on which the temple was built had long been regarded as a consecrated place. It was here that Abraham, the father of the faithful, had revealed his willingness to sacrifice his only son in obedience to the command of Jehovah. Here God had renewed with Abraham the covenant of blessing, which included the glorious Messianic promise to the human race of deliverance through the sacrifice of the Son of the Most High. See Genesis 22:9, 16-18. Here it was that when David offered burnt offerings and peace offerings to stay the avenging sword of the destroying angel, God had answered him by fire from heaven. See 1 Chronicles 21. And now once more the worshipers of Jehovah were here to meet their God and renew their vows of allegiance to Him.

The time chosen for the dedication was a most favorable one—the seventh month, when the people from every part of the kingdom were accustomed to assemble at Jerusalem to celebrate the Feast of Tabernacles. This feast was preeminently an occasion of rejoicing. The labors of the harvest being ended and the toils of the new year not yet begun, the people were free from care and could give themselves up to the sacred, joyous influences of the hour. [38]

At the appointed time the hosts of Israel, with richly clad representatives from many foreign nations, assembled in the temple courts. The scene was one of unusual splendor. Solomon, with the elders of Israel and the most influential men among the people, had returned from another part of the city, whence they had brought the ark of the testament. From the sanctuary on the heights of Gibeon had been transferred the ancient "tabernacle of the congregation, and all the holy vessels that were in the tabernacle" (2 Chronicles 5:5); and these cherished reminders of the earlier experiences of the children of Israel during their wanderings in the wilderness and their conquest of Canaan, now found a permanent home in the splendid building that had been erected to take the place of the portable structure.

In bringing to the temple the sacred ark containing the two tables of stone on which were written by the finger of God the precepts of the Decalogue, Solomon had followed the example of his father David. Every six paces he sacrificed. With singing and with music and with great ceremony, "the priests brought in the ark of the covenant of the Lord unto his place, to the oracle of the house, into the most holy place." Verse 7. As they came out of the inner sanctuary, they took the positions assigned them. The singers—Levites arrayed in white linen, having cymbals and psalteries and harps—stood at the east end of the altar, and with them a hundred and twenty priests sounding with trumpets. See Verse 12.

"It came even to pass, as the trumpeters and singers were as one, to make one sound to be heard in praising and [39] thanking the Lord; and when they lifted up their voice with the trumpets and cymbals and instruments of music, and praised the Lord, saying, For He is good; for His mercy endureth forever: that then the house was filled with a cloud, even the house of the Lord; so that the priests could not stand to minister by reason of the cloud: for the glory of the Lord had filled the house of God." Verses 13, 14.

Realizing the significance of this cloud, Solomon declared: "The Lord hath said that He would dwell in the thick darkness. But I have built an house of habitation for Thee, and a place for Thy dwelling forever." 2 Chronicles 6:1, 2.

"The Lord reigneth; Let the people tremble: He sitteth between the cherubims; Let the earth be moved. "The Lord is great in Zion; And He is high above all the people. Let them praise Thy great and terrible name; For it is holy.... "Exalt ye the Lord our God, And worship at His footstool; For He is holy."

Psalm 99:1-5.

"In the midst of the court" of the temple had been erected "a brazen scaffold," or platform, "five cubits long, and five cubits broad, and three cubits high." Upon this Solomon stood and with uplifted hands blessed the vast multitude before him. "And all the congregation of Israel stood." 2 Chronicles 6:13, 3.

"Blessed be the Lord God of Israel," Solomon exclaimed, "who hath with His hands fulfilled that which He spake [40] with His mouth to my father David, saying, ... I have chosen Jerusalem, that My name might be there." Verses 4-6.

Solomon then knelt upon the platform, and in the hearing of all the people offered the dedicatory prayer. Lifting his hands toward heaven, while the congregation were bowed with their faces to the ground, the king pleaded: "Lord God of Israel, there is no God like Thee in the heaven, nor in the earth; which keepest covenant, and showest mercy unto Thy servants, that walk before Thee with all their heart."

"Will God in very deed dwell with men on the earth? Behold, heaven and the heaven of heavens cannot contain Thee; how much less this house which I have built? Have respect therefore to the prayer of Thy servant, and to his supplication, O Lord my God, to hearken unto the cry and the prayer which Thy servant prayeth before Thee: that Thine eyes may be open upon this house day and night, upon the place whereof Thou hast said that Thou wouldest put Thy name there; to hearken unto the prayer which Thy servant prayeth toward this place. Hearken therefore unto the supplications of Thy servant, and of Thy people Israel, which they shall make toward this place: hear Thou from Thy dwelling place, even from heaven; and when Thou hearest, forgive...."

"If Thy people Israel be put to the worse before the enemy, because they have sinned against Thee; and shall return and confess Thy name, and pray and make supplication before Thee in this house; then hear Thou from the heavens, and forgive the sin of Thy people Israel, and bring them again unto the land which Thou gavest to them and to their fathers. [41]

"When the heaven is shut up, and there is no rain, because they have sinned against Thee; yet if they pray toward this place, and confess Thy name, and turn from their sin, when Thou dost afflict them; then hear Thou from heaven, and forgive the sin of Thy servants, and of Thy people Israel, when Thou hast taught them the good way, wherein they should walk; and send rain upon Thy land, which Thou hast given unto Thy people for an inheritance.

"If there be dearth in the land, if there be pestilence, if there be blasting, or mildew, locusts, or caterpillars; if their enemies besiege them in the cities of their land; whatsoever sore or whatsoever sickness there be: then what prayer or what supplication soever shall be made of any man, or of all Thy people Israel, when everyone shall know his own sore and his own grief, and shall spread forth his hands in his house: then hear Thou from heaven Thy dwelling place, and forgive, and render unto every man according unto all his ways, whose heart Thou knowest; ... that they may fear Thee, to walk in Thy ways, so long as they live in the land which Thou gavest unto our fathers.

"Moreover concerning the stranger, which is not of Thy people Israel, but is come from a far country for Thy great name's sake, and Thy mighty hand, and Thy stretched-out arm; if they come and pray in this house; then hear Thou from the heavens, even from Thy dwelling place, and do according to all that the stranger calleth to Thee for; that all people of the earth may know Thy name, and fear Thee, as doth Thy people Israel, and may know that this house which I have built is called by Thy name. [42]

"If Thy people go out to war against their enemies by the way that Thou shalt send them, and they pray unto Thee toward this city which Thou hast chosen, and the house which I have built for Thy name; then hear Thou from the heavens their prayer and their supplication, and maintain their cause.

"If they sin against Thee, (for there is no man which sinneth not,) and Thou be angry with them, and deliver them over before their enemies, and they carry them away captives unto a land far off or near; yet if they bethink themselves in the land whither they are carried captive, and turn and pray unto Thee in the land of their captivity, saying, We have sinned, we have done amiss, and have dealt wickedly; if they return to Thee with all their heart and with all their soul in the land of their captivity, whither they have carried them captives, and pray toward their land, which Thou gavest unto their fathers, and toward the city which Thou hast chosen, and toward the house which I have built for Thy name: then hear Thou from the heavens, even from Thy dwelling place, their prayer and their supplications, and maintain their cause, and forgive Thy people which have sinned against Thee.

"Now, my God, let, I beseech Thee, Thine eyes be open, and let Thine ears be attent unto the prayer that is made in this place. Now therefore arise, O Lord God, into Thy resting place, Thou, and the ark of Thy strength: let Thy priests, O Lord God, be clothed with salvation, and let Thy saints rejoice in goodness. O Lord God, turn not away the face of Thine anointed: remember the mercies of David Thy servant." Verses 14-42. [43] [44] [45]

As Solomon ended his prayer, "fire came down from heaven, and consumed the burnt offering and the sacrifices." The priests could not enter the temple because "the glory of the Lord had filled the Lord's house." "When all the children of Israel saw ... the glory of the Lord upon the house, they bowed themselves with their faces to the ground upon the pavement, and worshiped, and praised the Lord, saying, For He is good; for His mercy endureth forever."

Then king and people offered sacrifices before the Lord. "So the king and all the people dedicated the house of God." 2 Chronicles 7:1-5. For seven days the multitudes from every part of the kingdom, from the borders "of Hamath unto the river of Egypt," "a very great congregation," kept a joyous feast. The week following was spent by the happy throng in observing the Feast of Tabernacles. At the close of the season of reconsecration and rejoicing the people returned to their homes, "glad and merry in heart for the goodness that the Lord had showed unto David, and to Solomon, and to Israel His people." Verses 8, 10.

The king had done everything within his power to encourage the people to give themselves wholly to God and His service, and to magnify His holy name. And now once more, as at Gibeon early in his reign, Israel's ruler was given evidence of divine acceptance and blessing. In a night vision the Lord appeared to him with the message: "I have heard thy prayer, and have chosen this place to Myself for an house of sacrifice. If I shut up heaven that there be no rain, or if I command the locusts to devour the land, or if I [46] send pestilence among My people; if My people, which are called by My name, shall humble themselves, and pray, and seek My face, and turn from their wicked ways; then will I hear from heaven, and will forgive their sin, and will heal their land. Now Mine eyes shall be open, and Mine ears attent unto the prayer that is made in this place. For now have I chosen and sanctified this house, that My name may be there forever: and Mine eyes and Mine heart shall be there perpetually." Verses 12-16.

Had Israel remained true to God, this glorious building would have stood forever, a perpetual sign of God's especial favor to His chosen people. "The sons of the stranger," God declared, "that join themselves to the Lord, to serve Him, and to love the name of the Lord, to be His servants, everyone that keepeth the Sabbath from polluting it, and taketh hold of My covenant; even them will I bring to My holy mountain, and make them joyful in My house of prayer: their burnt offerings and their sacrifices shall be accepted upon Mine altar; for Mine house shall be called an house of prayer for all people." Isaiah 56:6, 7.

In connection with these assurances of acceptance, the Lord made very plain the path of duty before the king. "As for thee," He declared, "if thou wilt walk before Me, as David thy father walked, and do according to all that I have commanded thee, and shalt observe My statutes and My judgments; then will I establish the throne of thy kingdom, according as I have covenanted with David thy father, saying, There shall not fail thee a man to be ruler in Israel." 2 Chronicles 7:17, 18. [47]

Had Solomon continued to serve the Lord in humility, his entire reign would have exerted a powerful influence for good over the surrounding nations, nations that had been so favorably impressed by the reign of David his father and by the wise words and the magnificent works of the earlier years of his own reign. Foreseeing the terrible temptations that attend prosperity and worldly honor, God warned Solomon against the evil of apostasy and foretold the awful results of sin. Even the beautiful temple that had just been dedicated, He declared, would become "a proverb and a byword among all nations" should the Israelites forsake "the Lord God of their fathers" and persist in idolatry. Verses 20, 22.

Strengthened in heart and greatly cheered by the message from heaven that his prayer in behalf of Israel had been heard, Solomon now entered upon the most glorious period of his reign, when "all the kings of the earth" began to seek his presence, "to hear his wisdom, that God had put in his heart." 2 Chronicles 9:23. Many came to see the manner of his government and to receive instruction regarding the conduct of difficult affairs.

As these people visited Solomon, he taught them of God as the Creator of all things, and they returned to their homes with clearer conceptions of the God of Israel and of His love for the human race. In the works of nature they now beheld an expression of His love and a revelation of His character; and many were led to worship Him as their God.

The humility of Solomon at the time he began to bear the burdens of state, when he acknowledged before God, [48] "I am but a little child" (1 Kings 3:7), his marked love of God, his profound reverence for things divine, his distrust of self, and his exaltation of the infinite Creator of all—all these traits of character, so worthy of emulation, were revealed during the services connected with the completion of the temple, when during his dedicatory prayer he knelt in the humble position of a petitioner. Christ's followers today should guard against the tendency to lose the spirit of reverence and godly fear. The Scriptures teach men how they should approach their Maker—with humility and awe, through faith in a divine Mediator. The psalmist has declared:

"The Lord is a great God, And a great King above all gods.... O come, let us worship and bow down: Let us kneel before the Lord our Maker."

Psalm 95:3-6.

Both in public and in private worship it is our privilege to bow on our knees before God when we offer our petitions to Him. Jesus, our example, "kneeled down, and prayed." Luke 22:41. Of His disciples it is recorded that they, too, "kneeled down, and prayed." Acts 9:40. Paul declared, "I bow my knees unto the Father of our Lord Jesus Christ." Ephesians 3:14. In confessing before God the sins of Israel, Ezra knelt. See Ezra 9:5. Daniel "kneeled upon his knees three times a day, and prayed, and gave thanks before his God." Daniel 6:10.

True reverence for God is inspired by a sense of His infinite greatness and a realization of His presence. With this sense of the Unseen, every heart should be deeply impressed. The hour and place of prayer are sacred, because God is [49] there. And as reverence is manifested in attitude and demeanor, the feeling that inspires it will be deepened. "Holy and reverend is His name," the psalmist declares. Psalm 111:9. Angels, when they speak that name, veil their faces. With what reverence, then, should we, who are fallen and sinful, take it upon our lips!

Well would it be for old and young to ponder those words of Scripture that show how the place marked by God's special presence should be regarded. "Put off thy shoes from off thy feet," He commanded Moses at the burning bush, "for the place whereon thou standest is holy ground." Exodus 3:5. Jacob, after beholding the vision of the angel, exclaimed, "The Lord is in this place; and I knew it not.... This is none other but the house of God, and this is the gate of heaven." Genesis 28:16, 17.

In that which was said during the dedicatory services, Solomon had sought to remove from the minds of those present the superstitions in regard to the Creator, that had beclouded the minds of the heathen. The God of heaven is not, like the gods of the heathen, confined to temples made with hands; yet He would meet with His people by His Spirit when they should assemble at the house dedicated to His worship.

Centuries later Paul taught the same truth in the words: "God that made the world and all things therein, seeing that He is Lord of heaven and earth, dwelleth not in temples made with hands; neither is worshiped with men's hands, as though He needed anything, seeing He giveth to all life, and breath, and all things; ... that they should seek the Lord, if haply they might feel after Him, and find [50] Him, though He be not far from every one of us: for in Him we live, and move, and have our being." Acts 17:24-28.

"Blessed is the nation whose God is the Lord; And the people whom He hath chosen for His own inheritance. The Lord looketh from heaven; He beholdeth all the sons of men. From the place of His habitation He looketh upon all the inhabitants of the earth."

"The Lord hath prepared His throne in the heavens; And His kingdom ruleth over all."

"Thy way, O God, is in the sanctuary: Who is so great a God as our God? Thou art the God that doest wonders: Thou hast declared Thy strength among the people."

Psalm 33:12-14; 103:19; Psalm 77:13, 14.

Although God dwells not in temples made with hands, yet He honors with His presence the assemblies of His people. He has promised that when they come together to seek Him, to acknowledge their sins, and to pray for one another, He will meet with them by His Spirit. But those who assemble to worship Him should put away every evil thing. Unless they worship Him in spirit and truth and in the beauty of holiness, their coming together will be of no avail. Of such the Lord declares, "This people draweth nigh unto Me with their mouth, and honoreth Me with their lips; but their heart is far from Me." Matthew 15:8, 9. Those who worship God must worship Him "in spirit and in truth: for the Father seeketh such to worship Him." John 4:23.

"The Lord is in His holy temple: let all the earth keep silence before Him." Habakkuk 2:20. [51]

Chapter 3

Pride of Prosperity

While Solomon exalted the law of heaven, God was with him, and wisdom was given him to rule over Israel with impartiality and mercy. At first, as wealth and worldly honor came to him, he remained humble, and great was the extent of his influence. "Solomon reigned over all kingdoms from the river [Euphrates] unto the land of the Philistines, and unto the border of Egypt." "He ... had peace on all sides round about him. And Judah and Israel dwelt safely, every man under his vine and under his fig tree, ... all the days of Solomon." 1 Kings 4:21, 24, 25.

But after a morning of great promise his life was darkened by apostasy. History records the melancholy fact that he who had been called Jedidiah,—"Beloved of the Lord" (2 Samuel 12:25, margin),—he who had been honored by God with tokens of divine favor so remarkable that his wisdom and uprightness gained for him world-wide fame, he who had led others to ascribe honor to the God of [52] Israel, turned from the worship of Jehovah to bow before the idols of the heathen.

Hundreds of years before Solomon came to the throne, the Lord, foreseeing the perils that would beset those who might be chosen as rulers of Israel, gave Moses instruction for their guidance. Directions were given that he who should sit on the throne of Israel should "write him a copy" of the statutes of Jehovah "in a book out of that which is before the priests the Levites." "It shall be with him," the Lord said, "and he shall read therein all the days of his life: that he may learn to fear the Lord his God, to keep all the words of this law and these statutes, to do them: that his heart be not lifted up above his brethren, and that he turn not aside from the commandment, to the right hand, or to the left: to the end that he may prolong his days in his kingdom, he, and his children, in the midst of Israel." Deuteronomy 17:18-20.

In connection with this instruction the Lord particularly cautioned the one who might be anointed king not to "multiply wives to himself, that his heart turn not away: neither shall he greatly multiply to himself silver and gold." Verse 17.

With these warnings Solomon was familiar, and for a time he heeded them. His greatest desire was to live and rule in accordance with the statutes given at Sinai. His manner of conducting the affairs of the kingdom was in striking contrast with the customs of the nations of his time—nations who feared not God and whose rulers trampled underfoot His holy law. [53]

In seeking to strengthen his relations with the powerful kingdom lying to the southward of Israel, Solomon ventured upon forbidden ground. Satan knew the results that would attend obedience; and during the earlier years of Solomon's reign—years glorious because of the wisdom, the beneficence, and the uprightness of the king—he sought to bring in influences that would insidiously undermine Solomon's loyalty to principle and cause him to separate from God. That the enemy was successful in this effort, we know from the record: "Solomon made affinity with Pharaoh king of Egypt, and took Pharaoh's daughter, and brought her into the City of David." 1 Kings 3:1.

From a human point of view, this marriage, though contrary to the teachings of God's law, seemed to prove a blessing; for Solomon's heathen wife was converted and united with him in the worship of the true God. Furthermore, Pharaoh rendered signal service to Israel by taking Gezer, slaying "the Canaanites that dwelt in the city," and giving it "for a present unto his daughter, Solomon's wife." 1 Kings 9:16. This city Solomon rebuilt and thus apparently greatly strengthened his kingdom along the Mediterranean seacoast. But in forming an alliance with a heathen nation, and sealing the compact by marriage with an idolatrous princess, Solomon rashly disregarded the wise provision that God had made for maintaining the purity of His people. The hope that his Egyptian wife might be converted was but a feeble excuse for the sin.

For a time God in His compassionate mercy overruled this terrible mistake; and the king, by a wise course, could [54] have checked at least in a large measure the evil forces that his imprudence had set in operation. But Solomon had begun to lose sight of the Source of his power and glory. As inclination gained the ascendancy over reason, self-confidence increased, and he sought to carry out the Lord's purpose in his own way. He reasoned that political and commercial alliances with the surrounding nations would bring these nations to a knowledge of the true God; and he entered into unholy alliance with nation after nation. Often these alliances were sealed by marriages with heathen princesses. The commands of Jehovah were set aside for the customs of surrounding peoples.

Solomon flattered himself that his wisdom and the power of his example would lead his wives from idolatry to the worship of the true God, and also that the alliances thus formed would draw the nations round about into close touch with Israel. Vain hope! Solomon's mistake in regarding himself as strong enough to resist the influence of heathen associates was fatal. And fatal, too, the deception that led him to hope that notwithstanding a disregard of God's law on his part, others might be led to revere and obey its sacred precepts.

The king's alliances and commercial relations with heathen nations brought him renown, honor, and the riches of this world. He was enabled to bring gold from Ophir and silver from Tarshish in great abundance. "The king made silver and gold at Jerusalem as plenteous as stones, and cedar trees made he as the sycamore trees that are in the vale for abundance." 2 Chronicles 1:15. Wealth, with [55] all its attendant temptations, came in Solomon's day to an increasingly large number of people; but the fine gold of character was dimmed and marred.

So gradual was Solomon's apostasy that before he was aware of it, he had wandered far from God. Almost imperceptibly he began to trust less and less in divine guidance and blessing, and to put confidence in his own strength. Little by little he withheld from God that

PROPHETS AND KINGS

unswerving obedience which was to make Israel a peculiar people, and he conformed more and more closely to the customs of the surrounding nations. Yielding to the temptations incident to his success and his honored position, he forgot the Source of his prosperity. An ambition to excel all other nations in power and grandeur led him to pervert for selfish purposes the heavenly gifts hitherto employed for the glory of God. The money which should have been held in sacred trust for the benefit of the worthy poor and for the extension of principles of holy living throughout the world, was selfishly absorbed in ambitious projects.

Engrossed in an overmastering desire to surpass other nations in outward display, the king overlooked the need of acquiring beauty and perfection of character. In seeking to glorify himself before the world, he sold his honor and integrity. The enormous revenues acquired through commerce with many lands were supplemented by heavy taxes. Thus pride, ambition, prodigality, and indulgence bore fruit in cruelty and exaction. The conscientious, considerate spirit that had marked his dealings with the people during the early part of his reign, was now changed. From the wisest [56] and most merciful of rulers, he degenerated into a tyrant. Once the compassionate, God-fearing guardian of the people, he became oppressive and despotic. Tax after tax was levied upon the people, that means might be forthcoming to support the luxurious court.

The people began to complain. The respect and admiration they had once cherished for their king was changed into disaffection and abhorrence.

As a safeguard against dependence on the arm of flesh, the Lord had warned those who should rule over Israel not to multiply horses to themselves. But in utter disregard of this command, "Solomon had horses brought out of Egypt." "And they brought unto Solomon horses out of Egypt, and out of all lands." "Solomon gathered together chariots and horsemen: and he had a thousand and four hundred chariots, and twelve thousand horsemen, whom he bestowed in the cities for chariots, and with the king at Jerusalem." 2 Chronicles 1:16; 9:28; 1 Kings 10:26.

More and more the king came to regard luxury, self-indulgence, and the favor of the world as indications of greatness. Beautiful and attractive women were brought from Egypt, Phoenicia, Edom, and Moab, and from many other places. These women were numbered by hundreds. Their religion was idol worship, and they had been taught to practice cruel and degrading rites. Infatuated with their beauty, the king neglected his duties to God and to his kingdom.

His wives exerted a strong influence over him and gradually prevailed on him to unite with them in their worship. Solomon had disregarded the instruction that God had given to serve as a barrier against apostasy, and [57] now he gave himself up to the worship of the false gods. "It came to pass, when Solomon was old, that his wives turned away his heart after other gods: and his heart was not perfect with the Lord his God, as was the heart of David his father. For Solomon went after Ashtoreth the goddess of the Zidonians, and after Milcom the abomination of the Ammonites." 1 Kings 11:4, 5.

On the southern eminence of the Mount of Olives, opposite Mount Moriah, where stood the beautiful temple of Jehovah, Solomon erected an imposing pile of buildings to be used as idolatrous shrines. To please his wives, he placed huge idols, unshapely images of wood and stone, amidst the groves of myrtle and olive. There, before the altars of heathen deities,

"Chemosh, the abomination of Moab," and "Molech, the abomination of the children of Ammon," were practiced the most degrading rites of heathenism. Verse 7.

Solomon's course brought its sure penalty. His separation from God through communication with idolaters was his ruin. As he cast off his allegiance to God, he lost the mastery of himself. His moral efficiency was gone. His fine sensibilities became blunted, his conscience seared. He who in his early reign had displayed so much wisdom and sympathy in restoring a helpless babe to its unfortunate mother (see 1 Kings 3:16-28), fell so low as to consent to the erection of an idol to whom living children were offered as sacrifices. He who in his youth was endowed with discretion and understanding, and who in his strong manhood had been inspired to write, "There is a way which seemeth right unto a man, but the end thereof are the ways of death" (Proverbs 14:12), in later years departed so far [58] from purity as to countenance licentious, revolting rites connected with the worship of Chemosh and Ashtoreth. He who at the dedication of the temple had said to his people, "Let your heart therefore be perfect with the Lord our God" (1 Kings 8:61), became himself an offender, in heart and life denying his own words. He mistook license for liberty. He tried—but at what cost!—to unite light with darkness, good with evil, purity with impurity, Christ with Belial.

From being one of the greatest kings that ever wielded a scepter, Solomon became a profligate, the tool and slave of others. His character, once noble and manly, became enervated and effeminate. His faith in the living God was supplanted by atheistic doubts. Unbelief marred his happiness, weakened his principles, and degraded his life. The justice and magnanimity of his early reign were changed to despotism and tyranny. Poor, frail human nature! God can do little for men who lose their sense of dependence upon Him.

During these years of apostasy, the spiritual decline of Israel progressed steadily. How could it be otherwise when their king had united his interests with satanic agencies? Through these agencies the enemy worked to confuse the minds of the Israelites in regard to true and false worship, and they became an easy prey. Commerce with other nations brought them into intimate contact with those who had no love for God, and their own love for Him was greatly lessened. Their keen sense of the high, holy character of God was deadened. Refusing to follow in the path of [59] obedience, they transferred their allegiance to the enemy of righteousness. It came to be a common practice to intermarry with idolaters, and the Israelites rapidly lost their abhorrence of idol worship. Polygamy was countenanced. Idolatrous mothers brought their children up to observe heathen rites. In the lives of some, the pure religious service instituted by God was replaced by idolatry of the darkest hue.

Christians are to keep themselves distinct and separate from the world, its spirit, and its influences. God is fully able to keep us in the world, but we are not to be of the world. His love is not uncertain and fluctuating. Ever He watches over His children with a care that is measureless. But He requires undivided allegiance. "No man can serve two masters: for either he will hate the one, and love the other; or else he will hold to the one, and despise the other. Ye cannot serve God and mammon." Matthew 6:24.

Solomon was endued with wonderful wisdom, but the world drew him away from God. Men today are no stronger than he; they are as prone to yield to the influences that caused his downfall. As God warned Solomon of his danger, so today He warns His children not to imperil their souls by affinity with the world. "Come out from among them," He pleads, "and be ye separate, ... and touch not the unclean thing, and I will receive you, and will be a Father unto you, and ye shall be My sons and daughters, saith the Lord Almighty." 2 Corinthians 6:17, 18.

In the midst of prosperity lurks danger. Throughout the ages, riches and honor have ever been attended with peril to humility and spirituality. It is not the empty cup [60] that we have difficulty in carrying; it is the cup full to the brim that must be carefully balanced. Affliction and adversity may cause sorrow, but it is prosperity that is most dangerous to spiritual life. Unless the human subject is in constant submission to the will of God, unless he is sanctified by the truth, prosperity will surely arouse the natural inclination to presumption.

In the valley of humiliation, where men depend on God to teach them and to guide their every step, there is comparative safety. But the men who stand, as it were, on a lofty pinnacle, and who, because of their position, are supposed to possess great wisdom—these are in gravest peril. Unless such men make God their dependence, they will surely fall.

Whenever pride and ambition are indulged, the life is marred, for pride, feeling no need, closes the heart against the infinite blessings of Heaven. He who makes self-glorification his aim will find himself destitute of the grace of God, through whose efficiency the truest riches and the most satisfying joys are won. But he who gives all and does all for Christ will know the fulfillment of the promise, "The blessing of the Lord, it maketh rich, and He addeth no sorrow with it." Proverbs 10:22. With the gentle touch of grace the Saviour banishes from the soul unrest and unholy ambition, changing enmity to love and unbelief to confidence. When He speaks to the soul, saying, "Follow Me," the spell of the world's enchantment is broken. At the sound of His voice the spirit of greed and ambition flees from the heart, and men arise, emancipated, to follow Him. [61]

Chapter 4
Results of Transgression

Prominent among the primary causes that led Solomon into extravagance and oppression was his failure to maintain and foster the spirit of self-sacrifice.

When, at the foot of Sinai, Moses told the people of the divine command, "Let them make Me a sanctuary; that I may dwell among them," the response of the Israelites was accompanied by the appropriate gifts. "They came, everyone whose heart stirred him up, and everyone whom his spirit made willing," and brought offerings. Exodus 25:8; 35:21. For the building of the sanctuary, great and extensive preparations were necessary; a large amount of the most precious and costly material was required, but the Lord accepted only freewill offerings. "Of every man that giveth it willingly with his heart ye shall take My offering," was the command repeated by Moses to the congregation. Exodus 25:2. Devotion to God and a spirit of sacrifice were the [62] first requisites in preparing a dwelling place for the Most High.

A similar call to self-sacrifice was made when David turned over to Solomon the responsibility of building the temple. Of the assembled multitude David asked, "Who then is willing to consecrate his service this day unto the Lord?" 1 Chronicles 29:5. This call to consecration and willing service should ever have been kept in mind by those who had to do with the erection of the temple.

For the construction of the wilderness tabernacle, chosen men were endowed by God with special skill and wisdom. "Moses said unto the children of Israel, See, the Lord hath called by name Bezaleel, ... of the tribe of Judah; and He hath filled him with the Spirit of God, in wisdom, in understanding, and in knowledge, and in all manner of workmanship.... And He hath put in his heart that he may teach, both he, and Aholiab, ... of the tribe of Dan. Them hath He filled with wisdom of heart, to work all manner of work, of the engraver, and of the cunning workman, and of the embroiderer, ... and of the weaver, even of them that do any work.... Then wrought Bezaleel and Aholiab, and every wisehearted man, in whom the Lord put wisdom and understanding." Exodus 35:30-35; 36:1. Heavenly intelligences co-operated with the workmen whom God Himself had chosen.

The descendants of these workmen inherited to a large degree the talents conferred on their forefathers. For a time these men of Judah and Dan remained humble and unselfish; but gradually, almost imperceptibly, they lost their hold upon God and their desire to serve Him unselfishly. They [63] asked higher wages for their services, because of their superior skill as workmen in the finer arts. In some instances their request was granted, but more often they found employment in the surrounding nations. In place of the noble spirit of self-sacrifice that had filled the hearts of their illustrious ancestors, they indulged a spirit of covetousness, of grasping for more and more. That their selfish desires might be gratified, they used their God-given skill in the service of heathen kings, and lent their talent to the perfecting of works which were a dishonor to their Maker.

It was among these men that Solomon looked for a master workman to superintend the construction of the temple on Mount Moriah. Minute specifications, in writing, regarding every portion of the sacred structure, had been entrusted to the king; and he could have looked to God in faith for consecrated helpers, to whom would have been granted special skill for doing with exactness the work required. But Solomon lost sight of this opportunity to exercise faith in God. He sent to the king of Tyre for a man, "cunning to work in gold, and in silver, and in brass, and in iron, and in purple, and crimson, and blue, and that can skill to grave with the cunning men ... in Judah and in Jerusalem." 2 Chronicles 2:7.

The Phoenician king responded by sending Huram, "the son of a woman of the daughters of Dan, and his father was a man of Tyre." Verse 14. Huram was a descendant, on his mother's side, of Aholiab, to whom, hundreds of years before, God had given special wisdom for the construction of the tabernacle.

Thus at the head of Solomon's company of workmen [64] there was placed a man whose efforts were not prompted by an unselfish desire to render service to God. He served the god of this world, mammon. The very fibers of his being were inwrought with the principles of selfishness.

Because of his unusual skill, Huram demanded large wages. Gradually the wrong principles that he cherished came to be accepted by his associates. As they labored with him day after day, they yielded to the inclination to compare his wages with their own, and they began to lose sight of the holy character of their work. The spirit of self-denial left them, and in its place came the spirit of covetousness. The result was a demand for higher wages, which was granted.

The baleful influences thus set in operation permeated all branches of the Lord's service, and extended throughout the kingdom. The high wages demanded and received gave to many an opportunity to indulge in luxury and extravagance. The poor were oppressed by the rich; the spirit of self-sacrifice was well-nigh lost. In the far-reaching effects of these influences may be traced one of the principal causes of the terrible apostasy of him who once was numbered among the wisest of mortals.

The sharp contrast between the spirit and motives of the people building the wilderness tabernacle, and of those engaged in erecting Solomon's temple, has a lesson of deep significance. The self-seeking that characterized the workers on the temple finds its counterpart today in the selfishness that rules in the world. The spirit of covetousness, of seeking for the highest position and the highest wage, is rife. [65] The willing service and joyous self-denial of the tabernacle workers is seldom met with. But this is the only spirit that should actuate the followers of Jesus. Our divine Master has given an example of how His disciples are to work. To those whom He bade, "Follow Me, and I will make you fishers of men" (Matthew 4:19), He offered no stated sum as a reward for their services. They were to share with Him in self-denial and sacrifice.

Not for the wages we receive are we to labor. The motive that prompts us to work for God should have in it nothing akin to self-serving. Unselfish devotion and a spirit of sacrifice have always been and always will be the first requisite of acceptable service. Our Lord and Master designs that not one thread of selfishness shall be woven into His work. Into our efforts we are to bring the tact and skill, the exactitude and wisdom, that the God of perfection required of the builders of the earthly tabernacle; yet in all our labors we are to remember that the greatest talents or the most splendid services are acceptable only when self is laid upon the altar, a living, consuming sacrifice.

Another of the deviations from right principles that finally led to the downfall of Israel's king was his yielding to the temptation to take to himself the glory that belongs to God alone.

From the day that Solomon was entrusted with the work of building the temple, to the time of its completion, his avowed purpose was "to build an house for the name of the Lord God of Israel." 2 Chronicles 6:7. This purpose was fully recognized before the assembled hosts of Israel [66] at the time of the dedication of the temple. In his prayer the king acknowledged that Jehovah had said, "My name shall be there." 1 Kings 8:29.

One of the most touching portions of Solomon's dedicatory prayer was his plea to God for the strangers that should come from countries afar to learn more of Him whose fame had been spread abroad among the nations. "They shall hear," the king pleaded, "of Thy great name, and of Thy strong hand, and of Thy stretched-out arm." In behalf of every one of these stranger worshipers Solomon had petitioned: "Hear Thou, ... and do according to all that the stranger calleth to Thee for: that all people of the earth may know Thy name, to fear Thee, as do Thy people Israel; and that they may know that this house, which I have builded, is called by Thy name." Verses 42, 43.

At the close of the service, Solomon had exhorted Israel to be faithful and true to God, in order that "all the people of the earth may know," he said, "that the Lord is God, and that there is none else." Verse 60.

A Greater than Solomon was the designer of the temple; the wisdom and glory of God stood there revealed. Those who were unacquainted with this fact naturally admired and praised Solomon as the architect and builder; but the king disclaimed any honor for its conception or erection.

Thus it was when the Queen of Sheba came to visit Solomon. Hearing of his wisdom and of the magnificent temple he had built, she determined "to prove him with hard questions" and to see for herself his famous works. Attended by a retinue of servants, and with camels bearing [67] "spices, and gold in abundance, and precious stones," she made the long journey to Jerusalem. "And when she was come to Solomon, she communed with him of all that was in her heart." She talked with him of the mysteries of nature; and Solomon taught her of the God of nature, the great Creator, who dwells in the highest heaven and rules over all.

"Solomon told her all her questions: there was not anything hid from the king, which he told her not." 1 Kings 10:1-3; 2 Chronicles 9:1, 2.

"When the Queen of Sheba had seen all Solomon's wisdom, and the house that he had built, ... there was no more spirit in her." "It was a true report," she acknowledged, "which I heard in mine own land of thine acts, and of thy wisdom: howbeit I believed not their words, until I came, and mine eyes had seen it:" "and, behold, the half was not told me: thy wisdom and prosperity exceedeth the fame which I heard. Happy are thy men, happy are these thy servants, which stand continually before thee, and that hear thy wisdom." 1 Kings 10:4-8; 2 Chronicles 9:3-7.

By the time of the close of her visit the queen had been so fully taught by Solomon as to the source of his wisdom and prosperity that she was constrained, not to extol the human agent, but to exclaim, "Blessed be the Lord thy God, which delighted in thee, to set thee on the throne of Israel: because the Lord loved Israel forever, therefore made He thee king, to do judgment and justice." 1 Kings 10:9. This is the impression that God designed should be made upon all peoples. And when "all the kings of the earth sought the presence of Solomon, to hear his wisdom, that God had [68] put in his heart" (2 Chronicles 9:23), Solomon for a time honored God by reverently pointing them to the Creator of the heavens and the earth, the Ruler of the universe, the All-wise.

Had Solomon continued in humility of mind to turn the attention of men from himself to the One who had given him wisdom and riches and honor, what a history might have been his! But while the pen of inspiration records his virtues, it also bears faithful witness to his downfall. Raised to a pinnacle of greatness and surrounded with the gifts of fortune, Solomon became dizzy, lost his balance, and fell. Constantly extolled by men of the world, he was at length unable to withstand the flattery offered him. The wisdom entrusted to him that he might glorify the Giver, filled him with pride. He finally permitted men to speak of him as the one most worthy of praise for the matchless splendor of the building planned and erected for the honor of "the name of the Lord God of Israel."

Thus it was that the temple of Jehovah came to be known throughout the nations as "Solomon's temple." The human agent had taken to himself the glory that belonged to the One "higher than the highest." Ecclesiastes 5:8. Even to this day the temple of which Solomon declared, "This house which I have built is called by Thy name" (2 Chronicles 6:33), is oftenest spoken of, not as the temple of Jehovah, but as "Solomon's temple."

Man cannot show greater weakness than by allowing men to ascribe to him the honor for gifts that are Heaven-bestowed. The true Christian will make God first and [69] last and best in everything. No ambitious motives will chill his love for God; steadily, perseveringly, will he cause honor to redound to his heavenly Father. It is when we are faithful in exalting the name of God that our impulses are under divine supervision, and we are enabled to develop spiritual and intellectual power.

Jesus, the divine Master, ever exalted the name of His heavenly Father. He taught His disciples to pray, "Our Father who art in heaven, hallowed be Thy name." Matthew 6:9, A.R.V. And they were not to forget to acknowledge, "Thine is ... the glory." Verse 13. So careful was the great Healer to direct attention from Himself to the Source of His power, that the wondering multitude, "when they saw the dumb to speak, the maimed to be whole, the lame to walk, and the blind to see," did not glorify Him, but "glorified the God of Israel." Matthew 15:31. In the wonderful prayer that Christ offered just before His crucifixion, He declared, "I have glorified Thee on the earth." "Glorify Thy Son," He pleaded, "that Thy Son also may glorify Thee." "O righteous Father, the world hath not known Thee: but I have known Thee, and these have known that Thou hast sent Me. And I have declared unto them Thy name, and will declare it: that the love wherewith Thou hast loved Me may be in them, and I in them." John 17:4, 1, 25, 26.

"Thus saith the Lord, Let not the wise man glory in his wisdom, neither let the mighty man glory in his might, let not the rich man glory in his riches: but let him that glorieth glory in this, that he understandeth and knoweth Me, [70] that I am the Lord which exercise loving-kindness, judgment, and righteousness, in the earth: for in these things I delight, saith the Lord." Jeremiah 9:23, 24.

"I will praise the name of God, ... And will magnify Him with thanksgiving."

"Thou art worthy, O Lord, to receive glory and honor and power."

"I will praise Thee, O Lord my God, with all my heart: And I will glorify Thy name forevermore."

"O magnify the Lord with me, And let us exalt His name together."

Psalm 69:30; Revelation 4:11; Psalm 86:12; 34:3.

The introduction of principles leading away from a spirit of sacrifice and tending toward self-glorification, was accompanied by yet another gross perversion of the divine plan for Israel. God had designed that His people should be the light of the world. From them was to shine forth the glory of His law as revealed in the life practice. For the carrying out of this design, He had caused the chosen nation to occupy a strategic position among the nations of earth.

In the days of Solomon the kingdom of Israel extended from Hamath on the north to Egypt on the south, and from the Mediterranean Sea to the river Euphrates. Through this territory ran many natural highways of the world's commerce, and caravans from distant lands were constantly passing to and fro. Thus there was given to Solomon and his people opportunity to reveal to men of all nations the character of the King of kings, and to teach them to reverence and obey Him. To all the world this knowledge was [71] to be given. Through the teaching of the sacrificial offerings, Christ was to be uplifted before the nations, that all who would might live.

Placed at the head of a nation that had been set as a beacon light to the surrounding nations, Solomon should have used his God-given wisdom and power of influence in organizing and directing a great movement for the enlightenment of those who were ignorant of God and His truth. Thus multitudes would have been won to allegiance to the divine precepts, Israel would have been shielded from the evils practiced by the heathen, and the Lord of glory would have been greatly honored. But Solomon lost sight of this high purpose. He failed of improving his splendid opportunities for enlightening those who were continually passing through his territory or tarrying at the principal cities.

The missionary spirit that God had implanted in the heart of Solomon and in the hearts of all true Israelites was supplanted by a spirit of commercialism. The opportunities afforded by contact with many nations were used for personal aggrandizement. Solomon sought to strengthen his position politically by building fortified cities at the gateways of commerce. He rebuilt Gezer, near Joppa, lying along the road between Egypt and Syria; Beth-horon, to the westward of Jerusalem, commanding the passes of the highway leading from the heart of Judea to Gezer and the seacoast; Megiddo, situated on the caravan road from Damascus to Egypt, and from Jerusalem to the northward; and "Tadmor in the wilderness" (2 Chronicles 8:4), along the route of caravans from the east. All these cities were strongly [72] fortified. The commercial advantages of an outlet at the head of the Red Sea were developed by the construction of "a navy of ships in Ezion-geber, ... on the shore of the Red Sea, in the land of Edom." Trained sailors from Tyre, "with the servants of Solomon," manned these vessels on voyages "to Ophir, and fetched from thence gold," and "great plenty of almug trees, and precious stones." Verse 18; 1 Kings 9:26, 28; 10:11.

The revenue of the king and of many of his subjects was greatly increased, but at what a cost! Through the cupidity and shortsightedness of those to whom had been entrusted the oracles of God, the countless multitudes who thronged [73] the highways of travel were allowed to remain in ignorance of Jehovah.

In striking contrast to the course pursued by Solomon was the course followed by Christ when He was on this earth. The Saviour, though possessing "all power," never used this power for self-aggrandizement. No dream of earthly conquest, of worldly greatness, marred the perfection of His service for mankind. "Foxes have holes, and the birds of the air have nests," He said, "but the Son of man hath not where to lay His head." Matthew 8:20. Those who, in response to the call of the hour, have entered the service of the Master Worker, may well study His methods. He took advantage of the opportunities to be found along the great thoroughfares of travel.

In the intervals of His journeys to and fro, Jesus dwelt at Capernaum, which came to be known as "His own city." Matthew 9:1. Situated on the highway from Damascus to Jerusalem and Egypt and to the Mediterranean Sea, it was well adapted to be the center of the Saviour's work. People from many lands passed through the city or tarried for rest. There Jesus met with those of all nations and all ranks, and thus His lessons were carried to other countries and into many households. By this means interest was aroused in the prophecies pointing forward to the Messiah, attention was directed to the Saviour, and His mission was brought before the world.

In this our day the opportunities for coming into contact with men and women of all classes and many nationalities are much greater than in the days of Israel. The thoroughfares of travel have multiplied a thousandfold. [74]

Like Christ, the messengers of the Most High today should take their position in these great thoroughfares, where they can meet the passing multitudes from all parts of the world. Like Him, hiding self in God, they are to sow the gospel seed, presenting before others the precious truths of Holy Scripture that will take deep root in mind and heart, and spring up unto life eternal.

Solemn are the lessons of Israel's failure during the years when ruler and people turned from the high purpose they had been called to fulfill. Wherein they were weak, even to the point of failure, the Israel of God today, the representatives of heaven that make up the true church of Christ, must be strong; for upon them devolves the task of finishing the work that has been committed to man, and of ushering in the day of final awards. Yet the same influences that prevailed against Israel in the time when Solomon reigned are to be met with still. The forces of the enemy of all righteousness are strongly entrenched; only by the power of God can the victory be gained. The conflict before us calls for the exercise of a spirit of self-denial, for distrust of self and for dependence on God alone, for the wise use of every opportunity for the saving of souls. The Lord's blessing will attend His church as they advance unitedly, revealing to a world lying in the darkness of error the beauty of holiness as manifested in a Christlike spirit of self-sacrifice, in an exaltation of the divine rather than the human, and in loving and untiring service for those so much in need of the blessings of the gospel. [75]

Chapter 5

Solomon's Repentance

Twice during Solomon's reign the Lord had appeared to him with words of approval and counsel—in the night vision at Gibeon, when the promise of wisdom, riches, and honor was accompanied by an admonition to remain humble and obedient; and after the dedication of the temple, when once more the Lord exhorted him to faithfulness. Plain were the admonitions, wonderful the promises, given to Solomon; yet of him who in circumstances, in character, and in life seemed abundantly fitted to heed the charge and meet the expectation of Heaven, it is recorded: "He kept not that which the Lord commanded." "His heart was turned from the Lord God of Israel, which had appeared unto him twice, and had commanded him concerning this thing, that he should not go after other gods." 1 Kings 11:9, 10. And so complete was his apostasy, so hardened his heart in transgression, that his case seemed well-nigh hopeless. [76]

From the joy of divine communion, Solomon turned to find satisfaction in the pleasures of sense. Of this experience he says:

"I made me great works; I builded me houses; I planted me vineyards: I made me gardens and orchards: ... I got me servants and maidens: ... I gathered me also silver and gold, and the peculiar treasure of kings and of the provinces: I gat me men singers and women singers, and the delights of the sons of men, as musical instruments, and that of all sorts. So I was great, and increased more than all that were before me in Jerusalem....

"And whatsoever mine eyes desired I kept not from them, I withheld not my heart from any joy; for my heart rejoiced in all my labor.... Then I looked on all the works that my hands had wrought, and on the labor that I had labored to do: and, behold, all was vanity and vexation of spirit, and there was no profit under the sun.

"And I turned myself to behold wisdom, and madness, and folly: for what can the man do that cometh after the king? even that which hath been already done.... I hated life.... Yea, I hated all my labor which I had taken under the sun." Ecclesiastes 2:4-18.

By his own bitter experience, Solomon learned the emptiness of a life that seeks in earthly things its highest good. He erected altars to heathen gods, only to learn how vain is their promise of rest to the spirit. Gloomy and soul-harassing thoughts troubled him night and day. For him there was no longer any joy of life or peace of mind, and the future was dark with despair. [77]

Yet the Lord forsook him not. By messages of reproof and by severe judgments, He sought to arouse the king to a realization of the sinfulness of his course. He removed His protecting care and permitted adversaries to harass and weaken the kingdom. "The Lord stirred up an adversary unto Solomon, Hadad the Edomite.... And God stirred him up another adversary, Rezon, ... captain over a band," who "abhorred Israel, and reigned over Syria. And Jeroboam, ... Solomon's servant," "a mighty man of valor," "even he lifted up his hand against the king." 1 Kings 11:14-28.

At last the Lord, through a prophet, delivered to Solomon the startling message: "Forasmuch as this is done of thee, and thou hast not kept My covenant and My statutes, which I have commanded thee, I will surely rend the kingdom from thee, and will give it to thy servant. Notwithstanding in thy days I will not do it for David thy father's sake: but I will rend it out of the hand of thy son." Verses 11, 12.

Awakened as from a dream by this sentence of judgment pronounced against him and his house, Solomon with quickened conscience began to see his folly in its true light. Chastened in spirit, with mind and body enfeebled, he turned wearied and thirsting from earth's broken cisterns, to drink once more at the fountain of life. For him at last the discipline of suffering had accomplished its work. Long had he been harassed by the fear of utter ruin because of inability to turn from folly; but now he discerned in the message given him a ray of hope. God had not utterly cut him off, but stood ready to deliver him from a bondage more cruel [78] than the grave, and from which he had had no power to free himself.

In gratitude Solomon acknowledged the power and the loving-kindness of the One who is "higher than the highest" (Ecclesiastes 5:8); in penitence he began to retrace his steps toward the exalted plane of purity and holiness from whence he had fallen so far. He could never hope to escape the blasting results of sin, he could never free his mind from all remembrance of the self-indulgent course he had been pursuing, but he would endeavor earnestly to dissuade others from following after folly. He would humbly confess the error of his ways and lift his voice in warning lest others be lost irretrievably because of the influences for evil he had been setting in operation.

The true penitent does not put his past sins from his remembrance. He does not, as soon as he has obtained peace, grow unconcerned in regard to the mistakes he has made. He thinks of those who have been led into evil by his course, and tries in every possible way to lead them back into the true path. The clearer the light that he has entered into, the stronger is his desire to set the feet of others in the right way. He does not gloss over his wayward course, making his wrong a light thing, but lifts the danger signal, that others may take warning.

Solomon acknowledged that "the heart of the sons of men is full of evil, and madness is in their heart." Ecclesiastes 9:3. And again he declared, "Because sentence against an evil work is not executed speedily, therefore the heart of the sons of men is fully set in them to do evil. Though a sinner do evil an hundred times, and his days be prolonged, [79] yet surely I know that it shall be well with them that fear God, which fear before Him: but it shall not be well with the wicked, neither shall he prolong his days, which are as a shadow; because he feareth not before God." Ecclesiastes 8:11-13.

By the spirit of inspiration the king recorded for after generations the history of his wasted years with their lessons of warning. And thus, although the seed of his sowing was reaped by his people in harvests of evil, his life-work was not wholly lost. With meekness and lowliness Solomon in his later years "taught the people knowledge; yea, he gave good heed, and sought out, and set in order [80] many proverbs." He "sought to find out acceptable words: and that which was written was upright, even words of truth." "The words of the wise are as goads, and as nails fastened by the masters of assemblies, which are given from one shepherd. And further, by these, my son, be admonished." Ecclesiastes 12:9-12.

"Let us hear the conclusion of the whole matter," he wrote: "Fear God, and keep His commandments: for this is the whole duty of man. For God shall bring every work into judgment, with every secret thing, whether it be good, or whether it be evil." Verses 13, 14.

Solomon's later writings reveal that as he realized more and still more the wickedness of his course, he gave special attention to warning the youth against falling into the errors that had led him to squander for nought Heaven's choicest gifts. With sorrow and shame he confessed that in the prime of manhood, when he should have found God his comfort, his support, his life, he turned from the light of Heaven and the wisdom of God, and put idolatry in the place of the worship of Jehovah. And now, having learned through sad experience the folly of such a life, his yearning desire was to save others from entering into the bitter experience through which he had passed.

With touching pathos he wrote concerning the privileges and responsibilities before the youth in God's service:

"Truly the light is sweet, and a pleasant thing it is for the eyes to behold the sun: but if a man live many years, and rejoice in them all; yet let him remember the days of darkness; for they shall be many. All that cometh is vanity. Rejoice, O young man, in thy youth; and let thy heart [81] cheer thee in the days of thy youth, and walk in the ways of thine heart, and in the sight of thine eyes: but know thou, that for all these things God will bring thee into judgment. Therefore remove sorrow from thy heart, and put away evil from thy flesh: for childhood and youth are vanity." Ecclesiastes 11:7-10.

"Remember now thy Creator in the days of thy youth, While the evil days come not, Nor the years draw nigh, When thou shalt say, I have no pleasure in them;

"While the sun, Or the light, Or the moon, Or the stars, Be not darkened, Nor the clouds return after the rain:

"In the day when the keepers of the house shall tremble, And the strong men shall bow themselves, And the grinders cease because they are few, And those that look out of the windows be darkened, And the doors shall be shut in the streets,

"When the sound of the grinding is low, And he shall rise up at the voice of the bird, And all the daughters of music shall be brought low;

"Also when they shall be afraid of that which is high, And fears shall be in the way,

"And the almond tree shall flourish, And the grasshopper shall be a burden, And desire shall fail:

"Because man goeth to his long home, And the mourners go about the streets:

"Or ever the silver cord be loosed, Or the golden bowl be broken, Or the pitcher be broken at the fountain, Or the wheel broken at the cistern. [82]

"Then shall the dust return to the earth As it was: And the spirit shall return unto God Who gave it."

Ecclesiastes 12:1-7.

Not only to the youth, but to those of mature years, and to those who are descending the hill of life and facing the western sun, the life of Solomon is full of warning. We see and hear of unsteadiness in youth, the young wavering between right and wrong, and the current of evil passions proving too strong for them. In those of maturer years, we do not look for this unsteadiness and unfaithfulness; we expect the character to be established, the principles firmly rooted. But this is not always so. When Solomon should have been in character as a sturdy oak, he fell from his steadfastness under the power of temptation. When his strength should have been the firmest, he was found to be the weakest.

From such examples we should learn that in watchfulness and prayer is the only safety for both young and old. Security does not lie in exalted position and great privileges. One may for many years have enjoyed a genuine Christian experience, but he is still exposed to Satan's attacks. In the battle with inward sin and outward temptation, even the wise and powerful Solomon was vanquished. His failure teaches us that, whatever a man's intellectual qualities may be, and however faithfully he may have served God in the past, he can never with safety trust in his own wisdom and integrity.

In every generation and in every land the true foundation [83] and pattern for character building have been the same. The divine law, "Thou shalt love the Lord thy God with all thy heart, ... and thy neighbor as thyself," the great principle made manifest in the character and life of our Saviour, is the only secure foundation, the only sure guide. Luke 10:27. "Wisdom and knowledge shall be the stability of thy times, and strength of salvation," the wisdom and knowledge which God's word alone can impart. Isaiah 33:6.

It is as true now as when the words were spoken to Israel of obedience to His commandments: "This is your wisdom and your understanding in the sight of the nations." Deuteronomy 4:6. Here is the only safeguard for individual integrity, for the purity of the home, the well-being of society, or the stability of the nation. Amidst all life's perplexities and dangers and conflicting claims, the one safe and sure rule is to do what God says. "The statutes of the Lord are right," and "he that doeth these things shall never be moved." Psalm 19:8; 15:5.

Those who heed the warning of Solomon's apostasy will shun the first approach of those sins that overcame him. Only obedience to the requirements of Heaven will keep man from apostasy. God has bestowed upon man great light and many blessings; but unless this light and these blessings are accepted, they are no security against disobedience and apostasy. When those whom God has exalted to positions of high trust turn from Him to human wisdom, their light becomes darkness. Their entrusted capabilities become a snare.

Till the conflict is ended, there will be those who will depart from God. Satan will so shape circumstances that [84] unless we are kept by divine power, they will almost imperceptibly weaken the fortifications of the soul. We need to inquire at every step, "Is this the way of the Lord?" So long as life shall last, there will be need of guarding the affections and the passions with a firm purpose. Not one moment can we be secure except as we rely upon God, the life hidden with Christ. Watchfulness and prayer are the safeguards of purity.

All who enter the City of God will enter through the strait gate—by agonizing effort; for "there shall in no wise enter into it anything that defileth." Revelation 21:27. But none who have fallen need give up to despair. Aged men, once honored of God, may have defiled their souls, sacrificing virtue on the altar of lust; but if they repent, forsake sin, and turn to God, there is still hope for them. He who declares, "Be thou faithful unto death, and I will give thee a crown of life," also gives the invitation, "Let the wicked forsake his way, and the unrighteous man his thoughts: and let him return unto the Lord, and He will have mercy upon him; and to our God, for He will abundantly pardon." Revelation 2:10; Isaiah 55:7. God hates sin, but He loves the sinner. "I will heal their backsliding," He declares; "I will love them freely." Hosea 14:4.

Solomon's repentance was sincere; but the harm that his example of evil-doing had wrought could not be undone. During his apostasy there were in the kingdom men who remained true to their trust, maintaining their purity and loyalty. But many were led astray; and the forces of evil set in operation by the introduction of idolatry and worldly practices could not easily be stayed by the penitent king. [85] his influence for good was greatly weakened. Many hesitated to place full confidence in his leadership. Though the king confessed his sin and wrote out for the benefit of after generations a record of his folly and repentance, he could never hope entirely to destroy the baleful influence of his wrong deeds. Emboldened by his apostasy, many continued to do evil, and evil only. And in the downward course of many of the rulers who followed him may be traced the sad influence of the prostitution of his God-given powers.

In the anguish of bitter reflection on the evil of his course, Solomon was constrained to declare, "Wisdom is better than weapons of war: but one sinner destroyeth much good." "There is an evil which I have seen under the sun, as an error which proceedeth from the ruler: folly is set in great dignity."

"Dead flies cause the ointment of the apothecary to send forth a stinking savor: so doth a little folly him that is in reputation for wisdom and honor." Ecclesiastes 9:18; 10:5, 6, 1.

Among the many lessons taught by Solomon's life, none is more strongly emphasized than the power of influence for good or for ill. However contracted may be our sphere, we still exert an influence for weal or woe. Beyond our knowledge or control, it tells upon others in blessing or cursing. It may be heavy with the gloom of discontent and selfishness, or poisonous with the deadly taint of some cherished sin; or it may be charged with the life-giving power of faith, courage, and hope, and sweet with the fragrance of love. But potent for good or for ill it will surely be. [86]

That our influence should be a savor of death unto death is a fearful thought, yet it is possible. One soul misled, forfeiting eternal bliss—who can estimate the loss! And yet one rash act, one thoughtless word, on our part may exert so deep an influence on the life of another that it will prove the ruin of his soul. One blemish on the character may turn many away from Christ.

As the seed sown produces a harvest, and this in turn is sown, the harvest is multiplied. In our relation to others, this law holds true. Every act, every word, is a seed that will bear fruit. Every deed of thoughtful kindness, of obedience, of self-denial, will reproduce itself in others, and through them in still others. So every act of envy, malice, or dissension is a seed that will spring up in a "root of bitterness" whereby many shall be defiled. Hebrews 12:15. And how much larger number will the "many" poison! Thus the sowing of good and evil goes on for time and for eternity. [87]

Chapter 6

The Rending of the Kingdom

"Solomon slept with his fathers, and was buried in the City of David his father: and Rehoboam his son reigned in his stead." 1 Kings 11:43.

Soon after his accession to the throne, Rehoboam went to Shechem, where he expected to receive formal recognition from all the tribes. "To Shechem were all Israel come to make him king." 2 Chronicles 10:1.

Among those present was Jeroboam the son of Nebat—the same Jeroboam who during Solomon's reign had been known as "a mighty man of valor," and to whom the prophet Ahijah the Shilonite had delivered the startling message, "Behold, I will rend the kingdom out of the hand of Solomon, and will give ten tribes to thee." 1 Kings 11:28, 31.

The Lord through His messenger had spoken plainly to Jeroboam regarding the necessity of dividing the kingdom. This division must take place, He had declared, "because that they have forsaken Me, and have worshiped [88] Ashtoreth the goddess of the Zidonians, Chemosh the god of the Moabites, and Milcom the god of the children of Ammon, and have not walked in My ways, to do that which is right in Mine eyes, and to keep My statutes and My judgments, as did David." Verse 33.

Jeroboam had been further instructed that the kingdom was not to be divided before the close of Solomon's reign. "I will not take the whole kingdom out of his hand," the Lord had declared; "but I will make him prince all the days of his life for David My servant's sake, whom I chose, because he kept My commandments and My statutes: but I will take the kingdom out of his son's hand, and will give it unto thee, even ten tribes." Verses 34, 35.

Although Solomon had longed to prepare the mind of Rehoboam, his chosen successor, to meet with wisdom the crisis foretold by the prophet of God, he had never been able to exert a strong molding influence for good over the mind of his son, whose early training had been so grossly neglected. Rehoboam had received from his mother, an Ammonitess, the stamp of a vacillating character. At times he endeavored to serve God and was granted a measure of prosperity; but he was not steadfast, and at last he yielded to the influences for evil that had surrounded him from infancy. In the mistakes of Rehoboam's life and in his final apostasy is revealed the fearful result of Solomon's union with idolatrous women.

The tribes had long suffered grievous wrongs under the oppressive measures of their former ruler. The extravagance of Solomon's reign during his apostasy had led him [89] to tax the people heavily and to require of them much menial service. Before going forward with the coronation of a new ruler, the leading men from among the tribes determined to ascertain whether or not it was the purpose of Solomon's son to lessen these burdens. "So Jeroboam and all Israel came and spake to Rehoboam, saying, Thy father made our yoke grievous: now therefore ease thou somewhat the grievous servitude of thy father, and his heavy yoke that he put upon us, and we will serve thee."

Desirous of taking counsel with his advisers before outlining his policy, Rehoboam answered, "Come again unto me after three days. And the people departed.

"And King Rehoboam took counsel with the old men that had stood before Solomon his father while he yet lived, saying, What counsel give ye me to return answer to this people? And they spake unto him, saying, If thou be kind to this people, and please them, and speak good words to them, they will be thy servants forever." 2 Chronicles 10:3-7.

Dissatisfied, Rehoboam turned to the younger men with whom he had associated during his youth and early manhood, and inquired of them, "What counsel give ye that we may answer this people, who have spoken to me, saying, Make the yoke which thy father did put upon us lighter?" 1 Kings 12:9. The young men suggested that he deal sternly with the subjects of his kingdom and make plain to them that from the very beginning he would brook no interference with his personal wishes.

Flattered by the prospect of exercising supreme authority, Rehoboam determined to disregard the counsel of the older [90] men of his realm, and to make the younger men his advisers. Thus it came to pass that on the day appointed, when "Jeroboam and all the people came to Rehoboam" for a statement concerning the policy he intended to pursue, Rehoboam "answered the people roughly, ... saying, My father made your yoke heavy, and I will add to your yoke: my father also chastised you with whips, but I will chastise you with scorpions." Verses 12-14.

Had Rehoboam and his inexperienced counselors understood the divine will concerning Israel, they would have listened to the request of the people for decided reforms in the administration of the government. But in the hour of opportunity that came to them during the meeting in Shechem, they failed to reason from cause to effect, and thus forever weakened their influence over a large number of the people. Their expressed determination to perpetuate and add to the oppression introduced during Solomon's reign was in direct conflict with God's plan for Israel, and gave the people ample occasion to doubt the sincerity of their motives. In this unwise and unfeeling attempt to exercise power, the king and his chosen counselors revealed the pride of position and authority.

The Lord did not allow Rehoboam to carry out the policy he had outlined. Among the tribes were many thousands who had become thoroughly aroused over the oppressive measures of Solomon's reign, and these now felt that they could not do otherwise than rebel against the house of David. "When all Israel saw that the king hearkened not unto them, the people answered the king, saying, What [91] portion have we in David? neither have we inheritance in the son of Jesse: to your tents, O Israel: now see to thine own house, David. So Israel departed unto their tents." Verse 16.

The breach created by the rash speech of Rehoboam proved irreparable. Thenceforth the twelve tribes of Israel were divided, the tribes of Judah and Benjamin composing the lower or southern kingdom of Judah, under the rulership of Rehoboam; while the ten northern tribes formed and maintained a separate government, known as the kingdom of Israel, with Jeroboam as their ruler. Thus was fulfilled the prediction of the prophet concerning the rending of the kingdom. "The cause was from the Lord." Verse 15.

When Rehoboam saw the ten tribes withdrawing their allegiance from him, he was aroused to action. Through one of the influential men of his kingdom, "Adoram, who was over the tribute," he made an effort to conciliate them. But the ambassador of peace received treatment which bore witness to the feeling against Rehoboam. "All Israel stoned him with stones, that he died." Startled by this evidence of the strength of revolt, "King Rehoboam made speed to get him up to his chariot, to flee to Jerusalem." Verse 18.

At Jerusalem "he assembled all the house of Judah, with the tribe of Benjamin, an hundred and fourscore thousand chosen men, which were warriors, to fight against the house of Israel, to bring the kingdom again to Rehoboam the son of Solomon. But the word of God came unto Shemaiah the man of God, saying, Speak unto Rehoboam, the son of Solomon, king of Judah, and unto all the house [92] of Judah and Benjamin, and to the remnant of the people, saying, Thus saith the Lord, Ye shall not go up, nor fight against your brethren the children of Israel: return every man to his house; for this thing is from Me. They hearkened therefore to the word of the Lord, and returned to depart, according to the word of the Lord." Verses 21-24.

For three years Rehoboam tried to profit by his sad experience at the beginning of his reign; and in this effort he was prospered. He "built cities for defense in Judah," and "fortified the strongholds, and put captains in them, [93] and store of victual, and of oil and wine." He was careful to make these fortified cities "exceeding strong." 2 Chronicles 11:5, 11, 12. But the secret of Judah's prosperity during the first years of Rehoboam's reign lay not in these measures. It was their recognition of God as the Supreme Ruler that placed the tribes of Judah and Benjamin on vantage ground. To their number were added many God-fearing men from the northern tribes. "Out of all the tribes of Israel," the record reads, "such as set their hearts to seek the Lord God of Israel came to Jerusalem, to sacrifice unto the Lord God of their fathers. So they strengthened the kingdom of Judah, and made Rehoboam the son of Solomon strong, three years: for three years they walked in the way of David and Solomon." Verses 16, 17.

In continuing this course lay Rehoboam's opportunity to redeem in large measure the mistakes of the past and to restore confidence in his ability to rule with discretion. But the pen of inspiration has traced the sad record of Solomon's successor as one who failed to exert a strong influence for loyalty to Jehovah. Naturally headstrong, confident, self-willed, and inclined to idolatry, nevertheless, had he placed his trust wholly in God, he would have developed strength of character, steadfast faith, and submission to the divine requirements. But as time passed, the king put his trust in the power of position and in the strongholds he had fortified. Little by little he gave way to inherited weakness, until he threw his influence wholly on the side of idolatry. "It came to pass, when Rehoboam had established the kingdom, and had strengthened himself, he forsook [94] the law of the Lord, and all Israel with him." 2 Chronicles 12:1.

How sad, how filled with significance, the words, "and all Israel with him"! The people whom God had chosen to stand as a light to the surrounding nations were turning from their Source of strength and seeking to become like the nations about them. As with Solomon, so with Rehoboam—the influence of wrong example led many astray. And as with them, so to a greater or less degree is it today with everyone who gives himself up to work evil—the influence of wrongdoing is not confined to the doer. No man liveth unto himself. None perish alone in their iniquity. Every life is a light that brightens and cheers the pathway of others, or a dark and desolating influence that tends toward despair and ruin. We lead others either upward to happiness and immortal life, or downward to sorrow and eternal death. And if by our deeds we strengthen or force into activity the evil powers of those around us, we share their sin.

God did not allow the apostasy of Judah's ruler to remain unpunished. "In the fifth year of King Rehoboam Shishak king of Egypt came up against Jerusalem, because they had transgressed against the Lord, with twelve hundred chariots, and three score thousand horsemen: and the people were without number that came with him out of Egypt.... And he took the fenced cities which pertained to Judah, and came to Jerusalem.

"Then came Shemaiah the prophet to Rehoboam, and to the princes of Judah, that were gathered together to [95] Jerusalem because of Shishak, and said unto them, Thus saith the Lord, Ye have forsaken Me, and therefore have I also left you in the hand of Shishak." Verses 2-5.

The people had not yet gone to such lengths in apostasy that they despised the judgments of God. In the losses sustained by the invasion of Shishak, they recognized the hand of God and for a time humbled themselves. "The Lord is righteous," they acknowledged.

"And when the Lord saw that they humbled themselves, the word of the Lord came to Shemaiah, saying, They have humbled themselves; therefore I will not destroy them, but I will grant them some deliverance; and My wrath shall not be poured out upon Jerusalem by the hand of Shishak. Nevertheless they shall be his servants; that they may know My service, and the service of the kingdoms of the countries.

"So Shishak king of Egypt came up against Jerusalem, and took away the treasures of the house of the Lord, and the treasures of the king's house; he took all: he carried away also the shields of gold which Solomon had made. Instead of which King Rehoboam made shields of brass, and committed them to the hands of the chief of the guard, that kept the entrance of the king's house.... And when he humbled himself, the wrath of the Lord turned from him, that He would not destroy him altogether: and also in Judah things went well." Verses 6-12.

But as the hand of affliction was removed, and the nation prospered once more, many forgot their fears and turned again to idolatry. Among these was King Rehoboam himself. Though humbled by the calamity that had befallen [96] him, he failed to make this experience a decisive turning point in his life. Forgetting the lesson that God had endeavored to teach him, he relapsed into the sins that had brought judgments on the nation. After a few inglorious years, during which the king "did evil, because he prepared not his heart to seek the Lord," "Rehoboam slept with his fathers, and was buried in the City of David: and Abijah his son reigned in his stead." Verses 14, 16.

With the rending of the kingdom early in Rehoboam's reign the glory of Israel began to depart, never again to be regained in its fullness. At times during the centuries that followed, the throne of David was occupied by men of moral worth and far-seeing judgment, and under the rulership of these sovereigns the blessings resting upon the men of Judah were extended to the surrounding nations. At times the name of Jehovah was exalted above every false god, and His law was held in reverence. From time to time mighty prophets arose to strengthen the hands of the rulers and to encourage the people to continued faithfulness. But the seeds of evil already springing up when Rehoboam ascended the throne were never to be wholly uprooted; and at times the once-favored people of God were to fall so low as to become a byword among the heathen.

Yet notwithstanding the perversity of those who leaned toward idolatrous practices, God in mercy would do everything in His power to save the divided kingdom from utter ruin. And as the years rolled on and His purpose concerning Israel seemed to be utterly thwarted by the devices of men inspired by satanic agencies, He still manifested His [97] beneficent designs through the captivity and restoration of the chosen nation.

The rending of the kingdom was but the beginning of a wonderful history, wherein are revealed the long-sufferance and tender mercy of God. From the crucible of affliction through which they were to pass because of hereditary and cultivated tendencies to evil, those whom God was seeking to purify unto Himself a peculiar people, zealous of good works, were finally to acknowledge:

"There is none like unto Thee, O Lord; Thou art great, and Thy name is great in might. Who would not fear Thee, O King of nations? ... Among all the wise men of the nations, and in all their kingdoms, there is none like unto Thee." "The Lord is the true God, He is the living God, and an everlasting King." Jeremiah 10:6, 7, 10.

And the worshipers of idols were at last to learn the lesson that false gods are powerless to uplift and save. "The gods that have not made the heavens and the earth, even they shall perish from the earth, and from under these heavens." Verse 11. Only in allegiance to the living God, the Creator of all and the Ruler over all, can man find rest and peace.

With one accord the chastened and penitent of Israel and Judah were at last to renew their covenant relationship with Jehovah of hosts, the God of their fathers; and of Him they were to declare:

"He hath made the earth by His power, He hath established the world by His wisdom, And hath stretched out the heavens by His discretion. [98]

"When He uttereth His voice, there is a multitude of waters in the heavens.

And He causeth the vapors to ascend from the ends of the earth; He maketh lightnings with rain, and bringeth forth the wind out of His treasures.

"Every man is brutish in his knowledge: Every founder is confounded by the graven image: For his molten image is falsehood, and there is no breath in them.

"They are vanity, and the work of errors: In the time of their visitation they shall perish. The portion of Jacob is not like them:

"For He is the former of all things; And Israel is the rod of His inheritance: The Lord of hosts is His name."

Verse 12-16. [99]

Chapter 7

Jeroboam

Placed on the throne by the ten tribes of Israel who had rebelled against the house of David, Jeroboam, the former servant of Solomon, was in a position to bring about wise reforms in both civil and religious affairs. Under the rulership of Solomon he had shown aptitude and sound judgment; and the knowledge he had gained during years of faithful service fitted him to rule with discretion. But Jeroboam failed to make God his trust.

Jeroboam's greatest fear was that at some future time the hearts of his subjects might be won over by the ruler occupying the throne of David. He reasoned that if the ten tribes should be permitted to visit often the ancient seat of the Jewish monarchy, where the services of the temple were still conducted as in the years of Solomon's reign, many might feel inclined to renew their allegiance to the government centering at Jerusalem. Taking counsel with his advisers, Jeroboam determined by one bold stroke to [100] lessen, so far as possible, the probability of a revolt from his rule. He would bring this about by creating within the borders of his newly formed kingdom two centers of worship, one at Bethel and the other at Dan. In these places the ten tribes should be invited to assemble, instead of at Jerusalem, to worship God.

In arranging this transfer, Jeroboam thought to appeal to the imagination of the Israelites by setting before them some visible representation to symbolize the presence of the invisible God. Accordingly he caused to be made two calves of gold, and these were placed within shrines at the appointed centers of worship. In this effort to represent the Deity, Jeroboam violated the plain command of Jehovah: "Thou shalt not make unto thee any graven image.... Thou shalt not bow down thyself to them, nor serve them." Exodus 20:4, 5.

So strong was Jeroboam's desire to keep the ten tribes away from Jerusalem that he lost sight of the fundamental weakness of his plan. He failed to take into consideration the great peril to which he was exposing the Israelites by setting before them the idolatrous symbol of the deity with which their ancestors had been so familiar during the centuries of Egyptian bondage. Jeroboam's recent residence in Egypt should have taught him the folly of placing before the people such heathen representations. But his set purpose of inducing the northern tribes to discontinue their annual visits to the Holy City led him to adopt the most imprudent of measures. "It is too much for you to go up to Jerusalem," he urged; "behold thy gods, O Israel, which brought thee up out of the land of Egypt." 1 Kings 12:28. [101] Thus they were invited to bow down before the golden images and adopt strange forms of worship.

The king tried to persuade the Levites, some of whom were living within his realm, to serve as priests in the newly erected shrines at Bethel and Dan; but in this effort he met with failure. He was therefore compelled to elevate to the priesthood men from "the lowest of the people." Verse 31. Alarmed over the prospect, many of the faithful, including a great number of the Levites, fled to Jerusalem, where they might worship in harmony with the divine requirements.

"Jeroboam ordained a feast in the eighth month, on the fifteenth day of the month, like unto the feast that is in Judah, and he offered upon the altar. So did he in Bethel, sacrificing unto the calves that he had made: and he placed in Bethel the priests of the high places which he had made." Verse 32.

The king's bold defiance of God in thus setting aside divinely appointed institutions was not allowed to pass unrebuked. Even while he was officiating and burning incense during the dedication of the strange altar he had set up at Bethel, there appeared before him a man of God from the kingdom of Judah, sent to denounce him for presuming to introduce new forms of worship. The prophet "cried against the altar, ... and said, O altar, altar, thus saith the Lord; Behold, a child shall be born unto the house of David, Josiah by name; and upon thee shall he offer the priests of the high places that burn incense upon thee, and men's bones shall be burnt upon thee.

"And he gave a sign the same day, saying, This is the sign which the Lord hath spoken; Behold, the altar shall [102] be rent, and the ashes that are upon it shall be poured out." Immediately the altar "was rent, and the ashes poured out from the altar, according to the sign which the man of God had given by the word of the Lord." 1 Kings 13:2, 3, 5.

On seeing this, Jeroboam was filled with a spirit of defiance against God and attempted to restrain the one who had delivered the message. In wrath "he put forth his hand from the altar" and cried out, "Lay hold on him." His impetuous act met with swift rebuke. The hand outstretched against the messenger of Jehovah suddenly became powerless and withered, and could not be withdrawn.

Terror-stricken, the king appealed to the prophet to intercede with God in his behalf. "Entreat now the face of the Lord thy God," he pleaded, "and pray for me, that my hand may be restored me again. And the man of God besought the Lord, and the king's hand was restored him again, and became as it was before." Verses 4, 6.

Vain had been Jeroboam's effort to invest with solemnity the dedication of a strange altar, respect for which would have led to disrespect for the worship of Jehovah in the temple at Jerusalem. By the message of the prophet, the king of Israel should have been led to repent and to renounce his wicked purposes, which were turning the people away from the true worship of God. But he hardened his heart and determined to follow a way of his own choosing.

At the time of the feast at Bethel the hearts of the Israelites were not fully hardened. Many were susceptible to the influence of the Holy Spirit. The Lord designed that those [103] [104] [105] who were taking rapid steps in apostasy should be checked in their course before it should be too late. He sent His messenger to interrupt the idolatrous proceedings and to reveal to king and people what the outworking of this apostasy would be. The rending of the altar was a sign of God's displeasure at the abomination that was being wrought in Israel.

The Lord seeks to save, not to destroy. He delights in the rescue of sinners. "As I live, saith the Lord God, I have no pleasure in the death of the wicked." Ezekiel 33:11. By warnings and entreaties He calls the wayward to cease from their evil-doing and to turn to Him and live. He gives His chosen messengers a holy boldness, that those who hear may fear and be brought to repentance. How firmly the man of God rebuked the king! And this firmness was essential; in no other way could the existing evils have been rebuked. The Lord gave His servant boldness, that an abiding impression might be made on those who heard. The messengers of the Lord are never to fear the face of man, but are to stand unflinchingly for the right. So long as they put their trust in God, they need not fear; for He who gives them their commission gives them also the assurance of His protecting care.

Having delivered his message, the prophet was about to return, when Jeroboam said to him, "Come home with me, and refresh thyself, and I will give thee a reward." "If thou wilt give me half thine house," the prophet replied, "I will not go in with thee, neither will I eat bread nor drink water in this place: for so was it charged me by the [106] word of the Lord, saying, Eat no bread, nor drink water, nor turn again by the same way that thou camest." 1 Kings 13:7-9.

Well would it have been for the prophet had he adhered to his purpose to return to Judea without delay. While traveling homeward by another route, he was overtaken by an aged man who claimed to be a prophet and who made false representations to the man of God, declaring, "I am a prophet also as thou art; and an angel spake unto me by the word of the Lord, saying, Bring him back with thee into thine house, that he may eat bread and drink water." Again and again the lie was repeated and the invitation urged until the man of God was persuaded to return.

Because the true prophet allowed himself to take a course contrary to the line of duty, God permitted him to suffer the penalty of transgression. While he and the one who had invited him to return to Bethel were sitting together at the table, the inspiration of the Almighty came upon the false prophet, "and he cried unto the man of God that came from Judah, saying, Thus saith the Lord, Forasmuch as thou hast disobeyed the mouth of the Lord, and hast not kept the commandment which the Lord thy God commanded thee, ... thy carcass shall not come unto the sepulcher of thy fathers." Verses 18-22.

This prophecy of doom was soon literally fulfilled. "It came to pass, after he had eaten bread, and after he had drunk, that he saddled for him the ass.... And when he was gone, a lion met him by the way, and slew him: and his carcass was cast in the way, and the ass stood by it, the lion also stood by the carcass. And, behold, men passed by, and [107] saw the carcass cast in the way, ... and they came and told it in the city where the old prophet dwelt. And when the prophet that brought him back from the way heard thereof, he said, It is the man of God, who was disobedient unto the word of the Lord." Verses 23-26.

The penalty that overtook the unfaithful messenger was a still further evidence of the truth of the prophecy uttered over the altar. If, after disobeying the word of the Lord, the prophet had been permitted to go on in safety, the king would have used this fact in an attempt to vindicate his own disobedience. In the rent altar, in the palsied arm, and in the terrible fate of the one who dared disobey an express command of Jehovah, Jeroboam should have discerned the swift displeasure of an offended God, and these judgments should have warned him not to persist in wrongdoing. But, far from repenting, Jeroboam "made again of the lowest of the people priests of the high places: whosoever would, he consecrated him, and he became one of the priests of the high places." Thus he not only sinned greatly himself, but "made Israel to sin;" and "this thing became sin unto the house of Jeroboam, even to cut it off, and to destroy it from off the face of the earth." Verses 33, 34; 14:16.

Toward the close of a troubled reign of twenty-two years, Jeroboam met with a disastrous defeat in a war with Abijah, the successor of Rehoboam. "Neither did Jeroboam recover strength again in the days of Abijah: and the Lord struck him, and he died." 2 Chronicles 13:20.

The apostasy introduced during Jeroboam's reign became more and more marked, until finally it resulted in the utter ruin of the kingdom of Israel. Even before the death of [108] Jeroboam, Ahijah, the aged prophet at Shiloh who many years before had predicted the elevation of Jeroboam to the throne, declared: "The Lord shall smite Israel, as a reed is shaken in the water, and He shall root up Israel out of this good land, which He gave to their fathers, and shall scatter them beyond the river, because they have made their groves, provoking the Lord to anger. And He shall give Israel up because of the sins of Jeroboam, who did sin, and who made Israel to sin." 1 Kings 14:15, 16.

Yet the Lord did not give Israel up without first doing all that could be done to lead them back to their allegiance to Him. Through long, dark years when ruler after ruler stood up in bold defiance of Heaven and led Israel deeper and still deeper into idolatry, God sent message after message to His backslidden people. Through His prophets He gave them every opportunity to stay the tide of apostasy and to return to Him. During the years that were to follow the rending of the kingdom, Elijah and Elisha were to live and labor, and the tender appeals of Hosea and Amos and Obadiah were to be heard in the land. Never was the kingdom of Israel to be left without noble witnesses to the mighty power of God to save from sin. Even in the darkest hours some would remain true to their divine Ruler and in the midst of idolatry would live blameless in the sight of a holy God. These faithful ones were numbered among the goodly remnant through whom the eternal purpose of Jehovah was finally to be fulfilled. [109]

Chapter 8

National Apostasy

From the time of Jeroboam's death to Elijah's appearance before Ahab the people of Israel suffered a steady spiritual decline. Ruled by men who did not fear Jehovah and who encouraged strange forms of worship, the larger number of the people rapidly lost sight of their duty to serve the living God and adopted many of the practices of idolatry.

Nadab, the son of Jeroboam, occupied the throne of Israel for only a few months. His career of evil was suddenly stopped by a conspiracy headed by Baasha, one of his generals, to gain control of the government. Nadab was slain, with all his kindred in the line of succession, "according unto the saying of the Lord, which He spake by His servant Ahijah the Shilonite: because of the sins of Jeroboam which he sinned, and which he made Israel sin." 1 Kings 15:29, 30.

Thus perished the house of Jeroboam. The idolatrous worship introduced by him had brought upon the guilty offenders the retributive judgments of Heaven; and yet the [110] rulers who followed—Baasha, Elah, Zimri, and Omri—during a period of nearly forty years, continued in the same fatal course of evil-doing.

During the greater part of this time of apostasy in Israel, Asa was ruling in the kingdom of Judah. For many years "Asa did that which was good and right in the eyes of the Lord his God: for he took away the altars of the strange gods, and the high places, and brake down the images, and cut down the groves: and commanded Judah to seek the Lord God of their fathers, and to do the law and the commandment. Also he took away out of all the cities of Judah the high places and the sun [margin] images: and the kingdom was quiet before him." 2 Chronicles 14:2-5.

The faith of Asa was put to a severe test when "Zerah the Ethiopian with an host of a thousand thousand, and three hundred chariots," invaded his kingdom. Verse 9. In this crisis Asa did not put his trust in the "fenced cities in Judah" that he had built, with "walls, and towers, gates, and bars," nor in the "mighty men of valor" in his carefully trained army. Verses 6-8. The king's trust was in Jehovah of hosts, in whose name marvelous deliverances had been wrought in behalf of Israel of old. Setting his forces in battle array, he sought the help of God.

The opposing armies now stood face to face. It was a time of test and trial to those who served the Lord. Had every sin been confessed? Had the men of Judah full confidence in God's power to deliver? Such thoughts as these were in the minds of the leaders. From every human viewpoint the vast host from Egypt would sweep everything before it. But in time of peace Asa had not been giving [111] himself to amusement and pleasure; he had been preparing for any emergency. He had an army trained for conflict; he had endeavored to lead his people to make their peace with God. And now, although his forces were fewer in number than the enemy, his faith in the One whom he had made his trust did not weaken.

Having sought the Lord in the days of prosperity, the king could now rely upon Him in the day of adversity. His petitions showed that he was not a stranger to God's wonderful power. "It is nothing with Thee to help," he pleaded, "whether with many, or with them that have no power: help us, O Lord our God; for we rest on Thee, and in Thy name we go against this multitude. O Lord, Thou art our God; let not man prevail against Thee." Verse 11.

The prayer of Asa is one that every Christian believer may fittingly offer. We fight in a warfare, not against flesh and blood, but against principalities and powers, and against spiritual wickedness in high places. See Ephesians 6:12. In life's conflict we must meet evil agencies that have arrayed themselves against the right. Our hope is not in man, but in the living God. With full assurance of faith we may expect that He will unite His omnipotence with the efforts of human instrumentalities, for the glory of His name. Clad with the armor of His righteousness, we may gain the victory over every foe.

King Asa's faith was signally rewarded. "The Lord smote the Ethiopians before Asa, and before Judah; and the Ethiopians fled. And Asa and the people that were with him pursued them unto Gerar: and the Ethiopians were overthrown, that they could not recover themselves; [112] for they were destroyed before the Lord, and before His host." 2 Chronicles 14:12, 13.

As the victorious armies of Judah and Benjamin were returning to Jerusalem, "the Spirit of God came upon Azariah the son of Oded: and he went out to meet Asa, and said unto him, Hear ye me, Asa, and all Judah and Benjamin; The Lord is with you, while ye be with Him; and if ye seek Him, He will be found of you; but if ye forsake Him, He will forsake you." "Be ye strong therefore, and let not your hands be weak: for your work shall be rewarded." 2 Chronicles 15:1, 2, 7.

Greatly encouraged by these words, Asa soon led out in a second reformation in Judah. He "put away the abominable idols out of all the land of Judah and Benjamin, and out of the cities which he had taken from Mount Ephraim, and renewed the altar of the Lord, that was before the porch of the Lord.

"And he gathered all Judah and Benjamin, and the strangers with them out of Ephraim and Manasseh, and out of Simeon: for they fell to him out of Israel in abundance, when they saw that the Lord his God was with him. So they gathered themselves together at Jerusalem in the third month, in the fifteenth year of the reign of Asa. And they offered unto the Lord the same time, of the spoil which they had brought, seven hundred oxen and seven thousand sheep. And they entered into a covenant to seek the Lord God of their fathers with all their heart and with all their soul." "And He was found of them: and the Lord gave them rest round about." Verses 8-12, 15. [113]

Asa's long record of faithful service was marred by some mistakes, made at times when he failed to put his trust fully in God. When, on one occasion, the king of Israel entered the kingdom of Judah and seized Ramah, a fortified city only five miles from Jerusalem, Asa sought deliverance by forming an alliance with Benhadad, king of Syria. This failure to trust God alone in time of need was sternly rebuked by Hanani the prophet, who appeared before Asa with the message:

"Because thou hast relied on the king of Syria, and not relied on the Lord thy God, therefore is the host of the king of Syria escaped out of thine hand. Were not the Ethiopians and the Lubims a huge host, with very many chariots and horsemen? yet, because thou didst rely on the Lord, He delivered them into thine hand. For the eyes of the Lord run to and fro throughout the whole earth, to show Himself strong in the behalf of them whose heart is perfect toward Him. Herein thou hast done foolishly: therefore from henceforth thou shalt have wars." 2 Chronicles 16:7-9.

Instead of humbling himself before God because of his mistake, "Asa was wroth with the seer, and put him in a prison house; for he was in a rage with him because of this thing. And Asa oppressed some of the people the same time." Verse 10.

"In the thirty and ninth year of his reign," Asa was "diseased in his feet, until his disease was exceeding great: yet in his disease he sought not to the Lord, but to the physicians." Verse 12. The king died in the forty-first year of his reign and was succeeded by Jehoshaphat, his son. [114]

Two years before the death of Asa, Ahab began to rule in the kingdom of Israel. From the beginning his reign was marked by a strange and terrible apostasy. His father, Omri, the founder of Samaria, had "wrought evil in the eyes of the Lord, and did worse than all that were before him" (1 Kings 16:25); but the sins of Ahab were even greater. He "did more to provoke the Lord God of Israel to anger than all the kings of Israel that were before him," acting "as if it had been a light thing for him to walk in the sins of Jeroboam the son of Nebat." Verses 33, 31. Not content with encouraging the forms of religious service followed at Bethel and Dan, he boldly led the people into the grossest heathenism, by setting aside the worship of Jehovah for Baal worship.

Taking to wife Jezebel, "the daughter of Ethbaal king of the Zidonians" and high priest of Baal, Ahab "served Baal, and worshiped him. And he reared up an altar for Baal in the house of Baal, which he had built in Samaria." Verses 31, 32.

Not only did Ahab introduce Baal worship at the capital city, but under the leadership of Jezebel he erected heathen altars in many "high places," where in the shelter of surrounding groves the priests and others connected with this seductive form of idolatry exerted their baleful influence, until well-nigh all Israel were following after Baal. "There was none like unto Ahab," who "did sell himself to work wickedness in the sight of the Lord, whom Jezebel his wife stirred up. And he did very abominably in following idols, according to all things as did the Amorites, whom the Lord [115] cast out before the children of Israel." 1 Kings 21:25, 26.

Ahab was weak in moral power. His union by marriage with an idolatrous woman of decided character and positive temperament resulted disastrously both to himself and to the nation. Unprincipled, and with no high standard of rightdoing, his character was easily molded by the determined spirit of Jezebel. His selfish nature was incapable of appreciating the mercies of God to Israel and his own obligations as the guardian and leader of the chosen people.

Under the blighting influence of Ahab's rule, Israel wandered far from the living God and corrupted their ways before Him. For many years they had been losing their sense of reverence and godly fear; and now it seemed as if there were none who dared expose their lives by openly standing forth in opposition to the prevailing blasphemy. The dark shadow of apostasy covered the whole land. Images of Baalim and Ashtoreth were everywhere to be seen. Idolatrous temples and consecrated groves, wherein were worshiped the works of men's hands, were multiplied. The air was polluted with the smoke of the sacrifices offered to false gods. Hill and vale resounded with the drunken cries of a heathen priesthood who sacrificed to the sun, moon, and stars.

Through the influence of Jezebel and her impious priests, the people were taught that the idol gods that had been set up were deities, ruling by their mystic power the elements of earth, fire, and water. All the bounties of heaven—the running brooks, the streams of living water, the gentle dew, the showers of rain which refreshed the earth and caused [116] the fields to bring forth abundantly—were ascribed to the favor of Baal and Ashtoreth, instead of to the Giver of every good and perfect gift. The people forgot that the hills and valleys, the streams and fountains, were in the hand of the living God, that He controlled the sun, the clouds of heaven, and all the powers of nature.

Through faithful messengers the Lord sent repeated warnings to the apostate king and the people, but in vain were these words of reproof. In vain did the inspired messengers assert Jehovah's right to be the only God in Israel; in vain did they exalt the laws that He had entrusted to them. Captivated by the gorgeous display and the fascinating rites of idol worship, the people followed the example of the king and his court, and gave themselves up to the intoxicating, degrading pleasures of a sensual worship. In their blind folly they chose to reject God and His worship. The light so graciously given them had become darkness. The fine gold had become dim.

Alas, how had the glory of Israel departed! Never before had the chosen people of God fallen so low in apostasy. Of "the prophets of Baal" there were "four hundred and fifty," besides four hundred "prophets of the groves." 1 Kings 18:19. Nothing short of the miracle-working power of God could preserve the nation from utter destruction. Israel had voluntarily separated herself from Jehovah, yet the Lord in compassion still yearned after those who had been led into sin, and He was about to send to them one of the mightiest of His prophets, through whom many were to be led back to allegiance to the God of their fathers. [117]

Chapter 9

Elijah the Tishbite

Beginning of Section 2 — Prophets of the Northern Kingdom. This chapter is based on 1 Kings 17:1-7.

Among the mountains of Gilead, east of the Jordan, there dwelt in the days of Ahab a man of faith and prayer whose fearless ministry was destined to check the rapid spread of apostasy in Israel. Far removed from any city of renown, and occupying no high station in life, Elijah the Tishbite nevertheless entered upon his mission confident in God's purpose to prepare the way before him and to give him abundant success. The word of faith and power was upon his lips, and his whole life was devoted to the work of reform. His was the voice of one crying in the wilderness to rebuke sin and press back the tide of evil. And while he came to the people as a reprover of sin, his message offered the balm of Gilead to the sin-sick souls of all who desired to be healed.

As Elijah saw Israel going deeper and deeper into idolatry, his soul was distressed and his indignation aroused. God had done great things for His people. He had delivered [120] them from bondage and given them "the lands of the heathen, ... that they might observe His statutes, and keep His laws." Psalm 105:44, 45. But the beneficent designs of Jehovah were now well-nigh forgotten. Unbelief was fast separating the chosen nation from the Source of their strength. Viewing this apostasy from his mountain retreat, Elijah was overwhelmed with sorrow. In anguish of soul he besought God to arrest the once-favored people in their wicked course, to visit them with judgments, if need be, that they might be led to see in its true light their departure from Heaven. He longed to see them brought to repentance before they should go to such lengths in evil-doing as to provoke the Lord to destroy them utterly.

Elijah's prayer was answered. Oft-repeated appeals, remonstrances, and warnings had failed to bring Israel to repentance. The time had come when God must speak to them by means of judgments. Inasmuch as the worshipers of Baal claimed that the treasures of heaven, the dew and the rain, came not from Jehovah, but from the ruling forces of nature, and that it was through the creative energy of the sun that the earth was enriched and made to bring forth abundantly, the curse of God was to rest heavily upon the polluted land. The apostate tribes of Israel were to be shown the folly of trusting to the power of Baal for temporal blessings. Until they should turn to God with repentance, and acknowledge Him as the source of all blessing, there should fall upon the land neither dew nor rain.

To Elijah was entrusted the mission of delivering to Ahab Heaven's message of judgment. He did not seek to [121] be the Lord's messenger; the word of the Lord came to him. And jealous for the honor of God's cause, he did not hesitate to obey the divine summons, though to obey seemed to invite swift destruction at the hand of the wicked king. The prophet set out at once and traveled night and day until he reached Samaria. At the palace he solicited no admission, nor waited to be formally announced. Clad in the coarse garments usually worn by the prophets of that time, he passed the guards, apparently unnoticed, and stood for a moment before the astonished king.

Elijah made no apology for his abrupt appearance. A Greater than the ruler of Israel had commissioned him to speak; and, lifting his hand toward heaven, he solemnly affirmed by the living God that the judgments of the Most High were about to fall upon Israel. "As the Lord God of Israel liveth, before whom I stand," he declared, "there shall not be dew nor rain these years, but according to my word."

It was only by the exercise of strong faith in the unfailing power of God's word that Elijah delivered his message. Had he not possessed implicit confidence in the One whom he served, he would never have appeared before Ahab. On his way to Samaria, Elijah had passed by ever-flowing streams, hills covered with verdure, and stately forests that seemed beyond the reach of drought. Everything on which the eye rested was clothed with beauty. The prophet might have wondered how the streams that had never ceased their flow could become dry, or how those hills and valleys could be burned with drought. But he gave no place to [122] unbelief. He fully believed that God would humble apostate Israel, and that through judgments they would be brought to repentance. The fiat of Heaven had gone forth; God's word could not fail; and at the peril of his life Elijah fearlessly fulfilled his commission. Like a thunderbolt from a clear sky, the message of impending judgment fell upon the ears of the wicked king; but before Ahab could recover from his astonishment, or frame a reply, Elijah disappeared as abruptly as he had come, without waiting to witness the effect of his message. And the Lord went before him, [123] making plain the way. "Turn thee eastward," the prophet was bidden, "and hide thyself by the brook Cherith, that is before Jordan. And it shall be, that thou shalt drink of the brook; and I have commanded the ravens to feed thee."

The king made diligent inquiry, but the prophet was not to be found. Queen Jezebel, angered over the message that had locked up the treasures of heaven, lost no time in conferring with the priests of Baal, who united with her in cursing the prophet and in defying the wrath of Jehovah. But notwithstanding their desire to find him who had uttered the word of woe, they were destined to meet with disappointment. Nor could they conceal from others a knowledge of the judgment pronounced in consequence of the prevailing apostasy. Tidings of Elijah's denunciation of the sins of Israel, and of his prophecy of swift-coming punishment, quickly spread throughout the land. The fears of some were aroused, but in general the heavenly message was received with scorn and ridicule.

The prophet's words went into immediate effect. Those who were at first inclined to scoff at the thought of calamity, soon had occasion for serious reflection; for after a few months the earth, unrefreshed by dew or rain, became dry, and vegetation withered. As time passed, streams that had never been known to fail began to decrease, and brooks began to dry up. Yet the people were urged by their leaders to have confidence in the power of Baal and to set aside as idle words the prophecy of Elijah. The priests still insisted that it was through the power of Baal that the showers of rain fell. Fear not the God of Elijah, nor tremble at [124] His word, they urged, it is Baal that brings forth the harvest in its season and provides for man and beast.

God's message to Ahab gave Jezebel and her priests and all the followers of Baal and Ashtoreth opportunity to test the power of their gods, and, if possible, to prove the word of Elijah false. Against the assurances of hundreds of idolatrous priests, the prophecy of Elijah stood alone. If, notwithstanding the prophet's declaration, Baal could still give dew and rain, causing the streams to continue to flow and vegetation to flourish, then let the king of Israel worship him and the people say that he is god.

Determined to keep the people in deception, the priests of Baal continue to offer sacrifices to their gods and to call upon them night and day to refresh the earth. With costly offerings the priests attempt to appease the anger of their gods; with a zeal and a perseverance worthy of a better cause they linger round their pagan altars and pray earnestly for rain. Night after night, throughout the doomed land, their cries and entreaties arise. But no clouds appear in the heavens by day to hide the burning rays of the sun. No dew or rain refreshes the thirsty earth. The word of Jehovah stands unchanged by anything the priests of Baal can do.

A year passes, and yet there is no rain. The earth is parched as if with fire. The scorching heat of the sun destroys what little vegetation has survived. Streams dry up, and lowing herds and bleating flocks wander hither and thither in distress. Once-flourishing fields have become like burning desert sands, a desolate waste. The groves dedicated to idol worship are leafless; the forest trees, gaunt skeletons [125] of nature, afford no shade. The air is dry and suffocating; dust storms blind the eyes and nearly stop the breath. Once-prosperous cities and villages have become places of mourning. Hunger and thirst are telling upon man and beast with fearful mortality. Famine, with all its horror, comes closer and still closer.

Yet notwithstanding these evidences of God's power, Israel repented not, nor learned the lesson that God would have them learn. They did not see that He who created nature controls her laws, and can make of them instruments of blessing or of destruction. Proud-hearted, enamored of [126] their false worship, they were unwilling to humble themselves under the mighty hand of God, and they began to cast about for some other cause to which to attribute their sufferings.

Jezebel utterly refused to recognize the drought as a judgment from Jehovah. Unyielding in her determination to defy the God of heaven, she, with nearly the whole of Israel, united in denouncing Elijah as the cause of all their misery. Had he not borne testimony against their forms of worship? If only he could be put out of the way, she argued, the anger of their gods would be appeased, and their troubles would end.

Urged on by the queen, Ahab instituted a most diligent search for the hiding place of the prophet. To the surrounding nations, far and near, he sent messengers to seek for the man whom he hated, yet feared; and in his anxiety to make the search as thorough as possible, he required of these kingdoms and nations an oath that they knew nothing of the whereabouts of the prophet. But the search was in vain. The prophet was safe from the malice of the king whose sins had brought upon the land the denunciation of an offended God.

Failing in her efforts against Elijah, Jezebel determined to avenge herself by slaying all the prophets of Jehovah in Israel. Not one should be left alive. The infuriated woman carried out her purpose in the massacre of many of God's servants. Not all, however, perished. Obadiah, the governor of Ahab's house, yet faithful to God, "took an hundred prophets," and at the risk of his own life, "hid them by fifty in a cave, and fed them with bread and water." 1 Kings 18:4. [127]

The second year of famine passed, and still the pitiless heavens gave no sign of rain. Drought and famine continued their devastation throughout the kingdom. Fathers and mothers, powerless to relieve the sufferings of their children, were forced to see them die. Yet still apostate Israel refused to humble their hearts before God and continued to murmur against the man by whose word these terrible judgments had been brought upon them. They seemed unable to discern in their suffering and distress a call to repentance, a divine interposition to save them from taking the fatal step beyond the boundary of Heaven's forgiveness.

The apostasy of Israel was an evil more dreadful than all the multiplied horrors of famine. God was seeking to free the people from their delusion and lead them to understand their accountability to the One to whom they owed their life and all things. He was trying to help them to recover their lost faith, and He must needs bring upon them great affliction.

"Have I any pleasure at all that the wicked should die? saith the Lord God: and not that he should return from his ways, and live?" "Cast away from you all your transgressions, whereby ye have transgressed; and make you a new heart and a new spirit: for why will ye die, O house of Israel? For I have no pleasure in the death of him that dieth, saith the Lord God: wherefore turn yourselves, and live ye." "Turn ye, turn ye from your evil ways; for why will ye die, O house of Israel?" Ezekiel 18:23, 31, 32; 33:11.

God had sent messengers to Israel, with appeals to return to their allegiance. Had they heeded these appeals, had [128] they turned from Baal to the living God, Elijah's message of judgment would never have been given. But the warnings that might have been a savor of life unto life had proved to them a savor of death unto death. Their pride had been wounded, their anger had been aroused against the messengers, and now they regarded with intense hatred the prophet Elijah. If only he should fall into their hands, gladly they would deliver him to Jezebel—as if by silencing his voice they could stay the fulfillment of his words! In the face of calamity they continued to stand firm in their idolatry. Thus they were adding to the guilt that had brought the judgments of Heaven upon the land.

For stricken Israel there was but one remedy—a turning away from the sins that had brought upon them the chastening hand of the Almighty, and a turning to the Lord with full purpose of heart. To them had been given the assurance, "If I shut up heaven that there be no rain, or if I command the locusts to devour the land, or if I send pestilence among My people; if My people, which are called by My name, shall humble themselves, and pray, and seek My face, and turn from their wicked ways; then will I hear from heaven, and will forgive their sin, and will heal their land." 2 Chronicles 7:13, 14. It was to bring to pass this blessed result that God continued to withhold from them the dew and the rain until a decided reformation should take place. [129]

Chapter 10

The Voice of Stern Rebuke

This chapter is based on 1 Kings 17:8-24; 18:1-19.

For a time Elijah remained hidden in the mountains by the brook Cherith. There for many months he was miraculously provided with food. Later on, when, because of the continued drought, the brook became dry, God bade His servant find refuge in a heathen land. "Arise," He bade him, "get thee to Zarephath, [known in New Testament times as Sarepta], which belongeth to Zidon, and dwell there: behold, I have commanded a widow woman there to sustain thee."

This woman was not an Israelite. She had never had the privileges and blessings that the chosen people of God had enjoyed; but she was a believer in the true God and had walked in all the light that was shining on her pathway. And now, when there was no safety for Elijah in the land of Israel, God sent him to this woman to find an asylum in her home.

"So he arose and went to Zarephath. And when he came to the gate of the city, behold, the widow woman was [130] there gathering of sticks: and he called to her, and said, Fetch me, I pray thee, a little water in a vessel, that I may drink. And as she was going to fetch it, he called to her, and said, Bring me, I pray thee, a morsel of bread in thine hand."

In this poverty-stricken home the famine pressed sore, and the pitifully meager fare seemed about to fail. The coming of Elijah on the very day when the widow feared that she must give up the struggle to sustain life tested to the utmost her faith in the power of the living God to provide for her necessities. But even in her dire extremity she bore witness to her faith by a compliance with the request of the stranger who was asking her to share her last morsel with him.

In response to Elijah's request for food and drink, the widow said, "As the Lord thy God liveth, I have not a cake, but an handful of meal in a barrel, and a little oil in a cruse: and, behold, I am gathering two sticks, that I may go in and dress it for me and my son, that we may eat it, and die." Elijah said to her, "Fear not; go and do as thou hast said: but make me thereof a little cake first, and bring it unto me, and after make for thee and for thy son. For thus saith the Lord of Israel, The barrel of meal shall not waste, neither shall the cruse of oil fail, until the day that the Lord sendeth rain upon the earth."

No greater test of faith than this could have been required. The widow had hitherto treated all strangers with kindness and liberality. Now, regardless of the suffering that might result to herself and child, and trusting in the God of Israel [131] to supply her every need, she met this supreme test of hospitality by doing "according to the saying of Elijah."

Wonderful was the hospitality shown to God's prophet by this Phoenician woman, and wonderfully were her faith and generosity rewarded. "She, and he, and her house, did eat many days. And the barrel of meal wasted not, neither did the cruse of oil fail, according to the word of the Lord, which He spake by Elijah.

"And it came to pass after these things, that the son of the woman, the mistress of the house, fell sick; and his sickness was so sore, that there was no breath left in him. And she said unto Elijah, What have I to do with thee, O thou man of God? art thou come unto me to call my sin to remembrance, and to slay my son?

"And he said unto her, Give me thy son. And he took him out of her bosom, and carried him up into a loft, where he abode, and laid him upon his own bed.... And he stretched himself upon the child three times, and cried unto the Lord.... And the Lord heard the voice of Elijah; and the soul of the child came into him again, and he revived.

"And Elijah took the child, and brought him down out of the chamber into the house, and delivered him unto his mother: and Elijah said, See, thy son liveth. And the woman said to Elijah, Now by this I know that thou art a man of God, and that the word of the Lord in thy mouth is truth."

The widow of Zarephath shared her morsel with Elijah, and in return her life and that of her son were preserved. And to all who, in time of trial and want, give sympathy [132] and assistance to others more needy, God has promised great blessing. He has not changed. His power is no less now than in the days of Elijah. No less sure now than when spoken by our Saviour is the promise, "He that receiveth a prophet in the name of a prophet shall receive a prophet's reward." Matthew 10:41.

"Be not forgetful to entertain strangers: for thereby some have entertained angels unawares." Hebrews 13:2. These words have lost none of their force through the lapse of time. Our heavenly Father still continues to place in the pathway of His children opportunities that are blessings in disguise; and those who improve these opportunities find great joy. "If thou draw out thy soul to the hungry, and satisfy the afflicted soul; then shall thy light rise in obscurity, and thy darkness be as the noonday: and the Lord shall guide thee continually, and satisfy thy soul in drought, and make fat thy bones: and thou shalt be like a watered garden, and like a spring of water, whose waters fail not." Isaiah 58:10, 11.

To His faithful servants today Christ says, "He that receiveth you receiveth Me, and he that receiveth Me receiveth Him that sent Me." No act of kindness shown in His name will fail to be recognized and rewarded. And in the same tender recognition Christ includes even the feeblest and lowliest of the family of God. "Whosoever shall give to drink," He says, "unto one of these little ones"—those who are as children in their faith and their knowledge of Christ—"a cup of cold water only in the name of a disciple, verily I say unto you, he shall in no wise lose his reward." Matthew 10:40, 42. [133]

Through the long years of drought and famine, Elijah prayed earnestly that the hearts of Israel might be turned from idolatry to allegiance to God. Patiently the prophet waited, while

PROPHETS AND KINGS

the hand of the Lord rested heavily on the stricken land. As he saw evidences of suffering and want multiplying on every side, his heart was wrung with sorrow, and he longed for power to bring about a reformation quickly. But God Himself was working out His plan, and all that His servant could do was to pray on in faith and await the time for decided action.

The apostasy prevailing in Ahab's day was the result of many years of evil-doing. Step by step, year after year, Israel had been departing from the right way. For generation after generation they had refused to make straight paths for their feet, and at last the great majority of the people had yielded themselves to the leadership of the powers of darkness.

About a century had passed since, under the rulership of King David, Israel had joyfully united in chanting hymns of praise to the Most High, in recognition of their entire dependence on Him for daily mercies. Listen to their words of adoration as then they sang:

"O God of our salvation, ... Thou makest the outgoings of the morning and evening to rejoice. Thou visitest the earth, and waterest it: Thou greatly enrichest it with the river of God, which is full of water: Thou preparest them corn, when Thou hast so provided for it. [134]

Thou waterest the ridges thereof abundantly: Thou causest rain to descend into the furrows thereof: Thou makest it soft with showers: Thou blessest the springing thereof. Thou crownest the year with Thy goodness; And Thy paths drop fatness. They drop upon the pastures of the wilderness: And the little hills rejoice on every side. The pastures are clothed with flocks; The valleys also are covered over with corn; They shout for joy, they also sing."

Psalm 65:5, 8-13, margin.

Israel had then recognized God as the One who "laid the foundations of the earth." In expression of their faith they had sung:

"Thou coveredst it with the deep as with a garment: The waters stood above the mountains. At Thy rebuke they fled; At the voice of Thy thunder they hasted away. They go up by the mountains; they go down by the valleys Unto the place which Thou hast founded for them. Thou hast set a bound that they may not pass over; That they turn not again to cover the earth."

Psalm 104:5-9.

It is by the mighty power of the Infinite One that the elements of nature in earth and sea and sky are kept within bounds. And these elements He uses for the happiness of His creatures. "His good treasure" is freely expended "to give the rain ... in his season, and to bless all the work" of man's hands. Deuteronomy 28:12.

"He sendeth the springs into the valleys, Which run among the hills. They give drink to every beast of the field: The wild asses quench their thirst. By them shall the fowls of the heaven have their habitation, Which sing among the branches.... [135]

He causeth the grass to grow for the cattle, And herb for the service of man: That He may bring forth food out of the earth; And wine that maketh glad the heart of man, And oil to make his face to shine, And bread which strengtheneth man's heart....

"O Lord, how manifold are Thy works! In wisdom has Thou made them all: The earth is full of Thy riches. So is this great and wide sea, Wherein are things creeping innumerable,

Both small and great beasts.... These wait all upon Thee; That Thou mayest give them their meat in due season. That Thou givest them they gather:

"Thou openest Thine hand, They are filled with good."

Psalm 104:10-15, 24-28.

Israel had had abundant occasion for rejoicing. The land to which the Lord had brought them was a land flowing with milk and honey. During the wilderness wandering, God had assured them that He was guiding them to a country where they need never suffer for lack of rain. "The land, whither thou goest in to possess it," He had told them, "is not as the land of Egypt, from whence ye came out, where thou sowedst thy seed, and wateredst it with thy foot, as a garden of herbs: but the land, whither ye go to possess it, is a land of hills and valleys, and drinketh water of the rain of heaven: a land which the Lord thy God careth for: the eyes of the Lord thy God are always upon it, from the beginning of the year even unto the end of the year."

The promise of abundance of rain had been given on [136] condition of obedience. "It shall come to pass," the Lord had declared, "if ye shall hearken diligently unto My commandments which I command you this day, to love the Lord your God, and to serve Him with all your heart and with all your soul, that I will give you the rain of your land in his due season, the first rain and the latter rain, that thou mayest gather in thy corn, and thy wine, and thine oil. And I will send grass in thy fields for thy cattle, that thou mayest eat and be full.

"Take heed to yourselves," the Lord had admonished His people, "that your heart be not deceived, and ye turn aside, and serve other gods, and worship them; and then the Lord's wrath be kindled against you, and He shut up the heaven, that there be no rain, and that the land yield not her fruit; and lest ye perish quickly from off the good land which the Lord giveth you." Deuteronomy 11:10-17.

"If thou wilt not hearken unto the voice of the Lord thy God, to observe to do all His commandments and His statutes," the Israelites had been warned, "thy heaven that is over thy head shall be brass, and the earth that is under thee shall be iron. The Lord shall make the rain of thy land powder and dust: from heaven shall it come down upon thee, until thou be destroyed." Deuteronomy 28:15, 23, 24.

These were among the wise counsels of Jehovah to ancient Israel. "Lay up these My words in your heart and in your soul," He had commanded His chosen people, "and bind them for a sign upon your hand, that they may be as frontlets between your eyes. And ye shall teach them your children, speaking of them when thou sittest in thine house, [137] and when thou walkest by the way, when thou liest down, and when thou risest up." Deuteronomy 11:18, 19. Plain were these commands, yet as the centuries passed, and generation after generation lost sight of the provision made for their spiritual welfare, the ruinous influences of apostasy threatened to sweep aside every barrier of divine grace.

Thus it had come to pass that God was now visiting His people with the severest of His judgments. The prediction of Elijah was meeting with terrible fulfillment. For three years the messenger of woe was sought for in city after city and nation after nation. At the mandate of Ahab, many rulers had given their oath of honor that the strange prophet could not be found in their dominions. Yet the search was continued, for Jezebel and the prophets of Baal hated Elijah with a deadly hatred, and they spared no effort to bring him within reach of their power. And still there was no rain.

At last, "after many days," the word of the Lord came to Elijah, "Go, show thyself unto Ahab; and I will send rain upon the earth."

In obedience to the command, "Elijah went to show himself unto Ahab." About the time that the prophet set forth on his journey to Samaria, Ahab had proposed to Obadiah, the governor of his household, that they make thorough search for springs and brooks of water, in the hope of finding pasture for their starving flocks and herds. Even in the royal court the effect of the long-continued drought was keenly felt. The king, deeply concerned over the outlook for his household, decided to unite personally with his servant in a search for some favored spots where [138] pasture might be had. "So they divided the land between them to pass throughout it: Ahab went one way by himself, and Obadiah went another way by himself."

"As Obadiah was in the way, behold, Elijah met him: and he knew him, and fell on his face, and said, Art thou that my lord Elijah?"

During the apostasy of Israel, Obadiah had remained faithful. His master, the king, had been unable to turn him from his allegiance to the living God. Now he was honored with a commission from Elijah, who said, "Go, tell thy lord, Behold, Elijah is here."

Greatly terrified, Obadiah exclaimed, "What have I sinned, that thou wouldest deliver thy servant into the hand of Ahab, to slay me?" To take such a message as this to Ahab was to court certain death. "As the Lord thy God liveth," he explained to the prophet, "there is no nation or kingdom, whither my lord hath not sent to seek thee: and when they said, He is not there; he took an oath of the kingdom and nation, that they found thee not. And now thou sayest, Go, tell thy lord, Behold, Elijah is here. And it shall come to pass, as soon as I am gone from thee, that the Spirit of the Lord shall carry thee whither I know not; and so when I come and tell Ahab, and he cannot find thee, he shall slay me."

Earnestly Obadiah pleaded with the prophet not to urge him. "I thy servant," he urged, "fear the Lord from my youth. Was it not told my lord what I did when Jezebel slew the prophets of the Lord, how I hid an hundred men of the Lord's prophets by fifty in a cave, and fed them [139] with bread and water? And now thou sayest, Go, tell thy lord, Behold, Elijah is here: and he shall slay me."

With a solemn oath Elijah promised Obadiah that the errand should not be in vain. "As the Lord of hosts liveth, before whom I stand," he declared, "I will surely show myself unto him today." Thus assured, "Obadiah went to meet Ahab, and told him."

In astonishment mingled with terror the king listened to the message from the man whom he feared and hated, and for whom he had sought so untiringly. Well he knew that Elijah would not endanger his life merely for the sake of meeting him. Could it be possible that the prophet was about to utter another woe against Israel? The king's heart was seized with dread. He remembered the withered arm of Jeroboam. Ahab could not avoid obeying the summons, neither dared he lift up his hand against the messenger of God. And so, accompanied by a bodyguard of soldiers, the trembling monarch went to meet the prophet.

The king and the prophet stand face to face. Though Ahab is filled with passionate hatred, yet in the presence of Elijah he seems unmanned, powerless. In his first faltering words, "Art thou he that troubleth Israel?" he unconsciously reveals the inmost feelings of his heart. Ahab knew that it was by the word of God that the heavens had become as brass, yet he sought to cast upon the prophet the blame for the heavy judgments resting on the land.

It is natural for the wrongdoer to hold the messengers of God responsible for the calamities that come as the sure result of a departure from the way of righteousness. Those [140] who place themselves in Satan's power are unable to see things as God sees them. When the mirror of truth is held up before them, they become indignant at the thought of receiving reproof. Blinded by sin, they refuse to repent; they feel that God's servants have turned against them and are worthy of severest censure.

Standing in conscious innocence before Ahab, Elijah makes no attempt to excuse himself or to flatter the king. Nor does he seek to evade the king's wrath by the good news that the drought is almost over. He has no apology to offer. Indignant, and jealous for the honor of God, he casts back the imputation of Ahab, fearlessly declaring to the king that it is his sins, and the sins of his fathers, that have brought upon Israel this terrible calamity. "I have not troubled Israel," Elijah boldly asserts, "but thou, and thy father's house, in that ye have forsaken the commandments of the Lord, and thou hast followed Baalim."

Today there is need of the voice of stern rebuke; for grievous sins have separated the people from God. Infidelity is fast becoming fashionable. "We will not have this man to reign over us," is the language of thousands. Luke 19:14. The smooth sermons so often preached make no lasting impression; the trumpet does not give a certain sound. Men are not cut to the heart by the plain, sharp truths of God's word.

There are many professed Christians who, if they should express their real feelings, would say, What need is there of speaking so plainly? They might as well ask, Why need John the Baptist have said to the Pharisees, "O generation of vipers, who hath warned you to flee from the wrath to [141] come?" Luke 3:7. Why need he have provoked the anger of Herodias by telling Herod that it was unlawful for him to live with his brother's wife? The forerunner of Christ lost his life by his plain speaking. Why could he not have moved along without incurring the displeasure of those who were living in sin?

So men who should be standing as faithful guardians of God's law have argued, till policy has taken the place of faithfulness, and sin is allowed to go unreproved. When will the voice of faithful rebuke be heard once more in the church?

"Thou art the man." 2 Samuel 12:7. Words as unmistakably plain as these spoken by Nathan to David are seldom heard in the pulpits of today, seldom seen in the public press. If they were not so rare, we should see more of the power of God revealed among men. The Lord's messengers should not complain that their efforts are without fruit until they repent of their own love of approbation and their desire to please men, which leads them to suppress truth.

Those ministers who are men pleasers, who cry, Peace, peace, when God has not spoken peace, might well humble their hearts before God, asking pardon for their insincerity and their lack of moral courage. It is not from love for their neighbor that they smooth down the message entrusted to them, but because they are self-indulgent and ease-loving. True love seeks first the honor of God and the salvation of souls. Those who have this love will not evade the truth to save themselves from the unpleasant results of plain speaking. When souls are in peril, God's ministers will not [142] consider self, but will speak the word given them to speak, refusing to excuse or palliate evil.

Would that every minister might realize the sacredness of his office and the holiness of his work, and show the courage that Elijah showed! As divinely appointed messengers, ministers are in a position of awful responsibility. They are to "reprove, rebuke, exhort with all long-suffering." 2 Timothy 4:2. In Christ's stead they are to labor as stewards of the mysteries of heaven, encouraging the obedient and warning the disobedient. With them worldly policy is to have no weight. Never are they to swerve from the path in which Jesus has bidden them walk. They are to go forward in faith, remembering that they are surrounded by a cloud of witnesses. They are not to speak their own words, but words which One greater than the potentates of earth has bidden them speak. Their message is to be, "Thus saith the Lord." God calls for men like Elijah, Nathan, and John the Baptist—men who will bear His message with faithfulness, regardless of the consequences; men who will speak the truth bravely, though it call for the sacrifice of all they have.

God cannot use men who, in time of peril, when the strength, courage, and influence of all are needed, are afraid to take a firm stand for the right. He calls for men who will do faithful battle against wrong, warring against principalities and powers, against the rulers of the darkness of this world, against spiritual wickedness in high places. It is to such as these that He will speak the words: "Well done, good and faithful servant; ... enter thou into the joy of thy Lord." Matthew 25:23. [143]

Chapter 11

Carmel

This chapter is based on 1 Kings 18:19-40.

Standing before Ahab, Elijah demanded that all Israel be assembled to meet him and the prophets of Baal and Ashtoreth on Mount Carmel. "Send," he commanded, "and gather to me all Israel unto Mount Carmel, and the prophets of Baal four hundred and fifty, and the prophets of the groves four hundred, which eat at Jezebel's table."

The command was issued by one who seemed to stand in the very presence of Jehovah; and Ahab obeyed at once, as if the prophet were monarch, and the king a subject. Swift messengers were sent throughout the kingdom with the summons to meet Elijah and the prophets of Baal and Ashtoreth. In every town and village the people prepared to assemble at the appointed time. As they journeyed toward the place, the hearts of many were filled with strange forebodings. Something unusual was about to happen; else why this summons to gather at Carmel? What [144] new calamity was about to fall upon the people and the land?

Before the drought, Mount Carmel had been a place of beauty, its streams fed from never-failing springs, and its fertile slopes covered with fair flowers and flourishing groves. But now its beauty languished under a withering curse. The altars erected to the worship of Baal and Ashtoreth stood now in leafless groves. On the summit of one of the highest ridges, in sharp contrast with these was the broken-down altar of Jehovah.

Carmel overlooked a wide expanse of country; its heights were visible from many parts of the kingdom of Israel. At the foot of the mount there were vantage points from which could be seen much of what took place above. God had been signally dishonored by the idolatrous worship carried on under cover of its wooded slopes; and Elijah chose this elevation as the most conspicuous place for the display of God's power and for the vindication of the honor of His name.

Early on the morning of the day appointed, the hosts of apostate Israel, in eager expectancy, gather near the top of the mountain. Jezebel's prophets march up in imposing array. In regal pomp the king appears and takes his position at the head of the priests, and the idolaters shout his welcome. But there is apprehension in the hearts of the priests as they remember that at the word of the prophet the land of Israel for three years and a half has been destitute of dew and rain. Some fearful crisis is at hand, they feel sure. The gods in whom they have trusted have been unable to prove Elijah a false prophet. To their frantic cries, their [145]

[146] [147] prayers, their tears, their humiliation, their revolting ceremonies, their costly and ceaseless sacrifices, the objects of their worship have been strangely indifferent.

Facing King Ahab and the false prophets, and surrounded by the assembled hosts of Israel, Elijah stands, the only one who has appeared to vindicate the honor of Jehovah. He whom the whole kingdom has charged with its weight of woe is now before them, apparently defenseless in the presence of the monarch of Israel, the prophets of Baal, the men of war, and the surrounding thousands. But Elijah is not alone. Above and around him are the protecting hosts of heaven, angels that excel in strength.

Unashamed, unterrified, the prophet stands before the multitude, fully aware of his commission to execute the divine command. His countenance is lighted with an awful solemnity. In anxious expectancy the people wait for him to speak. Looking first upon the broken-down altar of Jehovah, and then upon the multitude, Elijah cries out in clear, trumpetlike tones, "How long halt ye between two opinions? if the Lord be God, follow Him: but if Baal, then follow him."

The people answer him not a word. Not one in that vast assembly dare reveal loyalty to Jehovah. Like a dark cloud, deception and blindness had overspread Israel. Not all at once had this fatal apostasy closed about them, but gradually, as from time to time they had failed to heed the words of warning and reproof that the Lord sent them. Each departure from rightdoing, each refusal to repent, had deepened their guilt and driven them farther from Heaven. And now, in this crisis, they persisted in refusing to take their stand for God. [148]

The Lord abhors indifference and disloyalty in a time of crisis in His work. The whole universe is watching with inexpressible interest the closing scenes of the great controversy between good and evil. The people of God are nearing the borders of the eternal world; what can be of more importance to them than that they be loyal to the God of heaven? All through the ages, God has had moral heroes, and He has them now—those who, like Joseph and Elijah and Daniel, are not ashamed to acknowledge themselves His peculiar people. His special blessing accompanies the labors of men of action, men who will not be swerved from the straight line of duty, but who with divine energy will inquire, "Who is on the Lord's side?" (Exodus 32:26), men who will not stop merely with the inquiry, but who will demand that those who choose to identify themselves with the people of God shall step forward and reveal unmistakably their allegiance to the King of kings and Lord of lords. Such men make their wills and plans subordinate to the law of God. For love of Him they count not their lives dear unto themselves. Their work is to catch the light from the Word and let it shine forth to the world in clear, steady rays. Fidelity to God is their motto.

While Israel on Carmel doubt and hesitate, the voice of Elijah again breaks the silence: "I, even I only, remain a prophet of the Lord; but Baal's prophets are four hundred and fifty men. Let them therefore give us two bullocks; and let them choose one bullock for themselves, and cut it in pieces, and lay it on wood, and put no fire under: and I will dress the other bullock, and lay it on wood, and put no fire under: and call ye on the name of your gods, and [149] I will call on the name of the Lord: and the God that answereth by fire, let him be God."

The proposal of Elijah is so reasonable that the people cannot well evade it, so they find courage to answer, "It is well spoken." The prophets of Baal dare not lift their voices in dissent; and, addressing them, Elijah directs, "Choose you one bullock for yourselves, and dress it first; for ye are many; and call on the name of your gods, but put no fire under."

Outwardly bold and defiant, but with terror in their guilty hearts, the false priests prepare their altar, laying on the wood and the victim; and then they begin their incantations. Their shrill cries echo and re-echo through the forests and the surrounding heights, as they call on the name of their god, saying, "O Baal, hear us." The priests gather about their altar, and with leaping and writhing and screaming, with tearing of hair and cutting of flesh, they beseech their god to help them.

The morning passes, noon comes, and yet there is no evidence that Baal hears the cries of his deluded followers. There is no voice, no reply to their frantic prayers. The sacrifice remains unconsumed.

As they continue their frenzied devotions, the crafty priests are continually trying to devise some means by which they may kindle a fire upon the altar and lead the people to believe that the fire has come direct from Baal. But Elijah watches every movement; and the priests, hoping against hope for some opportunity to deceive, continue to carry on their senseless ceremonies.

"It came to pass at noon, that Elijah mocked them, and [150] said, Cry aloud: for he is a god; either he is talking, or he is pursuing, or he is in a journey, or peradventure he sleepeth, and must be awaked. And they cried aloud, and cut themselves after their manner with knives and lancets, till the blood gushed out upon them. And it came to pass, when midday was past, and they prophesied until the time of the offering of the evening sacrifice, that there was neither voice, nor any to answer, nor any that regarded."

Gladly would Satan have come to the help of those whom he had deceived, and who were devoted to his service. Gladly would he have sent the lightning to kindle their sacrifice. But Jehovah has set Satan's bounds, restrained his power, and not all the enemy's devices can convey one spark to Baal's altar.

At last, their voices hoarse with shouting, their garments stained with blood from self-inflicted wounds, the priests become desperate. With unabated frenzy they now mingle with their pleading terrible cursings of their sun-god, and Elijah continues to watch intently; for he knows that if by any device the priests should succeed in kindling their altar fire, he would instantly be torn in pieces.

Evening draws on. The prophets of Baal are weary, faint, confused. One suggests one thing, and another something else, until finally they cease their efforts. Their shrieks and curses no longer resound over Carmel. In despair they retire from the contest.

All day long the people have witnessed the demonstrations of the baffled priests. They have beheld their wild leaping round the altar, as if they would grasp the burning rays of the sun to serve their purpose. They have looked [151] with horror on the frightful, self-inflicted mutilations of the priests, and have had opportunity to reflect on the follies of idol worship. Many in the throng are weary of the exhibitions of demonism, and they now await with deepest interest the movements of Elijah.

It is the hour of the evening sacrifice, and Elijah bids the people, "Come near unto me." As they tremblingly draw near, he turns to the broken-down altar where once men worshiped the God of heaven, and repairs it. To him this heap of ruins is more precious than all the magnificent altars of heathendom.

In the reconstruction of this ancient altar, Elijah revealed his respect for the covenant that the Lord made with Israel when they crossed the Jordan into the Promised Land. Choosing "twelve stones, according to the number of the tribes of the sons of Jacob, ... he built an altar in the name of the Lord."

The disappointed priests of Baal, exhausted by their vain efforts, wait to see what Elijah will do. They hate the prophet for proposing a test that has exposed the weakness and inefficiency of their gods; yet they fear his power. The people, fearful also, and almost breathless with expectancy, watch while Elijah continues his preparations. The calm demeanor of the prophet stands out in sharp contrast with the fanatical, senseless frenzy of the followers of Baal.

The altar completed, the prophet makes a trench about it, and, having put the wood in order and prepared the bullock, he lays the victim on the altar and commands the people to flood the sacrifice and the altar with water. "Fill four barrels," he directed, "and pour it on the burnt sacrifice, [152] and on the wood. And he said, Do it the second time. And they did it the second time. And he said, Do it the third time. And they did it the third time. And the water ran round about the altar; and he filled the trench also with water."

Reminding the people of the long-continued apostasy that has awakened the wrath of Jehovah, Elijah calls upon them to humble their hearts and turn to the God of their fathers, that the curse upon the land of Israel may be removed. Then, bowing reverently before the unseen God, he raises his hands toward heaven and offers a simple prayer. Baal's priests have screamed and foamed and leaped, from early morning until late in the afternoon; but as Elijah prays, no senseless shrieks resound over Carmel's height. He prays as if he knows Jehovah is there, a witness to the scene, a listener to his appeal. The prophets of Baal have prayed wildly, incoherently. Elijah prays simply and fervently, asking God to show His superiority over Baal, that Israel may be led to turn to Him.

"Lord God of Abraham, Isaac, and of Israel," the prophet pleads, "let it be known this day that Thou art God in Israel, and that I am Thy servant, and that I have done all these things at Thy word. Hear me, O Lord, hear me, that this people may know that Thou art the Lord God, and that Thou hast turned their heart back again."

A silence, oppressive in its solemnity, rests upon all. The priests of Baal tremble with terror. Conscious of their guilt, they look for swift retribution.

No sooner is the prayer of Elijah ended than flames of [153] fire, like brilliant flashes of lightning, descend from heaven upon the upreared altar, consuming the sacrifice, licking up the water in the trench, and consuming even the stones of the altar. The brilliancy of the blaze illumines the mountain and dazzles the eyes of the multitude. In the valleys below, where many are watching in anxious suspense the movements of those above, the descent of fire is clearly seen, and all are amazed at the sight. It resembles the pillar of fire which at the Red Sea separated the children of Israel from the Egyptian host.

The people on the mount prostrate themselves in awe before the unseen God. They dare not continue to look upon the Heaven-sent fire. They fear that they themselves will be consumed; and, convicted of their duty to acknowledge the God of Elijah as the God of their fathers, to whom they owe allegiance, they cry out together as with one voice, "The Lord, He is the God; the Lord, He is the God." With startling distinctness the cry resounds over the mountain and echoes in the plain below. At last Israel is aroused, undeceived, penitent. At last the people see how greatly they have dishonored God. The character of Baal worship, in contrast with the reasonable service required by the true God, stands fully revealed. The people recognize God's justice and mercy in withholding the dew and the rain until they have been brought to confess His name. They are ready now to admit that the God of Elijah is above every idol.

The priests of Baal witness with consternation the wonderful revelation of Jehovah's power. Yet even in their [154] discomfiture and in the presence of divine glory, they refuse to repent of their evil-doing. They would still remain the prophets of Baal. Thus they showed themselves ripe for destruction. That repentant Israel may be protected from the allurements of those who have taught them to worship Baal, Elijah is directed by the Lord to destroy these false teachers. The anger of the people has already been aroused against the leaders in transgression; and when Elijah gives the command, "Take the prophets of Baal; let not one of them escape," they are ready to obey. They seize the priests, and take them to the brook Kishon, and there, before the close of the day that marked the beginning of decided reform, the ministers of Baal are slain. Not one is permitted to live. [155]

Chapter 12

From Jezreel to Horeb

This chapter is based on 1 Kings 18:41-46; 19:1-8.

With the slaying of the prophets of Baal, the way was opened for carrying forward a mighty spiritual reformation among the ten tribes of the northern kingdom. Elijah had set before the people their apostasy; he had called upon them to humble their hearts and turn to the Lord. The judgments of Heaven had been executed; the people had confessed their sins, and had acknowledged the God of their fathers as the living God; and now the curse of Heaven was to be withdrawn, and the temporal blessings of life renewed. The land was to be refreshed with rain. "Get thee up, eat and drink," Elijah said to Ahab; "for there is a sound of abundance of rain." Then the prophet went to the top of the mount to pray.

It was not because of any outward evidence that the showers were about to fall, that Elijah could so confidently bid Ahab prepare for rain. The prophet saw no clouds in the heavens; he heard no thunder. He simply spoke the [156] word that the Spirit of the Lord had moved him to speak in response to his own strong faith. Throughout the day he had unflinchingly performed the will of God and had revealed his implicit confidence in the prophecies of God's word; and now, having done all that was in his power to do, he knew that Heaven would freely bestow the blessings foretold. The same God who had sent the drought had promised an abundance of rain as the reward of rightdoing; and now Elijah waited for the promised outpouring. In an attitude of humility, "his face between his knees," he interceded with God in behalf of penitent Israel.

Again and again Elijah sent his servant to a point overlooking the Mediterranean, to learn whether there were any visible token that God had heard his prayer. Each time the servant returned with the word, "There is nothing." The prophet did not become impatient or lose faith, but continued his earnest pleading. Six times the servant returned with the word that there was no sign of rain in the brassy heavens. Undaunted, Elijah sent him forth once more; and this time the servant returned with the word, "Behold, there ariseth a little cloud out of the sea like a man's hand."

This was enough. Elijah did not wait for the heavens to gather blackness. In that small cloud he beheld by faith an abundance of rain; and he acted in harmony with his faith, sending his servant quickly to Ahab with the message, "Prepare thy chariot, and get thee down, that the rain stop thee not."

It was because Elijah was a man of large faith that God could use him in this grave crisis in the history of Israel. [157] As he prayed, his faith reached out and grasped the promises of Heaven, and he persevered in prayer until his petitions were answered. He did not wait for the full evidence that God had heard him, but was willing to venture all on the slightest token of divine favor. And yet what he was enabled to do under God, all may do in their sphere of activity in God's service; for of the prophet from the mountains of Gilead it is written: "Elias was a man subject to like passions as we are, and he prayed earnestly that it might not rain: and it rained not on the earth by the space of three years and six months." James 5:17.

Faith such as this is needed in the world today—faith that will lay hold on the promises of God's word and refuse to let go until Heaven hears. Faith such as this connects us closely with Heaven, and brings us strength for coping with the powers of darkness. Through faith God's children have "subdued kingdoms, wrought righteousness, obtained promises, stopped the mouths of lions, quenched the violence of fire, escaped the edge of the sword, out of weakness were made strong, waxed valiant in fight, turned to flight the armies of the aliens." Hebrews 11:33, 34. And through faith we today are to reach the heights of God's purpose for us. "If thou canst believe, all things are possible to him that believeth." Mark 9:23.

Faith is an essential element of prevailing prayer. "He that cometh to God must believe that He is, and that He is a rewarder of them that diligently seek Him." "If we ask anything according to His will, He heareth us: and if we know that He hear us, whatsoever we ask, we know [158] that we have the petitions that we desired of Him." Hebrews 11:6; 1 John 5:14, 15. With the persevering faith of Jacob, with the unyielding persistence of Elijah, we may present our petitions to the Father, claiming all that He has promised. The honor of His throne is staked for the fulfillment of His word.

The shades of night were gathering about Mount Carmel as Ahab prepared for the descent. "It came to pass in the meanwhile, that the heaven was black with clouds and wind, and there was a great rain. And Ahab rode, and went to Jezreel." As he journeyed toward the royal city through the darkness and the blinding rain, Ahab was unable to see his way before him. Elijah, who, as the prophet of God, had that day humiliated Ahab before his subjects and slain his idolatrous priests, still acknowledged him as Israel's king; and now, as an act of homage, and strengthened by the power of God, he ran before the royal chariot, guiding the king to the entrance of the city.

In this gracious act of God's messenger shown to a wicked king is a lesson for all who claim to be servants of God, but who are exalted in their own estimation. There are those who feel above performing duties that to them appear menial. They hesitate to perform even needful service, fearing that they will be found doing the work of a servant. These have much to learn from the example of Elijah. By his word the treasures of heaven had been for three years withheld from the earth; he had been signally honored of God as, in answer to his prayer on Carmel, fire had flashed from heaven and consumed the sacrifice; his [159] hand had executed the judgment of God in slaying the idolatrous prophets; his petition for rain had been granted. And yet, after the signal triumphs with which God had been pleased to honor his public ministry, he was willing to perform the service of a menial.

At the gate of Jezreel, Elijah and Ahab separated. The prophet, choosing to remain outside the walls, wrapped himself in his mantle, and lay down upon the bare earth to sleep. The king, passing within, soon reached the shelter of his palace and there related to his wife the wonderful events of the day and the marvelous revelation of divine power that had proved to Israel that Jehovah is the true God and Elijah His chosen messenger. As Ahab told the queen of the slaying of the idolatrous prophets, Jezebel, hardened and impenitent, became infuriated. She refused to recognize in the events on Carmel the overruling providence of God, and, still defiant, she boldly declared that Elijah should die.

That night a messenger aroused the weary prophet and delivered to him the word of Jezebel: "So let the gods do to me, and more also, if I make not thy life as the life of one of them by tomorrow about this time."

It would seem that after showing courage so undaunted, after triumphing so completely over king and priests and people, Elijah could never afterward have given way to despondency nor been awed into timidity. But he who had been blessed with so many evidences of God's loving care was not above the frailties of mankind, and in this dark hour his faith and courage forsook him. Bewildered, he [160] started from his slumber. The rain was pouring from the heavens, and darkness was on every side. Forgetting that three years before, God had directed his course to a place of refuge from the hatred of Jezebel and the search of Ahab, the prophet now fled for his life. Reaching Beersheba, he "left his servant there. But he himself went a day's journey into the wilderness."

Elijah should not have fled from his post of duty. He should have met the threat of Jezebel with an appeal for protection to the One who had commissioned him to vindicate the honor of Jehovah. He should have told the messenger that the God in whom he trusted would protect him against the hatred of the queen. Only a few hours had passed since he had witnessed a wonderful manifestation of divine power, and this should have given him assurance that he would not now be forsaken. Had he remained where he was, had he made God his refuge and strength, standing steadfast for the truth, he would have been shielded from harm. The Lord would have given him another signal victory by sending His judgments on Jezebel; and the impression made on the king and the people would have wrought a great reformation.

Elijah had expected much from the miracle wrought on Carmel. He had hoped that after this display of God's power, Jezebel would no longer have influence over the mind of Ahab, and that there would be a speedy reform throughout Israel. All day on Carmel's height he had toiled without food. Yet when he guided the chariot of Ahab to the gate of Jezreel, his courage was strong, despite the physical strain under which he had labored. [161]

But a reaction such as frequently follows high faith and glorious success was pressing upon Elijah. He feared that the reformation begun on Carmel might not be lasting; and depression seized him. He had been exalted to Pisgah's top; now he was in the valley. While under the inspiration of the Almighty, he had stood the severest trial of faith; but in this time of discouragement, with Jezebel's threat [162] sounding in his ears, and Satan still apparently prevailing through the plotting of this wicked woman, he lost his hold on God. He had been exalted above measure, and the reaction was tremendous. Forgetting God, Elijah fled on and on, until he found himself in a dreary waste, alone. Utterly wearied, he sat down to rest under a juniper tree. And sitting there, he requested for himself that he might die. "It is enough; now, O Lord," he said, "take away my life; for I am not better than my fathers." A fugitive, far from the dwelling places of men, his spirits crushed by bitter disappointment, he desired never again to look upon the face of man. At last, utterly exhausted, he fell asleep.

Into the experience of all there come times of keen disappointment and utter discouragement—days when sorrow is the portion, and it is hard to believe that God is still the kind benefactor of His earthborn children; days when troubles harass the soul, till death seems preferable to life. It is then that many lose their hold on God and are brought into the slavery of doubt, the bondage of unbelief. Could we at such times discern with spiritual insight the meaning of God's providences we should see angels seeking to save us from ourselves, striving to plant our feet upon a foundation more firm than the everlasting hills, and new faith, new life, would spring into being.

The faithful Job, in the day of his affliction and darkness, declared:

"Let the day perish wherein I was born." "O that my grief were throughly weighed, And my calamity laid in the balances together!" [163]

"O that I might have my request; And that God would grant me the thing that I long for! Even that it would please God to destroy me; That He would let loose His hand, and cut me off! Then should I yet have comfort."

"I will not refrain my mouth; I will speak in the anguish of my spirit; I will complain in the bitterness of my soul."

"My soul chooseth ... death rather than my life. I loathe it; I would not live alway: Let me alone; For my days are vanity."

Job 3:3; 6:2, 8-10; Job 7:11, 15, 16.

But though weary of life, Job was not allowed to die. To him were pointed out the possibilities of the future, and there was given him the message of hope:

"Thou shalt be steadfast, and shalt not fear: Because thou shalt forget thy misery, And remember it as waters that pass away: And thine age shall be clearer than the noonday; Thou shalt shine forth, thou shalt be as the morning. And thou shalt be secure, Because there is hope.... Thou shalt lie down, And none shall make thee afraid; Yea, many shall make suit unto thee. But the eyes of the wicked shall fail, And they shall not escape, And their hope shall be as the giving up of the ghost."

Job 11:15-20.

From the depths of discouragement and despondency Job rose to the heights of implicit trust in the mercy and the saving power of God. Triumphantly he declared: [164]

"Though He slay me, yet will I trust in Him: ... He also shall be my salvation." "I know that my Redeemer liveth, And that He shall stand at the latter day upon the earth: And though after my skin worms destroy this body, Yet in my flesh shall I see God: Whom I shall see for myself, And mine eyes shall behold, and not another."

Job 13:15, 16; 19:25-27.

"The Lord answered Job out of the whirlwind" (Job 38:1), and revealed to His servant the might of His power. When Job caught a glimpse of his Creator, he abhorred himself and repented in dust and ashes. Then the Lord was able to bless him abundantly and to make his last years the best of his life.

Hope and courage are essential to perfect service for God. These are the fruit of faith. Despondency is sinful and unreasonable. God is able and willing "more abundantly" (Hebrews 6:17) to bestow upon His servants the strength they need for test and trial. The plans of the enemies of His work may seem to be well laid and firmly established, but God can overthrow the strongest of these. And this He does in His own time and way, when He sees that the faith of His servants has been sufficiently tested.

For the disheartened there is a sure remedy—faith, prayer, work. Faith and activity will impart assurance and satisfaction that will increase day by day. Are you tempted to give way to feelings of anxious foreboding or utter despondency? In the darkest days, when appearances seem most forbidding, fear not. Have faith in God. He knows your need. He has all power. His infinite love and compassion never weary. Fear not that He will fail of fulfilling His promise. He is eternal truth. Never will He change the covenant He has made with those who love Him. And He will bestow upon His faithful servants the measure of efficiency that their need demands. The apostle Paul has testified: "He said unto me, My grace is sufficient for thee: for My strength is made perfect in weakness.... Therefore I take pleasure in infirmities, in reproaches, in necessities, in persecutions, in distresses for Christ's sake: for when I am weak, then am I strong." 2 Corinthians 12:9, 10. [165] [166]

Did God forsake Elijah in his hour of trial? Oh, no! He loved His servant no less when Elijah felt himself forsaken of God and man than when, in answer to his prayer, fire flashed from heaven and illuminated the mountaintop. And now, as Elijah slept, a soft touch and a pleasant voice awoke him. He started up in terror, as if to flee, fearing that the enemy had discovered him. But the pitying face bending over him was not the face of an enemy, but of a friend. God had sent an angel from heaven with food for His servant. "Arise and eat," the angel said. "And he looked, and, behold, there was a cake baken on the coals, and a cruse of water at his head."

After Elijah had partaken of the refreshment prepared for him, he slept again. A second time the angel came. Touching the exhausted man, he said with pitying tenderness, "Arise and eat; because the journey is too great for thee." "And he arose, and did eat and drink;" and in the strength of that food he was able to journey "forty days and forty nights unto Horeb the mount of God," where he found refuge in a cave. [167]

Chapter 13

"What Doest Thou Here?"

This chapter is based on 1 Kings 19:9-18.

Elijah's retreat on Mount Horeb, though hidden from man, was known to God; and the weary and discouraged prophet was not left to struggle alone with the powers of darkness that were pressing upon him. At the entrance to the cave wherein Elijah had taken refuge, God met with him, through a mighty angel sent to inquire into his needs and to make plain the divine purpose for Israel.

Not until Elijah had learned to trust wholly in God could he complete his work for those who had been seduced into Baal worship. The signal triumph on the heights of Carmel had opened the way for still greater victories; yet from the wonderful opportunities opening before him, Elijah had been turned away by the threat of Jezebel. The man of God must be made to understand the weakness of his present position as compared with the vantage ground the Lord would have him occupy. [168]

God met His tried servant with the inquiry, What doest thou here, Elijah? I sent you to the brook Cherith and afterward to the widow of Sarepta. I commissioned you to return to Israel and to stand before the idolatrous priests on Carmel, and I girded you with strength to guide the chariot of the king to the gate of Jezreel. But who sent you on this hasty flight into the wilderness? What errand have you here?

In bitterness of soul Elijah mourned out his complaint: "I have been very jealous for the Lord God of hosts: for the children of Israel have forsaken Thy covenant, thrown down Thine altars, and slain Thy prophets with the sword; and I, even I only, am left; and they seek my life, to take it away."

Calling upon the prophet to leave the cave, the angel bade him stand before the Lord on the mount, and listen to His word. "And, behold, the Lord passed by, and a great and strong wind rent the mountains, and brake in pieces the rocks before the Lord; but the Lord was not in the wind: and after the wind an earthquake; but the Lord was not in the earthquake: and after the earthquake a fire; but the Lord was not in the fire: and after the fire a still small voice. And it was so, when Elijah heard it, that he wrapped his face in his mantle, and went out, and stood in the entering in of the cave."

Not in mighty manifestations of divine power, but by "a still small voice," did God choose to reveal Himself to His servant. He desired to teach Elijah that it is not always the work that makes the greatest demonstration that is most successful in accomplishing His purpose. While Elijah waited [169] for the revelation of the Lord, a tempest rolled, the lightnings flashed, and a devouring fire swept by; but God was not in all this. Then there came a still, small voice, and the prophet covered his head before the presence of the Lord. His petulance was silenced, his spirit softened and subdued. He now knew that a quiet trust, a firm reliance on God, would ever find for him a present help in time of need.

It is not always the most learned presentation of God's truth that convicts and converts the soul. Not by eloquence or logic are men's hearts reached, but by the sweet influences of the Holy Spirit, which operate quietly yet surely in transforming and developing character. It is the still, small voice of the Spirit of God that has power to change the heart.

"What doest thou here, Elijah?" the voice inquired; and again the prophet answered, "I have been very jealous for the Lord God of hosts: because the children of Israel have forsaken Thy covenant, thrown down Thine altars, and slain Thy prophets with the sword; and I, even I only, am left; and they seek my life, to take it away."

The Lord answered Elijah that the wrongdoers in Israel should not go unpunished. Men were to be especially chosen to fulfill the divine purpose in the punishment of the idolatrous kingdom. There was stern work to be done, that all might be given opportunity to take their position on the side of the true God. Elijah himself was to return to Israel, and share with others the burden of bringing about a reformation.

"Go," the Lord commanded Elijah, "return on thy way to the wilderness of Damascus: and when thou comest, [170] anoint Hazael to be king over Syria: and Jehu the son of Nimshi shalt thou anoint to be king over Israel: and Elisha the son of Shaphat of Abel-meholah shalt thou anoint to be prophet in thy room. And it shall come to pass, that him that escapeth the sword of Hazael shall Jehu slay: and him that escapeth from the sword of Jehu shall Elisha slay."

Elijah had thought that he alone in Israel was a worshiper of the true God. But He who reads the hearts of all revealed to the prophet that there were many others who, through the long years of apostasy, had remained true to Him. "I have left Me," God said, "seven thousand in Israel, all the knees which have not bowed unto Baal, and every mouth which hath not kissed him."

From Elijah's experience during those days of discouragement and apparent defeat there are many lessons to be drawn, lessons invaluable to the servants of God in this age, marked as it is by general departure from right. The apostasy prevailing today is similar to that which in the prophet's day overspread Israel. In the exaltation of the human above the divine, in the praise of popular leaders, in the worship of mammon, and in the placing of the teachings of science above the truths of revelation, multitudes today are following after Baal. Doubt and unbelief are exercising their baleful influence over mind and heart, and many are substituting for the oracles of God the theories of men. It is publicly taught that we have reached a time when human reason should be exalted above the teachings of the Word. The law of God, the divine standard of righteousness, is declared to be of no effect. The enemy of all truth [171] is working with deceptive power to cause men and women to place human institutions where God should be, and to forget that which was ordained for the happiness and salvation of mankind.

Yet this apostasy, widespread as it has come to be, is not universal. Not all in the world are lawless and sinful; not all have taken sides with the enemy. God has many thousands who have not bowed the knee to Baal, many who long to understand more fully in regard to Christ and the law, many who are hoping against hope that Jesus will come soon to end the reign of sin and death. And there are many who have been worshiping Baal ignorantly, but with whom the Spirit of God is still striving.

These need the personal help of those who have learned to know God and the power of His word. In such a time as this, every child of God should be actively engaged in helping others. As those who have an understanding of Bible truth try to seek out the men and women who are longing for light, angels of God will attend them. And where angels go, none need fear to move forward. As a result of the faithful efforts of consecrated workers, many will be turned from idolatry to the worship of the living God. Many will cease to pay homage to man-made institutions and will take their stand fearlessly on the side of God and His law.

Much depends on the unceasing activity of those who are true and loyal, and for this reason Satan puts forth every possible effort to thwart the divine purpose to be wrought out through the obedient. He causes some to lose [172] sight of their high and holy mission, and to become satisfied with the pleasures of this life. He leads them to settle down at ease, or, for the sake of greater worldly advantages, to remove from places where they might be a power for good. Others he causes to flee in discouragement from duty, because of opposition or persecution. But all such are regarded by Heaven with tenderest pity. To every child of God whose voice the enemy of souls had succeeded in silencing, the question is addressed, "What doest thou here?" I commissioned you to go into all the world and preach the gospel, to prepare a people for the day of God. Why are you here? Who sent you?

The joy set before Christ, the joy that sustained Him through sacrifice and suffering, was the joy of seeing sinners saved. This should be the joy of every follower of His, the spur to his ambition. Those who realize, even in a limited degree, what redemption means to them and to their fellow men, will comprehend in some measure the vast needs of humanity. Their hearts will be moved to compassion as they see the moral and spiritual destitution of thousands who are under the shadow of a terrible doom, in comparison with which physical suffering fades into nothingness.

Of families, as of individuals, the question is asked, "What doest thou here?" In many churches there are families well instructed in the truths of God's word, who might widen the sphere of their influence by moving to places in need of the ministry they are capable of giving. God calls for Christian families to go into the dark places of the earth and work wisely and perseveringly for those who are [173] enshrouded in spiritual gloom. To answer this call requires self-sacrifice. While many are waiting to have every obstacle removed, souls are dying, without hope and without God. For the sake of worldly advantage, for the sake of acquiring scientific knowledge, men are willing to venture into pestilential regions and to endure hardship and privation. Where are those who are willing to do as much for the sake of telling others of the Saviour?

If, under trying circumstances, men of spiritual power, pressed beyond measure, become discouraged and desponding, if at times they see nothing desirable in life, that they should choose it, this is nothing strange or new. Let all such remember that one of the mightiest of the prophets fled for his life before the rage of an infuriated woman. A fugitive, weary and travel-worn, bitter disappointment crushing his spirits, he asked that he might die. But it was when hope was gone and his lifework seemed threatened with defeat, that he learned one of the most precious lessons of his life. In the hour of his greatest weakness he learned the need and the possibility of trusting God under circumstances the most forbidding.

Those who, while spending their life energies in self-sacrificing labor, are tempted to give way to despondency and distrust, may gather courage from the experience of Elijah. God's watchful care, His love, His power, are especially manifest in behalf of His servants whose zeal is misunderstood or unappreciated, whose counsels and reproofs are slighted, and whose efforts toward reform are repaid with hatred and opposition. [174]

It is at the time of greatest weakness that Satan assails the soul with the fiercest temptations. It was thus that he hoped to prevail over the Son of God; for by this policy he had gained many victories over man. When the will power weakened and faith failed, then those who had stood long and valiantly for the right yielded to temptation. Moses, wearied with forty years of wandering and unbelief, lost for a moment his hold on Infinite Power. He failed just on the borders of the Promised Land. So with Elijah. He who had maintained his trust in Jehovah during the years of drought and famine, he who had stood undaunted before Ahab, he who throughout that trying day on Carmel had stood before the whole nation of Israel the sole witness to the true God, in a moment of weariness allowed the fear of death to overcome his faith in God.

And so it is today. When we are encompassed with doubt, perplexed by circumstances, or afflicted by poverty or distress, Satan seeks to shake our confidence in Jehovah. It is then that he arrays before us our mistakes and tempts us to distrust God, to question His love. He hopes to discourage the soul and break our hold on God.

Those who, standing in the forefront of the conflict, are impelled by the Holy Spirit to do a special work, will frequently feel a reaction when the pressure is removed. Despondency may shake the most heroic faith and weaken the most steadfast will. But God understands, and He still pities and loves. He reads the motives and the purposes of the heart. To wait patiently, to trust when everything looks dark, is the lesson that the leaders in God's work need to learn. Heaven will not fail them in their day of adversity. [175] Nothing is apparently more helpless, yet really more invincible, than the soul that feels its nothingness and relies wholly on God.

Not alone for men in positions of large responsibility is the lesson of Elijah's experience in learning anew how to trust God in the hour of trial. He who was Elijah's strength is strong to uphold every struggling child of His, no matter how weak. Of everyone He expects loyalty, and to everyone He grants power according to the need. In his own strength man is strengthless; but in the might of God he may be strong to overcome evil and to help others to overcome. Satan can never gain advantage of him who makes God his defense. "Surely, shall one say, in the Lord have I righteousness and strength." Isaiah 45:24.

Fellow Christian, Satan knows your weakness; therefore cling to Jesus. Abiding in God's love, you may stand every test. The righteousness of Christ alone can give you power to stem the tide of evil that is sweeping over the world. Bring faith into your experience. Faith lightens every burden, relieves every weariness. Providences that are now mysterious you may solve by continued trust in God. Walk by faith in the path He marks out. Trials will come, but go forward. This will strengthen your faith and fit you for service. The records of sacred history are written, not merely that we may read and wonder, but that the same faith which wrought in God's servants of old may work in us. In no less marked manner will the Lord work now, wherever there are hearts of faith to be channels of His power.

To us, as to Peter, the word is spoken, "Satan hath desired [176] to have you, that he may sift you as wheat: but I have prayed for thee, that thy faith fail not." Luke 22:31, 32. Christ will never abandon those for whom He has died. We may leave Him and be overwhelmed with temptation, but Christ can never turn from one for whom He has paid the ransom of His own life. Could our spiritual vision be quickened, we should see souls bowed under oppression and burdened with grief, pressed as a cart beneath sheaves, and ready to die in discouragement. We should see angels flying quickly to the aid of these tempted ones, forcing back the hosts of evil that encompass them, and placing their feet on the sure foundation. The battles waging between the two armies are as real as those fought by the armies of this world, and on the issue of the spiritual conflict eternal destinies depend.

In the vision of the prophet Ezekiel there was the appearance of a hand beneath the wings of the cherubim. This is to teach God's servants that it is divine power that gives success. Those whom God employs as His messengers are not to feel that His work is dependent on them. Finite beings are not left to carry this burden of responsibility. He who slumbers not, who is continually at work for the accomplishment of His designs, will carry forward His work. He will thwart the purposes of wicked men and will bring to confusion the counsels of those who plot mischief against His people. He who is the King, the Lord of hosts, sitteth between the cherubim, and amidst the strife and tumult of nations He guards His children still. When the strongholds of kings shall be overthrown, when the arrows of wrath shall strike through the hearts of His enemies, His people will be safe in His hands. [177]

Chapter 14

"In the Spirit and Power of Elias"

Through the long centuries that have passed since Elijah's time, the record of his lifework has brought inspiration and courage to those who have been called to stand for the right in the midst of apostasy. And for us, "upon whom the ends of the world are come" (1 Corinthians 10:11), it has special significance. History is being repeated. The world today has its Ahabs and its Jezebels. The present age is one of idolatry, as verily as was that in which Elijah lived. No outward shrine may be visible; there may be no image for the eye to rest upon; yet thousands are following after the gods of this world—after riches, fame, pleasure, and the pleasing fables that permit man to follow the inclinations of the unregenerate heart. Multitudes have a wrong conception of God and His attributes, and are as truly serving a false god as were the worshipers of Baal. Many even of those who claim to be Christians have allied themselves with influences that are unalterably opposed to God and [178] His truth. Thus they are led to turn away from the divine and to exalt the human.

The prevailing spirit of our time is one of infidelity and apostasy—a spirit of avowed illumination because of a knowledge of truth, but in reality of the blindest presumption. Human theories are exalted and placed where God and His law should be. Satan tempts men and women to disobey, with the promise that in disobedience they will find liberty and freedom that will make them as gods. There is seen a spirit of opposition to the plain word of God, of idolatrous exaltation of human wisdom above divine revelation. Men have allowed their minds to become so darkened and confused by conformity to worldly customs and influences that they seem to have lost all power to discriminate between light and darkness, truth and error. So far have they departed from the right way that they hold the opinions of a few philosophers, so-called, to be more trustworthy than the truths of the Bible. The entreaties and promises of God's word, its threatenings against disobedience and idolatry—these seem powerless to melt their hearts. A faith such as actuated Paul, Peter, and John they regard as old-fashioned, mystical, and unworthy of the intelligence of modern thinkers.

In the beginning, God gave His law to mankind as a means of attaining happiness and eternal life. Satan's only hope of thwarting the purpose of God is to lead men and women to disobey this law, and his constant effort has been to misrepresent its teachings and belittle its importance. His master stroke has been an attempt to change the law itself, so as to lead men to violate its precepts while professing to obey it. [179]

One writer has likened the attempt to change the law of God to an ancient mischievous practice of turning in a wrong direction a signpost erected at an important junction where two roads met. The perplexity and hardship which this practice often caused was great.

A signpost was erected by God for those journeying through this world. One arm of this signpost pointed out willing obedience to the Creator as the road to felicity and life, while the other arm indicated disobedience as the path to misery and death. The way to happiness was as clearly defined as was the way to the city of refuge under the Jewish dispensation. But in an evil hour for our race, the great enemy of all good turned the signpost around, and multitudes have mistaken the way.

Through Moses the Lord instructed the Israelites: "Verily My Sabbaths ye shall keep: for it is a sign between Me and you throughout your generations; that ye may know that I am the Lord that doth sanctify you. Ye shall keep the Sabbath therefore; for it is holy unto you: everyone that defileth it shall surely be put to death: for whosoever doeth any work ... in the Sabbath day, he shall surely be put to death. Wherefore the children of Israel shall keep the Sabbath, to observe the Sabbath throughout their generations, for a perpetual covenant. It is a sign between Me and the children of Israel forever: for in six days the Lord made heaven and earth, and on the seventh day He rested, and was refreshed." Exodus 31:13-17.

In these words the Lord clearly defined obedience as the way to the City of God; but the man of sin has changed the signpost, making it point in the wrong direction. He [180] has set up a false sabbath and has caused men and women to think that by resting on it they were obeying the command of the Creator.

God has declared that the seventh day is the Sabbath of the Lord. When "the heavens and the earth were finished," He exalted this day as a memorial of His creative work. Resting on the seventh day "from all His work which He had made," "God blessed the seventh day, and sanctified it." Genesis 2:1-3.

At the time of the Exodus from Egypt, the Sabbath institution was brought prominently before the people of God. While they were still in bondage, their taskmasters had attempted to force them to labor on the Sabbath by increasing [181] the amount of work required each week. Again and again the conditions of labor had been made harder and more exacting. But the Israelites were delivered from bondage and brought to a place where they might observe unmolested all the precepts of Jehovah. At Sinai the law was spoken; and a copy of it, on two tables of stone, "written with the finger of God" was delivered to Moses. Exodus 31:18. And through nearly forty years of wandering the Israelites were constantly reminded of God's appointed rest day, by the withholding of the manna every seventh day and the miraculous preservation of the double portion that fell on the preparation day.

Before entering the Promised Land, the Israelites were [182] admonished by Moses to "keep the Sabbath day to sanctify it." Deuteronomy 5:12. The Lord designed that by a faithful observance of the Sabbath command, Israel should continually be reminded of their accountability to Him as their Creator and their Redeemer. While they should keep the Sabbath in the proper spirit, idolatry could not exist; but should the claims of this precept of the Decalogue be set aside as no longer binding, the Creator would be forgotten and men would worship other gods. "I gave them My Sabbaths," God declared, "to be a sign between Me and them, that they might know that I am the Lord that sanctify them." Yet "they despised My judgments, and walked not in My statutes, but polluted My Sabbaths: for their heart went after their idols." And in His appeal to them to return to Him, He called their attention anew to the importance of keeping the Sabbath holy. "I am the Lord your God," He said; "walk in My statutes, and keep My judgments, and do them; and hallow My Sabbaths; and they shall be a sign between Me and you, that ye may know that I am the Lord your God." Ezekiel 20:12, 16, 19, 20.

In calling the attention of Judah to the sins that finally brought upon them the Babylonian Captivity, the Lord declared: "Thou hast ... profaned My Sabbaths." "Therefore have I poured out Mine indignation upon them; I have consumed them with the fire of My wrath: their own way have I recompensed upon their heads." Ezekiel 22:8, 31.

At the restoration of Jerusalem, in the days of Nehemiah, Sabbathbreaking was met with the stern inquiry, "Did not your fathers thus, and did not our God bring all this evil [183] upon us, and upon this city? yet ye bring more wrath upon Israel by profaning the Sabbath." Nehemiah 13:18.

Christ, during His earthly ministry, emphasized the binding claims of the Sabbath; in all His teaching He showed reverence for the institution He Himself had given. In His days the Sabbath had become so perverted that its observance reflected the character of selfish and arbitrary men rather than the character of God. Christ set aside the false teaching by which those who claimed to know God had misrepresented Him. Although followed with merciless hostility by the rabbis, He did not even appear to conform to their requirements, but went straight forward keeping the Sabbath according to the law of God.

In unmistakable language He testified to His regard for the law of Jehovah. "Think not that I am come to destroy the law, or the prophets," He said; "I am not come to destroy, but to fulfill. For verily I say unto you, Till heaven and earth pass, one jot or one tittle shall in no wise pass from the law, till all be fulfilled. Whosoever therefore shall break one of these least commandments, and shall teach men so, he shall be called the least in the kingdom of heaven: but whosoever shall do and teach them, the same shall be called great in the kingdom of heaven." Matthew 5:17-19.

During the Christian dispensation, the great enemy of man's happiness has made the Sabbath of the fourth commandment an object of special attack. Satan says, "I will work at cross purposes with God. I will empower my followers to set aside God's memorial, the seventh-day Sabbath. Thus I will show the world that the day sanctified [184] and blessed by God has been changed. That day shall not live in the minds of the people. I will obliterate the memory of it. I will place in its stead a day that does not bear the credentials of God, a day that cannot be a sign between God and His people. I will lead those who accept this day to place upon it the sanctity that God placed upon the seventh day.

"Through my vicegerent, I will exalt myself. The first day will be extolled, and the Protestant world will receive this spurious sabbath as genuine. Through the nonobservance of the Sabbath that God instituted, I will bring His law into contempt. The words, 'A sign between Me and you throughout your generations,' I will make to serve on the side of my sabbath.

"Thus the world will become mine. I will be the ruler of the earth, the prince of the world. I will so control the minds under my power that God's Sabbath shall be a special object of contempt. A sign? I will make the observance of the seventh day a sign of disloyalty to the authorities of earth. Human laws will be made so stringent that men and women will not dare to observe the seventh-day Sabbath. For fear of wanting food and clothing, they will join with the world in transgressing God's law. The earth will be wholly under my dominion."

Through the setting up of a false sabbath, the enemy thought to change times and laws. But has he really succeeded in changing God's law? The words of the thirty-first chapter of Exodus are the answer. He who is the same yesterday, today, and forever, has declared of the seventh-day Sabbath: "It is a sign between Me and you throughout your [185] generations." "It is a sign ... forever." Exodus 31:13, 17. The changed signpost is pointing the wrong way, but God has not changed. He is still the mighty God of Israel. "Behold, the nations are as a drop of a bucket, and are counted as the small dust of the balance: behold, He taketh up the isles as a very little thing. And Lebanon is not sufficient to burn, nor the beasts thereof sufficient for a burnt offering. All nations before Him are as nothing; and they are counted to Him less than nothing, and vanity." Isaiah 40:15-17. And He is just as jealous for His law now as He was in the days of Ahab and Elijah.

But how is that law disregarded! Behold the world today in open rebellion against God. This is in truth a froward generation, filled with ingratitude, formalism, insincerity, pride, and apostasy. Men neglect the Bible and hate truth. Jesus sees His law rejected, His love despised, His ambassadors treated with indifference. He has spoken by His mercies, but these have been unacknowledged; He has spoken by warnings, but these have been unheeded. The temple courts of the human soul have been turned into places of unholy traffic. Selfishness, envy, pride, malice—all are cherished.

Many do not hesitate to sneer at the word of God. Those who believe that word just as it reads are held up to ridicule. There is a growing contempt for law and order, directly traceable to a violation of the plain commands of Jehovah. Violence and crime are the result of turning aside from the path of obedience. Behold the wretchedness and misery of multitudes who worship at the shrine of idols and who seek in vain for happiness and peace. [186]

Behold the well-nigh universal disregard of the Sabbath commandment. Behold also the daring impiety of those who, while enacting laws to safeguard the supposed sanctity of the first day of the week, at the same time are making laws legalizing the liquor traffic. Wise above that which is written, they attempt to coerce the consciences of men, while lending their sanction to an evil that brutalizes and destroys the beings created in the image of God. It is Satan himself who inspires such legislation. He well knows that the curse of God will rest on those who exalt human enactments above the divine, and he does all in his power to lead men into the broad road that ends in destruction.

So long have men worshiped human opinions and human institutions that almost the whole world is following after idols. And he who has endeavored to change God's law is using every deceptive artifice to induce men and women to array themselves against God and against the sign by which the righteous are known. But the Lord will not always suffer His law to be broken and despised with impunity. There is a time coming when "the lofty looks of man shall be humbled, and the haughtiness of men shall be bowed down, and the Lord alone shall be exalted in that day." Isaiah 2:11. Skepticism may treat the claims of God's law with jest, scoffing, and denial. The spirit of worldliness may contaminate the many and control the few, the cause of God may hold its ground only by great exertion and continual sacrifice, yet in the end the truth will triumph gloriously.

In the closing work of God in the earth, the standard of His law will be again exalted. False religion may prevail, [187] iniquity may abound, the love of many may wax cold, the cross of Calvary may be lost sight of, and darkness, like the pall of death, may spread over the world; the whole force of the popular current may be turned against the truth; plot after plot may be formed to overthrow the people of God; but in the hour of greatest peril the God of Elijah will raise up human instrumentalities to bear a message that will not be silenced. In the populous cities of the land, and in the places where men have gone to the greatest lengths in speaking against the Most High, the voice of stern rebuke will be heard. Boldly will men of God's appointment denounce the union of the church with the world. Earnestly will they call upon men and women to turn from the observance of a man-made institution to the observance of the true Sabbath. "Fear God, and give glory to Him," they will proclaim to every nation; "for the hour of His judgment is come: and worship Him that made heaven, and earth, and the sea, and the fountains of waters.... If any man worship the beast and his image, and receive his mark in his forehead, or in his hand, the same shall drink of the wine of the wrath of God, which is poured out without mixture into the cup of His indignation." Revelation 14:7-10.

God will not break His covenant, nor alter the thing that has gone out of His lips. His word will stand fast forever as unalterable as His throne. At the judgment this covenant will be brought forth, plainly written with the finger of God, and the world will be arraigned before the bar of Infinite Justice to receive sentence.

Today, as in the days of Elijah, the line of demarcation [188] between God's commandment-keeping people and the worshipers of false gods is clearly drawn. "How long halt ye between two opinions?" Elijah cried; "if the Lord be God, follow Him: but if Baal, then follow him." 1 Kings 18:21. And the message for today is: "Babylon the great is fallen, is fallen.... Come out of her, My people, that ye be not partakers of her sins, and that ye receive not of her plagues. For her sins have reached unto heaven, and God hath remembered her iniquities." Revelation 18:2, 4, 5.

The time is not far distant when the test will come to every soul. The observance of the false sabbath will be urged upon us. The contest will be between the commandments of God and the commandments of men. Those who have yielded step by step to worldly demands and conformed to worldly customs will then yield to the powers that be, rather than subject themselves to derision, insult, threatened imprisonment, and death. At that time the gold will be separated from the dross. True godliness will be clearly distinguished from the appearance and tinsel of it. Many a star that we have admired for its brilliance will then go out in darkness. Those who have assumed the ornaments of the sanctuary, but are not clothed with Christ's righteousness, will then appear in the shame of their own nakedness.

Among earth's inhabitants, scattered in every land, there are those who have not bowed the knee to Baal. Like the stars of heaven, which appear only at night, these faithful ones will shine forth when darkness covers the earth and gross darkness the people. In heathen Africa, in the Catholic lands of Europe and of South America, in China, in India, [189] in the islands of the sea, and in all the dark corners of the earth, God has in reserve a firmament of chosen ones that will yet shine forth amidst the darkness, revealing clearly to an apostate world the transforming power of obedience to His law. Even now they are appearing in every nation, among every tongue and people; and in the hour of deepest apostasy, when Satan's supreme effort is made to cause "all, both small and great, rich and poor, free and bond," to receive, under penalty of death, the sign of allegiance to a false rest day, these faithful ones, "blameless and harmless, the sons of God, without rebuke," will "shine as lights in the world." Revelation 13:16; Philippians 2:15. The darker the night, the more brilliantly will they shine.

What strange work Elijah would have done in numbering Israel at the time when God's judgments were falling upon the backsliding people! He could count only one on the Lord's side. But when he said, "I, even I only, am left; and they seek my life," the word of the Lord surprised him, "Yet I have left Me seven thousand in Israel, all the knees which have not bowed unto Baal." 1 Kings 19:14, 18.

Then let no man attempt to number Israel today, but let everyone have a heart of flesh, a heart of tender sympathy, a heart that, like the heart of Christ, reaches out for the salvation of a lost world. [190]

Chapter 15

Jehoshaphat

Until called to the throne at the age of thirty-five, Jehoshaphat had before him the example of good King Asa, who in nearly every crisis had done "that which was right in the eyes of the Lord." 1 Kings 15:11. During a prosperous reign of twenty-five years, Jehoshaphat sought to walk "in all the ways of Asa his father; he turned not aside."

In his efforts to rule wisely, Jehoshaphat endeavored to persuade his subjects to take a firm stand against idolatrous practices. Many of the people in his realm "offered and burnt incense yet in the high places." 1 Kings 22:43. The king did not at once destroy these shrines; but from the beginning he tried to safeguard Judah from the sins characterizing the northern kingdom under the rule of Ahab, of whom he was a contemporary for many years. Jehoshaphat himself was loyal to God. He "sought not unto Baalim; [191] but sought to the Lord God of his father, and walked in His commandments, and not after the doings of Israel." Because of his integrity, the Lord was with him, and "stablished the kingdom in his hand." 2 Chronicles 17:3-5.

"All Judah brought to Jehoshaphat presents; and he had riches and honor in abundance. And his heart was lifted up in the ways of the Lord." As time passed and reformations were wrought, the king "took away the high places and groves out of Judah." Verses 5, 6. "And the remnant of the Sodomites, which remained in the days of his father Asa, he took out of the land." 1 Kings 22:46. Thus gradually the inhabitants of Judah were freed from many of the perils that had been threatening to retard seriously their spiritual development.

Throughout the kingdom the people were in need of instruction in the law of God. In an understanding of this law lay their safety; by conforming their lives to its requirements they would become loyal both to God and to man. Knowing this, Jehoshaphat took steps to ensure to his people thorough instruction in the Holy Scriptures. The princes in charge of the different portions of his realm were directed to arrange for the faithful ministry of teaching priests. By royal appointment these instructors, working under the direct supervision of the princes, "went about throughout all the cities of Judah, and taught the people." 2 Chronicles 17:7-9. And as many endeavored to understand God's requirements and to put away sin, a revival was effected. [192]

To this wise provision for the spiritual needs of his subjects, Jehoshaphat owed much of his prosperity as a ruler. In obedience to God's law there is great gain. In conformity to the divine requirements there is a transforming power that brings peace and good will among men. If the teachings of God's word were made the controlling influence in the life of every man and woman, if mind and heart were brought under its restraining power, the evils that now exist in national and in social life would find no place. From every home would go forth an influence that would make men and women strong in spiritual insight and in moral power, and thus nations and individuals would be placed on vantage ground.

For many years Jehoshaphat lived in peace, unmolested by surrounding nations. "The fear of the Lord fell upon all the kingdoms of the lands that were round about Judah." Verse 10. From Philistia he received tribute money and presents; from Arabia, large flocks of sheep and goats. "Jehoshaphat waxed great exceedingly; and he built in Judah castles, and cities of stores.... Men of war, mighty men of valor, ... waited on the king, beside those whom the king put in the fenced cities throughout all Judah." Verses 12-19. Blessed abundantly with "riches and honor," he was enabled to wield a mighty influence for truth and righteousness. 2 Chronicles 18:1.

Some years after coming to the throne, Jehoshaphat, now in the height of his prosperity, consented to the marriage of his son, Jehoram, to Athaliah, daughter of Ahab and Jezebel. By this union there was formed between the kingdoms [193] [194] [195] of Judah and Israel an alliance which was not in the order of God and which in a time of crisis brought disaster to the king and to many of his subjects.

On one occasion Jehoshaphat visited the king of Israel at Samaria. Special honor was shown the royal guest from Jerusalem, and before the close of his visit he was persuaded to unite with the king of Israel in war against the Syrians. Ahab hoped that by joining his forces with those of Judah he might regain Ramoth, one of the old cities of refuge, which, he contended, rightfully belonged to the Israelites.

Although Jehoshaphat in a moment of weakness had rashly promised to join the king of Israel in his war against the Syrians, yet his better judgment led him to seek to learn the will of God concerning the undertaking. "Inquire, I pray thee, at the word of the Lord today," he suggested to Ahab. In response, Ahab called together four hundred of the false prophets of Samaria, and asked of them, "Shall we go to Ramoth-gilead to battle, or shall I forbear?" And they answered, "Go up; for God will deliver it into the kings's hand." Verses 4, 5.

Unsatisfied, Jehoshaphat sought to learn for a certainty the will of God. "Is there not here a prophet of the Lord," he asked, "that we might inquire of him?" Verse 6. "There is yet one man, Micaiah the son of Imlah, by whom we may inquire of the Lord," Ahab answered; "but I hate him; for he doth not prophesy good concerning me, but evil." 1 Kings 22:8. Jehoshaphat was firm in his request that the man of God be called; and upon appearing before them and being adjured by Ahab to tell "nothing but that which [196] is true in the name of the Lord," Micaiah said: "I saw all Israel scattered upon the hills, as sheep that have not a shepherd: and the Lord said, These have no master: let them return every man to his house in peace." Verses 16, 17.

The words of the prophet should have been enough to show the kings that their project was not favored by Heaven, but neither ruler felt inclined to heed the warning. Ahab had marked out his course, and he was determined to follow it. Jehoshaphat had given his word of honor, "We will be with thee in the war;" and after making such a promise, he was reluctant to withdraw his forces. 2 Chronicles 18:3. "So the king of Israel and Jehoshaphat the king of Judah went up to Ramoth-gilead." 1 Kings 22:29.

During the battle that followed, Ahab was shot by an arrow, and at eventide he died. "About the going down of the sun," "there went a proclamation throughout the host," "Every man to his city, and every man to his own country." Verse 36. Thus was fulfilled the word of the prophet.

From this disastrous battle Jehoshaphat returned to Jerusalem. As he approached the city, the prophet Jehu met him with the reproof: "Shouldest thou help the ungodly, and love them that hate the Lord? therefore is wrath upon thee from before the Lord. Nevertheless there are good things found in thee, in that thou hast taken away the groves out of the land, and hast prepared thine heart to seek God." 2 Chronicles 19:2, 3.

The later years of Jehoshaphat's reign were largely spent in strengthening the national and spiritual defenses of Judah. [197] He "went out again through the people from Beersheba to Mount Ephraim, and brought them back unto the Lord God of their fathers." Verse 4.

One of the important steps taken by the king was the establishment and maintenance of efficient courts of justice. He "set judges in the land throughout all the fenced cities of Judah, city by city;" and in the charge given them he urged: "Take heed what ye do: for ye judge not for man, but for the Lord, who is with you in the judgment. Wherefore now let the fear of the Lord be upon you; take heed and do it: for there is no iniquity with the Lord our God, nor respect of persons, nor taking of gifts." Verses 5-7.

The judicial system was perfected by the founding of a court of appeal at Jerusalem, where Jehoshaphat "set of the Levites, and of the priests, and of the chief of the fathers of Israel, for the judgment of the Lord, and for controversies." Verse 8.

The king exhorted these judges to be faithful. "Thus shall ye do in the fear of the Lord, faithfully, and with a perfect heart," he charged them. "And what cause soever shall come to you of your brethren that dwell in their cities, between blood and blood, between law and commandment, statutes and judgments, ye shall even warn them that they trespass not against the Lord, and so wrath come upon you, and upon your brethren: this do, and ye shall not trespass.

"And, behold, Amariah the chief priest is over you in all matters of the Lord; and Zebadiah the son of Ishmael, the [198] ruler of the house of Judah, for all the king's matters: also the Levites shall be officers before you.

"Deal courageously, and the Lord shall be with the good." Verses 9-11.

In his careful safeguarding of the rights and liberties of his subjects, Jehoshaphat emphasized the consideration that every member of the human family receives from the God of justice, who rules over all. "God standeth in the congregation of the mighty; He judgeth among the gods." And those who are appointed to act as judges under Him, are to "defend the poor and fatherless;" they are to "do justice to the afflicted and needy," and "rid them out of the hand of the wicked." Psalm 82:1, 3, 4.

Toward the close of Jehoshaphat's reign the kingdom of Judah was invaded by an army before whose approach the inhabitants of the land had reason to tremble. "The children of Moab, and the children of Ammon, and with them other beside the Ammonites, came against Jehoshaphat to battle." Tidings of this invasion reached the king through a messenger, who appeared with the startling word, "There cometh a great multitude against thee from beyond the sea on this side Syria: and, behold, they be in Hazazon-tamar, which is Engedi." 2 Chronicles 20:1, 2.

Jehoshaphat was a man of courage and valor. For years he had been strengthening his armies and his fortified cities. He was well prepared to meet almost any foe; yet in this crisis he put not his trust in the arm of flesh. Not by disciplined armies and fenced cities, but by a living faith in the God of Israel, could he hope to gain the victory over these [199] heathen who boasted of their power to humble Judah in the eyes of the nations.

"Jehoshaphat feared, and set himself to seek the Lord, and proclaimed a fast throughout all Judah. And Judah gathered themselves together, to ask help of the Lord: even out of all the cities of Judah they came to seek the Lord."

Standing in the temple court before his people, Jehoshaphat poured out his soul in prayer, pleading God's promises, with confession of Israel's helplessness. "O Lord God of our fathers" he petitioned, "art not Thou God in heaven? and rulest not Thou over all the kingdoms of the heathen? and in Thine hand is there not power and might, so that none is able to withstand Thee? Art not Thou our God, who didst drive out the inhabitants of this land before Thy people Israel, and gavest it to the seed of Abraham Thy friend forever? And they dwelt therein, and have built Thee a sanctuary therein for Thy name, saying, If, when evil cometh upon us, as the sword, judgment, or pestilence, or famine, we stand before this house, and in Thy presence, (for Thy name is in this house,) and cry unto Thee in our affliction, then Thou wilt hear and help.

"And now, behold, the children of Ammon and Moab and Mount Seir, whom Thou wouldest not let Israel invade, when they came out of the land of Egypt, but they turned from them, and destroyed them not; behold, I say, how they reward us, to come to cast us out of Thy possession, which Thou hast given us to inherit. O our God, wilt Thou not judge them? for we have no might against this great [200] company that cometh against us; neither know we what to do: but our eyes are upon Thee." Verses 3-12.

With confidence Jehoshaphat could say to the Lord, "Our eyes are upon thee." For years he had taught the people to trust in the One who in past ages had so often interposed to save His chosen ones from utter destruction; and now, when the kingdom was in peril, Jehoshaphat did not stand alone; "all Judah stood before the Lord, with their little ones, their wives, and their children." Verse 13. Unitedly they fasted and prayed; unitedly they besought the Lord to put their enemies to confusion, that the name of Jehovah might be glorified.

"Keep not Thou silence, O God: Hold not Thy peace, and be not still, O God. For, lo, Thine enemies make a tumult: And they that hate Thee have lifted up the head. They have taken crafty counsel against Thy people, And consulted against Thy hidden ones. They have said, Come, and let us cut them off from being a nation; That the name of Israel may be no more in remembrance. For they have consulted together with one consent: They are confederate against Thee: The tabernacles of Edom, and the Ishmaelites; Of Moab, and the Hagarenes; Gebal, and Ammon, and Amalek.... Do unto them as unto the Midianites; As to Sisera, as to Jabin, at the brook of Kison: ... Let them be confounded and troubled forever; Yea, let them be put to shame, and perish: That men may know that Thou, whose name alone is Jehovah, Art the Most High over all the earth."

Psalm 83. [201]

As the people joined with their king in humbling themselves before God, and asking Him for help, the Spirit of the Lord came upon Jahaziel, "a Levite of the sons of Asaph," and he said:

"Hearken ye, all Judah, and ye inhabitants of Jerusalem, and thou King Jehoshaphat, Thus saith the Lord unto you, Be not afraid nor dismayed by reason of this great multitude; for the battle is not yours, but God's. Tomorrow go ye down against them: behold, they come up by the cliff of Ziz; and ye shall find them at the end of the brook, before the wilderness of Jeruel. Ye shall not need to fight in this battle: set yourselves, stand ye still, and see the salvation of the Lord with you, O Judah and Jerusalem: fear not, nor be dismayed; tomorrow go out against them: for the Lord will be with you."

"Jehoshaphat bowed his head with his face to the ground: and all Judah and the inhabitants of Jerusalem fell before the Lord, worshiping the Lord. And the Levites, of the children of the Kohathites, and of the children of the Korhites, stood up to praise the Lord God of Israel with a loud voice on high."

Early in the morning they rose and went into the wilderness of Tekoa. As they advanced to the battle, Jehoshaphat said, "Hear me, O Judah, and ye inhabitants of Jerusalem; Believe in the Lord your God, so shall ye be established: believe His prophets, so shall ye prosper." "And when he had consulted with the people, he appointed singers unto the Lord, and that should praise the beauty of holiness." 2 Chronicles 20:14-21. These singers went before the army, lifting their voices in praise to God for the promise of victory. [202]

It was a singular way of going to battle against the enemy's army—praising the Lord with singing, and exalting the God of Israel. This was their battle song. They possessed the beauty of holiness. If more praising of God were engaged in now, hope and courage and faith would steadily increase. And would not this strengthen the hands of the valiant soldiers who today are standing in defense of truth?

"The Lord set ambushments against the children of Ammon, Moab, and Mount Seir, which were come against Judah; and they were smitten. For the children of Ammon and Moab stood up against the inhabitants of Mount Seir, utterly to slay and destroy them: and when they had made an end of the inhabitants of Seir, everyone helped to destroy another.

"And when Judah came toward the watchtower in the wilderness, they looked unto the multitude, and, behold, they were dead bodies fallen to the earth, and none escaped." Verses 22-24.

God was the strength of Judah in this crisis, and He is the strength of His people today. We are not to trust in princes, or to set men in the place of God. We are to remember that human beings are fallible and erring, and that He who has all power is our strong tower of defense. In every emergency we are to feel that the battle is His. His resources are limitless, and apparent impossibilities will make the victory all the greater.

"Save us, O God of our salvation, And gather us together, And deliver us from the heathen, That we may give thanks to Thy holy name, And glory in Thy praise."

1 Chronicles 16:35. [203]

Laden with spoil, the armies of Judah returned "with joy; for the Lord had made them to rejoice over their enemies. And they came to Jerusalem with psalteries and harps and trumpets unto the house of the Lord." 2 Chronicles 20:27, 28. Great was their cause for rejoicing. In obedience to the command, "Stand ye still, and see the salvation of the Lord: ... fear not, nor be dismayed," they had put their trust wholly in God, and He had proved to be their fortress and their deliverer. Verse 17. Now they could sing with understanding the inspired hymns of David:

"God is our refuge and strength, A very present help in trouble.... He breaketh the bow, and cutteth the spear in sunder; He burneth the chariot in the fire. Be still, and know that I am God: I will be exalted among the heathen, I will be exalted in the earth. The Lord of hosts is with us; The God of Jacob is our refuge."

Psalm 46.

"According to Thy name, O God, So is Thy praise unto the ends of the earth: Thy right hand is full of righteousness. Let Mount Zion rejoice, Let the daughters of Judah be glad, Because of Thy judgments....

"This God is our God for ever and ever: He will be our guide even unto death."

Psalm 48:10-14.

Through the faith of Judah's ruler and of his armies "the fear of God was on all the kingdoms of those countries, when they had heard that the Lord fought against the enemies of Israel. So the realm of Jehoshaphat was quiet: for his God gave him rest." 2 Chronicles 20:29, 30. [204]

Chapter 16

The Fall of the House of Ahab

This chapter is based on 1 Kings 21; 2 Kings 1.

The evil influence that Jezebel had exercised from the first over Ahab continued during the later years of his life and bore fruit in deeds of shame and violence such as have seldom been equaled in sacred history. "There was none like unto Ahab, which did sell himself to work wickedness in the sight of the Lord, whom Jezebel his wife stirred up."

Naturally of a covetous disposition, Ahab, strengthened and sustained in wrongdoing by Jezebel, had followed the dictates of his evil heart until he was fully controlled by the spirit of selfishness. He could brook no refusal of his wishes; the things he desired he felt should by right be his.

This dominant trait in Ahab, which influenced so disastrously the fortunes of the kingdom under his successors, is revealed in an incident which took place while Elijah was still a prophet in Israel. Hard by the palace of the king was a vineyard belonging to Naboth, a Jezreelite. Ahab set his [205] heart on possessing this vineyard, and he proposed to buy it or else to give in exchange for it another piece of land. "Give me thy vineyard," he said to Naboth, "that I may have it for a garden of herbs, because it is near unto my house: and I will give thee for it a better vineyard than it; or, if it seem good to thee, I will give thee the worth of it in money."

Naboth valued his vineyard highly because it had belonged to his fathers, and he refused to part with it. "The Lord forbid it me," he said to Ahab, "that I should give the inheritance of my fathers unto thee." According to the Levitical code no land could be transferred permanently by sale or exchange; every one of the children of Israel must "keep himself to the inheritance of the tribe of his fathers." Numbers 36:7.

Naboth's refusal made the selfish monarch ill. "Ahab came into his house heavy and displeased because of the word which Naboth the Jezreelite had spoken to him.... And he laid him down upon his bed, and turned away his face, and would eat no bread."

Jezebel soon learned the particulars, and, indignant that anyone should refuse the request of the king, she assured Ahab that he need no longer be sad. "Dost thou now govern the kingdom of Israel?" she said. "Arise, and eat bread, and let thine heart be merry: I will give thee the vineyard of Naboth the Jezreelite."

Ahab cared not by what means his wife might accomplish the desired object, and Jezebel immediately proceeded to carry out her wicked purpose. She wrote letters in the name of the king, sealed them with his signet, and sent [206] them to the elders and nobles of the city where Naboth dwelt, saying: "Proclaim a fast, and set Naboth on high among the people: and set two men, sons of Belial, before him, to bear witness against him, saying, Thou didst blaspheme God and the king. And then carry him out, and stone him, that he may die."

The command was obeyed. "The men of his city, even the elders and the nobles, ... did as Jezebel had ... written in the letters which she had sent unto them." Then Jezebel went to the king and bade him arise and take the vineyard. And Ahab, heedless of the consequences, blindly followed her counsel and went down to take possession of the coveted property.

The king was not allowed to enjoy unrebuked that which he had gained by fraud and bloodshed. "The word of the Lord came to Elijah the Tishbite, saying, Arise, go down to meet Ahab king of Israel, which is in Samaria: behold, he is in the vineyard of Naboth, whither he is gone down to possess it. And thou shalt speak unto him, saying, Thus saith the Lord, Hast thou killed, and also taken possession?" And the Lord further instructed Elijah to pronounce upon Ahab a terrible judgment.

The prophet hastened to carry out the divine command. The guilty ruler, meeting the stern messenger of Jehovah face to face in the vineyard, gave voice to his startled fear in the words, "Hast thou found me, O mine enemy?"

Without hesitation the messenger of the Lord replied, "I have found thee: because thou hast sold thyself to work evil in the sight of the Lord. Behold, I will bring evil upon thee, and will take away thy posterity." No mercy was to [207] be shown. The house of Ahab was to be utterly destroyed, "like the house of Jeroboam the son of Nebat, and like the house of Baasha the son of Ahijah," the Lord declared through His servant, "for the provocation wherewith thou hast provoked Me to anger, and made Israel to sin."

And of Jezebel the Lord declared, "The dogs shall eat Jezebel by the wall of Jezreel. Him that dieth of Ahab in the city the dogs shall eat; and him that dieth in the field shall the fowls of the air eat."

When the king heard this fearful message, "he rent his clothes, and put sackcloth upon his flesh, and fasted, and lay in sackcloth, and went softly.

"And the word of the Lord came to Elijah the Tishbite, saying, Seest thou how Ahab humbleth himself before Me? because he humbleth himself before Me, I will not bring the evil in his days: but in his son's days will I bring the evil upon his house."

It was less than three years later that King Ahab met his death at the hands of the Syrians. Ahaziah, his successor, "did evil in the sight of the Lord, and walked in the way of his father, and in the way of his mother, and in the way of Jeroboam." "He served Baal, and worshiped him, and provoked to anger the Lord God of Israel," as his father Ahab had done. 1 Kings 22:52, 53. But judgments followed close upon the sins of the rebellious king. A disastrous war with Moab, and then an accident by which his own life was threatened, attested to God's wrath against him.

Having fallen "through a lattice in his upper chamber," Ahaziah, seriously injured, and fearful of the possible outcome, sent some of his servants to make inquiry of Baalzebub, [208] the god of Ekron, whether he should recover or not. The god of Ekron was supposed to give information, through the medium of its priests, concerning future events. Large numbers of people went to inquire of it; but the predictions there uttered, and the information given, proceeded from the prince of darkness.

Ahaziah's servants were met by a man of God, who directed them to return to the king with the message: "Is it because there is no God in Israel, that ye go to inquire of Baal-zebub, the god of Ekron? Now therefore thus saith Jehovah, Thou shalt not come down from the bed whither thou art gone up, but shalt surely die." Having delivered his message, the prophet departed.

The astonished servants hastened back to the king, and repeated to him the words of the man of God. The king inquired, "What manner of man was he?" They answered, "He was an hairy man, and girt with a girdle of leather about his loins." "It is Elijah the Tishbite," Ahaziah exclaimed. He knew that if the stranger whom his messengers had met was indeed Elijah, the words of doom pronounced would surely come to pass. Anxious to avert, if possible, the threatened judgment, he determined to send for the prophet.

Twice Ahaziah sent a company of soldiers to intimidate the prophet, and twice the wrath of God fell upon them in judgment. The third company of soldiers humbled themselves before God; and their captain, as he approached the Lord's messenger, "fell on his knees before Elijah, and besought him, and said unto him, O man of God, I pray [209] thee, let my life, and the life of these fifty thy servants, be precious in thy sight."

"The angel of Jehovah said unto Elijah, Go down with him: be not afraid of him. And he arose, and went down with him unto the king. And he said unto him, Thus saith Jehovah, Forasmuch as thou hast sent messengers to inquire of Baal-zebub, the god of Ekron, is it because there is no God in Israel to inquire of His word? therefore thou shalt not come down from the bed whither thou art gone up, but shalt surely die."

During the father's reign, Ahaziah had witnessed the wondrous works of the Most High. He had seen the terrible evidences that God had given apostate Israel of the way in which He regards those who set aside the binding claims of His law. Ahaziah had acted as if these awful realities were but idle tales. Instead of humbling his heart before [210] the Lord, he had followed after Baal, and at last he had ventured upon this, his most daring act of impiety. Rebellious, and unwilling to repent, Ahaziah died, "according to the word of the Lord which Elijah had spoken."

The history of King Ahaziah's sin and its punishment has in it a warning which none can disregard with impunity. Men today may not pay homage to heathen gods, yet thousands are worshiping at Satan's shrine as verily as did the king of Israel. The spirit of idolatry is rife in the world today, although, under the influence of science and education, it has assumed forms more refined and attractive than in the days when Ahaziah sought to the god of Ekron. Every day adds its sorrowful evidence that faith in the sure word of prophecy is decreasing, and that in its stead superstition and satanic witchery are captivating the minds of many.

Today the mysteries of heathen worship are replaced by the secret association and seances, the obscurities and wonders, of spiritistic mediums. The disclosures of these mediums are eagerly received by thousands who refuse to accept light from God's word or through His Spirit. Believers in spiritism may speak with scorn of the magicians of old, but the great deceiver laughs in triumph as they yield to his arts under a different form.

There are many who shrink with horror from the thought of consulting spirit mediums, but who are attracted by more pleasing forms of spiritism. Others are led astray by the teachings of Christian Science, and by the mysticism of Theosophy and other Oriental religions. [211]

The apostles of nearly all forms of spiritism claim to have power to heal. They attribute this power to electricity, magnetism, the so-called "sympathetic remedies," or to latent forces within the mind of man. And there are not a few, even in this Christian age, who go to these healers, instead of trusting in the power of the living God and the skill of well-qualified physicians. The mother, watching by the sickbed of her child, exclaims, "I can do no more. Is there no physician who has power to restore my child?" She is told of the wonderful cures performed by some clairvoyant or magnetic healer, and she trusts her dear one to his charge, placing it as verily in the hand of Satan as if he were standing by her side. In many instances the future life of the child is controlled by a satanic power which it seems impossible to break.

God had cause for displeasure at Ahaziah's impiety. What had He not done to win the hearts of the people of Israel and to inspire them with confidence in Himself? For ages He had been giving His people manifestations of unexampled kindness and love. From the beginning He had shown that His "delights were with the sons of men." Proverbs 8:31. He had been a very present help to all who sought Him in sincerity. Yet now the king of Israel, turning from God to ask help of the worst enemy of His people, proclaimed to the heathen that he had more confidence in their idols than in the God of heaven. In the same manner do men and women dishonor Him when they turn from the Source of strength and wisdom to ask help or counsel from the powers of darkness. If God's wrath was kindled by Ahaziah's [212] act, how does He regard those who, having still greater light, choose to follow a similar course?

Those who give themselves up to the sorcery of Satan, may boast of great benefit received; but does this prove their course to be wise or safe? What if life should be prolonged? What if temporal gain should be secured? Will it pay in the end to have disregarded the will of God? All such apparent gain will prove at last an irrecoverable loss. We cannot with impunity break down a single barrier which God has erected to guard His people from Satan's power.

As Ahaziah had no son, he was succeeded by Jehoram, his brother, who reigned over the ten tribes for twelve years. Throughout these years his mother, Jezebel, was still living, and she continued to exercise her evil influence over the affairs of the nation. Idolatrous customs were still practiced by many of the people. Jehoram himself "wrought evil in the sight of the Lord; but not like his father, and like his mother: for he put away the image of Baal that his father had made. Nevertheless he cleaved unto the sins of Jereboam the son of Nebat, which made Israel to sin; he departed not therefrom." 2 Kings 3:2, 3.

It was during Jehoram's reign over Israel that Jehoshaphat died, and Jehoshaphat's son, also named Jehoram, ascended the throne of the kingdom of Judah. By his marriage with the daughter of Ahab and Jezebel, Jehoram of Judah was closely connected with the king of Israel; and in his reign he followed after Baal, "like as did the house of Ahab." "Moreover he made high places in the mountains of Judah, and caused the inhabitants of Jerusalem to [213] commit fornication, and compelled Judah thereto." 2 Chronicles 21:6, 11.

The king of Judah was not permitted to continue his terrible apostasy unreproved. The prophet Elijah had not yet been translated, and he could not remain silent while the kingdom of Judah was pursuing the same course that had brought the northern kingdom to the verge of ruin. The prophet sent to Jehoram of Judah a written communication, in which the wicked king read the awful words:

"Thus saith the Lord God of David thy father, Because thou hast not walked in the ways of Jehoshaphat thy father, nor in the ways of Asa king of Judah, but hast walked in the way of the kings of Israel, and hast made Judah and the inhabitants of Jerusalem to go a whoring, like to the whoredoms of the house of Ahab, and also hast slain thy brethren of thy father's house, which were better than thyself: behold, with a great plague will the Lord smite thy people, and thy children, and thy wives, and all thy goods: and thou shalt have great sickness."

In fulfillment of this prophecy "the Lord stirred up against Jehoram the spirit of the Philistines, and of the Arabians, that were near the Ethiopians: and they came up into Judah, and brake into it, and carried away all the substance that was found in the king's house, and his sons also, and his wives; so that there was never a son left him, save Jehoahaz [Ahaziah, Azariah], the youngest of his sons.

"And after all this the Lord smote him in his bowels with an incurable disease. And it came to pass, that in process of time, after the end of two years, ... he died of sore [214] diseases." "And Ahaziah [Jehoahaz] his son reigned in his stead." Verses 12-19; 2 Kings 8:24.

Jehoram the son of Ahab was still reigning in the kingdom of Israel when his nephew, Ahaziah, came to the throne of Judah. Ahaziah ruled only one year, and during this time, influenced by his mother, Athaliah, "his counselor to do wickedly," "he walked in the way of the house of Ahab, and did evil in the sight of the Lord." 2 Chronicles 22:3, 4; 2 Kings 8:27. Jezebel, his grandmother, was still living, and he allied himself boldly with Jehoram of Israel, his uncle.

Ahaziah of Judah soon met a tragic end. The surviving members of the house of Ahab were indeed "his counselors after the death of his father to his destruction." 2 Chronicles 22:3, 4. While Ahaziah was visiting his uncle at Jezreel, the prophet Elisha was divinely directed to send one of the sons of the prophets to Ramoth-gilead to anoint Jehu king of Israel. The combined forces of Judah and Israel were at that time engaged in a military campaign against the Syrians of Ramoth-gilead. Jehoram had been wounded in battle, and had returned to Jezreel, leaving Jehu in charge of the royal armies.

In anointing Jehu, the messenger of Elisha declared, "I have anointed thee king over the people of the Lord, even over Israel." And then he solemnly charged Jehu with a special commission from heaven. "Thou shalt smite the house of Ahab thy master," the Lord declared through His messenger, "that I may avenge the blood of My servants the prophets, and the blood of all the servants of the Lord, at the [215] hand of Jezebel. For the whole house of Ahab shall perish." 2 Kings 9:6-8.

After he had been proclaimed king by the army, Jehu hastened to Jezreel, where he began his work of execution on those who had deliberately chosen to continue in sin and to lead others into sin. Jehoram of Israel, Ahaziah of Judah, and Jezebel the queen mother, with "all that remained of the house of Ahab in Jezreel, and all his great men, and his kinsfolks, and his priests," were slain. "All the prophets of Baal, all his servants, and all his priests" dwelling at the center of Baal worship near Samaria, were put to the sword. The idolatrous images were broken down and burned, and the temple of Baal was laid in ruins. "Thus Jehu destroyed Baal out of Israel." 2 Kings 10:11, 19, 28.

Tidings of this general execution reached Athaliah, Jezebel's daughter, who still occupied a commanding position in the kingdom of Judah. When she saw that her son, the king of Judah, was dead, "she arose and destroyed all the seed royal of the house of Judah." In this massacre all the descendants of David who were eligible to the throne were destroyed, save one, a babe named Joash, whom the wife of Jehoiada the high priest hid within the precincts of the temple. For six years the child remained hidden, while "Athaliah reigned over the land." 2 Chronicles 22:10, 12.

At the end of this time, "the Levites and all Judah" (2 Chronicles 23:8) united with Jehoiada the high priest in crowning and anointing the child Joash and acclaiming him their king. "And they clapped their hands, and said, God save the king." 2 Kings 11:12. [216]

"Now when Athaliah heard the noise of the people running and praising the king, she came to the people into the house of the Lord." 2 Chronicles 23:12. "And when she looked, behold, the king stood by a pillar, as the manner was, and the princes and the trumpeters by the king, and all the people of the land rejoiced, and blew with trumpets."

"Athaliah rent her clothes, and cried, Treason, Treason." 2 Kings 11:14. But Jehoiada commanded the officers to lay hold of Athaliah and all her followers and lead them out of the temple to a place of execution, where they were to be slain.

Thus perished the last member of the house of Ahab. The terrible evil that had been wrought through his alliance with Jezebel, continued till the last of his descendants was destroyed. Even in the land of Judah, where the worship of the true God had never been formally set aside, Athaliah had succeeded in seducing many. Immediately after the execution of the impenitent queen "all the people of the land went into the house of Baal, and brake it down; his altars and his images brake they in pieces thoroughly, and slew Mattan the priest of Baal before the altars." Verse 18.

A reformation followed. Those who took part in acclaiming Joash king, had solemnly covenanted "that they should be the Lord's people." And now that the evil influence of the daughter of Jezebel had been removed from the kingdom of Judah, and the priests of Baal had been slain and their temple destroyed, "all the people of the land rejoiced: and the city was quiet." 2 Chronicles 23:16, 21. [217]

Chapter 17

The Call of Elisha

God had bidden Elijah anoint another to be prophet in his stead. "Elisha the son of Shaphat ... shalt thou anoint to be prophet in thy room" (1 Kings 19:16), He had said; and in obedience to the command, Elijah went to find Elisha. As he journeyed northward, how changed was the scene from what it had been only a short while before! Then the ground was parched, the farming districts unworked, for neither dew nor rain had fallen for three and a half years. Now on every hand vegetation was springing up as if to redeem the time of drought and famine.

Elisha's father was a wealthy farmer, a man whose household were among the number that in a time of almost universal apostasy had not bowed the knee to Baal. Theirs was a home where God was honored and where allegiance to the faith of ancient Israel was the rule of daily life. In such surroundings the early years of Elisha were passed. In the quietude of country life, under the teaching of God and [218] nature and the discipline of useful work, he received the training in habits of simplicity and of obedience to his parents and to God that helped to fit him for the high position he was afterward to occupy.

The prophetic call came to Elisha while, with his father's servants, he was plowing in the field. He had taken up the work that lay nearest. He possessed both the capabilities of a leader among men and the meekness of one who is ready to serve. Of a quiet and gentle spirit, he was nevertheless energetic and steadfast. Integrity, fidelity, and the love and fear of God were his, and in the humble round of daily toil he gained strength of purpose and nobleness of character, constantly increasing in grace and knowledge. While co-operating with his father in the home-life duties, he was learning to co-operate with God.

By faithfulness in little things, Elisha was preparing for weightier trusts. Day by day, through practical experience, he gained a fitness for a broader, higher work. He learned to serve; and in learning this, he learned also how to instruct and lead. The lesson is for all. None can know what may be God's purpose in His discipline; but all may be certain that faithfulness in little things is the evidence of fitness for greater responsibilities. Every act of life is a revelation of character, and he only who in small duties proves himself "a workman that needeth not to be ashamed" can be honored by God with higher service. 2 Timothy 2:15.

He who feels that it is of no consequence how he performs the smaller tasks proves himself unfit for a more honored position. He may think himself fully competent to take up the larger duties; but God looks deeper than the surface. [219] After test and trial, there is written against him the sentence, "Thou art weighed in the balances, and art found wanting." His unfaithfulness reacts upon himself. He fails of gaining the grace, the power, the force of character, which is received through unreserved surrender.

Because they are not connected with some directly religious work, many feel that their lives are useless, that they are doing nothing for the advancement of God's kingdom. If they could do some great thing how gladly they would undertake it! But because they can serve only in little things, they think themselves justified in doing nothing. In this they err. A man may be in the active service of God while engaged in the ordinary, everyday duties—while felling trees, clearing the ground, or following the plow. The mother who trains her children for Christ is as truly working for God as is the minister in the pulpit.

Many long for special talent with which to do a wonderful work, while the duties lying close at hand, the performance of which would make the life fragrant, are lost sight of. Let such ones take up the duties lying directly in their pathway. Success depends not so much on talent as on energy and willingness. It is not the possession of splendid talents that enables us to render acceptable service, but the conscientious performance of daily duties, the contented spirit, the unaffected, sincere interest in the welfare of others. In the humblest lot true excellence may be found. The commonest tasks, wrought with loving faithfulness, are beautiful in God's sight.

As Elijah, divinely directed in seeking a successor, passed the field in which Elisha was plowing, he cast upon the [220] young man's shoulders the mantle of consecration. During the famine the family of Shaphat had become familiar with the work and mission of Elijah, and now the Spirit of God impressed Elisha's heart as to the meaning of the prophet's act. To him it was the signal that God had called him to be the successor of Elijah.

"And he left the oxen, and ran after Elijah, and said, Let me, I pray thee, kiss my father and my mother, and then I will follow thee." "Go back again," was Elijah's answer, "for what have I done to thee?" This was not a repulse, but a test of faith. Elisha must count the cost—decide for himself to accept or reject the call. If his desires clung to his home and its advantages, he was at liberty to remain there. But Elisha understood the meaning of the call. He knew it was from God, and he did not hesitate to obey. Not for any worldly advantage would he forgo the opportunity of becoming God's messenger or sacrifice the privilege of association with His servant. He "took a yoke of oxen, and slew them, and boiled their flesh with the instruments of the oxen, and gave unto the people, and they did eat. Then he arose, and went after Elijah, and ministered unto him." 1 Kings 19:20, 21. Without hesitation he left a home where he was beloved, to attend the prophet in his uncertain life.

Had Elisha asked Elijah what was expected of him,—what would be his work,—he would have been answered: God knows; He will make it known to you. If you wait upon the Lord, He will answer your every question. You may come with me if you have evidence that God has called you. Know for yourself that God stands back of me, and [221] that it is His voice you hear. If you can count everything but dross that you may win the favor of God, come.

Similar to the call that came to Elisha was the answer given by Christ to the young ruler who asked Him the question, "What good thing shall I do, that I may have eternal life?" "If thou wilt be perfect," Christ replied, "go and sell that thou hast, and give to the poor, and thou shalt have treasure in heaven: and come and follow Me." Matthew 19:16, 21.

Elisha accepted the call to service, casting no backward glance at the pleasures and comforts he was leaving. The young ruler, when he heard the Saviour's words, "went away sorrowful: for he had great possessions." Verse 22. He was not willing to make the sacrifice. His love for his possessions was greater than his love for God. By his refusal to renounce all for Christ, he proved himself unworthy of a place in the Master's service.

The call to place all on the altar of service comes to each one. We are not all asked to serve as Elisha served, nor are we all bidden to sell everything we have; but God asks us to give His service the first place in our lives, to allow no day to pass without doing something to advance His work in the earth. He does not expect from all the same kind of service. One may be called to ministry in a foreign land; another may be asked to give of his means for the support of gospel work. God accepts the offering of each. It is the consecration of the life and all its interests, that is necessary. Those who make this consecration will hear and obey the call of Heaven. [222]

To everyone who becomes a partaker of His grace, the Lord appoints a work for others. Individually we are to stand in our lot, saying, "Here am I; send me." Whether a man be a minister of the Word or a physician, whether he be merchant or farmer, professional man or mechanic, the responsibility rests upon him. It is his work to reveal to others the gospel of their salvation. Every enterprise in which he engages should be a means to this end.

It was no great work that was at first required of Elisha; commonplace duties still constituted his discipline. He is spoken of as pouring water on the hands of Elijah, his master. He was willing to do anything that the Lord directed, and at every step he learned lessons of humility and service. As the prophet's personal attendant, he continued to prove faithful in little things, while with daily strengthening purpose he devoted himself to the mission appointed him by God.

Elisha's life after uniting with Elijah was not without temptations. Trials he had in abundance; but in every emergency he relied on God. He was tempted to think of the home that he had left, but to this temptation he gave no heed. Having put his hand to the plow, he was resolved not to turn back, and through test and trial he proved true to his trust.

Ministry comprehends far more than preaching the word. It means training young men as Elijah trained Elisha, taking them from their ordinary duties, and giving them responsibilities to bear in God's work—small responsibilities at first, and larger ones as they gain strength and experience. There are in the ministry men of faith and prayer, men who can [223] say, "That which was from the beginning, which we have heard, which we have seen with our eyes, which we have looked upon, and our hands have handled, of the Word of life; ... that which we have seen and heard declare we unto you." 1 John 1:1-3. Young, inexperienced workers should be trained by actual labor in connection with these experienced servants of God. Thus they will learn how to bear burdens.

Those who undertake this training of young workers are doing noble service. The Lord Himself co-operates with their efforts. And the young men to whom the word of consecration has been spoken, whose privilege it is to be brought into close association with earnest, godly workers, should make the most of their opportunity. God has honored them by choosing them for His service and by placing them where they can gain greater fitness for it, and they should be humble, faithful, obedient, and willing to sacrifice. If they submit to

God's discipline, carrying out His directions and choosing His servants as their counselors, they will develop into righteous, high-principled, steadfast men, whom God can entrust with responsibilities.

As the gospel is proclaimed in its purity, men will be called from the plow and from the common commercial business vocations that largely occupy the mind and will be educated in connection with men of experience. As they learn to labor effectively, they will proclaim the truth with power. Through most wonderful workings of divine providence, mountains of difficulty will be removed and cast into the sea. The message that means so much to the dwellers upon the earth will be heard and understood. Men will [224] know what is truth. Onward and still onward the work will advance until the whole earth shall have been warned, and then shall the end come.

For several years after the call of Elisha, Elijah and Elisha labored together, the younger man daily gaining greater preparedness for his work. Elijah had been God's instrument for the overthrow of gigantic evils. The idolatry which, supported by Ahab and the heathen Jezebel, had seduced the nation, had been given a decided check. Baal's prophets had been slain. The whole people of Israel had been deeply stirred, and many were returning to the worship of God. As Elijah's successor, Elisha, by careful, patient instruction, must endeavor to guide Israel in safe paths. His association with Elijah, the greatest prophet since the days of Moses, prepared him for the work that he was soon to take up alone.

During these years of united ministry, Elijah from time to time was called upon to meet flagrant evils with stern rebuke. When wicked Ahab seized Naboth's vineyard, it was the voice of Elijah that prophesied his doom and the doom of all his house. And when Ahaziah, after the death of his father Ahab, turned from the living God to Baal-zebub, the god of Ekron, it was Elijah's voice that was heard once more in earnest protest.

The schools of the prophets, established by Samuel, had fallen into decay during the years of Israel's apostasy. Elijah re-established these schools, making provision for young men to gain an education that would lead them to magnify the law and make it honorable. Three of these schools, one at Gilgal, one at Bethel, and one at Jericho, are mentioned [225] in the record. Just before Elijah was taken to heaven, he and Elisha visited these centers of training. The lessons that the prophet of God had given them on former visits, he now repeated. Especially did he instruct them concerning their high privilege of loyally maintaining their allegiance to the God of heaven. He also impressed upon their minds the importance of letting simplicity mark every feature of their education. Only in this way could they receive the mold of heaven and go forth to work in the ways of the Lord.

The heart of Elijah was cheered as he saw what was being accomplished by means of these schools. The work of reformation was not complete, but he could see throughout the kingdom a verification of the word of the Lord, "Yet I have left Me seven thousand in Israel, all the knees which have not bowed unto Baal." 1 Kings 19:18.

As Elisha accompanied the prophet on his round of service from school to school, his faith and resolution were once more tested. At Gilgal, and again at Bethel and Jericho, he was invited by the prophet to turn back. "Tarry here, I pray thee," Elijah said; "for the Lord hath sent me to Bethel." But in his early labor of guiding the plow, Elisha had learned not to fail or to become discouraged, and now that he had set his hand to the plow in another line of duty he would not be diverted from his purpose. He would not be parted from his master, so long as opportunity remained for gaining a further fitting up for service. Unknown to Elijah, the revelation that he was to be translated had been made known to his disciples in the schools of the prophets, and in particular to Elisha. And now the tried servant of the man of God kept close beside him. As [226] often as the invitation to turn back was given, his answer was, "As the Lord liveth, and as thy soul liveth, I will not leave thee."

"And they two went on.... And they two stood by Jordan. And Elijah took his mantle, and wrapped it together, and smote the waters, and they were divided hither and thither, so that they two went over on dry ground. And it came to pass, when they were gone over, that Elijah said unto Elisha, Ask what I shall do for thee, before I be taken away from thee."

Elisha asked not for worldly honor, or for a high place among the great men of earth. That which he craved was a large measure of the Spirit that God had bestowed so freely upon the one about to be honored with translation. [227] He knew that nothing but the Spirit which had rested upon Elijah could fit him to fill the place in Israel to which God had called him, and so he asked, "I pray thee, let a double portion of thy Spirit be upon me."

In response to this request, Elijah said, "Thou hast asked a hard thing: nevertheless, if thou see me when I am taken from thee, it shall be so unto thee; but if not, it shall not be so. And it came to pass, as they still went on, and talked, that, behold, there appeared a chariot of fire, and horses of fire, and parted them both asunder; and Elijah went up by a whirlwind into heaven." See 2 Kings 2:1-11.

Elijah was a type of the saints who will be living on the earth at the time of the second advent of Christ and who will be "changed, in a moment, in the twinkling of an eye, at the last trump," without tasting of death. 1 Corinthians 15:51, 52. It was as a representative of those who shall be thus translated that Elijah, near the close of Christ's earthly ministry, was permitted to stand with Moses by the side of the Saviour on the mount of transfiguration. In these glorified ones, the disciples saw in miniature a representation of the kingdom of the redeemed. They beheld Jesus clothed with the light of heaven; they heard the "voice out of the cloud" (Luke 9:35), acknowledging Him as the Son of God; they saw Moses, representing those who will be raised from the dead at the time of the second advent; and there also stood Elijah, representing those who at the close of earth's history will be changed from mortal to immortal and be translated to heaven without seeing death. [228]

In the desert, in loneliness and discouragement, Elijah had said that he had had enough of life and had prayed that he might die. But the Lord in His mercy had not taken him at his word. There was yet a great work for Elijah to do; and when his work was done, he was not to perish in discouragement and solitude. Not for him the descent into the tomb, but the ascent with God's angels to the presence of His glory.

"And Elisha saw it, and he cried, My father, my father, the chariot of Israel, and the horsemen thereof. And he saw him no more: and he took hold of his own clothes, and rent them in two pieces. He took up also the mantle of Elijah that fell from him, and went back, and stood by the bank of Jordan; and he took the mantle of Elijah that fell from him, and smote the waters, and said, Where is the Lord God of Elijah? and when he also had smitten the waters, they parted hither and thither: and Elisha went over. And when the sons of the prophets which were to view at Jericho saw him, they said, The Spirit of Elijah doth rest on

Elisha. And they came to meet him, and bowed themselves to the ground before him." 2 Kings 2:12-15.

When the Lord in His providence sees fit to remove from His work those to whom He has given wisdom, He helps and strengthens their successors, if they will look to Him for aid and will walk in His ways. They may be even wiser than their predecessors; for they may profit by their experience and learn wisdom from their mistakes.

Henceforth Elisha stood in Elijah's place. He who had been faithful in that which was least was to prove himself faithful also in much. [229]

Chapter 18

The Healing of the Waters

In Patriarchal times the Jordan Valley was "well watered everywhere, ... even as the garden of the Lord." It was in this fair valley that Lot chose to make his home when he "pitched his tent toward Sodom." Genesis 13:10, 12. At the time that the cities of the plain were destroyed, the region round about became a desolate waste, and it has since formed a part of the wilderness of Judea.

A portion of the beautiful valley remained, with its life-giving springs and streams, to gladden the heart of man. In this valley, rich with fields of grain and forests of date palms and other fruit-bearing trees, the hosts of Israel had encamped after crossing the Jordan and had first partaken of the fruits of the Promised Land. Before them had stood the walls of Jericho, a heathen stronghold, the center of the worship of Ashtoreth, vilest and most degrading of all Canaanitish forms of idolatry. Soon its walls were thrown [230] down and its inhabitants slain, and at the time of its fall the solemn declaration was made, in the presence of all Israel: "Cursed be the man before the Lord, that riseth up and buildeth this city Jericho: he shall lay the foundation thereof in his first-born, and in his youngest son shall he set up the gates of it." Joshua 6:26.

Five centuries passed. The spot lay desolate, accursed of God. Even the springs that had made residence in this portion of the valley so desirable suffered the blighting effects of the curse. But in the days of Ahab's apostasy, when through Jezebel's influence the worship of Ashtoreth was revived, Jericho, the ancient seat of this worship, was rebuilt, though at a fearful cost to the builder. Hiel the Bethelite "laid the foundation thereof in Abiram his first-born, and set up the gates thereof in his youngest son Segub, according to the word of the Lord." 1 Kings 16:34.

Not far from Jericho, in the midst of fruitful groves, was one of the schools of the prophets, and thither, after the ascension of Elijah, Elisha went. During his sojourn among them the men of the city came to the prophet and said, "Behold, I pray thee, the situation of this city is pleasant, as my lord seeth: but the water is nought, and the ground barren." The spring that in former years had been pure and life-giving, and had contributed largely to the water supply of the city and the surrounding district, was now unfit for use.

In response to the plea of the men of Jericho, Elisha said, "Bring me a new cruse, and put salt therein." Having received this, "he went forth unto the spring of the waters, [231] and cast the salt in there, and said, Thus saith the Lord, I have healed these waters; there shall not be from thence any more death or barren land." 2 Kings 2:19-21.

The healing of the waters of Jericho was accomplished, not by any wisdom of man, but by the miraculous interposition of God. Those who had rebuilt the city were undeserving of the favor of Heaven; yet He who "maketh His sun to rise on the evil and on the good, and sendeth rain on the just and on the unjust," saw fit in this instance to reveal, through this token of compassion, His willingness to heal Israel of their spiritual maladies. Matthew 5:45.

The restoration was permanent; "the waters were healed unto this day, according to the saying of Elisha which he spake." 2 Kings 2:22. From age to age the waters have flowed on, making that portion of the valley an oasis of beauty.

Many are the spiritual lessons to be gathered from the story of the healing of the waters. The new cruse, the salt, the spring—all are highly symbolic.

In casting salt into the bitter spring, Elisha taught the same spiritual lesson imparted centuries later by the Saviour to His disciples when He declared, "Ye are the salt of the earth." Matthew 5:13. The salt mingling with the polluted spring purified its waters and brought life and blessing where before had been blighting and death. When God compares His children to salt, He would teach them that His purpose in making them the subjects of His grace is that they may become agents in saving others. The object of God in choosing a people before all the world was not [232] only that He might adopt them as His sons and daughters, but that through them the world might receive the grace that bringeth salvation. When the Lord chose Abraham, it was not simply to be the special friend of God, but to be a medium of the peculiar privileges the Lord desired to bestow upon the nations.

The world needs evidences of sincere Christianity. The poison of sin is at work at the heart of society. Cities and towns are steeped in sin and moral corruption. The world is full of sickness, suffering, and iniquity. Nigh and afar off are souls in poverty and distress, weighed down with a sense of guilt and perishing for want of a saving influence. The gospel of truth is kept ever before them, yet they perish because the example of those who should be a savor of life to them is a savor of death. Their souls drink in bitterness because the springs are poisoned, when they should be like a well of water springing up unto everlasting life.

Salt must be mingled with the substance to which it is added; it must penetrate, infuse it, that it may be preserved. So it is through personal contact and association that men are reached by the saving power of the gospel. They are not saved as masses, but as individuals. Personal influence is a power. It is to work with the influence of Christ, to lift where Christ lifts, to impart correct principles, and to stay the progress of the world's corruption. It is to diffuse that grace which Christ alone can impart. It is to uplift, to sweeten the lives and characters of others by the power of a pure example united with earnest faith and love. [233]

Of the hitherto polluted spring at Jericho, the Lord declared, "I have healed these waters; there shall not be from thence any more death or barren land." The polluted stream represents the soul that is separate from God. Sin not only shuts away from God, but destroys in the human soul both the desire and the capacity for knowing Him. Through sin, the whole human organism is deranged, the mind is perverted, the imagination corrupted; the faculties of the soul are degraded. There is an absence of pure religion, of heart holiness. The converting power of God has not wrought in transforming the character. The soul is weak, and for want of moral force to overcome, is polluted and debased.

To the heart that has become purified, all is changed. Transformation of character is the testimony to the world of an indwelling Christ. The Spirit of God produces a new life in the soul, bringing the thoughts and desires into obedience to the will of Christ; and the inward man is renewed in the image of God. Weak and erring men and women show to the world that the redeeming power of grace can cause the faulty character to develop into symmetry and abundant fruitfulness.

The heart that receives the word of God is not as a pool that evaporates, not like a broken cistern that loses its treasure. It is like the mountain stream, fed by unfailing springs, whose cool, sparkling waters leap from rock to rock, refreshing the weary, the thirsty, the heavy-laden. It is like a river constantly flowing and, as it advances, becoming deeper and wider, until its life-giving waters are spread over all the [234] earth. The stream that goes singing on its way leaves behind its gift of verdure and fruitfulness. The grass on its banks is a fresher green, the trees have a richer verdure, the flowers are more abundant. When the earth lies bare and brown under the summer's scorching heat, a line of verdure marks the river's course.

So it is with the true child of God. The religion of Christ reveals itself as a vitalizing, pervading principle, a living, working, spiritual energy. When the heart is opened to the heavenly influence of truth and love, these principles will flow forth again like streams in the desert, causing fruitfulness to appear where now are barrenness and dearth.

As those who have been cleansed and sanctified through a knowledge of Bible truth engage heartily in the work of soulsaving, they will become indeed a savor of life unto life. And as daily they drink of the inexhaustible fountain of grace and knowledge, they will find that their own hearts are filled to overflowing with the Spirit of their Master, and that through their unselfish ministry many are benefited physically, mentally, and spiritually. The weary are refreshed, the sick restored to health, and the sin-burdened relieved. In far-off countries thanksgiving is heard from the lips of those whose hearts are turned from the service of sin unto righteousness.

"Give, and it shall be given unto you;" for the word of God is "a fountain of gardens, a well of living waters, and streams from Lebanon." Luke 6:38; Song of Solomon 4:15. [235]

Chapter 19

A Prophet of Peace

This chapter is based on 2 Kings 4.

The work of Elisha as a prophet was in some respects very different from that of Elijah. To Elijah had been committed messages of condemnation and judgment; his was the voice of fearless reproof, calling king and people to turn from their evil ways. Elisha's was a more peaceful mission; his it was to build up and strengthen the work that Elijah had begun; to teach the people the way of the Lord. Inspiration pictures him as coming into personal touch with the people, surrounded by the sons of the prophets, bringing by his miracles and his ministry healing and rejoicing.

Elisha was a man of mild and kindly spirit; but that he could also be stern is shown by his course when, on the way to Bethel, he was mocked by ungodly youth who had come out of the city. These youth had heard of Elijah's ascension, and they made this solemn event the subject of their jeers, saying to Elisha, "Go up, thou bald head; go up, [236] thou bald head." At the sound of their mocking words the prophet turned back, and under the inspiration of the Almighty he pronounced a curse upon them. The awful judgment that followed was of God. "There came forth two she-bears out of the wood, and tare forty and two" of them. 2 Kings 2:23, 24.

Had Elisha allowed the mockery to pass unnoticed, he would have continued to be ridiculed and reviled by the rabble, and his mission to instruct and save in a time of grave national peril might have been defeated. This one instance of terrible severity was sufficient to command respect throughout his life. For fifty years he went in and out of the gate of Bethel, and to and fro in the land, from city to city, passing through crowds of idle, rude, dissolute youth; but none mocked him or made light of his qualifications as the prophet of the Most High.

Even kindness should have its limits. Authority must be maintained by a firm severity, or it will be received by many with mockery and contempt. The so-called tenderness, the coaxing and indulgence, used toward youth by parents and guardians, is one of the worst evils which can come upon them. In every family, firmness, decision, positive requirements, are essential.

Reverence, in which the youth who mocked Elisha were so lacking, is a grace that should be carefully cherished. Every child should be taught to show true reverence for God. Never should His name be spoken lightly or thoughtlessly. Angels, as they speak it, veil their faces. With what reverence should we, who are fallen and sinful, take it upon our lips! [237]

Reverence should be shown for God's representatives—for ministers, teachers, and parents, who are called to speak and act in His stead. In the respect shown them, God is honored.

Courtesy, also, is one of the graces of the Spirit and should be cultivated by all. It has power to soften natures which without it would grow hard and rough. Those who profess to be followers of Christ, and are at the same time rough, unkind, and uncourteous, have not learned of Jesus. Their sincerity may not be doubted, their uprightness may not be questioned; but sincerity and uprightness will not atone for a lack of kindness and courtesy.

The kindly spirit that enabled Elisha to exert a powerful influence over the lives of many in Israel, is revealed in the story of his friendly relations with a family dwelling at Shunem. In his journeyings to and fro throughout the kingdom "it fell on a day, that Elisha passed to Shunem, where was a great woman; and she constrained him to eat bread. And so it was, that as oft as he passed by, he turned in thither to eat bread." The mistress of the house perceived that Elisha was "an holy man of God," and she said to her husband: "Let us make a little chamber, I pray thee, on the wall; and let us set for him there a bed, and a table, and a stool, and a candlestick: and it shall be, when he cometh to us, that he shall turn in thither." To this retreat Elisha often came, thankful for its quiet peace. Nor was God unmindful of the woman's kindness. Her home had been childless; and now the Lord rewarded her hospitality by the gift of a son. [238]

Years passed. The child was old enough to be out in the field with the reapers. One day he was stricken down by the heat, "and he said unto his father, My head, my head." The father bade a lad carry the child to his mother; "and when he had taken him, and brought him to his mother, he sat on her knees till noon, and then died. And she went up, and laid him on the bed of the man of God, and shut the door upon him, and went out."

In her distress, the Shunammite determined to go to Elisha for help. The prophet was then at Mount Carmel, and the woman, accompanied by her servant, set forth immediately. "And it came to pass, when the man of God saw her afar off, that he said to Gehazi his servant, Behold, yonder is that Shunammite: run now, I pray thee, to meet her, and say unto her, Is it well with thee? is it well with thy husband? is it well with the child?" The servant did as he was bidden, but not till she had reached Elisha did the stricken mother reveal the cause of her sorrow. Upon hearing of her loss, Elisha bade Gehazi: "Gird up thy loins, and take my staff in thine hand, and go thy way: if thou meet any man, salute him not; and if any salute thee, answer him not again: and lay my staff upon the face of the child."

But the mother would not be satisfied till Elisha himself came with her. "As the Lord liveth, and as thy soul liveth, I will not leave thee," she declared. "And he arose, and followed her. And Gehazi passed on before them, and laid the staff upon the face of the child; but there was neither voice, nor hearing. Wherefore he went again to meet him, and told him, saying, The child is not awaked." [239]

When they reached the house, Elisha went into the room where the dead child lay, "and shut the door upon them twain, and prayed unto the Lord. And he went up, and lay upon the child, and put his mouth upon his mouth, and his eyes upon his eyes, and his hands upon his hands: and he stretched himself upon the child; and the flesh of the child waxed warm. Then he returned, and walked in the house to and fro; and went up, and stretched himself upon him: and the child sneezed seven times, and the child opened his eyes."

Calling Gehazi, Elisha bade him send the mother to him. "And when she was come in unto him, he said, Take up thy son. Then she went in, and fell at his feet, and bowed herself to the ground, and took up her son, and went out."

So was the faith of this woman rewarded. Christ, the great Life-giver, restored her son to her. In like manner will His faithful ones be rewarded, when, at His coming, death loses its sting and the grave is robbed of the victory it has claimed. Then will He restore to His servants the children that have been taken from them by death. "Thus saith the Lord; A voice was heard in Ramah, lamentation, and bitter weeping; Rachel weeping for her children refused to be comforted for her children, because they were not. Thus saith the Lord; Refrain thy voice from weeping, and thine eyes from tears: for thy work shall be rewarded, ... and they shall come again from the land of the enemy. And there is hope in thine end, saith the Lord, that thy children shall come again to their own border." Jeremiah 31:15-17. [240]

Jesus comforts our sorrow for the dead with a message of infinite hope: "I will ransom them from the power of the grave; I will redeem them from death: O death, I will be thy plagues; O grave, I will be thy destruction." Hosea 13:14. "I am He that liveth, and was dead; and, behold, I am alive for evermore, ... and have the keys of hell and of death." Revelation 1:18. "The Lord Himself shall descend from heaven with a shout, with the voice of the Archangel, and with the trump of God: and the dead in Christ shall rise first: then we which are alive and remain shall be caught up together with them in the clouds, to meet the Lord in the air: and so shall we ever be with the Lord." 1 Thessalonians 4:16, 17.

Like the Saviour of mankind, of whom he was a type, Elisha in his ministry among men combined the work of healing with that of teaching. Faithfully, untiringly, throughout his long and effective labors, Elisha endeavored to foster and advance the important educational work carried on by the schools of the prophets. In the providence of God his words of instruction to the earnest groups of young men assembled were confirmed by the deep movings of the Holy Spirit, and at times by other unmistakable evidences of his authority as a servant of Jehovah.

It was on the occasion of one of his visits to the school established at Gilgal that he healed the poisoned pottage. "There was a dearth in the land; and the sons of the prophets were sitting before him: and he said unto his servant, Set on the great pot, and seethe pottage for the sons of the prophets. And one went out into the field to gather herbs, and found a wild vine, and gathered thereof wild gourds [241] his lap full, and came and shred them into the pot of pottage: for they knew them not. So they poured out for the men to eat. And it came to pass, as they were eating of the pottage, that they cried out, and said, O thou man of God, there is death in the pot. And they could not eat thereof. But he said, Then bring meal. And he cast it into the pot; and he said, Pour out for the people, that they may eat. And there was no harm in the pot."

At Gilgal, also, while the dearth was still in the land, Elisha fed one hundred men with the present brought to him by "a man from Baalshalisha," "bread of the first fruits, twenty loaves of barley, and full ears of corn in the husk thereof." There were those with him who were sorely in need of food. When the offering came, he said to his servant, "Give unto the people, that they may eat. And his servitor said, What, should I set this before an hundred men? He said again, Give the people, that they may eat: for thus saith the Lord, They shall eat, and shall leave thereof. So he set it before them, and they did eat, and left thereof, according to the word of the Lord."

What condescension it was on the part of Christ, through His messenger, to work this miracle to satisfy hunger! Again and again since that time, though not always in so marked and perceptible a manner, has the Lord Jesus worked to supply human need. If we had clearer spiritual discernment we would recognize more readily than we do God's compassionate dealing with the children of men.

It is the grace of God on the small portion that makes it all-sufficient. God's hand can multiply it a hundredfold. [242] From His resources He can spread a table in the wilderness. By the touch of His hand He can increase the scanty provision and make it sufficient for all. It was His power that increased the loaves and corn in the hands of the sons of the prophets.

In the days of Christ's earthly ministry, when He performed a similar miracle in feeding the multitudes, the same unbelief was manifested as was shown by those associated [243] with the prophet of old. "What!" said Elisha's servant; "should I set this before an hundred men?" And when Jesus bade His disciples give the multitude to eat, they answered, "We have no more but five loaves and two fishes; except we should go and buy meat for all this people." Luke 9:13. What is that among so many?

The lesson is for God's children in every age. When the Lord gives a work to be done, let not men stop to inquire into the reasonableness of the command or the probable result of their efforts to obey. The supply in their hands may seem to fall short of the need to be filled; but in the hands of the Lord it will prove more than sufficient. The servitor "set it before them, and they did eat, and left thereof, according to the word of the Lord."

A fuller sense of God's relationship to those whom He has purchased with the gift of His Son, a greater faith in the onward progress of His cause in the earth—this is the great need of the church today. Let none waste time in deploring the scantiness of their visible resources. The outward appearance may be unpromising, but energy and trust in God will develop resources. The gift brought to Him with thanksgiving and with prayer for His blessing, He will multiply as He multiplied the food given to the sons of the prophets and to the weary multitude. [244]

Chapter 20

Naaman

This chapter is based on 2 Kings 5.

"Now Naaman, captain of the host of the king of Syria, was a great man with his master, and honorable, because by him the Lord had given deliverance unto Syria: he was also a mighty man in valor, but he was a leper."

Ben-hadad, king of Syria, had defeated the armies of Israel in the battle which resulted in the death of Ahab. Since that time the Syrians had maintained against Israel a constant border warfare, and in one of their raids they had carried away a little maid who, in the land of her captivity, "waited on Naaman's wife." A slave, far from her home, this little maid was nevertheless one of God's witnesses, unconsciously fulfilling the purpose for which God had chosen Israel as His people. As she ministered in that heathen home, her sympathies were aroused in behalf of her master; and, remembering the wonderful miracles of [245] healing wrought through Elisha, she said to her mistress, "Would God my lord were with the prophet that is in Samaria! for he would recover him of his leprosy." She knew that the power of Heaven was with Elisha, and she believed that by this power Naaman could be healed.

The conduct of the captive maid, the way that she bore herself in that heathen home, is a strong witness to the power of early home training. There is no higher trust than that committed to fathers and mothers in the care and training of their children. Parents have to do with the very foundations of habit and character. By their example and teaching the future of their children is largely decided.

Happy are the parents whose lives are a true reflection of the divine, so that the promises and commands of God awaken in the child gratitude and reverence; the parents whose tenderness and justice and long-suffering interpret to the child the love and justice and long-suffering of God, and who by teaching the child to love and trust and obey them, are teaching him to love and trust and obey his Father in heaven. Parents who impart to the child such a gift have endowed him with a treasure more precious than the wealth of all the ages, a treasure as enduring as eternity.

We know not in what line our children may be called to serve. They may spend their lives within the circle of the home; they may engage in life's common vocations, or go as teachers of the gospel to heathen lands; but all are alike called to be missionaries for God, ministers of mercy to the world. They are to obtain an education that will help them to stand by the side of Christ in unselfish service. [246]

The parents of that Hebrew maid, as they taught her of God, did not know the destiny that would be hers. But they were faithful to their trust; and in the home of the captain of the Syrian host, their child bore witness to the God whom she had learned to honor.

Naaman heard of the words that the maid had spoken to her mistress; and, obtaining permission from the king, he went forth to seek healing, taking with him "ten talents of silver, and six thousand pieces of gold, and ten changes of raiment." He also carried a letter from the king of Syria to the king of Israel, in which was written the message, "Behold, I have ... sent Naaman my servant to thee, that thou mayest recover him of his leprosy." When the king of Israel read the letter, "he rent his clothes, and said, Am I God, to kill and to make alive, that this man doth send unto me to recover a man of his leprosy? wherefore consider, I pray you, and see how he seeketh a quarrel against me."

Tidings of the matter reached Elisha, and he sent word to the king, saying, "Wherefore has thou rent thy clothes? let him come now to me, and he shall know that there is a prophet in Israel."

"So Naaman came with his horses and with his chariot, and stood at the door of the house of Elisha." Through a messenger the prophet bade him, "Go and wash in Jordan seven times, and thy flesh shall come again to thee, and thou shalt be clean."

Naaman had expected to see some wonderful manifestation of power from heaven. "I thought," he said, "he will surely come out to me, and stand, and call on the name of [247] [248] [249] the Lord his God, and strike his hand over the place, and recover the leper." When told to wash in the Jordan, his pride was touched, and in mortification and disappointment he exclaimed, "Are not Abana and Pharpar, rivers of Damascus, better than all the waters of Israel? may I not wash in them, and be clean?" "So he turned and went away in a rage."

The proud spirit of Naaman rebelled against following the course outlined by Elisha. The rivers mentioned by the Syrian captain were beautified by surrounding groves, and many flocked to the banks of these pleasant streams to worship their idol gods. It would have cost Naaman no great humiliation of soul to descend into one of those streams. But it was only through following the specific directions of the prophet that he could find healing. Willing obedience alone would bring the desired result.

Naaman's servants entreated him to carry out Elisha's directions: "If the prophet had bid thee do some great thing," they urged, "wouldest thou not have done it? how much rather then, when he saith to thee, Wash, and be clean?" The faith of Naaman was being tested, while pride struggled for the mastery. But faith conquered, and the haughty Syrian yielded his pride of heart and bowed in submission to the revealed will of Jehovah. Seven times he dipped himself in Jordan, "according to the saying of the man of God." And his faith was honored; "his flesh came again like unto the flesh of a little child, and he was clean."

Gratefully "he returned to the man of God, he and all his company," with the acknowledgment, "Behold, now [250] I know that there is no God in all the earth, but in Israel."

In accordance with the custom of the times, Naaman now asked Elisha to accept a costly present. But the prophet refused. It was not for him to take payment for a blessing that God had in mercy bestowed. "As the Lord liveth," he said, "I will receive none." The Syrian "urged him to take it; but he refused.

"And Naaman said, Shall there not then, I pray thee, be given to thy servant two mules' burden of earth? for thy servant will henceforth offer neither burnt offering nor sacrifice unto other gods, but unto the Lord. In this thing the Lord pardon thy servant, that when my master goeth into the house of Rimmon to worship there, and he leaneth on my hand, and I bow myself in the house of Rimmon: when I bow down myself in the house of Rimmon, the Lord pardon thy servant in this thing.

"And he said unto him, Go in peace. So he departed from him a little way."

Gehazi, Elisha's servant, had had opportunity during the years to develop the spirit of self-denial characterizing his master's lifework. It had been his privilege to become a noble standard-bearer in the army of the Lord. The best gifts of Heaven had long been within his reach; yet, turning from these, he had coveted instead the base alloy of worldly wealth. And now the hidden longings of his avaricious spirit led him to yield to an overmastering temptation. "Behold," he reasoned within himself, "my master hath spared Naaman this Syrian, in not receiving at his hands that which he brought: but ... I will run after him, and [251] take somewhat of him." And thus it came about that in secrecy "Gehazi followed after Naaman."

"When Naaman saw him running after him, he lighted down from the chariot to meet him, and said, Is all well? And he said, All is well." Then Gehazi uttered a deliberate lie. "My master," he said, "hath sent me, saying, Behold, even now there be come to me from Mount Ephraim two young men of the sons of the prophets: give them, I pray thee, a talent of silver, and two changes of garments." To the request Naaman gladly acceded, pressing upon Gehazi two talents of silver instead of one, "with two changes of garments," and commissioning servants to bear the treasure back.

As Gehazi neared Elisha's home, he dismissed the servants and placed the silver and the garments in hiding. This accomplished, "he went in, and stood before his master;" and, to shield himself from censure, he uttered a second lie. In response to the inquiry of the prophet, "Whence comest thou?" Gehazi answered, "Thy servant went no whither."

Then came the stern denunciation, showing that Elisha knew all. "Went not mine heart with thee," he asked, "when the man turned again from his chariot to meet thee? Is it a time to receive money, and to receive garments, and olive yards, and vineyards, and sheep, and oxen, and menservants, and maidservants? The leprosy therefore of Naaman shall cleave unto thee, and unto thy seed forever." Swift was the retribution that overtook the guilty man. He went out from Elisha's presence "a leper as white as snow." [252]

Solemn are the lessons taught by this experience of one to whom had been given high and holy privileges. The course of Gehazi was such as to place a stumbling block in the pathway of Naaman, upon whose mind had broken a wonderful light, and who was favorably disposed toward the service of the living God. For the deception practiced by Gehazi there could be pleaded no excuse. To the day of his death he remained a leper, cursed of God and shunned by his fellow men.

"A false witness shall not be unpunished, and he that speaketh lies shall not escape." Proverbs 19:5. Men may think to hide their evil deeds from human eyes, but they cannot deceive God. "All things are naked and opened unto the eyes of Him with whom we have to do." Hebrews 4:13. Gehazi thought to deceive Elisha, but God revealed to His prophet the words that Gehazi had spoken to Naaman, and every detail of the scene between the two men.

Truth is of God; deception in all its myriad forms is of Satan, and whoever in any way departs from the straight line of truth is betraying himself into the power of the wicked one. Those who have learned of Christ will "have no fellowship with the unfruitful works of darkness." Ephesians 5:11. In speech, as in life, they will be simple, straightforward, and true, for they are preparing for the fellowship of those holy ones in whose mouth is found no guile. See Revelation 14:5.

Centuries after Naaman returned to his Syrian home, healed in body and converted in spirit, his wonderful faith was referred to and commended by the Saviour as an object [253] lesson for all who claim to serve God. "Many lepers were in Israel in the time of Eliseus the prophet," the Saviour declared; "and none of them was cleansed, saving Naaman the Syrian." Luke 4:27. God passed over the many lepers in Israel because their unbelief closed the door of good to them. A heathen nobleman who had been true to his convictions of right, and who felt his need of help, was in the sight of God more worthy of His blessing than were the afflicted in Israel, who had slighted and despised their God-given privileges. God works for those who appreciate His favors and respond to the light given them from heaven.

Today in every land there are those who are honest in heart, and upon these the light of heaven is shining. If they continue faithful in following that which they understand to be duty, they will be given increased light, until, like Naaman of old, they will be constrained to acknowledge that "there is no God in all the earth," save the living God, the Creator.

To every sincere soul "that walketh in darkness, and hath no light," is given the invitation, "Let him trust in the name of the Lord, and stay upon his God." "For since the beginning of the world men have not heard, nor perceived by the ear, neither hath the eye seen, O God, beside Thee, what He hath prepared for him that waiteth for Him. Thou meetest him that rejoiceth and worketh righteousness, those that remember Thee in Thy ways." Isaiah 50:10; 64:4, 5. [254]

Chapter 21

Elisha's Closing Ministry

Called to the prophetic office while Ahab was still reigning, Elisha had lived to see many changes take place in the kingdom of Israel. Judgment upon judgment had befallen the Israelites during the reign of Hazael the Syrian, who had been anointed to be the scourge of the apostate nation. The stern measures of reform instituted by Jehu had resulted in the slaying of all the house of Ahab. In continued wars with the Syrians, Jehoahaz, Jehu's successor, had lost some of the cities lying east of the Jordan. For a time it had seemed as if the Syrians might gain control of the entire kingdom. But the reformation begun by Elijah and carried forward by Elisha had led many to inquire after God. The altars of Baal were being forsaken, and slowly yet surely God's purpose was being fulfilled in the lives of those who chose to serve Him with all the heart.

It was because of His love for erring Israel that God permitted the Syrians to scourge them. It was because of [255] his compassion for those whose moral power was weak that He raised up Jehu to slay wicked Jezebel and all the house of Ahab. Once more, through a merciful providence, the priests of Baal and of Ashtoreth were set aside and their heathen altars thrown down. God in His wisdom foresaw that if temptation were removed, some would forsake heathenism and turn their faces heavenward, and this is why He permitted calamity after calamity to befall them. His judgments were tempered with mercy; and when His purpose was accomplished, He turned the tide in favor of those who had learned to inquire after Him.

While influences for good and for evil were striving for the ascendancy, and Satan was doing all in his power to complete the ruin he had wrought during the reign of Ahab and Jezebel, Elisha continued to bear his testimony. He met with opposition, yet none could gainsay his words. Throughout the kingdom he was honored and venerated. Many came to him for counsel. While Jezebel was still living, Joram, the king of Israel, sought his advice; and once, when in Damascus, he was visited by messengers from Benhadad, king of Syria, who desired to learn whether a sickness then upon him would result in death. To all the prophet bore faithful witness in a time when, on every hand, truth was being perverted and the great majority of the people were in open rebellion against Heaven.

And God never forsook His chosen messenger. On one occasion, during a Syrian invasion, the king of Syria sought to destroy Elisha because of his activity in apprising the king of Israel of the plans of the enemy. The Syrian king [256] had taken counsel with his servants, saying, "In such and such a place shall be my camp." This plan was revealed by the Lord to Elisha, who "sent unto the king of Israel, saying, Beware that thou pass not such a place; for thither the Syrians are come down. And the king of Israel sent to the place which the man of God told him and warned him of, and saved himself there, not once nor twice.

"Therefore the heart of the king of Syria was sore troubled for this thing; and he called his servants, and said unto them, Will ye not show me which of us is for the king of Israel? And one of his servants said, None, my lord, O king: but Elisha, the prophet that is in Israel, telleth the king of Israel the words that thou speakest in thy bedchamber."

Determined to make away with the prophet, the Syrian king commanded, "Go and spy where he is, that I may send and fetch him." The prophet was in Dothan; and, learning this, the king sent thither "horses, and chariots, and a great host: and they came by night, and compassed the city about. And when the servant of the man of God was risen early, and gone forth, behold, an host compassed the city both with horses and chariots."

In terror Elisha's servant sought him with the tidings. "Alas, my master!" he said, "how shall we do?"

"Fear not," was the answer of the prophet; "for they that be with us are more than they that be with them." And then, that the servant might know this for himself, "Elisha prayed, and said, Lord, I pray Thee, open his eyes, that he may see." "The Lord opened the eyes of the young [257] man; and he saw: and, behold, the mountain was full of horses and chariots of fire round about Elisha." Between the servant of God and the hosts of armed foemen was an encircling band of heavenly angels. They had come down in mighty power, not to destroy, not to exact homage, but to encamp round about and minister to the Lord's weak and helpless ones.

When the people of God are brought into strait places, and apparently there is no escape for them, the Lord alone must be their dependence.

As the company of Syrian soldiers boldly advanced, ignorant of the unseen hosts of heaven, "Elisha prayed unto the Lord, and said, Smite this people, I pray Thee, with blindness. And He smote them with blindness according to the word of Elisha. And Elisha said unto them, This is not the way, neither is this the city: follow me, and I will bring you to the man whom ye seek. But he led them to Samaria.

"And it came to pass, when they were come into Samaria, that Elisha said, Lord, open the eyes of these men, that they may see. And the Lord opened their eyes, and they saw; and, behold, they were in the midst of Samaria. And the king of Israel said unto Elisha, when he saw them, My father, shall I smite them? shall I smite them? And he answered, Thou shalt not smite them: wouldest thou smite those whom thou hast taken captive with thy sword and with thy bow? set bread and water before them, that they may eat and drink, and go to their master. And he prepared great provision for them: and when they had eaten [258] and drunk, he sent them away, and they went to their master." See 2 Kings 6.

For a time after this, Israel was free from the attacks of the Syrians. But later, under the energetic direction of a determined king, Hazael, the Syrian hosts surrounded Samaria and besieged it. Never had Israel been brought into so great a strait as during this siege. The sins of the fathers were indeed being visited upon the children and the children's children. The horrors of prolonged famine were driving the king of Israel to desperate measures, when Elisha predicted deliverance the following day.

As the next morning was about to dawn, the Lord "made the host of the Syrians to hear a noise of chariots, and a noise of horses, even the noise of a great host;" and they, seized with fear, "arose and fled in the twilight," leaving "their tents, and their horses, and their asses, even the camp as it was," with rich stores of food. They "fled for their life," not tarrying until after the Jordan had been crossed.

During the night of the flight, four leprous men at the gate of the city, made desperate by hunger, had proposed to visit the Syrian camp and throw themselves upon the mercy of the besiegers, hoping thereby to arouse sympathy and obtain food. What was their astonishment when, entering the camp, they found "no man there." With none to molest or forbid, "they went into one tent, and did eat and drink, and carried thence silver, and gold, and raiment, and went and hid it; and came again, and entered into another tent, and carried thence also, and went and hid it. Then they said one to another, We do not well: this day is [259] a day of good tidings, and we hold our peace." Quickly they returned to the city with the glad news.

Great was the spoil; so abundant were the supplies that on that day "a measure of fine flour was sold for a shekel, and two measures of barley for a shekel," as had been foretold by Elisha the day before. Once more the name of God was exalted before the heathen "according to the word of the Lord" through His prophet in Israel. See 2 Kings 7:5-16.

Thus the man of God continued to labor from year to year, drawing close to the people in faithful ministry, and in times of crisis standing by the side of kings as a wise counselor. The long years of idolatrous backsliding on the part of rulers and people had wrought their baleful work; the dark shadow of apostasy was still everywhere apparent, yet here and there were those who had steadfastly refused to bow the knee to Baal. As Elisha continued his work of reform, many were reclaimed from heathenism, and these learned to rejoice in the service of the true God. The prophet was cheered by these miracles of divine grace, and he was inspired with a great longing to reach all who were honest in heart. Wherever he was he endeavored to be a teacher of righteousness.

From a human point of view the outlook for the spiritual regeneration of the nation was as hopeless as is the outlook today before God's servants who are laboring in the dark places of the earth. But the church of Christ is God's agency for the proclamation of truth; she is empowered by Him to do a special work; and if she is loyal to God, obedient to His commandments, there will dwell within her the excellency of divine power. If she will be true to her [260] allegiance, there is no power that can stand against her. The forces of the enemy will be no more able to overwhelm her than is the chaff to resist the whirlwind.

There is before the church the dawn of a bright, glorious day, if she will put on the robe of Christ's righteousness, withdrawing from all allegiance to the world.

God calls upon His faithful ones, who believe in Him, to talk courage to those who are unbelieving and hopeless. Turn to the Lord, ye prisoners of hope. Seek strength from God, the living God. Show an unwavering, humble faith in His power and His willingness to save.

When in faith we take hold of His strength, He will change, wonderfully change, the most hopeless, discouraging outlook. He will do this for the glory of His name.

So long as Elisha was able to journey from place to place throughout the kingdom of Israel, he continued to take an active interest in the upbuilding of the schools of the prophets. Wherever he was, God was with him, giving him words to speak and power to work miracles. On one occasion "the sons of the prophets said unto Elisha, Behold now, the place where we dwell with thee is too strait for us. Let us go, we pray thee, unto Jordan, and take thence every man a beam, and let us make us a place there, where we may dwell." 2 Kings 6:1, 2. Elisha went with them to Jordan, encouraging them by his presence, giving them instruction, and even performing a miracle to aid them in their work. "As one was felling a beam, the axhead fell into the water: and he cried, and said, Alas, master! for it was borrowed. And the man of God said, Where fell it? [261] And he showed him the place. And he cut down a stick, and cast it in thither; and the iron did swim. Therefore said he, Take it up to thee. And he put out his hand, and took it." Verses 5-7.

So effectual had been his ministry and so widespread his influence that, as he lay upon his deathbed, even the youthful King Joash, an idolater with but little respect for God, recognized in the prophet a father in Israel, and acknowledged that his presence among them was of more value in time of trouble than the possession of an army of horses and chariots. The record reads: "Now Elisha was fallen sick of his sickness whereof he died. And Joash the king of Israel came down unto him, and wept over his face, and said, O my father, my father, the chariot of Israel, and the horsemen thereof." 2 Kings 13:14.

To many a troubled soul in need of help the prophet had acted the part of a wise, sympathetic father. And in this instance he turned not from the godless youth before him, so unworthy of the position of trust he was occupying, and yet so greatly in need of counsel. God in His providence was bringing to the king an opportunity to redeem the failures of the past and to place his kingdom on vantage ground. The Syrian foe, now occupying the territory east of the Jordan, was to be repulsed. Once more the power of God was to be manifested in behalf of erring Israel.

The dying prophet bade the king, "Take bow and arrows." Joash obeyed. Then the prophet said, "Put thine hand upon the bow." Joash "put his hand upon it: and Elisha put his hands upon the king's hands. And he said, [262] Open the window eastward"—toward the cities beyond the Jordan in possession of the Syrians. The king having opened the latticed window, Elisha bade him shoot. As the arrow sped on its way, the prophet was inspired to say, "The arrow of the Lord's deliverance, and the arrow of deliverance from Syria: for thou shalt smite the Syrians in Aphek, till thou have consumed them."

And now the prophet tested the faith of the king. Bidding Joash take up the arrows, he said, "Smite upon the ground." Thrice the king smote the ground, and then he stayed his hand. "Thou shouldest have smitten five or six times," Elisha exclaimed in dismay; "then hadst thou smitten Syria [263] till thou hadst consumed it: whereas now thou shalt smite Syria but thrice." 2 Kings 13:15-19.

The lesson is for all in positions of trust. When God opens the way for the accomplishment of a certain work and gives assurance of success, the chosen instrumentality must do all in his power to bring about the promised result. In proportion to the enthusiasm and perseverance with which the work is carried forward will be the success given. God can work miracles for His people only as they act their part with untiring energy. He calls for men of devotion to His work, men of moral courage, with ardent love for souls, and with a zeal that never flags. Such workers will find no task too arduous, no prospect too hopeless; they will labor on, undaunted, until apparent defeat is turned into glorious victory. Not even prison walls nor the martyr's stake beyond, will cause them to swerve from their purpose of laboring together with God for the upbuilding of His kingdom.

With the counsel and encouragement given Joash, the work of Elisha closed. He upon whom had fallen in full measure the spirit resting upon Elijah, had proved faithful to the end. Never had he wavered. Never had he lost his trust in the power of Omnipotence. Always, when the way before him seemed utterly closed, he had still advanced by faith, and God had honored his confidence and opened the way before him.

It was not given Elisha to follow his master in a fiery chariot. Upon him the Lord permitted to come a lingering illness. During the long hours of human weakness and [264] suffering his faith laid fast hold on the promises of God, and he beheld ever about him heavenly messengers of comfort and peace. As on the heights of Dothan he had seen the encircling hosts of heaven, the fiery chariots of Israel and the horsemen thereof, so now he was conscious of the presence of sympathizing angels, and he was sustained. Throughout his life he had exercised strong faith, and as he had advanced in a knowledge of God's providences and of His merciful kindness, faith had ripened into an abiding trust in his God, and when death called him he was ready to rest from his labors.

"Precious in the sight of the Lord is the death of His saints." Psalm 116:15. "The righteous hath hope in his death." Proverbs 14:32. With the psalmist, Elisha could say in all confidence, "God will redeem my soul from the power of the grave: for He shall receive me." Psalm 49:15. And with rejoicing he could testify, "I know that my Redeemer liveth, and that He shall stand at the latter day upon the earth." Job 19:25. "As for me, I will behold Thy face in righteousness: I shall be satisfied, when I awake, with Thy likeness." Psalm 17:15. [265]

Chapter 22

"Nineveh, That Great City"

Among the cities of the ancient world in the days of divided Israel one of the greatest was Nineveh, the capital of the Assyrian realm. Founded on the fertile bank of the Tigris, soon after the dispersion from the tower of Babel, it had flourished through the centuries until it had become "an exceeding great city of three days' journey." Jonah 3:3.

In the time of its temporal prosperity Nineveh was a center of crime and wickedness. Inspiration has characterized it as "the bloody city, ... full of lies and robbery." In figurative language the prophet Nahum compared the Ninevites to a cruel, ravenous lion. "Upon whom," he inquired, "hath not thy wickedness passed continually?" Nahum 3:1, 19.

Yet Nineveh, wicked though it had become, was not wholly given over to evil. He who "beholdeth all the sons of men" (Psalm 33:13) and "seeth every precious thing" (Job 28:10) perceived in that city many who were reaching [266] out after something better and higher, and who, if granted opportunity to learn of the living God, would put away their evil deeds and worship Him. And so in His wisdom God revealed Himself to them in an unmistakable manner, to lead them, if possible, to repentance.

The instrument chosen for this work was the prophet Jonah, the son of Amittai. To him came the word of the Lord, "Arise, go to Nineveh, that great city, and cry against it; for their wickedness is come up before Me." Jonah 1:1, 2.

As the prophet thought of the difficulties and seeming impossibilities of this commission, he was tempted to question the wisdom of the call. From a human viewpoint it seemed as if nothing could be gained by proclaiming such a message in that proud city. He forgot for the moment that the God whom he served was all-wise and all-powerful. While he hesitated, still doubting, Satan overwhelmed him with discouragement. The prophet was seized with a great dread, and he "rose up to flee unto Tarshish." Going to Joppa, and finding there a ship ready to sail, "he paid the fare thereof and went down into it, to go with them." Verse 3.

In the charge given him, Jonah had been entrusted with a heavy responsibility; yet He who had bidden him go was able to sustain His servant and grant him success. Had the prophet obeyed unquestioningly, he would have been spared many bitter experiences, and would have been blessed abundantly. Yet in the hour of Jonah's despair the Lord did not desert him. Through a series of trials and strange [267] providences, the prophet's confidence in God and in His infinite power to save was to be revived.

If, when the call first came to him, Jonah had stopped to consider calmly, he might have known how foolish would be any effort on his part to escape the responsibility placed upon him. But not for long was he permitted to go on undisturbed in his mad flight. "The Lord sent out a great wind into the sea, and there was a mighty tempest in the sea, so that the ship was like to be broken. Then the mariners were afraid, and cried every man unto his god, and cast forth the wares that were in the ship into the sea, to lighten it of them. But Jonah was gone down into the sides of the ship; and he lay, and was fast asleep." Verses 4, 5.

As the mariners were beseeching their heathen gods for help, the master of the ship, distressed beyond measure, sought out Jonah and said, "What meanest thou, O sleeper? arise, call upon thy God, if so be that God will think upon us, that we perish not." Verse 6.

But the prayers of the man who had turned aside from the path of duty brought no help. The mariners, impressed with the thought that the strange violence of the storm betokened the anger of their gods, proposed as a last resort the casting of lots, "that we may know," they said, "for whose cause this evil is upon us. So they cast lots, and the lot fell upon Jonah. Then said they unto him, Tell us, we pray thee, for whose cause this evil is upon us; what is thine occupation? and whence comest thou? what is thy country? and of what people art thou? [268]

"And he said unto them, I am an Hebrew; and I fear the Lord, the God of heaven, which hath made the sea and the dry land.

"Then were the men exceedingly afraid, and said unto him, Why hast thou done this? For the men knew that he fled from the presence of the Lord, because he had told them.

"Then said they unto him, What shall we do unto thee, that the sea may be calm unto us? for the sea wrought, and was tempestuous. And he said unto them, Take me up, and cast me forth into the sea; so shall the sea be calm unto you: for I know that for my sake this great tempest is upon you.

"Nevertheless the men rowed hard to bring it to the land; but they could not: for the sea wrought, and was tempestuous against them. Wherefore they cried unto the Lord, and said, We beseech Thee, O Lord, we beseech Thee, let us not perish for this man's life, and lay not upon us innocent blood: for Thou, O Lord, hast done as it pleased Thee. So they took up Jonah, and cast him forth into the sea: and the sea ceased from her raging. Then the men feared the Lord exceedingly, and offered a sacrifice unto the Lord, and made vows.

"Now the Lord had prepared a great fish to swallow up Jonah. And Jonah was in the belly of the fish three days and three nights.

"Then Jonah prayed unto the Lord his God out of the fish's belly, and said:

"I cried by reason of mine affliction unto the Lord, And He heard me; Out of the belly of hell cried I, And Thou heardest my voice. [269]

"For Thou hadst cast me into the deep, In the midst of the seas; And the floods compassed me about: And Thy billows and Thy waves passed over me.

"Then I said, I am cast out of Thy sight; Yet I will look again toward Thy holy temple. The waters compassed me about, Even to the soul:

"The depth closed me round about, The weeds were wrapped about my head. I went down to the bottoms of the mountains; The earth with her bars was about me forever:

"Yet hast Thou brought up my life from corruption, O Lord my God. When my soul fainted within me I remembered the Lord: And my prayer came in unto Thee, Into Thine holy temple.

"They that observe lying vanities forsake their own mercy. But I will sacrifice unto Thee with the voice of thanksgiving; I will pay that that I have vowed. Salvation is of the Lord." Verse 7 to 2:9.

At last Jonah had learned that "salvation belongeth unto the Lord." Psalm 3:8. With penitence and a recognition of the saving grace of God, came deliverance. Jonah was released from the perils of the mighty deep and was cast upon the dry land.

Once more the servant of God was commissioned to warn Nineveh. "The word of the Lord came unto Jonah the second time, saying, Arise, go unto Nineveh, that great city, and preach unto it the preaching that I bid thee." This time he did not stop to question or doubt, but obeyed [270] unhesitatingly. He "arose, and went unto Nineveh, according to the word of the Lord." Jonah 3:1-3.

As Jonah entered the city, he began at once to "cry against" it the message, "Yet forty days, and Nineveh shall be overthrown." Verse 4. From street to street he went, sounding the note of warning.

The message was not in vain. The cry that rang through the streets of the godless city was passed from lip to lip until all the inhabitants had heard the startling announcement. The Spirit of God pressed the message home to every heart and caused multitudes to tremble because of their sins and to repent in deep humiliation.

"The people of Nineveh believed God, and proclaimed a fast, and put on sackcloth, from the greatest of them even to the least of them. For word came unto the king of Nineveh, and he arose from his throne, and he laid his robe from him, and covered him with sackcloth, and sat in ashes. And he causeth it to be proclaimed and published through Nineveh by the decree of the king and his nobles, saying, Let neither man nor beast, herd nor flock, taste anything: let them not feed, nor drink water: but let man and beast be covered with sackcloth, and cry mightily unto God: yea, let them turn everyone from his evil way, and from the violence that is in their hands. Who can tell if God will turn and repent, and turn away from His fierce anger, that we perish not?" Verses 5-9.

As king and nobles, with the common people, the high and the low, "repented at the preaching of Jonas" (Matthew 12:41) and united in crying to the God of heaven, His [271] mercy was granted them. He "saw their works, that they turned from their evil way; and God repented of the evil, that He had said that He would do unto them; and He did it not." Jonah 3:10. Their doom was averted, the God of Israel was exalted and honored throughout the heathen world, and His law was revered. Not until many years later was Nineveh to fall a prey to the surrounding nations through forgetfulness of God and through boastful pride. [For an account of the downfall of Assyria, see chapter 30.]

When Jonah learned of God's purpose to spare the city that, notwithstanding its wickedness, had been led to repent in sackcloth and ashes, he should have been the first to rejoice because of God's amazing grace; but instead he allowed his mind to dwell upon the possibility of his being regarded as a false prophet. Jealous of his reputation, he lost sight of the infinitely greater value of the souls in that wretched city. The compassion shown by God toward the repentant Ninevites "displeased Jonah exceedingly, and he was very angry." "Was not this my saying," he inquired of the Lord, "when I was yet in my country? Therefore I fled before unto Tarshish: for I knew that Thou art a gracious God, and merciful, slow to anger, and of great kindness, and repentest Thee of the evil." Jonah 4:1, 2.

Once more he yielded to his inclination to question and doubt, and once more he was overwhelmed with discouragement. Losing sight of the interests of others, and feeling as if he would rather die than live to see the city spared, in his dissatisfaction he exclaimed, "Now, O Lord, take, I beseech Thee, my life from me; for it is better for me to die than to live." [272]

"Doest thou well to be angry?" the Lord inquired. "So Jonah went out of the city, and sat on the east side of the city, and there made him a booth, and sat under it in the shadow, till he might see what would become of the city. And the Lord God prepared a gourd, and made it to come up over Jonah, that it might be a shadow over his head, to deliver him from his grief. So Jonah was exceeding glad of the gourd." Verses 3-6.

Then the Lord gave Jonah an object lesson. He "prepared a worm when the morning rose the next day, and it smote the gourd that it withered. And it came to pass, when the sun did arise, that God prepared a vehement east wind; and the sun beat upon the head of Jonah, that he fainted, and wished in himself to die, and said, It is better for me to die than to live."

Again God spoke to His prophet, "Doest thou well to be angry for the gourd?" And he said, "I do well to be angry, even unto death."

"Then said the Lord, Thou hast had pity on the gourd, for the which thou hast not labored, neither madest it grow; which came up in a night, and perished in a night: and should not I spare Nineveh, that great city, wherein are more than sixscore thousand persons that cannot discern between their right hand and their left hand; and also much cattle?" Verses 7-11.

Confused, humiliated, and unable to understand God's purpose in sparing Nineveh, Jonah nevertheless had fulfilled the commission given him to warn that great city; and though the event predicted did not come to pass, yet the [273] message of warning was nonetheless from God. And it accomplished the purpose God designed it should. The glory of His grace was revealed among the heathen. Those who had long been sitting "in darkness and in the shadow of death, being bound in affliction and iron," "cried unto the Lord in their trouble," and "He saved them out of their distresses. He brought them out of darkness and the shadow of death, and brake their bands in sunder." "He sent His word, and healed them, and delivered them from their destructions." Psalm 107:10, 13, 14, 20.

Christ during His earthly ministry referred to the good wrought by the preaching of Jonah in Nineveh, and compared the inhabitants of that heathen center with the professed [274] people of God in His day. "The men of Nineveh," He declared, "shall rise in judgment with this generation, and shall condemn it: because they repented at the preaching of Jonas;

and, behold, a greater than Jonas is here." Matthew 12:40, 41. Into the busy world, filled with the din of commerce and the altercation of trade, where men were trying to get all they could for self, Christ had come; and above the confusion His voice, like the trump of God, was heard: "What shall it profit a man, if he shall gain the whole world, and lose his own soul? or what shall a man give in exchange for his soul?" Mark 8:36, 37.

As the preaching of Jonah was a sign to the Ninevites, so Christ's preaching was a sign to His generation. But what a contrast in the reception of the word! Yet in the face of indifference and scorn the Saviour labored on and on, until He had accomplished His mission.

The lesson is for God's messengers today, when the cities of the nations are as verily in need of a knowledge of the attributes and purposes of the true God as were the Ninevites of old. Christ's ambassadors are to point men to the nobler world, which has largely been lost sight of. According to the teaching of the Holy Scriptures, the only city that will endure is the city whose builder and maker is God. With the eye of faith man may behold the threshold of heaven, flushed with God's living glory. Through His ministering servants the Lord Jesus is calling upon men to strive with sanctified ambition to secure the immortal inheritance. He urges them to lay up treasure beside the throne of God. [275]

There is coming rapidly and surely an almost universal guilt upon the inhabitants of the cities, because of the steady increase of determined wickedness. The corruption that prevails is beyond the power of the human pen to describe. Every day brings fresh revelations of strife, bribery, and fraud; every day brings its heart-sickening record of violence and lawlessness, of indifference to human suffering, of brutal, fiendish destruction of human life. Every day testifies to the increase of insanity, murder, and suicide.

From age to age Satan has sought to keep men in ignorance of the beneficent designs of Jehovah. He has endeavored to remove from their sight the great things of God's law—the principles of justice, mercy, and love therein set forth. Men boast of the wonderful progress and enlightenment of the age in which we are now living; but God sees the earth filled with iniquity and violence. Men declare that the law of God has been abrogated, that the Bible is not authentic; and as a result, a tide of evil, such as has not been seen since the days of Noah and of apostate Israel, is sweeping over the world. Nobility of soul, gentleness, piety, are bartered away to gratify the lust for forbidden things. The black record of crime committed for the sake of gain is enough to chill the blood and fill the soul with horror.

Our God is a God of mercy. With long-sufferance and tender compassion He deals with the transgressors of His law. And yet, in this our day, when men and women have so many opportunities for becoming familiar with the divine law as revealed in Holy Writ, the great Ruler of the universe cannot behold with any satisfaction the wicked [276] cities, where reign violence and crime. The end of God's forbearance with those who persist in disobedience is approaching rapidly.

Ought men to be surprised over a sudden and unexpected change in the dealings of the Supreme Ruler with the inhabitants of a fallen world? Ought they to be surprised when punishment follows transgression and increasing crime? Ought they to be surprised that God should bring destruction and death upon those whose ill-gotten gains have been obtained through deception and fraud? Notwithstanding the fact that increasing light regarding God's requirements has been shining on their pathway, many have refused to recognize Jehovah's rulership, and have chosen to remain under the black banner of the originator of all rebellion against the government of heaven.

The forbearance of God has been very great—so great that when we consider the continuous insult to His holy commandments, we marvel. The Omnipotent One has been exerting a restraining power over His own attributes. But He will certainly arise to punish the wicked, who so boldly defy the just claims of the Decalogue.

God allows men a period of probation; but there is a point beyond which divine patience is exhausted, and the judgments of God are sure to follow. The Lord bears long with men, and with cities, mercifully giving warnings to save them from divine wrath; but a time will come when pleadings for mercy will no longer be heard, and the rebellious element that continues to reject the light of truth will be blotted out, in mercy to themselves and to those who would otherwise be influenced by their example. [277]

The time is at hand when there will be sorrow in the world that no human balm can heal. The Spirit of God is being withdrawn. Disasters by sea and by land follow one another in quick succession. How frequently we hear of earthquakes and tornadoes, of destruction by fire and flood, with great loss of life and property! Apparently these calamities are capricious outbreaks of disorganized, unregulated forces of nature, wholly beyond the control of man; but in them all, God's purpose may be read. They are among the agencies by which He seeks to arouse men and women to a sense of their danger.

God's messengers in the great cities are not to become discouraged over the wickedness, the injustice, the depravity, which they are called upon to face while endeavoring to proclaim the glad tidings of salvation. The Lord would cheer every such worker with the same message that He gave to the apostle Paul in wicked Corinth: "Be not afraid, but speak, and hold not thy peace: for I am with thee, and no man shall set on thee to hurt thee: for I have much people in this city." Acts 18:9, 10. Let those engaged in soul-saving ministry remember that while there are many who will not heed the counsel of God in His word, the whole world will not turn from light and truth, from the invitations of a patient, forbearing Saviour. In every city, filled though it may be with violence and crime, there are many who with proper teaching may learn to become followers of Jesus. Thousands may thus be reached with saving truth and be led to receive Christ as a personal Saviour. [278]

God's message for the inhabitants of earth today is, "Be ye also ready: for in such an hour as ye think not the Son of man cometh." Matthew 24:44. The conditions prevailing in society, and especially in the great cities of the nations, proclaim in thunder tones that the hour of God's judgment is come and that the end of all things earthly is at hand. We are standing on the threshold of the crisis of the ages. In quick succession the judgments of God will follow one another—fire, and flood, and earthquake, with war and bloodshed. We are not to be surprised at this time by events both great and decisive; for the angel of mercy cannot remain much longer to shelter the impenitent.

"Behold, the Lord cometh out of His place to punish the inhabitants of the earth for their iniquity: the earth also shall disclose her blood, and shall no more cover her slain." Isaiah 26:21. The storm of God's wrath is gathering; and those only will stand who respond to the invitations of mercy, as did the inhabitants of Nineveh under the preaching of Jonah, and become sanctified through obedience to the laws of the divine Ruler. The righteous alone shall be hid with Christ in God till the desolation be overpast. Let the language of the soul be:

"Other refuge have I none, Hangs my helpless soul on Thee; Leave, O, leave me not alone! Still support and comfort me.

"Hide me, O my Saviour, hide! Till the storm of life is past; Safe into the haven guide, O receive my soul at last!" [279]

Chapter 23

The Assyrian Captivity

The closing years of the ill-fated kingdom of Israel were marked with violence and bloodshed such as had never been witnessed even in the worst periods of strife and unrest under the house of Ahab. For two centuries and more the rulers of the ten tribes had been sowing the wind; now they were reaping the whirlwind. King after king was assassinated to make way for others ambitious to rule. "They have set up kings," the Lord declared of these godless usurpers, "but not by Me: they have made princes, and I knew it not." Hosea 8:4. Every principle of justice was set aside; those who should have stood before the nations of earth as the depositaries of divine grace, "dealt treacherously against the Lord" and with one another. Hosea 5:7.

With the severest reproofs, God sought to arouse the impenitent nation to a realization of its imminent danger of utter destruction. Through Hosea and Amos He sent [280] the ten tribes message after message, urging full and complete repentance, and threatening disaster as the result of continued transgression. "Ye have plowed wickedness," declared Hosea, "ye have reaped iniquity; ye have eaten the fruit of lies: because thou didst trust in thy way, in the multitude of thy mighty men. Therefore shall a tumult arise among thy people, and all thy fortresses shall be spoiled.... In a morning shall the king of Israel utterly be cut off." Hosea 10:13-15.

Of Ephraim the prophet testified, "Strangers have devoured his strength, and he knoweth it not: yea, gray hairs are here and there upon him, yet he knoweth not." [The prophet Hosea often referred to Ephraim, a leader in apostasy among the tribes of Israel, as a symbol of the apostate nation.] "Israel hath cast off the thing that is good." "Broken in judgment," unable to discern the disastrous outcome of their evil course, the ten tribes were soon to be "wanderers among the nations." Hosea 7:9; 8:3; Hosea 5:11; 9:17.

Some of the leaders in Israel felt keenly their loss of prestige and wished that this might be regained. But instead of turning away from those practices which had brought weakness to the kingdom, they continued in iniquity, flattering themselves that when occasion arose, they would attain to the political power they desired by allying themselves with the heathen. "When Ephraim saw his sickness, and Judah saw his wound, then went Ephraim to the

Assyrian." "Ephraim also is like a silly dove without heart: they call to Egypt, they go to Assyria." "They do make a covenant with the Assyrians." Hosea 5:13; 7:11; Hosea 12:1. [281]

Through the man of God that had appeared before the altar at Bethel, through Elijah and Elisha, through Amos and Hosea, the Lord had repeatedly set before the ten tribes the evils of disobedience. But notwithstanding reproof and entreaty, Israel had sunk lower and still lower in apostasy. "Israel slideth back as a backsliding heifer," the Lord declared; "My people are bent to backsliding from Me." Hosea 4:16; 11:7.

There were times when the judgments of Heaven fell very heavily on the rebellious people. "I hewed them by the prophets," God declared; "I have slain them by the words of My mouth: and thy judgments are as the light that goeth forth. For I desired mercy, and not sacrifice; and the knowledge of God more than burnt offerings. But they like men have transgressed the covenant: there have they dealt treacherously against Me." Hosea 6:5-7.

"Hear the word of the Lord, ye children of Israel," was the message that finally came to them: "Seeing thou hast forgotten the law of thy God, I will also forget thy children. As they were increased, so they sinned against Me: therefore will I change their glory into shame.... I will punish them for their ways, and reward them their doings." Hosea 4:1, 6-9.

The iniquity in Israel during the last half century before the Assyrian captivity was like that of the days of Noah, and of every other age when men have rejected God and have given themselves wholly to evil-doing. The exaltation of nature above the God of nature, the worship of the creature instead of the Creator, has always resulted in the grossest [282] of evils. Thus when the people of Israel, in their worship of Baal and Ashtoreth, paid supreme homage to the forces of nature, they severed their connection with all that is uplifting and ennobling, and fell an easy prey to temptation. With the defenses of the soul broken down, the misguided worshipers had no barrier against sin and yielded themselves to the evil passions of the human heart.

Against the marked oppression, the flagrant injustice, the unwonted luxury and extravagance, the shameless feasting and drunkenness, the gross licentiousness and debauchery, of their age, the prophets lifted their voices; but in vain were their protests, in vain their denunciation of sin. "Him that rebuketh in the gate," declared Amos, "they hate, ... and they abhor him that speaketh uprightly." "They afflict the just, they take a bribe, and they turn aside the poor in the gate from their right." Amos 5:10, 12.

Such were some of the results that had followed the setting up of two calves of gold by Jeroboam. The first departure from established forms of worship had led to the introduction of grosser forms of idolatry, until finally nearly all the inhabitants of the land had given themselves over to the alluring practices of nature worship. Forgetting their Maker, Israel "deeply corrupted themselves." Hosea 9:9.

The prophets continued to protest against these evils and to plead for rightdoing. "Sow to yourselves in righteousness, reap in mercy," Hosea urged; "break up your fallow ground: for it is time to seek the Lord, till He come and rain righteousness upon you." "Turn thou to thy God: keep mercy and judgment, and wait on thy God continually." [283] "O Israel, return unto the Lord thy God; for thou hast fallen by thine iniquity: ... say unto Him, Take away all iniquity, and receive us graciously." Hosea 10:12; 12:6; Hosea 14:1, 2.

The transgressors were given many opportunities to repent. In their hour of deepest apostasy and greatest need, God's message to them was one of forgiveness and hope. "O Israel," He declared, "thou hast destroyed thyself; but in Me is thine help. I will be thy King: where is any other that may save thee?" Hosea 13:9, 10.

"Come, and let us return unto the Lord," the prophet entreated; "for He hath torn, and He will heal us; He hath smitten, and He will bind us up. After two days will He revive us: in the third day He will raise us up, and we shall live in His sight. Then shall we know, if we follow on to know the Lord: His going forth is prepared as the morning; and He shall come unto us as the rain, as the latter and former rain unto the earth." Hosea 6:1-3.

To those who had lost sight of the plan of the ages for the deliverance of sinners ensnared by the power of Satan, the Lord offered restoration and peace. "I will heal their backsliding, I will love them freely," He declared: "for Mine anger is turned away from him. I will be as the dew unto Israel: he shall grow as the lily, and cast forth his roots as Lebanon. His branches shall spread, and his beauty shall be as the olive tree, and his smell as Lebanon. They that dwell under His shadow shall return; they shall revive as the corn, and grow as the vine: the scent thereof shall be as the wine of Lebanon. Ephraim shall say, What have I [284] to do any more with idols? I have heard him, and observed him: I am like a green fir tree. From Me is thy fruit found.

"Who is wise, and he shall understand these things? Prudent, and he shall know them? For the ways of the Lord are right, And the just shall walk in them: But the transgressors shall fall therein."

Hosea 14:4-9.

The benefits of seeking God were strongly urged. "Seek ye Me," the Lord invited, "and ye shall live: but seek not Bethel, nor enter into Gilgal, and pass not to Beersheba: for Gilgal shall surely go into captivity, and Bethel shall come to nought."

"Seek good, and not evil, that ye may live: and so the Lord, the God of hosts, shall be with you, as ye have spoken. Hate the evil, and love the good, and establish judgment in the gate: it may be that the Lord God of hosts will be gracious unto the remnant of Joseph." Amos 5:4, 5, 14, 15.

By far the greater number of those who heard these invitations refused to profit by them. So contrary to the evil desires of the impenitent were the words of God's messengers, that the idolatrous priest at Bethel sent to the ruler in Israel, saying, "Amos hath conspired against thee in the midst of the house of Israel: the land is not able to bear all his words." Amos 7:10.

Through Hosea the Lord declared, "When I would have healed Israel, then the iniquity of Ephraim was discovered, and the wickedness of Samaria." "The pride of Israel testifieth to his face: and they do not return to the Lord their God, nor seek Him for all this." Hosea 7:1, 10. [285]

From generation to generation the Lord had borne with His wayward children, and even now, in the face of defiant rebellion, He still longed to reveal Himself to them as willing to save. "O Ephraim," He cried, "what shall I do unto thee? O Judah, what shall I do unto thee? for your goodness is as a morning cloud, and as the early dew it goeth away." Hosea 6:4.

The evils that had overspread the land had become incurable; and upon Israel was pronounced the dread sentence: "Ephraim is joined to idols: let him alone." "The days of visitation are come, the days of recompense are come; Israel shall know it." Hosea 4:17; 9:7.

The ten tribes of Israel were now to reap the fruitage of the apostasy that had taken form with the setting up of the strange altars at Bethel and at Dan. God's message to them was: "Thy calf, O Samaria, hath cast thee off; Mine anger is kindled against them: how long will it be ere they attain to innocency? For from Israel was it also: the workman made it; therefore it is not God: but the calf of Samaria shall be broken in pieces." "The inhabitants of Samaria shall fear because of the calves of Beth-aven: for the people thereof shall mourn over it, and the priests thereof that rejoiced on it.... It shall be also carried unto Assyria for a present to King Jareb" (Sennacherib). Hosea 8:5, 6; 10:5, 6.

"Behold, the eyes of the Lord God are upon the sinful kingdom, and I will destroy it from off the face of the earth; saying that I will not utterly destroy the house of Jacob, saith the Lord. For, lo, I will command, and I will sift the [286] house of Israel among all nations, like as corn is sifted in a sieve, yet shall not the least grain fall upon the earth. All the sinners of My people shall die by the sword, which say, The evil shall not overtake nor prevent us."

"The houses of ivory shall perish, and the great houses shall have an end, saith the Lord." "The Lord God of hosts is He that toucheth the land, and it shall melt, and all that dwell therein shall mourn." "Thy sons and thy daughters shall fall by the sword, and thy land shall be divided by line; and thou shalt die in a polluted land: and Israel shall surely go into captivity forth of his land." "Because I will do this unto thee, prepare to meet thy God, O Israel." Amos 9:8-10; 3:15; Amos 9:5; 7:17; Amos 4:12.

For a season these predicted judgments were stayed, and during the long reign of Jeroboam II the armies of Israel gained signal victories; but this time of apparent prosperity wrought no change in the hearts of the impenitent, and it was finally decreed, "Jeroboam shall die by the sword, and Israel shall surely be led away captive out of their own land." Amos 7:11.

The boldness of this utterance was lost on king and people, so far had they gone in impenitence. Amaziah, a leader among the idolatrous priests at Bethel, stirred by the plain words spoken by the prophet against the nation and their king, said to Amos, "O thou seer, go, flee thee away into the land of Judah, and there eat bread, and prophesy there: but prophesy not again any more at Bethel: for it is the king's chapel, and it is the king's court." Verses 12, 13.

To this the prophet firmly responded: "Thus saith the Lord, ... Israel shall surely go into captivity." Verse 17. [287]

The words spoken against the apostate tribes were literally fulfilled; yet the destruction of the kingdom came gradually. In judgment the Lord remembered mercy, and at first, when "Pul the king of Assyria came against the land," Menahem, then king of Israel, was not taken captive, but was permitted to remain on the throne as a vassal of the Assyrian realm. "Menahem gave Pul a thousand talents of silver, that his hand might be with him to confirm the kingdom in his hand. And Menahem exacted the money of Israel, even of all the mighty men of wealth, of each man fifty shekels of silver, to give to the king of Assyria." 2 Kings

15:19, 20. The Assyrians, having humbled the ten tribes, returned for a season to their own land.

Menahem, far from repenting of the evil that had wrought ruin in his kingdom, continued in "the sins of Jeroboam the son of Nebat, who made Israel to sin." Pekahiah and Pekah, his successors, also "did that which was evil in the sight of the Lord." Verses 18, 24, 28. "In the days of Pekah," who reigned twenty years, Tiglath-pileser, king of Assyria, invaded Israel and carried away with him a multitude of captives from among the tribes living in Galilee and east of the Jordan. "The Reubenites, and the Gadites, and the half tribe of Manasseh," with others of the inhabitants of "Gilead, and Galilee, all the land of Naphtali" (1 Chronicles 5:26; 2 Kings 15:29), were scattered among the heathen in lands far removed from Palestine.

From this terrible blow the northern kingdom never recovered. The feeble remnant continued the forms of government, though no longer possessed of power. Only one more ruler, Hoshea, was to follow Pekah. Soon the kingdom [288] was to be swept away forever. But in that time of sorrow and distress God still remembered mercy, and gave the people another opportunity to turn from idolatry. In the third year of Hoshea's reign, good King Hezekiah began to rule in Judah and as speedily as possible instituted important reforms in the temple service at Jerusalem. A Passover celebration was arranged for, and to this feast were invited not only the tribes of Judah and Benjamin, over which Hezekiah had been anointed king, but all the northern tribes as well. A proclamation was sounded "throughout all Israel, from Beersheba even to Dan, that they should come to keep the Passover unto the Lord God of Israel at Jerusalem: for they had not done it of a long time in such sort as it was written.

"So the posts went with the letters from the king and his princes throughout all Israel and Judah," with the pressing invitation, "Ye children of Israel, turn again unto the Lord God of Abraham, Isaac, and Israel, and He will return to the remnant of you, that are escaped out of the hand of the kings of Assyria.... Be ye not stiff-necked, as your fathers were, but yield yourselves unto the Lord, and enter into His sanctuary, which He hath sanctified forever: and serve the Lord your God, that the fierceness of His wrath may turn away from you. For if ye turn again unto the Lord, your brethren and your children shall find compassion before them that lead them captive, so that they shall come again into this land: for the Lord your God is gracious and merciful, and will not turn away His face from you; if ye return unto Him." 2 Chronicles 30:5-9. [289] [290] [291]

"From city to city through the country of Ephraim and Manasseh even unto Zebulun," the couriers sent out by Hezekiah carried the message. Israel should have recognized in this invitation an appeal to repent and turn to God. But the remnant of the ten tribes still dwelling within the territory of the once-flourishing northern kingdom treated the royal messengers from Judah with indifference and even with contempt. "They laughed them to scorn, and mocked them." There were a few, however, who gladly responded. "Divers of Asher and Manasseh and of Zebulun humbled themselves, and came to Jerusalem, ... to keep the feast of unleavened bread." Verses 10-13.

About two years later, Samaria was invested by the hosts of Assyria under Shalmaneser; and in the siege that followed, multitudes perished miserably of hunger and disease as well as by the sword. The city and nation fell, and the broken remnant of the ten tribes were carried away captive and scattered in the provinces of the Assyrian realm.

The destruction that befell the northern kingdom was a direct judgment from Heaven. The Assyrians were merely the instruments that God used to carry out His purpose. Through Isaiah, who began to prophesy shortly before the fall of Samaria, the Lord referred to the Assyrian hosts as "the rod of Mine anger." "The staff in their hand," He said, "is Mine indignation." Isaiah 10:5.

Grievously had the children of Israel "sinned against the Lord their God, ... and wrought wicked things." "They would not hear, but ... rejected His statutes, and His covenant that He made with their fathers, and His [292] testimonies which He testified against them." It was because they had "left all the commandments of the Lord their God, and made them molten images, even two calves, and made a grove, and worshiped all the host of heaven, and served Baal," and refused steadfastly to repent, that the Lord "afflicted them, and delivered them into the hand of spoilers, until He had cast them out of His sight," in harmony with the plain warnings He had sent them "by all His servants the prophets."

"So was Israel carried away out of their own land to Assyria," "because they obeyed not the voice of the Lord their God, but transgressed His covenant, and all that Moses the servant of the Lord commanded." 2 Kings 17:7, 11, 14-16, 20, 23; 18:12.

In the terrible judgments brought upon the ten tribes the Lord had a wise and merciful purpose. That which He could no longer do through them in the land of their fathers He would seek to accomplish by scattering them among the heathen. His plan for the salvation of all who should choose to avail themselves of pardon through the Saviour of the human race must yet be fulfilled; and in the afflictions brought upon Israel, He was preparing the way for His glory to be revealed to the nations of earth. Not all who were carried captive were impenitent. Among them were some who had remained true to God, and others who had humbled themselves before Him. Through these, "the sons of the living God" (Hosea 1:10), He would bring multitudes in the Assyrian realm to a knowledge of the attributes of His character and the beneficence of His law. [293]

Chapter 24

"Destroyed for Lack of Knowledge"

God's favor toward Israel had always been conditional on their obedience. At the foot of Sinai they had entered into covenant relationship with Him as His "peculiar treasure... above all people." Solemnly they had promised to follow in the path of obedience. "All that the Lord hath spoken we will do," they had said. Exodus 19:5, 8. And when, a few days afterward, God's law was spoken from Sinai, and additional instruction in the form of statutes and judgments was communicated through Moses, the Israelites with one voice had again promised, "All the words which the Lord hath said will we do." At the ratification of the covenant, the people had once more united in declaring, "All that the Lord hath said will we do, and be obedient," Exodus 24:3, 7. God had chosen Israel as His people, and they had chosen Him as their King.

Near the close of the wilderness wandering the conditions of the covenant had been repeated. At Baalpeor, on the [294] very borders of the Promised Land, where many fell a prey to subtle temptation, those who remained faithful renewed their vows of allegiance. Through Moses they were warned against the temptations that would assail them in the future; and they were earnestly exhorted to remain separate from the surrounding nations and to worship God alone.

"Now therefore hearken," Moses had instructed Israel, "unto the statutes and unto the judgments, which I teach you, for to do them, that ye may live, and go in and possess the land which the Lord God of your fathers giveth you. Ye shall not add unto the word which I command you, neither shall ye diminish aught from it, that ye may keep the commandments of the Lord your God which I command you.... Keep therefore and do them; for this is your wisdom and your understanding in the sight of the nations, which shall hear all these statutes, and say, Surely this great nation is a wise and understanding people." Deuteronomy 4:1-6.

The Israelites had been specially charged not to lose sight of the commandments of God, in obedience to which they would find strength and blessing. "Take heed to thyself, and keep thy soul diligently," had been the word of the Lord to them through Moses, "lest thou forget the things which thine eyes have seen, and lest they depart from thy heart all the days of thy life: but teach them thy sons, and thy sons' sons." Verse 9. The awe-inspiring scenes connected with the giving of the law at Sinai were never to be forgotten. Plain and decided were the warnings that had been given Israel against the idolatrous customs [295] prevailing among the neighboring nations. "Take ye ... good heed unto yourselves," was the counsel given; "lest ye corrupt yourselves, and make you a graven image, the similitude of any figure," "and lest thou lift up thine eyes unto heaven, and when thou seest the sun, and the moon, and the stars, even all the host of heaven, shouldest be driven to worship them, and serve them, which the Lord thy God hath divided unto all nations under the whole heaven." "Take heed unto yourselves, lest ye forget the covenant of the Lord your God, which He made with you, and make you a graven image, or the likeness of anything, which the Lord thy God hath forbidden thee." Verses 15, 16, 19, 23.

Moses traced the evils that would result from a departure from the statutes of Jehovah. Calling heaven and earth to witness, he declared that if, after having dwelt long in the Land of Promise, the people should introduce corrupt forms of worship and bow down to graven images and should refuse to return to the worship of the true God, the anger of the Lord would be aroused, and they would be carried away captive and scattered among the heathen. "Ye shall soon utterly perish from off the land whereunto ye go over Jordan to possess it," he warned them; "ye shall not prolong your days upon it, but shall utterly be destroyed. And the Lord shall scatter you among the nations, and ye shall be left few in number among the heathen, whither the Lord shall lead you. And there ye shall serve gods, the work of men's hands, wood and stone, which neither see, nor hear, nor eat, nor smell." Verses 26-28. [296]

This prophecy, fulfilled in part in the time of the judges, met a more complete and literal fulfillment in the captivity of Israel in Assyria and of Judah in Babylon.

The apostasy of Israel had developed gradually. From generation to generation, Satan had made repeated attempts to cause the chosen nation to forget "the commandments, the statutes, and the judgments" that they had promised to keep forever. Deuteronomy 6:1. He knew that if he could only lead Israel to forget God, and to "walk after other gods, and serve them, and worship them," they would "surely perish." Deuteronomy 8:19.

The enemy of God's church upon the earth had not, however, taken fully into account the compassionate nature of Him who "will by no means clear the guilty," yet whose glory it is to be "merciful and gracious, long-suffering, and abundant in goodness and truth, keeping mercy for thousands, forgiving iniquity and transgression and sin." Exodus 34:6, 7. Despite the efforts of Satan to thwart God's purpose for Israel, nevertheless even in some of the darkest hours of their history, when it seemed as if the forces of evil were about to gain the victory, the Lord graciously revealed Himself. He spread before Israel the things that were for the welfare of the nation. "I have written to him the great things of My law," He declared through Hosea, "but they were counted as a strange thing." "I taught Ephraim also to go, taking them by their arms; but they knew not that I healed them." Hosea 8:12; 11:3. Tenderly had the Lord dealt with them, instructing them by His prophets line upon line, precept upon precept. [297]

Had Israel heeded the messages of the prophets, they would have been spared the humiliation that followed. It was because they had persisted in turning aside from His law that God was compelled to let them go into captivity. "My people are destroyed for lack of knowledge," was His message to them through Hosea. "Because thou hast rejected knowledge, I will also reject thee: ... seeing thou hast forgotten the law of thy God." Hosea 4:6.

In every age, transgression of God's law has been followed by the same result. In the days of Noah, when every principle of rightdoing was violated, and iniquity became so deep and widespread that God could no longer bear with it, the decree went forth, "I will destroy man whom I have created from the face of the earth." Genesis 6:7. In Abraham's day the people of Sodom openly defied God and His law; and there followed the same wickedness, the same corruption, the same unbridled indulgence, that had marked the antediluvian world. The inhabitants of Sodom passed the limits of divine forbearance, and there was kindled against them the fire of God's vengeance.

The time preceding the captivity of the ten tribes of Israel was one of similar disobedience and of similar wickedness. God's law was counted as a thing of nought, and this opened the floodgates of iniquity upon Israel. "The Lord hath a controversy with the inhabitants of the land," Hosea declared, "because there is no truth, nor mercy, nor knowledge of God in the land. By swearing, and lying, and killing, and stealing, and committing adultery, they break out, and blood toucheth blood." Hosea 4:1, 2. [298]

The prophecies of judgment delivered by Amos and Hosea were accompanied by predictions of future glory. To the ten tribes, long rebellious and impenitent, was given no promise of complete restoration to their former power in Palestine. Until the end of time, they were to be "wanderers among the nations." But through Hosea was given a prophecy that set before them the privilege of having a part in the final restoration that is to be made to the people of God at the close of earth's history, when Christ shall appear as King of kings and Lord of lords. "Many days," the prophet declared, the ten tribes were to abide "without a king, and without a prince, and without a sacrifice, and without an image, and without an ephod, and without teraphim." "Afterward," the prophet continued, "shall the children of Israel return, and seek the Lord their God, and David their king; and shall fear the Lord and His goodness in the latter days." Hosea 3:4, 5.

In symbolic language Hosea set before the ten tribes God's plan of restoring to every penitent soul who would unite with His church on earth, the blessings granted Israel in the days of their loyalty to Him in the Promised Land. Referring to Israel as one to whom He longed to show mercy, the Lord declared, "I will allure her, and bring her into the wilderness, and speak comfortably unto her. And I will give her her vineyards from thence, and the valley of Achor for a door of hope: and she shall sing there, as in the days of her youth, and as in the day when she came up out of the land of Egypt. And it shall be at that day, saith the Lord, that thou shalt call Me Ishi ["My [299] husband," margin]; and shalt call Me no more Baali ["My lord," margin]. For I will take away the names of Baalim out of her mouth, and they shall no more be remembered by their name." Hosea 2:14-17.

In the last days of this earth's history, God's covenant with His commandment-keeping people is to be renewed. "In that day will I make a covenant for them with the beasts of the field, and with the fowls of heaven, and with the creeping things of the ground: and I will break the bow and the sword and the battle out of the earth, and will make them to lie down safely. And I will betroth thee unto Me forever; yea, I will betroth thee unto Me in righteousness, and in judgment, and in loving-kindness, and in mercies. I will even betroth thee unto Me in faithfulness: and thou shalt know the Lord.

"And it shall come to pass in that day, I will hear, saith the Lord, I will hear the heavens, and they shall hear the earth; and the earth shall hear the corn, and the wine, and the oil; and they shall hear Jezreel. And I will sow her unto Me in the earth; and I will have mercy upon her that had not obtained mercy; and I will say to them which were not My people, Thou art My people; and they shall say, Thou art my God." Verses 18-23.

"In that day" "the remnant of Israel, and such as are escaped of the house of Jacob, ... shall stay upon the Lord, the Holy One of Israel, in truth." Isaiah 10:20. From "every nation, and kindred, and tongue, and people" there will be some who will gladly respond to the message, "Fear God, and give glory to Him; for the hour of His judgment [300] is come." They will turn from every idol that binds them to earth, and will "worship Him that made heaven, and earth, and the sea, and the fountains of waters." They will free themselves from every entanglement and will stand before the world as monuments of God's mercy. Obedient to the divine requirements, they will be recognized by angels and by men as those that have kept "the commandments of God, and the faith of Jesus." Revelation 14:6, 7, 12.

"Behold, the days come, saith the Lord, that the plowman shall overtake the reaper, and the treader of grapes him that soweth seed; and the mountains shall drop sweet wine, and all the hills shall melt. And I will bring again the captivity of My people of Israel, and they shall build the waste cities, and inhabit them; and they shall plant vineyards, and drink the wine thereof; they shall also make gardens, and eat the fruit of them. And I will plant them upon their land, and they shall no more be pulled up out of their land which I have given them, saith the Lord thy God." Amos 9:13-15. [301]

Chapter 25

The Call of Isaiah

Beginning of Section 3 — A Preacher of Righteousness

The long reign of Uzziah [also known as Azariah] in the land of Judah and Benjamin was characterized by a prosperity greater than that of any other ruler since the death of Solomon, nearly two centuries before. For many years the king ruled with discretion. Under the blessing of Heaven his armies regained some of the territory that had been lost in former years. Cities were rebuilt and fortified, and the position of the nation among the surrounding peoples was greatly strengthened. Commerce revived, and the riches of the nations flowed into Jerusalem. Uzziah's name "spread far abroad; for he was marvellously helped, till he was strong." 2 Chronicles 26:15.

This outward prosperity, however, was not accompanied by a corresponding revival of spiritual power. The temple services were continued as in former years, and multitudes assembled to worship the living God; but pride and formality [304] gradually took the place of humility and sincerity. Of Uzziah himself it is written: "When he was strong, his heart was lifted up to his destruction: for he transgressed against the Lord his God." Verse 16.

The sin that resulted so disastrously to Uzziah was one of presumption. In violation of a plain command of Jehovah, that none but the descendants of Aaron should officiate as priests, the king entered the sanctuary "to burn incense upon the altar." Azariah the high priest and his associates remonstrated, and pleaded with him to turn from his purpose. "Thou hast trespassed," they urged; "neither shall it be for thine honor." Verses 16, 18.

Uzziah was filled with wrath that he, the king, should be thus rebuked. But he was not permitted to profane the sanctuary against the united protest of those in authority. While standing there, in wrathful rebellion, he was suddenly smitten with a divine judgment. Leprosy appeared on his forehead. In dismay he fled, never again to enter the temple courts. Unto the day of his death, some years later, Uzziah remained a leper—a living example of the folly of departing from a plain "Thus saith the Lord." Neither his exalted position nor his long life of service could be pleaded as an excuse for the presumptuous sin by which he marred the closing years of his reign, and brought upon himself the judgment of Heaven.

God is no respecter of persons. "The soul that doeth aught presumptuously, whether he be born in the land, or a stranger, the same reproacheth the Lord; and that soul shall be cut off from among his people." Numbers 15:30. [305]

The judgment that befell Uzziah seemed to have a restraining influence on his son. Jotham bore heavy responsibilities during the later years of his father's reign and succeeded to the throne after Uzziah's death. Of Jotham it is written: "He did that which was right in the sight of the Lord: he did according to all that his father Uzziah had done. Howbeit the high places were not removed: the people sacrificed and burned incense still in the high places." 2 Kings 15:34, 35.

The reign of Uzziah was drawing to a close, and Jotham was already bearing many of the burdens of state, when Isaiah, of the royal line, was called, while yet a young man, to the prophetic mission. The times in which Isaiah was to labor were fraught with peculiar peril to the people of God. The prophet was to witness the invasion of Judah by the combined armies of northern Israel and of Syria; he was to behold the Assyrian hosts encamped before the chief cities of the kingdom. During his lifetime, Samaria was to fall, and the ten tribes of Israel were to be scattered among the nations. Judah was again and again to be invaded by the Assyrian armies, and Jerusalem was to suffer a siege that would have resulted in her downfall had not God miraculously interposed. Already grave perils were threatening the peace of the southern kingdom. The divine protection was being removed, and the Assyrian forces were about to overspread the land of Judah.

But the dangers from without, overwhelming though they seemed, were not so serious as the dangers from within. It was the perversity of his people that brought to the Lord's servant the greatest perplexity and the deepest depression. [306] By their apostasy and rebellion those who should have been standing as light bearers among the nations were inviting the judgments of God. Many of the evils which were hastening the swift destruction of the northern kingdom, and which had recently been denounced in unmistakable terms by Hosea and Amos, were fast corrupting the kingdom of Judah.

The outlook was particularly discouraging as regards the social conditions of the people. In their desire for gain, men were adding house to house and field to field. See Isaiah 5:8. Justice was perverted, and no pity was shown the poor. Of these evils God declared, "The spoil of the poor is in your houses." "Ye beat My people to pieces, and grind the faces of the poor." Isaiah 3:14, 15. Even the magistrates, whose duty it was to protect the helpless, turned a deaf ear to the cries of the poor and needy, the widows and the fatherless. See Isaiah 10:1, 2.

With oppression and wealth came pride and love of display, gross drunkenness, and a spirit of revelry. See Isaiah 2:11, 12; 3:16, 18-23; Isaiah 5:22, 11, 12. And in Isaiah's day idolatry itself no longer provoked surprise. See Isaiah 2:8, 9. Iniquitous practices had become so prevalent among all classes that the few who remained true to God were often tempted to lose heart and to give way to discouragement and despair. It seemed as if God's purpose for Israel were about to fail and that the rebellious nation was to suffer a fate similar to that of Sodom and Gomorrah.

In the face of such conditions it is not surprising that when, during the last year of Uzziah's reign, Isaiah was called to bear to Judah God's messages of warning and [307] reproof, he shrank from the responsibility. He well knew that he would encounter obstinate resistance. As he realized his own inability to meet the situation and thought of the stubbornness and unbelief of the people for whom he was to labor, his task seemed hopeless. Should he in despair relinquish his mission and leave Judah undisturbed to their idolatry? Were the gods of Nineveh to rule the earth in defiance of the God of heaven?

Such thoughts as these were crowding through Isaiah's mind as he stood under the portico of the temple. Suddenly the gate and the inner veil of the temple seemed to be uplifted or withdrawn, and he was permitted to gaze within, upon the holy of holies, where even the prophet's feet might not enter. There rose up before him a vision of Jehovah sitting upon a throne high and lifted up, while the train of His glory filled the temple. On each side of the throne hovered the seraphim, their faces veiled in adoration, as they ministered before their Maker and united in the solemn invocation, "Holy, holy, holy, is the Lord of hosts: the whole earth is full of His glory," until post and pillar and cedar gate seemed shaken with the sound, and the house was filled with their tribute of praise. Isaiah 6:3.

As Isaiah beheld this revelation of the glory and majesty of his Lord, he was overwhelmed with a sense of the purity and holiness of God. How sharp the contrast between the matchless perfection of his Creator, and the sinful course of those who, with himself, had long been numbered among the chosen people of Israel and Judah! "Woe is me!" he cried; "for I am undone; because I am a man of unclean lips, and I dwell in the midst of a people of unclean lips: [308] for mine eyes have seen the King, the Lord of hosts." Verse 5. Standing, as it were, in the full light of the divine presence within the inner sanctuary, he realized that if left to his own imperfection and inefficiency, he would be utterly unable to accomplish the mission to which he had been called. But a seraph was sent to relieve him of his distress and to fit him for his great mission. A living coal from the altar was laid upon his lips, with the words, "Lo, this hath touched thy lips; and thine iniquity is taken away, and thy sin purged." Then the voice of God was heard saying, "Whom shall I send, and who will go for Us?" and Isaiah responded, "Here am I; send me." Verses 7, 8.

The heavenly visitant bade the waiting messenger, "Go, and tell this people,

"Hear ye indeed, but understand not; And see ye indeed, but perceive not. Make the heart of this people fat, And make their ears heavy, and shut their eyes; Lest they see with their eyes, and hear with their ears, And understand with their heart, And convert, and be healed."

Verses 9, 10.

The prophet's duty was plain; he was to lift his voice in protest against the prevailing evils. But he dreaded to undertake the work without some assurance of hope. "Lord, how long?" he inquired. Verse 11. Are none of Thy chosen people ever to understand and repent and be healed?

His burden of soul in behalf of erring Judah was not to be borne in vain. His mission was not to be wholly fruitless. [309] Yet the evils that had been multiplying for many generations could not be removed in his day. Throughout his lifetime he must be a patient, courageous teacher—a prophet of hope as well as of doom. The divine purpose finally accomplished, the full fruitage of his efforts, and of the labors of all God's faithful messengers, would appear. A remnant should be saved. That this might be brought about, the messages of warning and entreaty were to be delivered to the rebellious nation, the Lord declared:

"Until the cities be wasted without inhabitant, And the houses without man, And the land be utterly desolate, And the Lord have removed men far away, And there be a great forsaking in the midst of the land."

Verse 11, 12.

The heavy judgments that were to befall the impenitent,—war, exile, oppression, the loss of power and prestige among the nations,—all these were to come in order that those who would recognize in them the hand of an offended God might be led to repent. The ten tribes of the northern kingdom were soon to be scattered among the nations and their cities left desolate; the destroying armies of hostile nations were to sweep over their land again and again; even Jerusalem was finally to fall, and Judah was to be carried away captive; yet the Promised Land was not to remain wholly forsaken forever. The assurance of the heavenly visitant to Isaiah was:

"In it shall be a tenth, And it shall return, and shall be eaten: [310]

As a teil tree, and as an oak, Whose substance is in them, when they cast their leaves: So the holy seed shall be the substance thereof."

Verse 13.

This assurance of the final fulfillment of God's purpose brought courage to the heart of Isaiah. What though earthly powers array themselves against Judah? What though the Lord's messenger meet with opposition and resistance? Isaiah had seen the King, the Lord of hosts; he had heard the song of the seraphim, "The whole earth is full of His glory;" he had the promise that the messages of Jehovah to backsliding Judah would be accompanied by the convicting power of the Holy Spirit; and the prophet was nerved for the work before him. Verse 3. Throughout his long and arduous mission he carried with him the memory of this vision. For sixty years or more he stood before the children of Judah as a prophet of hope, waxing bolder and still bolder in his predictions of the future triumph of the church. [311]

Chapter 26

"Behold Your God!"

In Isaiah's day the spiritual understanding of mankind was dark through misapprehension of God. Long had Satan sought to lead men to look upon their Creator as the author of sin and suffering and death. Those whom he had thus deceived, imagined that God was hard and exacting. They regarded Him as watching to denounce and condemn, unwilling to receive the sinner so long as there was a legal excuse for not helping him. The law of love by which heaven is ruled had been misrepresented by the archdeceiver as a restriction upon men's happiness, a burdensome yoke from which they should be glad to escape. He declared that its precepts could not be obeyed and that the penalties of transgression were bestowed arbitrarily.

In losing sight of the true character of Jehovah, the Israelites were without excuse. Often had God revealed Himself to them as one "full of compassion, and gracious, long-suffering, and plenteous in mercy and truth." [312] Psalm 86:15. "When Israel was a child," He testified, "then I loved him, and called My son out of Egypt." Hosea 11:1.

Tenderly had the Lord dealt with Israel in their deliverance from Egyptian bondage and in their journey to the Promised Land. "In all their affliction He was afflicted, and the angel of His presence saved them: in His love and in His pity He redeemed them; and He bare them, and carried them all the days of old." Isaiah 63:9.

"My presence shall go with thee," was the promise given during the journey through the wilderness. Exodus 33:14. This assurance was accompanied by a marvelous revelation of Jehovah's character, which enabled Moses to proclaim to all Israel the goodness of God, and to instruct them fully concerning the attributes of their invisible King. "The Lord passed by before him, and proclaimed, The Lord, The Lord God, merciful and gracious, long-suffering, and abundant in goodness and truth, keeping mercy for thousands, forgiving iniquity and transgression and sin, and that will by no means clear the guilty." Exodus 34:6, 7.

It was upon his knowledge of the long-sufferance of Jehovah and of His infinite love and mercy, that Moses based his wonderful plea for the life of Israel when, on the borders of the Promised Land, they refused to advance in obedience to the command of God. At the height of their rebellion the Lord had declared, "I will smite them with the pestilence, and disinherit them;" and He had proposed to make of the descendants of Moses "a greater nation and mightier than they." Numbers 14:12. But the prophet pleaded the marvelous providences and promises of God in [313] behalf of the chosen nation. And then, as the strongest of all pleas, he urged the love of God for fallen man. See verses 17-19.

Graciously the Lord responded, "I have pardoned according to thy word." And then He imparted to Moses, in the form of a prophecy, a knowledge of His purpose concerning the final triumph of Israel. "As truly as I live," He declared, "all the earth shall be filled with the glory of the Lord." Verses 20, 21. God's glory, His character, His merciful kindness and tender love—that which Moses had pleaded in behalf of Israel—were to be revealed to all mankind. And this promise of Jehovah was made doubly sure; it was confirmed by an oath. As surely as God lives and reigns, His glory should be declared "among the heathen, His wonders among all people." Psalm 96:3.

It was concerning the future fulfillment of this prophecy that Isaiah had heard the shining seraphim singing before the throne, "The whole earth is full of His glory." Isaiah 6:3. The prophet, confident of the certainty of these words, himself afterward boldly declared of those who were bowing down to the images of wood and stone, "They shall see the glory of the Lord, and the excellency of our God." Isaiah 35:2.

Today this prophecy is meeting rapid fulfillment. The missionary activities of the church of God on earth are bearing rich fruitage, and soon the gospel message will have been proclaimed to all nations. "To the praise of the glory of His grace," men and women from every kindred, tongue, and people are being made "accepted in the Beloved," "that [314] in the ages to come He might show the exceeding riches of His grace in His kindness toward us through Christ Jesus." Ephesians 1:6; 2:7. "Blessed be the Lord God, the God of Israel, who only doeth wondrous things. And blessed be His glorious name forever: and let the whole earth be filled with His glory." Psalm 72:18, 19.

In the vision that came to Isaiah in the temple court, he was given a clear view of the character of the God of Israel. "The high and lofty One that inhabiteth eternity, whose name is Holy," had appeared before him in great majesty; yet the prophet was made to understand the compassionate nature of his Lord. He who dwells "in the high and holy place" dwells "with him also that is of a contrite and humble spirit, to revive the spirit of the humble, and to revive the heart of the contrite ones." Isaiah 57:15. The angel commissioned to touch Isaiah's lips had brought to him the message, "Thine iniquity is taken away, and thy sin purged." Isaiah 6:7.

In beholding his God, the prophet, like Saul of Tarsus at the gate of Damascus, had not only been given a view of his own unworthiness; there had come to his humbled heart the assurance of forgiveness, full and free; and he had arisen a changed man. He had seen his Lord. He had caught a glimpse of the loveliness of the divine character. He could testify of the transformation wrought through beholding Infinite Love. Henceforth he was inspired with longing desire to see erring Israel set free from the burden and penalty of sin. "Why should ye be stricken any more?" the prophet inquired. "Come now, and let us reason together, [315] saith the Lord: though your sins be as scarlet, they shall be as white as snow; though they be red like crimson, they shall be as wool." "Wash you, make you clean; put away the evil of your doings from before Mine eyes; cease to do evil; learn to do well." Isaiah 1:5, 18, 16, 17.

The God whom they had been claiming to serve, but whose character they had misunderstood, was set before them as the great Healer of spiritual disease. What though the whole head was sick and the whole heart faint? what though from the sole of the foot even unto the crown of the head there was no soundness, but wounds, and bruises, and putrifying sores? See Isaiah 1:6. He who had been walking frowardly in the way of his heart might find healing by turning to the Lord. "I have seen his ways," the Lord declared, "and will heal him: I will lead him also, and restore comforts unto him.... Peace, peace to him that is far off, and to him that is near, saith the Lord; and I will heal him." Isaiah 57:18, 19.

The prophet exalted God as Creator of all. His message to the cities of Judah was, "Behold your God!" Isaiah 40:9. "Thus saith God the Lord, He that created the heavens, and stretched them out; He that spread forth the earth, and that which cometh out of it;" "I am the Lord that maketh all things;" "I form the light, and create darkness;" "I have made the earth, and created man upon it: I, even My hands, have stretched out the heavens, and all their host have I commanded." Isaiah 42:5; 44:24; Isaiah 45:7, 12. "To whom then will ye liken Me, or shall I be equal? saith the Holy One. Lift up your eyes on high, and behold who hath [316] created these things, that bringeth out their host by number: He calleth them all by names by the greatness of His might, for that He is strong in power; not one faileth." Isaiah 40:25, 26.

To those who feared they would not be received if they should return to God, the prophet declared:

"Why sayest thou, O Jacob, and speakest, O Israel, My way is hid from the Lord, and my judgment is passed over from my God? Hast thou not known? hast thou not heard, that the everlasting God, the Lord, the Creator of the ends of the earth, fainteth not, neither is weary? there is no searching of His understanding. He giveth power to the faint; and to them that have no might He increaseth strength. Even the youths shall faint and be weary, and the young men shall utterly fall: but they that wait upon the Lord shall renew their strength; they shall mount up with wings as eagles; they shall run, and not be weary; and they shall walk, and not faint." Verses 27-31.

The heart of Infinite Love yearns after those who feel powerless to free themselves from the snares of Satan; and He graciously offers to strengthen them to live for Him. "Fear thou not," He bids them; "for I am with thee: be not dismayed; for I am thy God: I will strengthen thee; yea, I will help thee; yea, I will uphold thee with the right hand of My righteousness." "I the Lord thy God will hold thy right hand, saying unto thee, Fear not; I will help thee. Fear not, thou worm Jacob, and ye man of Israel; I will help thee, saith the Lord, and thy Redeemer, the Holy One of Israel." Isaiah 41:10, 13, 14. [317] [318] [319]

The inhabitants of Judah were all undeserving, yet God would not give them up. By them His name was to be exalted among the heathen. Many who were wholly unacquainted with His attributes were yet to behold the glory of the divine character. It was for the purpose of making plain His merciful designs that He kept sending His servants the prophets with the message, "Turn ye again now everyone from his evil way." Jeremiah 25:5. "For My name's sake," He declared through Isaiah, "will I defer Mine anger, and for My praise will I refrain for thee, that I cut thee not off." "For Mine own sake, even for Mine own sake, will I do it:

for how should My name be polluted? and I will not give My glory unto another." Isaiah 48:9, 11.

The call to repentance was sounded with unmistakable clearness, and all were invited to return. "Seek ye the Lord while He may be found," the prophet pleaded; "call ye upon Him while He is near: let the wicked forsake his way, and the unrighteous man his thoughts: and let him return unto the Lord, and He will have mercy upon him; and to our God, for He will abundantly pardon." Isaiah 55:6, 7.

Have you, reader, chosen your own way? Have you wandered far from God? Have you sought to feast upon the fruits of transgression, only to find them turn to ashes upon your lips? And now, your life plans thwarted and your hopes dead, do you sit alone and desolate? That voice which has long been speaking to your heart, but to which you would not listen, comes to you distinct and clear, "Arise ye, and depart; for this is not your rest: because it is polluted, [320] it shall destroy you, even with a sore destruction." Micah 2:10. Return to your Father's house. He invites you, saying, "Return unto Me; for I have redeemed thee." "Come unto Me: hear, and your soul shall live; and I will make an everlasting covenant with you, even the sure mercies of David." Isaiah 44:22; 55:3.

Do not listen to the enemy's suggestion to stay away from Christ until you have made yourself better, until you are good enough to come to God. If you wait until then you will never come. When Satan points to your filthy garments, repeat the promise of the Saviour, "Him that cometh to Me I will in no wise cast out." John 6:37. Tell the enemy that the blood of Jesus Christ cleanses from all sin. Make the prayer of David your own: "Purge me with hyssop, and I shall be clean: wash me, and I shall be whiter than snow." Psalm 51:7.

The exhortations of the prophet to Judah to behold the living God, and to accept His gracious offers, were not in vain. There were some who gave earnest heed, and who turned from their idols to the worship of Jehovah. They learned to see in their Maker love and mercy and tender compassion. And in the dark days that were to come in the history of Judah, when only a remnant were to be left in the land, the prophet's words were to continue bearing fruit in decided reformation. "At that day," declared Isaiah, "shall a man look to his Maker, and his eyes shall have respect to the Holy One of Israel. And he shall not look to the altars, the work of his hands, neither shall respect that which his fingers have made, either the groves, or the images." Isaiah 17:7, 8. [321]

Many were to behold the One altogether lovely, the chiefest among ten thousand. "Thine eyes shall see the King in His beauty," was the gracious promise made them. Isaiah 33:17. Their sins were to be forgiven, and they were to make their boast in God alone. In that glad day of redemption from idolatry they would exclaim, "The glorious Lord will be unto us a place of broad rivers and streams.... The Lord is our judge, the Lord is our lawgiver, the Lord is our king; He will save us." Verses 21, 22.

The messages borne by Isaiah to those who chose to turn from their evil ways were full of comfort and encouragement. Hear the word of the Lord through His prophet:

"Remember these, O Jacob and Israel; For thou art My servant: I have formed thee; thou art My servant: O Israel, thou shalt not be forgotten of Me. I have blotted out, as a thick cloud, thy transgressions, And, as a cloud, thy sins: Return unto Me; for I have redeemed thee."

Isaiah 44:21, 22.

"In that day thou shalt say, O Lord, I will praise Thee: Though Thou wast angry with me, Thine anger is turned away, and Thou comfortedst me.

"Behold, God is my salvation; I will trust, and not be afraid: For the Lord Jehovah is my strength and my song; He also is become my salvation....

"Sing unto the Lord; for He hath done excellent things: This is known in all the earth. Cry out and shout, thou inhabitant of Zion: For great is the Holy One of Israel in the midst of thee."

Isaiah 12. [322]

Chapter 27

Ahaz

The accession of Ahaz to the throne brought Isaiah and his associates face to face with conditions more appalling than any that had hitherto existed in the realm of Judah. Many who had formerly withstood the seductive influence of idolatrous practices were now being persuaded to take part in the worship of heathen deities. Princes in Israel were proving untrue to their trust; false prophets were arising with messages to lead astray; even some of the priests were teaching for hire. Yet the leaders in apostasy still kept up the forms of divine worship and claimed to be numbered among the people of God.

The prophet Micah, who bore his testimony during those troublous times, declared that sinners in Zion, while claiming to "lean upon the Lord," and blasphemously boasting, "Is not the Lord among us? none evil can come upon us," continued to "build up Zion with blood, and Jerusalem with iniquity." Micah 3:11, 10. Against these evils the [323] prophet Isaiah lifted his voice in stern rebuke: "Hear the word of the Lord, ye rulers of Sodom; give ear unto the law of our God, ye people of Gomorrah. To what purpose is the multitude of your sacrifices unto Me? saith the Lord.... When ye come to appear before Me, who hath required this at your hand, to tread My courts?" Isaiah 1:10-12.

Inspiration declares, "The sacrifice of the wicked is abomination: how much more, when he bringeth it with a wicked mind?" Proverbs 21:27. The God of heaven is "of purer eyes than to behold evil," and cannot "look on iniquity." Habakkuk 1:13. It is not because He is unwilling to forgive that He turns from the transgressor; it is because the sinner refuses to make use of the abundant provisions of grace, that God is unable to deliver from sin. "The Lord's hand is not shortened, that it cannot save; neither His ear heavy, that it cannot hear: but your iniquities have separated between you and your God, and your sins have hid His face from you, that He will not hear." Isaiah 59:1, 2.

Solomon had written, "Woe to thee, O land, when thy king is a child!" Ecclesiastes 10:16. Thus it was with the land of Judah. Through continued transgression her rulers had become as children. Isaiah called the attention of the people to the weakness of their position among the nations of earth, and he showed that this was the result of wickedness in high places. "Behold," he said, "the Lord, the Lord of hosts, doth take away from Jerusalem and from Judah the stay and the staff, the whole stay of bread, and the whole stay of water, the mighty man, and the man of war, the judge, and the prophet, and the prudent, and the ancient, [324] the captain of fifty, and the honorable man, and the counselor, and the cunning artificer, and the eloquent orator. And I will give children to be their princes, and babes shall rule over them." "For Jerusalem is ruined, and Judah is fallen: because their tongue and their doings are against the Lord." Isaiah 3:1-4, 8.

"They which lead thee," the prophet continued, "cause thee to err, and destroy the way of thy paths." Verse 12. During the reign of Ahaz this was literally true; for of him it is written: "He walked in the ways of the kings of Israel, and made also molten images for Baalim. Moreover he burnt incense in the valley of the son of Hinnom;" "yea, and made his son to pass through the fire, according to the abominations of the heathen, whom the Lord cast out from before the children of Israel." 2 Chronicles 28:2, 3; 2 Kings 16:3.

This was indeed a time of great peril for the chosen nation. Only a few short years, and the ten tribes of the kingdom of Israel were to be scattered among the nations of heathendom. And in the kingdom of Judah also the outlook was dark. The forces for good were rapidly diminishing, the forces for evil multiplying. The prophet Micah, viewing the situation, was constrained to exclaim: "The good man is perished out of the earth: and there is none upright among men." "The best of them is as a brier: the most upright is sharper than a thorn hedge." Micah 7:2, 4. "Except the Lord of hosts had left unto us a very small remnant," declared Isaiah, "we should have been as Sodom, and ... Gomorrah." Isaiah 1:9.

In every age, for the sake of those who have remained true, as well as because of His infinite love for the erring, [325] God has borne long with the rebellious, and has urged them to forsake their course of evil and return to Him. "Precept upon precept; line upon line, ... here a little, and there a little," through men of His appointment, He has taught transgressors the way of righteousness. Isaiah 28:10.

And thus it was during the reign of Ahaz. Invitation upon invitation was sent to erring Israel to return to their allegiance to Jehovah. Tender were the pleadings of the prophets; and as they stood before the people, earnestly exhorting to repentance and reformation, their words bore fruit to the glory of God.

Through Micah came the wonderful appeal, "Hear ye now what the Lord saith; Arise, contend thou before the mountains, and let the hills hear thy voice. Hear ye, O mountains, the Lord's controversy, and ye strong foundations of the earth: for the Lord hath a controversy with His people, and He will plead with Israel.

"O My people, what have I done unto thee? and wherein have I wearied thee? testify against Me. For I brought thee up out of the land of Egypt, and redeemed thee out of the house of servants; and I sent before thee Moses, Aaron, and Miriam.

"O My people, remember now what Balak king of Moab consulted, and what Balaam the son of Beor answered him from Shittim unto Gilgal; that ye may know the righteousness of the Lord." Micah 6:1-5.

The God whom we serve is long-suffering; "His compassions fail not." Lamentations 3:22. Throughout the period of probationary time His Spirit is entreating men [326] to accept the gift of life. "As I live, saith the Lord God, I have no pleasure in the death of the wicked; but that the wicked turn from his way and live: turn ye, turn ye from your evil ways; for why will ye die?" Ezekiel 33:11. It is Satan's special device to lead man into sin and then leave him there, helpless and hopeless, fearing to seek for pardon. But God invites, "Let him take hold of My strength, that he may make peace with Me; and he shall make peace with Me." Isaiah 27:5. In Christ every provision has been made, every encouragement offered.

In the days of apostasy in Judah and Israel, many were inquiring: "Wherewith shall I come before the Lord, and bow myself before the high God? shall I come before Him with burnt offerings, with calves of a year old? will the Lord be pleased with thousands of rams, or with ten thousands of rivers of oil?" The answer is plain and positive: "He hath showed thee, O man, what is good; and what doth the Lord require of thee, but to do justly, and to love mercy, and to walk humbly with thy God?" Micah 6:6-8.

In urging the value of practical godliness, the prophet was only repeating the counsel given Israel centuries before. Through Moses, as they were about to enter the Promised Land, the word of the Lord had been: "And now, Israel, what doth the Lord thy God require of thee, but to fear the Lord thy God, to walk in all His ways, and to love Him, and to serve the Lord thy God with all thy heart and with all thy soul, to keep the commandments of the Lord, and His statutes, which I command thee this day for thy good?" Deuteronomy 10:12, 13. From age to age these counsels [327] were repeated by the servants of Jehovah to those who were in danger of falling into habits of formalism and of forgetting to show mercy. When Christ Himself, during His earthly ministry, was approached by a lawyer with the question, "Master, which is the great commandment in the law?" Jesus said to him, "Thou shalt love the Lord thy God with all thy heart, and with all thy soul, and with all thy mind. This is the first and great commandment. And the second is like unto it, Thou shalt love thy neighbor as thyself. On these two commandments hang all the law and the prophets." Matthew 22:36-40.

These plain utterances of the prophets and of the Master Himself, should be received by us as the voice of God to every soul. We should lose no opportunity of performing deeds of mercy, of tender forethought and Christian courtesy, for the burdened and the oppressed. If we can do no more, we may speak words of courage and hope to those who are unacquainted with God, and who can be approached most easily by the avenue of sympathy and love.

Rich and abundant are the promises made to those who are watchful of opportunities to bring joy and blessing into the lives of others. "If thou draw out thy soul to the hungry, and satisfy the afflicted soul; then shall thy light rise in obscurity, and thy darkness be as the noonday: and the Lord shall guide thee continually, and satisfy thy soul in drought, and make fat thy bones: and thou shalt be like a watered garden, and like a spring of water, whose waters fail not." Isaiah 58:10, 11.

The idolatrous course of Ahaz, in the face of the earnest appeals of the prophets, could have but one result. "The [328] wrath of the Lord was upon Judah and Jerusalem, and He ... delivered them to trouble, to astonishment, and to hissing." 2 Chronicles 29:8. The kingdom suffered a rapid decline, and its very existence was soon imperiled by invading armies. "Rezin king of Syria and Pekah son of Remaliah king of Israel came up to Jerusalem to war: and they besieged Ahaz." 2 Kings 16:5.

Had Ahaz and the chief men of his realm been true servants of the Most High, they would have had no fear of so unnatural an alliance as had been formed against them. But repeated transgression had shorn them of strength. Stricken with a nameless dread of the retributive judgments [329] of an offended God, the heart of the king "was moved, and the heart of his people, as the trees of the wood are moved with the wind." Isaiah 7:2. In this crisis the word of the Lord came to Isaiah, bidding him meet the trembling king and say:

"Take heed, and be quiet; fear not, neither be fainthearted .... Because Syria, Ephraim, and the son of Remaliah, have taken evil counsel against thee, saying, Let us go up against Judah, and vex it, and let us make a breach therein for us, and set a king in the midst of it: ... thus saith the Lord God, It shall not stand, neither shall it come to pass." The prophet declared that the kingdom of Israel, and Syria as well, would soon come to an end. "If ye will not believe," he concluded, "surely ye shall not be established." Verses 4-7, 9.

Well would it have been for the kingdom of Judah had Ahaz received this message as from heaven. But choosing to lean on the arm of flesh, he sought help from the heathen. In desperation he sent word to Tiglath-pileser, king of Assyria: "I am thy servant and thy son: come up, and save me out of the hand of the king of Syria, and out of the hand of the king of Israel, which rise up against me." 2 Kings 16:7. The request was accompanied by a rich present from the king's treasure and from the temple storehouse.

The help asked for was sent, and King Ahaz was given temporary relief, but at what a cost to Judah! The tribute offered aroused the cupidity of Assyria, and that treacherous nation soon threatened to overflow and spoil Judah. Ahaz and his unhappy subjects were now harassed by the fear of falling completely into the hands of the cruel Assyrians. [330]

"The Lord brought Judah low" because of continued transgression. In this time of chastisement Ahaz, instead of repenting, trespassed "yet more against the Lord: ... for he sacrificed unto the gods of Damascus." "Because the gods of the kings of Syria help them," he said, "therefore will I sacrifice to them, that they may help me." 2 Chronicles 28:19, 22, 23.

As the apostate king neared the end of his reign, he caused the doors of the temple to be closed. The sacred services were interrupted. No longer were the candlesticks kept burning before the altar. No longer were offerings made for the sins of the people. No longer did sweet incense ascend on high at the time of the morning and the evening sacrifice. Deserting the courts of the house of God and locking fast its doors, the inhabitants of the godless city boldly set up altars for the worship of heathen deities on the street corners throughout Jerusalem. Heathenism had seemingly triumphed; the powers of darkness had well-nigh prevailed.

But in Judah there dwelt some who maintained their allegiance to Jehovah, steadfastly refusing to be led into idolatry. It was to these that Isaiah and Micah and their associates looked in hope as they surveyed the ruin wrought during the last years of Ahaz. Their sanctuary was closed, but the faithful ones were assured: "God is with us." "Sanctify the Lord of hosts Himself; and let Him be your fear, and let Him be your dread. And He shall be for a sanctuary." Isaiah 8:10, 13, 14. [331]

Chapter 28

Hezekiah

In sharp contrast with the reckless rule of Ahaz was the reformation wrought during the prosperous reign of his son. Hezekiah came to the throne determined to do all in his power to save Judah from the fate that was overtaking the northern kingdom. The messages of the prophets offered no encouragement to halfway measures. Only by most decided reformation could the threatened judgments be averted.

In the crisis, Hezekiah proved to be a man of opportunity. No sooner had he ascended the throne than he began to plan and to execute. He first turned his attention to the restoration of the temple services, so long neglected; and in this work he earnestly solicited the co-operation of a band of priests and Levites who had remained true to their sacred calling. Confident of their loyal support, he spoke with them freely concerning his desire to institute immediate and far-reaching reforms. "Our fathers have trespassed," he confessed, "and done that which was evil in the eyes [332] of the Lord our God, and have forsaken Him, and have turned away their faces from the habitation of the Lord." "Now it is in mine heart to make a covenant with the Lord God of Israel, that His fierce wrath may turn away from us." 2 Chronicles 29:6, 10.

In a few well-chosen words the king reviewed the situation they were facing—the closed temple and the cessation of all services within its precincts; the flagrant idolatry practiced in the streets of the city and throughout the kingdom; the apostasy of multitudes who might have remained true to God had the leaders in Judah set before them a right example; and the decline of the kingdom and loss of prestige in the estimation of surrounding nations. The northern kingdom was rapidly crumbling to pieces; many were perishing by the sword; a multitude had already been carried away captive; soon Israel would fall completely into the hands of the Assyrians, and be utterly ruined; and this fate would surely befall Judah as well, unless God should work mightily through chosen representatives.

Hezekiah appealed directly to the priests to unite with him in bringing about the necessary reforms. "Be not now negligent," he exhorted them; "for the Lord hath chosen you to stand before Him, to serve Him, and that ye should minister unto Him, and burn incense." "Sanctify now yourselves, and sanctify the house of the Lord God of your fathers." Verses 11, 5.

It was a time for quick action. The priests began at once. Enlisting the co-operation of others of their number who had not been present during this conference, they engaged heartily in the work of cleansing and sanctifying [333] the temple. Because of the years of desecration and neglect, this was attended with many difficulties; but the priests and the Levites labored untiringly, and within a remarkably short time they were able to report their task completed. The temple doors had been repaired and thrown open; the sacred vessels had been assembled and put into place; and all was in readiness for the re-establishment of the sanctuary services.

In the first service held, the rulers of the city united with King Hezekiah and with the priests and Levites in seeking forgiveness for the sins of the nation. Upon the altar were placed sin offerings "to make an atonement for all Israel." "And when they had made an end of offering, the king and all that were present with him bowed themselves, and worshiped." Once more the temple courts resounded with words of praise and adoration. The songs of David and of Asaph were sung with joy, as the worshipers realized that they were being delivered from the bondage of sin and apostasy. "Hezekiah rejoiced, and all the people, that God had prepared the people: for the thing was done suddenly." Verses 24, 29, 36.

God had indeed prepared the hearts of the chief men of Judah to lead out in a decided reformatory movement, that the tide of apostasy might be stayed. Through His prophets He had sent to His chosen people message after message of earnest entreaty—messages that had been despised and rejected by the ten tribes of the kingdom of Israel, now given over to the enemy. But in Judah there remained a goodly remnant, and to these the prophets continued to appeal. Hear Isaiah urging, "Turn ye unto Him from whom [334] the children of Israel have deeply revolted." Isaiah 31:6. Hear Micah declaring with confidence: "I will look unto the Lord; I will wait for the God of my salvation: my God will hear me. Rejoice not against me, O mine enemy; when I fall, I shall arise; when I sit in darkness, the Lord shall be a light unto me. I will bear the indignation of the Lord, because I have sinned against Him, until He plead my cause, and execute judgment for me: He will bring me forth to the light, and I shall behold His righteousness." Micah 7:7-9.

These and other like messages revealing the willingness of God to forgive and accept those who turned to Him with full purpose of heart, had brought hope to many a fainting soul in the dark years when the temple doors remained closed; and now, as the leaders began to institute a reform, a multitude of the people, weary of the thralldom of sin, were ready to respond.

Those who entered the temple courts to seek forgiveness and to renew their vows of allegiance to Jehovah, had wonderful encouragement offered them in the prophetic portions of Scripture. The solemn warnings against idolatry, spoken through Moses in the hearing of all Israel, had been accompanied by prophecies of God's willingness to hear and forgive those who in times of apostasy should seek Him with all the heart. "If thou turn to the Lord thy God," Moses had said, "and shalt be obedient unto His voice; (for the Lord thy God is a merciful God;) He will not forsake thee, neither destroy thee, nor forget the covenant of thy fathers which He sware unto them." Deuteronomy 4:30, 31. [335]

And in the prophetic prayer offered at the dedication of the temple whose services Hezekiah and his associates were now restoring, Solomon had prayed, "When Thy people Israel be smitten down before the enemy, because they have sinned against Thee, and shall turn again to Thee, and confess Thy name, and pray, and make supplication unto Thee in this house: then hear Thou in heaven, and forgive the sin of Thy people Israel." 1 Kings

8:33, 34. The seal of divine approval had been placed upon this prayer; for at its close fire had come down from heaven to consume the burnt offering and the sacrifices, and the glory of the Lord had filled the temple. See 2 Chronicles 7:1. And by night the Lord had appeared to Solomon to tell him that his prayer had been heard, and that mercy would be shown those who should worship there. The gracious assurance was given: "If My people, which are called by My name, shall humble themselves, and pray, and seek My face, and turn from their wicked ways; then will I hear from heaven, and will forgive their sin, and will heal their land." Verse 14.

These promises met abundant fulfillment during the reformation under Hezekiah.

The good beginning made at the time of the purification of the temple was followed by a broader movement, in which Israel as well as Judah participated. In his zeal to make the temple services a real blessing to the people, Hezekiah determined to revive the ancient custom of gathering the Israelites together for the celebration of the Passover feast.

For many years the Passover had not been observed as a national festival. The division of the kingdom after the [336] close of Solomon's reign had made this seem impracticable. But the terrible judgments befalling the ten tribes were awakening in the hearts of some a desire for better things; and the stirring messages of the prophets were having their effect. By royal couriers the invitation to the Passover at Jerusalem was heralded far and wide, "from city to city through the country of Ephraim and Manasseh even unto Zebulun." The bearers of the gracious invitation were [337] usually repulsed. The impenitent turned lightly aside; nevertheless some, eager to seek God for a clearer knowledge of His will, "humbled themselves, and came to Jerusalem." 2 Chronicles 30:10, 11.

In the land of Judah the response was very general; for upon them was "the hand of God," "to give them one heart to do the commandment of the king and of the princes"—a command in accord with the will of God as revealed through His prophets. Verse 12.

The occasion was one of the greatest profit to the multitudes assembled. The desecrated streets of the city were cleared of the idolatrous shrines placed there during the reign of Ahaz. On the appointed day the Passover was observed, and the week was spent by the people in offering peace offerings and in learning what God would have them do. Daily the Levites "taught the good knowledge of the Lord;" and those who had prepared their hearts to seek God, found pardon. A great gladness took possession of the worshiping multitude; "the Levites and the priests praised the Lord day by day, singing with loud instruments;" all were united in their desire to praise Him who had proved so gracious and merciful. Verses 21, 22.

The seven days usually allotted to the Passover feast passed all too quickly, and the worshipers determined to spend another seven days in learning more fully the way of the Lord. The teaching priests continued their work of instruction from the book of the law; daily the people assembled at the temple to offer their tribute of praise and thanksgiving; and as the great meeting drew to a close, [338] it was evident that God had wrought marvelously in the conversion of backsliding Judah and in stemming the tide of idolatry which threatened to sweep all before it. The solemn warnings of the prophets had not been uttered in vain. "There was great joy in Jerusalem: for since the time of Solomon the son of David king of Israel there was not the like in Jerusalem." Verse 26.

The time had come for the return of the worshipers to their homes. "The priests the Levites arose and blessed the people: and their voice was heard, and their prayer came up to His holy dwelling place, even unto heaven." Verse 27. God had accepted those who with broken hearts had confessed their sins and with resolute purpose had turned to Him for forgiveness and help.

There now remained an important work in which those who were returning to their homes must take an active part, and the accomplishment of this work bore evidence to the genuineness of the reformation wrought. The record reads: "All Israel that were present went out to the cities of Judah, and brake the images in pieces, and cut down the groves, and threw down the high places and the altars out of all Judah and Benjamin, in Ephraim also and Manasseh, until they had utterly destroyed them all. Then all the children of Israel returned, every man to his possession, into their own cities." 2 Chronicles 31:1.

Hezekiah and his associates instituted various reforms for the upbuilding of the spiritual and temporal interests of the kingdom. "Throughout all Judah" the king "wrought that which was good and right and truth before the Lord [339] his God. And in every work that he began, ... he did it with all his heart, and prospered." "He trusted in the Lord God of Israel, ... and departed not from following Him, but kept His commandments, which the Lord commanded Moses. And the Lord was with him; and he prospered." Verses 20, 21; 2 Kings 18:5-7.

The reign of Hezekiah was characterized by a series of remarkable providences which revealed to the surrounding nations that the God of Israel was with His people. The success of the Assyrians in capturing Samaria and in scattering the shattered remnant of the ten tribes among the nations, during the earlier portion of his reign, was leading many to question the power of the God of the Hebrews. Emboldened by their successes, the Ninevites had long since set aside the message of Jonah and had become defiant in their opposition to the purposes of Heaven. A few years after the fall of Samaria the victorious armies reappeared in Palestine, this time directing their forces against the fenced cities of Judah, with some measure of success; but they withdrew for a season because of difficulties arising in other portions of their realm. Not until some years later, toward the close of Hezekiah's reign, was it to be demonstrated before the nations of the world whether the gods of the heathen were finally to prevail. [340]

Chapter 29

The Ambassadors From Babylon

In the midst of his prosperous reign King Hezekiah was suddenly stricken with a fatal malady. "Sick unto death," his case was beyond the power of man to help. And the last vestige of hope seemed removed when the prophet Isaiah appeared before him with the message, "Thus saith the Lord, Set thine house in order: for thou shalt die, and not live." Isaiah 38:1.

The outlook seemed utterly dark; yet the king could still pray to the One who had hitherto been his "refuge and strength, a very present help in trouble." Psalm 46:1. And so "he turned his face to the wall, and prayed unto the Lord, saying, I beseech Thee, O Lord, remember now how I have walked before Thee in truth and with a perfect heart, and have done that which is good in Thy sight. And Hezekiah wept sore." 2 Kings 20:2, 3.

Since the days of David there had reigned no king who had wrought so mightily for the upbuilding of the kingdom of God in a time of apostasy and discouragement as had [341] Hezekiah. The dying ruler had served his God faithfully, and had strengthened the confidence of the people in Jehovah as their Supreme Ruler. And, like David, he could now plead:

"Let my prayer come before Thee: Incline Thine ear unto my cry; For my soul is full of troubles: And my life draweth nigh unto the grave."

Psalm 88:2, 3.

"Thou art my hope, O Lord God: Thou art my trust from my youth. By Thee have I been holden up." "Forsake me not when my strength faileth." "O God, be not far from me: O my God, make haste for my help." "O God, forsake me not; Until I have showed Thy strength unto this generation, And Thy power to everyone that is to come."

Psalm 71:5, 6, 9, 12, 18.

He whose "compassions fail not," heard the prayer of His servant. Lamentations 3:22. "It came to pass, afore Isaiah was gone out into the middle court, that the word of the Lord came to him, saying, Turn again, and tell Hezekiah the captain of My people, Thus saith the Lord, the God of David thy father, I have heard thy prayer, I have seen thy tears: behold, I will heal thee: on the third day thou shalt go up unto the house of the Lord. And I will add unto thy days fifteen years; and I will deliver thee and this city out of the hand of the king of Assyria; and I will defend this city for Mine own sake, and for My servant David's sake." 2 Kings 20:4-6. [342]

Gladly the prophet returned with the words of assurance and hope. Directing that a lump of figs be laid upon the diseased part, Isaiah delivered to the king the message of God's mercy and protecting care.

Like Moses in the land of Midian, like Gideon in the presence of the heavenly messenger, like Elisha just before the ascension of his master, Hezekiah pleaded for some sign that the message was from heaven. "What shall be the sign," he inquired of the prophet, "that the Lord will heal me, and that I shall go up into the house of the Lord the third day?"

"This sign shalt thou have of the Lord," the prophet answered, "that the Lord will do the thing that He hath spoken: shall the shadow go forward ten degrees, or go back ten degrees?" "It is a light thing," Hezekiah replied, "for the shadow to go down ten degrees: nay, but let the shadow return backward ten degrees."

Only by the direct interposition of God could the shadow on the sundial be made to turn back ten degrees; and this was to be the sign to Hezekiah that the Lord had heard his prayer. Accordingly, "the prophet cried unto the Lord: and He brought the shadow ten degrees backward, by which it had gone down in the dial of Ahaz." Verses 8-11.

Restored to his wonted strength, the king of Judah acknowledged in words of song the mercies of Jehovah, and vowed to spend his remaining days in willing service to the King of kings. His grateful recognition of God's compassionate dealing with him is an inspiration to all who desire to spend their years to the glory of their Maker. [343]

"I said In the cutting off of my days, I shall go to the gates of the grave: I am deprived of the residue of my years.

"I said, I shall not see the Lord, even the Lord, in the land of the living; I shall behold man no more with the inhabitants of the world.

"Mine age is departed, And is removed from me as a shepherd's tent:

"I have cut off like a weaver my life: He will cut me off with pining sickness:

"From day even to night wilt Thou make an end of me. I reckoned till morning, that, As a lion, so will He break all my bones:

"From day even to night wilt Thou make an end of me. Like a crane or a swallow, so did I chatter: I did mourn as a dove: Mine eyes fail with looking upward: O Lord, I am oppressed; undertake for me.

"What shall I say? He hath both spoken unto me, And Himself hath done it: I shall go softly all my years in the bitterness of my soul.

"O Lord, by these things men live, And in all these things is the life of my spirit: So wilt Thou recover me, and make me to live.

"Behold, for peace I had great bitterness: But Thou hast in love to my soul delivered it from the pit of corruption: For Thou hast cast all my sins behind Thy back.

"For the grave cannot praise Thee, Death cannot celebrate Thee: They that go down into the pit cannot hope for Thy truth. [344]

"The living, the living, he shall praise Thee, As I do this day: The father to the children shall make known Thy truth.

"The Lord was ready to save me: Therefore we will sing my songs to the stringed instruments All the days of our life in the house of the Lord."
Isaiah 38:10-20.

In the fertile valleys of the Tigris and the Euphrates there dwelt an ancient race which, though at that time subject to Assyria, was destined to rule the world. Among its people were wise men who gave much attention to the study of astronomy; and when they noticed that the shadow on the sundial had been turned back ten degrees, they marveled greatly. Their king, Merodachbaladan, upon learning that this miracle had been wrought as a sign to the king of Judah that the God of heaven had granted him a new lease of life, sent ambassadors to Hezekiah to congratulate him on his recovery and to learn, if possible, more of the God who was able to perform so great a wonder.

The visit of these messengers from the ruler of a far-away land gave Hezekiah an opportunity to extol the living God. How easy it would have been for him to tell them of God, the upholder of all created things, through whose favor his own life had been spared when all other hope had fled! What momentous transformations might have taken place had these seekers after truth from the plains of Chaldea been led to acknowledge the supreme sovereignty of the living God!

But pride and vanity took possession of Hezekiah's heart, and in self-exaltation he laid open to covetous eyes the [345] treasures with which God had enriched His people. The king "showed them the house of his precious things, the silver, and the gold, and the spices, and the precious ointment, and all the house of his armor, and all that was found in his treasures: there was nothing in his house, nor in all his dominion, that Hezekiah showed them not." Isaiah 39:2. Not to glorify God did he do this, but to exalt himself in the eyes of the foreign princes. He did not stop to consider that these men were representatives of a powerful nation that had not the fear nor the love of God in their [346] hearts, and that it was imprudent to make them his confidants concerning the temporal riches of the nation.

The visit of the ambassadors to Hezekiah was a test of his gratitude and devotion. The record says, "Howbeit in the business of the ambassadors of the princes of Babylon, who sent unto him to inquire of the wonder that was done in the land, God left him, to try him, that He might know all that was in his heart." 2 Chronicles 32:31. Had Hezekiah improved the opportunity given him to bear witness to the power, the goodness, the compassion, of the God of Israel, the report of the ambassadors would have been as light piercing darkness. But he magnified himself above the Lord of hosts. He "rendered not again according to the benefit done unto him; for his heart was lifted up." Verse 25.

How disastrous the results which were to follow! To Isaiah it was revealed that the returning ambassadors were carrying with them a report of the riches they had seen, and that the king of Babylon and his counselors would plan to enrich their own country with the treasures of Jerusalem. Hezekiah had grievously sinned; "therefore there was wrath upon him, and upon Judah and Jerusalem." Verse 25.

"Then came Isaiah the prophet unto King Hezekiah, and said unto him, What said these men? and from whence came they unto thee? And Hezekiah said, They are come from a far country unto me, even from Babylon. Then said he, What have they seen in thine house?

And Hezekiah answered, All that is in mine house have they seen: there is nothing among my treasures that I have not showed them.

"Then said Isaiah to Hezekiah, Hear the word of the [347] Lord of hosts: Behold, the days come, that all that is in thine house, and that which thy fathers have laid up in store until this day, shall be carried to Babylon: nothing shall be left, saith the Lord. And of thy sons that shall issue from thee, which thou shalt beget, shall they take away; and they shall be eunuchs in the palace of the king of Babylon.

"Then said Hezekiah to Isaiah, Good is the word of the Lord which thou hast spoken." Isaiah 39:3-8.

Filled with remorse, "Hezekiah humbled himself for the pride of his heart, both he and the inhabitants of Jerusalem, so that the wrath of the Lord came not upon them in the days of Hezekiah." 2 Chronicles 32:26. But the evil seed had been sown and in time was to spring up and yield a harvest of desolation and woe. During his remaining years the king of Judah was to have much prosperity because of his steadfast purpose to redeem the past and to bring honor to the name of the God whom he served; yet his faith was to be severely tried, and he was to learn that only by putting his trust fully in Jehovah could he hope to triumph over the powers of darkness that were plotting his ruin and the utter destruction of his people.

The story of Hezekiah's failure to prove true to his trust at the time of the visit of the ambassadors is fraught with an important lesson for all. Far more than we do, we need to speak of the precious chapters in our experience, of the mercy and loving-kindness of God, of the matchless depths of the Saviour's love. When mind and heart are filled with the love of God, it will not be difficult to impart that which [348] enters into the spiritual life. Great thoughts, noble aspirations, clear perceptions of truth, unselfish purposes, yearnings for piety and holiness, will find expression in words that reveal the character of the heart treasure.

Those with whom we associate day by day need our help, our guidance. They may be in such a condition of mind that a word spoken in season will be as a nail in a sure place. Tomorrow some of these souls may be where we can never reach them again. What is our influence over these fellow travelers?

Every day of life is freighted with responsibilities which we must bear. Every day, our words and acts are making impressions upon those with whom we associate. How great the need that we set a watch upon our lips and guard carefully our steps! One reckless movement, one imprudent step, and the surging waves of some strong temptation may sweep a soul into the downward path. We cannot gather up the thoughts we have planted in human minds. If they have been evil, we may have set in motion a train of circumstances, a tide of evil, which we are powerless to stay.

On the other hand, if by our example we aid others in the development of good principles, we give them power to do good. In their turn they exert the same beneficial influence over others. Thus hundreds and thousands are helped by our unconscious influence. The true follower of Christ strengthens the good purposes of all with whom he comes in contact. Before an unbelieving, sin-loving world he reveals the power of God's grace and the perfection of His character. [349]

Chapter 30

Deliverance From Assyria

In a time of grave national peril, when the hosts of Assyria were invading the land of Judah and it seemed as if nothing could save Jerusalem from utter destruction, Hezekiah rallied the forces of his realm to resist with unfailing courage their heathen oppressors and to trust in the power of Jehovah to deliver. "Be strong and courageous, be not afraid nor dismayed for the king of Assyria, nor for all the multitude that is with him," Hezekiah exhorted the men of Judah; "for there be more with us than with him: with him is an arm of flesh; but with us is the Lord our God to help us, and to fight our battles." 2 Chronicles 32:7, 8.

It was not without reason that Hezekiah could speak with certainty of the outcome. The boastful Assyrian, while used by God for a season as the rod of His anger for the punishment of the nations, was not always to prevail. See Isaiah 10:5. "Be not afraid of the Assyrian," had been the message of the Lord through Isaiah some years before to [350] those that dwelt in Zion; "for yet a very little while, ... and the Lord of hosts shall stir up a scourge for him according to the slaughter of Midian at the rock of Oreb: and as His rod was upon the sea, so shall He lift it up after the manner of Egypt. And it shall come to pass in that day, that his burden shall be taken away from off thy shoulder, and his yoke from off thy neck, and the yoke shall be destroyed because of the anointing." Verses 24-27.

In another prophetic message, given "in the year that King Ahaz died," the prophet had declared: "The Lord of hosts hath sworn, saying, Surely as I have thought, so shall it come to pass; and as I have purposed, so shall it stand: that I will break the Assyrian in My land, and upon My mountains tread him underfoot: then shall his yoke depart from off them, and his burden depart from off their shoulders. This is the purpose that is purposed upon the whole earth: and this is the hand that is stretched out upon all the nations. For the Lord of hosts hath purposed, and who shall disannul it? and His hand is stretched out, and who shall turn it back?" Isaiah 14:28, 24-27.

The power of the oppressor was to be broken. Yet Hezekiah, in the earlier years of his reign, had continued to pay tribute to Assyria, in harmony with the agreement entered into by Ahaz. Meanwhile the king had taken "counsel with his princes and his mighty men," and had done everything possible for the defense of his kingdom. He had made sure of a bountiful supply of water within the walls of Jerusalem, while without the city there should be a scarcity. "Also he strengthened himself, and built up all the wall that was broken, and raised it up to the towers, [351] and another wall without, and repaired Millo in the city of David, and made darts and shields in abundance. And he set captains of war over the people." 2 Chronicles 32:3, 5, 6. Nothing had been left undone that could be done in preparation for a siege.

At the time of Hezekiah's accession to the throne of Judah, the Assyrians had already carried captive a large number of the children of Israel from the northern kingdom; and a few years after he had begun to reign, and while he was still strengthening the defenses of Jerusalem, the Assyrians besieged and captured Samaria and scattered the ten tribes among the many provinces of the Assyrian realm. The borders of Judah were only a few miles distant, with Jerusalem less than fifty miles away; and the rich spoils to be found within the temple would tempt the enemy to return.

But the king of Judah had determined to do his part in preparing to resist the enemy; and, having accomplished all that human ingenuity and energy could do, he had assembled his forces and had exhorted them to be of good courage. "Great is the Holy One of Israel in the midst of thee" had been the message of the prophet Isaiah to Judah; and the king with unwavering faith now declared, "With us is the Lord our God to help us, and to fight our battles." Isaiah 12:6; 2 Chronicles 32:8.

Nothing more quickly inspires faith than the exercise of faith. The king of Judah had prepared for the coming storm; and now, confident that the prophecy against the Assyrians would be fulfilled, he stayed his soul upon God. "And the people rested themselves upon the words of Hezekiah." 2 Chronicles 32:8. What though the armies of [352] Assyria, fresh from the conquest of the greatest nations of earth, and triumphant over Samaria in Israel, should now turn their forces against Judah? What though they should boast, "As my hand hath found the kingdoms of the idols, and whose graven images did excel them of Jerusalem and of Samaria; shall I not, as I have done unto Samaria and her idols, so do to Jerusalem and her idols?" Isaiah 10:10, 11. Judah had nothing to fear; for their trust was in Jehovah.

The long-expected crisis finally came. The forces of Assyria, advancing from triumph to triumph, appeared in Judea. Confident of victory, the leaders divided their forces into two armies, one of which was to meet the Egyptian army to the southward, while the other was to besiege Jerusalem.

Judah's only hope was now in God. All possible help from Egypt had been cut off, and no other nations were near to lend a friendly hand.

The Assyrian officers, sure of the strength of their disciplined forces, arranged for a conference with the chief men of Judah, during which they insolently demanded the surrender of the city. This demand was accompanied by blasphemous revilings against the God of the Hebrews. Because of the weakness and apostasy of Israel and Judah, the name of God was no longer feared among the nations, but had become a subject for continual reproach. See Isaiah 52:5.

"Speak ye now to Hezekiah," said Rabshakeh, one of Sennacherib's chief officers, "Thus saith the great king, the king of Assyria, What confidence is this wherein thou trustest? Thou

PROPHETS AND KINGS

sayest, (but they are but vain words,) I have [353] counsel and strength for the war. Now on whom dost thou trust, that thou rebellest against me?" 2 Kings 18:19, 20.

The officers were conferring outside the gates of the city, but within the hearing of the sentries on the wall; and as the representatives of the Assyrian king loudly urged their proposals upon the chief men of Judah, they were requested to speak in the Syrian rather than the Jewish language, in order that those upon the wall might not have knowledge of the proceedings of the conference. Rabshakeh, scorning this suggestion, lifted his voice still higher, and, continuing to speak in the Jewish language, said:

"Hear ye the words of the great king, the king of Assyria. Thus saith the king, Let not Hezekiah deceive you: for he shall not be able to deliver you. Neither let Hezekiah make you trust in the Lord, saying, The Lord will surely deliver us: this city shall not be delivered into the hand of the king of Assyria.

"Hearken not to Hezekiah: for thus saith the king of Assyria, Make an agreement with me by a present, and come out to me: and eat ye everyone of his vine, and everyone of his fig tree, and drink ye everyone the waters of his own cistern; until I come and take you away to a land like your own land, a land of corn and wine, a land of bread and vineyards.

"Beware lest Hezekiah persuade you, saying, The Lord will deliver us. Hath any of the gods of the nations delivered his land out of the hand of the king of Assyria? Where are the gods of Hamath and Arphad? where are the gods of Sepharvaim? and have they delivered Samaria out of my hand? Who are they among all the gods of these lands, [354] that have delivered their land out of my hand, that the Lord should deliver Jerusalem out of my hand?" Isaiah 36:13-20.

To these taunts the children of Judah "answered him not a word." The conference was at an end. The Jewish representatives returned to Hezekiah "with their clothes rent, and told him the words of Rabshakeh." Verses 21, 22. The king, upon learning of the blasphemous challenge, "rent his clothes, and covered himself with sackcloth, and went into the house of the Lord." 2 Kings 19:1.

A messenger was dispatched to Isaiah to inform him of the outcome of the conference. "This day is a day of trouble, and of rebuke, and blasphemy," was the word the king sent. "It may be the Lord thy God will hear all the words of Rabshakeh, whom the king of Assyria his master hath sent to reproach the living God; and will reprove the words which the Lord thy God hath heard: wherefore lift up thy prayer for the remnant that are left." Verses 3, 4.

"For this cause Hezekiah the king, and the prophet Isaiah the son of Amoz, prayed and cried to Heaven." 2 Chronicles 32:20.

God answered the prayers of His servants. To Isaiah was given the message for Hezekiah: "Thus saith the Lord, Be not afraid of the words which thou hast heard, with which the servants of the king of Assyria have blasphemed Me. Behold, I will send a blast upon him, and he shall hear a rumor, and shall return to his own land; and I will cause him to fall by the sword in his own land." 2 Kings 19:6, 7.

The Assyrian representatives, after taking leave of the chief men of Judah, communicated direct with their king, [355] who was with the division of his army guarding the approach from Egypt. Upon hearing the report, Sennacherib wrote "letters to rail on the Lord God of Israel, and to speak against Him, saying, As the gods of the nations of other lands have not delivered their people out of mine hand, so shall not the God of Hezekiah deliver His people out of mine hand." 2 Chronicles 32:17.

The boastful threat was accompanied by the message: "Let not thy God in whom thou trustest deceive thee, saying, Jerusalem shall not be delivered into the hand of the king of Assyria. Behold, thou hast heard what the kings of Assyria have done to all lands, by destroying them utterly: and shalt thou be delivered? Have the gods of the nations delivered them which my fathers have destroyed; as Gozan, and Haran, and Rezeph, and the children of Eden which were in Thelasar? Where is the king of Hamath, and the king of Arpad, and the king of the city of Sepharvaim, of Hena, and Ivah?" 2 Kings 19:10-13.

When the king of Judah received the taunting letter, he took it into the temple and "spread it before the Lord" and prayed with strong faith for help from heaven, that the nations of earth might know that the God of the Hebrews still lived and reigned. Verse 14. The honor of Jehovah was at stake; He alone could bring deliverance.

"O Lord God of Israel, which dwellest between the cherubims," Hezekiah pleaded, "Thou art the God, even Thou alone, of all the kingdoms of the earth; Thou hast made heaven and earth. Lord, bow down Thine ear, and hear: open, Lord, Thine eyes, and see: and hear the words [356] of Sennacherib, which hath sent him to reproach the living God. Of a truth, Lord, the kings of Assyria have destroyed the nations and their lands, and have cast their gods into the fire: for they were no gods, but the work of men's hands, wood and stone: therefore they have destroyed them. Now therefore, O Lord our God, I beseech Thee, save Thou us out of his hand, that all the kingdoms of the earth may know that Thou art the Lord God, even Thou only." 2 Kings 19:15-19.

"Give ear, O Shepherd of Israel, Thou that leadest Joseph like a flock; Thou that dwellest between the cherubims, shine forth. Before Ephraim and Benjamin and Manasseh stir up Thy strength, And come and save us. Turn us again, O God, And cause Thy face to shine; and we shall be saved.

"O Lord God of hosts, How long wilt Thou be angry against the prayer of Thy people? Thou feedest them with the bread of tears; And givest them tears to drink in great measure. Thou makest us a strife unto our neighbors: And our enemies laugh among themselves. Turn us again, O God of hosts, And cause Thy face to shine; and we shall be saved.

"Thou hast brought a vine out of Egypt: Thou hast cast out the heathen, and planted it. Thou preparedst room before it, And didst cause it to take deep root, and it filled the land. The hills were covered with the shadow of it, And the boughs thereof were like the goodly cedars. She sent out her boughs unto the sea, And her branches unto the river. [357] [358] [359]

"Why hast Thou then broken down her hedges, So that all they which pass by the way do pluck her? The boar out of the wood doth waste it, And the wild beast of the field doth devour it. Return, we beseech Thee, O God of hosts: Look down from heaven, and behold, and visit this vine; And the vineyard which Thy right hand hath planted, And the branch that Thou madest strong for Thyself....

"Quicken us, and we will call upon Thy name. Turn us again, O Lord God of hosts, Cause Thy face to shine; and we shall be saved." Psalm 80.

Hezekiah's pleadings in behalf of Judah and of the honor of their Supreme Ruler were in harmony with the mind of God. Solomon, in his benediction at the dedication of the temple, had prayed the Lord to maintain "the cause of His people Israel at all times, as the matter shall require: that all the people of the earth may know that the Lord is God, and that there is none else." 1 Kings 8:59, 60. Especially was the Lord to show favor when, in times of war or of oppression by an army, the chief men of Israel should enter the house of prayer and plead for deliverance. Verses 33, 34.

Hezekiah was not left without hope. Isaiah sent to him, saying, "Thus saith the Lord God of Israel, That which thou hast prayed to Me against Sennacherib king of Assyria I have heard. This is the word that the Lord hath spoken concerning him:

"The virgin the daughter of Zion hath despised thee, and laughed thee to scorn; the daughter of Jerusalem hath shaken her head at thee.

"Whom hast thou reproached and blasphemed? and against whom hast thou exalted thy voice, and lifted up thine eyes on high? even against the Holy One of Israel. [360] By thy messengers thou hast reproached the Lord, and hast said, With the multitude of my chariots I am come up to the height of the mountains, to the sides of Lebanon, and will cut down the tall cedar trees thereof, and the choice fir trees thereof: and I will enter into the lodgings of his borders, and into the forest of his Carmel. I have digged and drunk strange waters, and with the sole of my feet have I dried up all the rivers of besieged places.

"Hast thou not heard long ago how I have done it, and of ancient times that I have formed it? now have I brought it to pass, that thou shouldest be to lay waste fenced cities into ruinous heaps. Therefore their inhabitants were of small power, they were dismayed and confounded; they were as the grass of the field, and as the green herb, as the grass on the housetops, and as corn blasted before it be grown up.

"But I know thy abode, and thy going out, and thy coming in, and thy rage against Me. Because thy rage against Me and thy tumult is come up into Mine ears, therefore I will put My hook in thy nose, and My bridle in thy lips, and I will turn thee back by the way by which thou camest." 2 Kings 19:20-28.

The land of Judah had been laid waste by the army of occupation, but God had promised to provide miraculously for the needs of the people. To Hezekiah came the message: "This shall be a sign unto thee, Ye shall eat this year such things as grow of themselves, and in the second year that which springeth of the same; and in the third year sow ye, and reap, and plant vineyards, and eat the fruits thereof. And the remnant that is escaped of the house of [361] Judah shall yet again take root downward, and bear fruit upward. For out of Jerusalem shall go forth a remnant, and they that escape out of Mount Zion: the zeal of the Lord of hosts shall do this.

"Therefore thus saith the Lord concerning the king of Assyria, He shall not come into this city, nor shoot an arrow there, nor come before it with shield, nor cast a bank against it. By the way that he came, by the same shall he return, and shall not come into this city, saith the Lord. For I will defend this city, to save it, for Mine own sake, and for My servant David's sake." Verses 29-34.

That very night deliverance came. "The angel of the Lord went out, and smote in the camp of the Assyrians an hundred fourscore and five thousand." Verse 35. "All the mighty men of valor, and the leaders and captains in the camp of the king of Assyria," were slain. 2 Chronicles 32:21.

Tidings of this terrible judgment upon the army that had been sent to take Jerusalem, soon reached Sennacherib, who was still guarding the approach to Judea from Egypt. Stricken with fear, the Assyrian king hasted to depart and "returned with shame of face to his own land." Verse 21. But he had not long to reign. In harmony with the prophecy that had been uttered concerning his sudden end, he was assassinated by those of his own home, "and Esarhaddon his son reigned in his stead." Isaiah 37:38.

The God of the Hebrews had prevailed over the proud Assyrian. The honor of Jehovah was vindicated in the eyes of the surrounding nations. In Jerusalem the hearts of the people were filled with holy joy. Their earnest [362] entreaties for deliverance had been mingled with confession of sin and with many tears. In their great need they had trusted wholly in the power of God to save, and He had not failed them. Now the temple courts resounded with songs of solemn praise.

"In Judah is God known: His name is great in Israel. In Salem also is His tabernacle, And His dwelling place in Zion. There brake He the arrows of the bow, The shield, and the sword, and the battle.

"Thou art more glorious and excellent Than the mountains of prey. The stouthearted are spoiled, they have slept their sleep: And none of the men of might have found their hands. At Thy rebuke, O God of Jacob, Both the chariot and horse are cast into a dead sleep.

"Thou, even Thou, art to be feared: And who may stand in Thy sight when once Thou art angry? Thou didst cause judgment to be heard from heaven; The earth feared, and was still, When God arose to judgment, To save all the meek of the earth.

"Surely the wrath of man shall praise Thee: The remainder of wrath shalt Thou restrain. Vow, and pay unto the Lord your God: Let all that be round about Him bring presents unto Him that ought to be feared. He shall cut off the spirit of princes: He is terrible to the kings of the earth."

Psalm 76.

The rise and fall of the Assyrian Empire is rich in lessons for the nations of earth today. Inspiration has likened the glory of Assyria at the height of her prosperity to a [363] noble tree in the garden of God, towering above the surrounding trees.

"The Assyrian was a cedar in Lebanon with fair branches, and with a shadowing shroud, and of an high stature; and his top was among the thick boughs.... Under his shadow dwelt all great nations. Thus was he fair in his greatness, in the length of his branches: for his root was by great waters. The cedars in the garden of God could not hide him: the fir trees were not like his boughs, and the chestnut trees were not like his branches; nor any tree in the garden of God was like unto him in his beauty.... All the trees of Eden, that were in the garden of God, envied him." Ezekiel 31:3-9.

But the rulers of Assyria, instead of using their unusual blessings for the benefit of mankind, became the scourge of many lands. Merciless, with no thought of God or their fellow men, they pursued the fixed policy of causing all nations to acknowledge the supremacy of the gods of Nineveh, whom they exalted above the Most High. God had sent Jonah to them with a message of warning, and for a season they humbled themselves before the Lord of hosts and sought forgiveness. But soon they turned again to idol worship and to the conquest of the world.

The prophet Nahum, in his arraignment of the evildoers in Nineveh, exclaimed:

"Woe to the bloody city! It is all full of lies and robbery; The prey departeth not;

"The noise of a whip, and the noise of the rattling of the wheels, And of the prancing horses, and of the jumping chariots. [364]

The horseman lifteth up both the bright sword and the glittering spear: And there is a multitude of slain....

"Behold, I am against thee, Saith the Lord of hosts."
Nahum 3:1-5.

With unerring accuracy the Infinite One still keeps account with the nations. While His mercy is tendered, with calls to repentance, this account remains open; but when the figures reach a certain amount which God has fixed, the ministry of His wrath begins. The account is closed. Divine patience ceases. Mercy no longer pleads in their behalf.

"The Lord is slow to anger, and great in power, and will not at all acquit the wicked: the Lord hath His way in the whirlwind and in the storm, and the clouds are the dust of His feet. He rebuketh the sea, and maketh it dry, and drieth up all the rivers: Bashan languisheth, and Carmel, and the flower of Lebanon languisheth. The mountains quake at Him, and the hills melt, and the earth is burned at His presence, yea, the world, and all that dwell therein. Who can stand before His indignation? and who can abide in the fierceness of His anger? His fury is poured out like fire, and the rocks are thrown down by Him." Nahum 1:3-6.

It was thus that Nineveh, "the rejoicing city that dwelt carelessly, that said in her heart, I am, and there is none beside me," became a desolation, "empty, and void, and waste," "the dwelling of the lions, and the feeding place of the young lions, where the lion, even the old lion, walked, and the lion's whelp, and none made them afraid." Zephaniah 2:15; Nahum 2:10, 11. [365]

Looking forward to the time when the pride of Assyria should be brought low, Zephaniah prophesied of Nineveh: "Flocks shall lie down in the midst of her, all the beasts of the nations: both the cormorant and the bittern shall lodge in the upper lintels of it; their voice shall sing in the windows; desolation shall be in the thresholds: for He shall uncover the cedar work." Zephaniah 2:14.

Great was the glory of the Assyrian realm; great was its downfall. The prophet Ezekiel, carrying farther the figure of a noble cedar tree, plainly foretold the fall of Assyria because of its pride and cruelty. He declared:

"Thus saith the Lord God; ... He hath shot up his top among the thick boughs, and his heart is lifted up in his height; I have therefore delivered him into the hand of the mighty one of the heathen; he shall surely deal with him: I have driven him out for his wickedness. And strangers, the terrible of the nations, have cut him off, and have left him: upon the mountains and in all the valleys his branches are fallen, and his boughs are broken by all the rivers of the land; and all the people of the earth are gone down from his shadow, and have left him. Upon his ruin shall all the fowls of the heaven remain, and all the beasts of the field shall be upon his branches: to the end that none of all the trees by the waters exalt themselves for their height....

"Thus saith the Lord God; In the day when he went down to the grave I caused a mourning: ... and all the trees of the field fainted for him. I made the nations to shake at the sound of his fall." Ezekiel 31:10-16. [366]

The pride of Assyria and its fall are to serve as an object lesson to the end of time. Of the nations of earth today who in arrogance and pride array themselves against Him, God inquires, "To whom art thou thus like in glory and in greatness among the trees of Eden? yet shalt thou be brought down with the trees of Eden unto the nether parts of the earth." Verse 18.

"The Lord is good, a stronghold in the day of trouble; and He knoweth them that trust in Him. But with an overrunning flood He will make an utter end" of all who endeavor to exalt themselves above the Most High. Nahum 1:7, 8.

"The pride of Assyria shall be brought down, and the scepter of Egypt shall depart away." Zechariah 10:11. This is true not only of the nations that arrayed themselves against God in ancient times, but also of nations today who fail of fulfilling the divine purpose. In the day of final awards, when the righteous Judge of all the earth shall "sift the nations" (Isaiah 30:28), and those that have kept the truth shall be permitted to enter the City of God, heaven's arches will ring with the triumphant songs of the redeemed. "Ye shall have a song," the prophet declares, "as in the night when a holy solemnity is kept; and gladness of heart, as when one goeth with a pipe to come into the mountain of the Lord, to the Mighty One of Israel. And the Lord shall cause His glorious voice to be heard.... Through the voice of the Lord shall the Assyrian be beaten down, which smote with a rod. And in every place where the grounded staff shall pass, which the Lord shall lay upon him, it shall be with tabrets and harps." Verses 29-32. [367]

Chapter 31

Hope for the Heathen

Throughout his ministry Isaiah bore a plain testimony concerning God's purpose for the heathen. Other prophets had made mention of the divine plan, but their language was not always understood. To Isaiah it was given to make very plain to Judah the truth that among the Israel of God were to be numbered many who were not descendants of Abraham after the flesh. This teaching was not in harmony with the theology of his age, yet he fearlessly proclaimed the messages given him of God and brought hope to many a longing heart reaching out after the spiritual blessings promised to the seed of Abraham.

The apostle to the Gentiles, in his letter to the believers in Rome, calls attention to this characteristic of Isaiah's teaching. "Isaiah is very bold," Paul declares, "and saith, I was found of them that sought Me not; I was made manifest unto them that asked not after Me." Romans 10:20.

Often the Israelites seemed unable or unwilling to understand God's purpose for the heathen. Yet it was this very [368] purpose that had made them a separate people and had established them as an independent nation among the nations of the earth. Abraham, their father, to whom the covenant promise was first given, had been called to go forth from his kindred, to the regions beyond, that he might be a light bearer to the heathen. Although the promise to him included a posterity as numerous as the sand by the sea, yet it was for no selfish purpose that he was to become the founder of a great nation in the land of Canaan. God's covenant with him embraced all the nations of earth. "I will bless thee," Jehovah declared, "and make thy name great; and thou shalt be a blessing: and I will bless them that bless thee, and curse him that curseth thee: and in thee shall all families of the earth be blessed." Genesis 12:2, 3.

In the renewal of the covenant shortly before the birth of Isaac, God's purpose for mankind was again made plain. "All the nations of the earth shall be blessed in him," was the assurance of the Lord concerning the child of promise. Genesis 18:18. And later the heavenly visitant once more declared, "In thy seed shall all the nations of the earth be blessed." Genesis 22:18.

The all-embracing terms of this covenant were familiar to Abraham's children and to his children's children. It was in order that the Israelites might be a blessing to the nations, and that God's name might be made known "throughout all the earth" (Exodus 9:16), that they were delivered from Egyptian bondage. If obedient to His requirements, they were to be placed far in advance of other peoples in wisdom and understanding; but this supremacy was to [369] be reached and maintained only in order that through them the purpose of God for "all nations of the earth" might be fulfilled.

The marvelous providences connected with Israel's deliverance from Egyptian bondage and with their occupancy of the Promised Land led many of the heathen to recognize the God of Israel as the Supreme Ruler. "The Egyptians shall know," had been the promise, "that I am the Lord, when I stretch forth Mine hand upon Egypt, and bring out the children of Israel from among them." Exodus 7:5. Even proud Pharaoh was constrained to acknowledge Jehovah's power. "Go, serve the Lord," he urged Moses and Aaron, "and bless me also." Exodus 12:31, 32.

The advancing hosts of Israel found that knowledge of the mighty workings of the God of the Hebrews had gone before them, and that some among the heathen were learning that He alone was the true God. In wicked Jericho the testimony of a heathen woman was, "The Lord your God, He is God in heaven above, and in earth beneath." Joshua 2:11. The knowledge of Jehovah that had thus come to her, proved her salvation. By faith "Rahab perished not with them that believed not." Hebrews 11:31. And her conversion was not an isolated case of God's mercy toward idolaters who acknowledged His divine authority. In the midst of the land a numerous people—the Gibeonites—renounced their heathenism and united with Israel, sharing in the blessings of the covenant.

No distinction on account of nationality, race, or caste, is recognized by God. He is the Maker of all mankind. [370] All men are of one family by creation, and all are one through redemption. Christ came to demolish every wall of partition, to throw open every compartment of the temple courts, that every soul may have free access to God. His love is so broad, so deep, so full, that it penetrates everywhere. It lifts out of Satan's influence those who have been deluded by his deceptions, and places them within reach of the throne of God, the throne encircled by the rainbow of promise. In Christ there is neither Jew nor Greek, bond nor free.

In the years that followed the occupation of the Promised Land, the beneficent designs of Jehovah for the salvation of the heathen were almost wholly lost sight of, and it became necessary for Him to set forth His plan anew. "All the ends of the world," the psalmist was inspired to sing, "shall remember and turn unto the Lord: and all the kindreds of the nations shall worship before Thee." "Princes shall come out of Egypt; Ethiopia shall soon stretch out her hands unto God." "The heathen shall fear the name of the Lord, and all the kings of the earth Thy glory." "This shall be written for the generation to come: and the people which shall be created shall praise the Lord. For He hath looked down from the height of His sanctuary; from heaven did the Lord behold the earth; to hear the groaning of the prisoner; to loose those that are appointed to death; to declare the name of the Lord in Zion, and His praise in Jerusalem; when the people are gathered together, and the kingdoms, to serve the Lord." Psalm 22:27; 68:31; Psalm 102:15, 18-22. [371]

Had Israel been true to her trust, all the nations of earth would have shared in her blessings. But the hearts of those to whom had been entrusted a knowledge of saving truth, were untouched by the needs of those around them. As God's purpose was lost sight of, the heathen came to be looked upon as beyond the pale of His mercy. The light of truth was withheld, and darkness prevailed. The nations were overspread with a veil of ignorance; the love of God was little known; error and superstition flourished.

Such was the prospect that greeted Isaiah when he was called to the prophetic mission; yet he was not discouraged, for ringing in his ears was the triumphal chorus of the angels surrounding the throne of God, "The whole earth is full of His glory." Isaiah 6:3. And his faith was strengthened by visions of glorious conquests by the church of God, when "the earth shall be full of the knowledge of the Lord, as the waters cover the sea." Isaiah 11:9. "The face of the covering cast over all people, and the veil that is spread over all nations," was finally to be destroyed. Isaiah 25:7. The Spirit of God was to be poured out upon all flesh. Those who hunger and thirst after righteousness were to be numbered among the Israel of God. "They shall spring up as among the grass, as willows by the watercourses," said the prophet. "One shall say, I am the Lord's; and another shall call himself by the name of Jacob; and another shall subscribe with his hand unto the Lord, and surname himself by the name of Israel." Isaiah 44:4, 5.

To the prophet was given a revelation of the beneficent design of God in scattering impenitent Judah among the [372] nations of earth. "My people shall know My name," the Lord declared; "they shall know in that day that I am He that doth speak." Isaiah 52:6. And not only were they themselves to learn the lesson of obedience and trust; in their places of exile they were also to impart to others a knowledge of the living God. Many from among the sons of the strangers were to learn to love Him as their Creator and their Redeemer; they were to begin the observance of His holy Sabbath day as a memorial of His creative power; and when He should make "bare His holy arm in the eyes of all the nations," to deliver His people from captivity, "all the ends of the earth" should see of the salvation of God. Verse 10. Many of these converts from heathenism would wish to unite themselves fully with the Israelites and accompany them on the return journey to Judea. None of these were to say, "The Lord hath utterly separated me from His people" (Isaiah 56:3), for the word of God through His prophet to those who should yield themselves to Him and observe His law was that they should thenceforth be numbered among spiritual Israel—His church on earth.

"The sons of the stranger, that join themselves to the Lord, to serve Him, and to love the name of the Lord, to be His servants, everyone that keepeth the Sabbath from polluting it, and taketh hold of My covenant; even them will I bring to My holy mountain, and make them joyful in My house of prayer: their burnt offerings and their sacrifices shall be accepted upon Mine altar; for Mine house shall be called an house of prayer for all people. The Lord God which gathereth the outcasts of Israel saith, Yet will [373] I gather others to Him, beside those that are gathered unto Him." Verses 6-8.

The prophet was permitted to look down the centuries to the time of the advent of the promised Messiah. At first he beheld only "trouble and darkness, dimness of anguish." Isaiah 8:22. Many who were longing for the light of truth were being led astray by false teachers into the bewildering mazes of philosophy and spiritism; others were placing their trust in a form of godliness, but were not bringing true holiness into the life practice. The outlook seemed hopeless; but soon the scene changed, and before the eyes of the prophet was spread a wondrous vision. He saw the Sun of Righteousness arise with healing in His wings; and, lost in admiration, he exclaimed: "The dimness shall not be such as was in her vexation, when at the first He lightly afflicted the land of Zebulun and the land of Naphtali, and afterward did more grievously afflict her by the way of the sea, beyond Jordan, in Galilee of the nations. The people that walked in darkness have seen a great light: they that dwell in the land of the shadow of death, upon them hath the light shined." Isaiah 9:1, 2.

This glorious Light of the world was to bring salvation to every nation, kindred, tongue, and people. Of the work before Him, the prophet heard the eternal Father declare: "It is a light thing that Thou shouldest be My servant to raise up the tribes of Jacob, and to restore the preserved of Israel: I will also give Thee for a light to the Gentiles, that Thou mayest be My salvation unto the end of the earth." "In an acceptable time have I heard Thee, and in a day of [374] salvation have I helped Thee: and I will preserve Thee, and give Thee for a covenant of the people, to establish the earth, to cause to inherit the desolate heritages; that Thou mayest say to the prisoners, Go forth; to them that are in darkness, Show yourselves." "Behold, these shall come from far: and, lo, these from the north and from the west; and these from the land of Sinim." Isaiah 49:6, 8, 9, 12.

Looking on still farther through the ages, the prophet beheld the literal fulfillment of these glorious promises. He saw the bearers of the glad tidings of salvation going to the ends of the earth, to every kindred and people. He heard the Lord saying of the gospel church, "Behold, I will extend peace to her like a river, and the glory of the Gentiles like a flowing stream;" and he heard the commission, "Enlarge the place of thy tent, and let them stretch forth the curtains of thine habitations: spare not, lengthen thy cords, and strengthen thy stakes; for thou shalt break forth on the right hand and on the left; and thy seed shall inherit the Gentiles." Isaiah 66:12; 54:2, 3.

Jehovah declared to the prophet that He would send His witnesses "unto the nations, to Tarshish, Pul, and Lud, ... to Tubal, and Javan, to the isles afar off." Isaiah 66:19.

"How beautiful upon the mountains Are the feet of him that bringeth good tidings, That publisheth peace; That bringeth good tidings of good, That publisheth salvation; That saith unto Zion, Thy God reigneth!"

Isaiah 52:7. [375]

The prophet heard the voice of God calling His church to her appointed work, that the way might be prepared for the ushering in of His everlasting kingdom. The message was unmistakably plain:

"Arise, shine; for thy light is come, And the glory of the Lord is risen upon thee.

"For, behold, the darkness shall cover the earth, And gross darkness the people: But the Lord shall arise upon thee, And His glory shall be seen upon thee. And the Gentiles shall come to thy light, And kings to the brightness of thy rising.

"Lift up thine eyes round about, and see: All they gather themselves together, they come to thee: Thy sons shall come from far, And thy daughters shall be nursed at thy side."

"And the sons of strangers shall build up thy walls, And their kings shall minister unto thee: For in My wrath I smote thee, But in My favor have I had mercy on thee. Therefore thy gates shall be open continually; They shall not be shut day nor night; That men may bring unto thee the forces of the Gentiles, And that their kings may be brought."

"Look unto Me, and be ye saved, all the ends of the earth: For I am God, and there is none else."

Isaiah 60:1-4, 10, 11; 45:22.

These prophecies of a great spiritual awakening in a time of gross darkness are today meeting fulfillment in the advancing lines of mission stations that are reaching out into the benighted regions of earth. The groups of missionaries in heathen lands have been likened by the prophet to ensigns [376] set up for the guidance of those who are looking for the light of truth.

"In that day," says Isaiah, "there shall be a root of Jesse, which shall stand for an ensign of the people; to it shall the Gentiles seek: and His rest shall be glorious. And it shall come to pass in that day, that the Lord shall set His hand again the second time to recover the remnant of His people.... And He shall set up an ensign for the nations, and shall assemble the outcasts of Israel, and gather together the dispersed of Judah from the four corners of the earth." Isaiah 11:10-12.

The day of deliverance is at hand. "The eyes of the Lord run to and fro throughout the whole earth, to show Himself strong in the behalf of them whose heart is perfect toward Him." 2 Chronicles 16:9. Among all nations, kindreds, and tongues, He sees men and women who are praying for light and knowledge. Their souls are unsatisfied; long have they fed on ashes. See Isaiah 44:20. The enemy of all righteousness has turned them aside, and they grope as blind men. But they are honest in heart and desire to learn a better way. Although in the depths of heathenism, with no knowledge of the written law of God nor of His Son Jesus, they have revealed in manifold ways the working of a divine power on mind and character.

At times those who have no knowledge of God aside from that which they have received under the operations of divine grace have been kind to His servants, protecting them at the risk of their own lives. The Holy Spirit is implanting the grace of Christ in the heart of many a noble [377] seeker after truth, quickening his sympathies contrary to his nature, contrary to his former education. The "Light, which lighteth every man that cometh into the world" (John 1:9), is shining in his soul; and this Light, if heeded, will guide his feet to the kingdom of God. The prophet Micah said: "When I sit in darkness, the Lord shall be a light unto me.... He will bring me forth to the light, and I shall behold His righteousness." Micah 7:8, 9.

Heaven's plan of salvation is broad enough to embrace the whole world. God longs to breathe into prostrate humanity the breath of life. And He will not permit any soul to [378] be disappointed who is sincere in his longing for something higher and nobler than anything the world can offer. Constantly He is sending His angels to those who, while surrounded by circumstances the most discouraging, pray in faith for some power higher than themselves to take possession of them and bring deliverance and peace. In various ways God will reveal Himself to them and will place them in touch with providences that will establish their confidence in the One who has given Himself a ransom for all, "that they might set their hope in God, and not forget the works of God, but keep His commandments." Psalm 78:7.

"Shall the prey be taken from the mighty, or the lawful captive delivered?" "Thus saith the Lord, Even the captives of the mighty shall be taken away, and the prey of the terrible shall be delivered." Isaiah 49:24, 25. "They shall be greatly ashamed, that trust in graven images, that say to the molten images, Ye are our gods." Isaiah 42:17.

"Happy is he that hath the God of Jacob for his help, whose hope is in the Lord his God!" Psalm 146:5. "Turn you to the stronghold, ye prisoners of hope!" Zechariah 9:12. Unto all the honest in heart in heathen lands—"the upright" in the sight of Heaven—"there ariseth light in the darkness." Psalm 112:4. God hath spoken: "I will bring the blind by a way that they knew not; I will lead them in paths that they have not known: I will make darkness light before them, and crooked things straight. These things will I do unto them, and not forsake them." Isaiah 42:16. [379]

Chapter 32

Manasseh and Josiah

Beginning of Section 4 — National Retribution

The kingdom of Judah, prosperous throughout the times of Hezekiah, was once more brought low during the long years of Manasseh's wicked reign, when paganism was revived, and many of the people were led into idolatry. "Manasseh made Judah and the inhabitants of Jerusalem to err, and to do worse than the heathen." 2 Chronicles 33:9. The glorious light of former generations was followed by the darkness of superstition and error. Gross evils sprang up and flourished—tyranny, oppression, hatred of all that is good. Justice was perverted; violence prevailed.

Yet those evil times were not without witnesses for God and the right. The trying experiences through which Judah had safely passed during Hezekiah's reign had developed, in the hearts of many, a sturdiness of character that now served as a bulwark against the prevailing iniquity. Their testimony in behalf of truth and righteousness aroused the anger of Manasseh and his associates in authority, who [382] endeavored to establish themselves in evil-doing by silencing every voice of disapproval. "Manasseh shed innocent blood very much, till he had filled Jerusalem from one end to another." 2 Kings 21:16.

One of the first to fall was Isaiah, who for over half a century had stood before Judah as the appointed messenger of Jehovah. "Others had trial of cruel mockings and scourgings, yea, moreover of bonds and imprisonment: they were stoned, they were sawn asunder, were tempted, were slain with the sword: they wandered about in sheepskins and goatskins; being destitute, afflicted, tormented; (of whom the world was not worthy:) they wandered in deserts, and in mountains, and in dens and caves of the earth." Hebrews 11:36-38.

Some of those who suffered persecution during Manasseh's reign were commissioned to bear special messages of reproof and of judgment. The king of Judah, the prophets declared, "hath done wickedly above all ... which were before him." Because of this wickedness, his kingdom was nearing a crisis; soon the inhabitants of the land were to be carried captive to Babylon, there to become "a prey and a spoil to all their enemies." 2 Kings 21:11, 14. But the Lord would not utterly forsake those who in a strange land should acknowledge Him as their Ruler; they might suffer great tribulation, yet He would bring deliverance to them in His appointed time and way. Those who should put their trust wholly in Him would find a sure refuge.

Faithfully the prophets continued their warnings and their exhortations; fearlessly they spoke to Manasseh and [383] to his people; but the messages were scorned; backsliding

Judah would not heed. As an earnest of what would befall the people should they continue impenitent, the Lord permitted their king to be captured by a band of Assyrian soldiers, who "bound him with fetters, and carried him to Babylon," their temporary capital. This affliction brought the king to his senses; "he besought the Lord his God, and humbled himself greatly before the God of his fathers, and prayed unto Him: and He was entreated of him, and heard his supplication, and brought him again to Jerusalem into his kingdom. Then Manasseh knew that the Lord He was God." 2 Chronicles 33:11-13. But this repentance, remarkable though it was, came too late to save the kingdom from the corrupting influence of years of idolatrous practices. Many had stumbled and fallen, never again to rise.

Among those whose life experience had been shaped beyond recall by the fatal apostasy of Manasseh, was his own son, who came to the throne at the age of twenty-two. Of King Amon it is written: "He walked in all the way that his father walked in, and served the idols that his father served, and worshiped them: and he forsook the Lord God of his fathers" (2 Kings 21:21, 22); he "humbled not himself before the Lord, as Manasseh his father had humbled himself; but Amon trespassed more and more." The wicked king was not permitted to reign long. In the midst of his daring impiety, only two years from the time he ascended the throne, he was slain in the palace by his own servants; and "the people of the land made Josiah his son king in his stead." 2 Chronicles 33:23, 25. [384]

With the accession of Josiah to the throne, where he was to rule for thirty-one years, those who had maintained the purity of their faith began to hope that the downward course of the kingdom was checked; for the new king, though only eight years old, feared God, and from the very beginning "he did that which was right in the sight of the Lord, and walked in all the way of David his father, and turned not aside to the right hand or to the left." 2 Kings 22:2. Born of a wicked king, beset with temptations to follow in his father's steps, and with few counselors to encourage him in the right way, Josiah nevertheless was true to the God of Israel. Warned by the errors of past generations, he chose to do right, instead of descending to the low level of sin and degradation to which his father and his grandfather had fallen. He "turned not aside to the right hand or to the left." As one who was to occupy a position of trust, he resolved to obey the instruction that had been given for the guidance of Israel's rulers, and his obedience made it possible for God to use him as a vessel unto honor.

At the time Josiah began to rule, and for many years before, the truehearted in Judah were questioning whether God's promises to ancient Israel could ever be fulfilled. From a human point of view the divine purpose for the chosen nation seemed almost impossible of accomplishment. The apostasy of former centuries had gathered strength with the passing years; ten of the tribes had been scattered among the heathen; only the tribes of Judah and Benjamin remained, and even these now seemed on the verge of [385] moral and national ruin. The prophets had begun to foretell the utter destruction of their fair city, where stood the temple built by Solomon, and where all their earthly hopes of national greatness had centered. Could it be that God was about to turn aside from His avowed purpose of bringing deliverance to those who should put their trust in Him? In the face of the long-continued persecution of the righteous, and of the apparent prosperity of the wicked, could those who had remained true to God hope for better days?

These anxious questionings were voiced by the prophet Habakkuk. Viewing the situation of the faithful in his day, he expressed the burden of his heart in the inquiry: "O Lord, how long shall I cry, and Thou wilt not hear! even cry out unto Thee of violence, and Thou wilt not save! Why dost Thou show me iniquity, and cause me to behold grievance? for spoiling and violence are before me: and there are that raise up strife and contention. Therefore the law is slacked, and judgment doth never go forth: for the wicked doth compass about the righteous; therefore wrong judgment proceedeth." Habakkuk 1:2-4.

God answered the cry of His loyal children. Through His chosen mouthpiece He revealed His determination to bring chastisement upon the nation that had turned from Him to serve the gods of the heathen. Within the lifetime of some who were even then making inquiry regarding the future, He would miraculously shape the affairs of the ruling nations of earth and bring the Babylonians into the ascendancy. These Chaldeans, "terrible and dreadful," were to fall suddenly upon the land of Judah as a divinely [386] appointed scourge. Verse 7. The princes of Judah and the fairest of the people were to be carried captive to Babylon; the Judean cities and villages and the cultivated fields were to be laid waste; nothing was to be spared.

Confident that even in this terrible judgment the purpose of God for His people would in some way be fulfilled, Habakkuk bowed in submission to the revealed will of Jehovah. "Art Thou not from everlasting, O Lord my God, mine Holy One?" he exclaimed. And then, his faith reaching out beyond the forbidding prospect of the immediate future, and laying fast hold on the precious promises that reveal God's love for His trusting children, the prophet added, "We shall not die." Verse 12. With this declaration of faith he rested his case, and that of every believing Israelite, in the hands of a compassionate God.

This was not Habakkuk's only experience in the exercise of strong faith. On one occasion, when meditating concerning the future, he said, "I will stand upon my watch, and set me upon the tower, and will watch to see what He will say unto me." Graciously the Lord answered him: "Write the vision, and make it plain upon tables, that he may run that readeth it. For the vision is yet for an appointed time, but at the end it shall speak, and not lie: though it tarry, wait for it; because it will surely come, it will not tarry. Behold, his soul which is lifted up is not upright in him: but the just shall live by his faith." Habakkuk 2:1-4.

The faith that strengthened Habakkuk and all the holy and the just in those days of deep trial was the same faith that sustains God's people today. In the darkest hours, under circumstances the most forbidding, the Christian believer [387] may keep his soul stayed upon the source of all light and power. Day by day, through faith in God, his hope and courage may be renewed. "The just shall live by his faith." In the service of God there need be no despondency, no wavering, no fear. The Lord will more than fulfill the highest expectations of those who put their trust in Him. He will give them the wisdom their varied necessities demand.

Of the abundant provision made for every tempted soul, the apostle Paul bears eloquent testimony. To him was given the divine assurance, "My grace is sufficient for thee: for My strength is made perfect in weakness." In gratitude and confidence the tried servant of God responded: "Most gladly therefore will I rather glory in my infirmities, that the power of Christ may rest upon me. Therefore I take pleasure in infirmities, in reproaches, in necessities, in persecutions, in distresses for Christ's sake: for when I am weak, then am I strong." 2 Corinthians 12:9, 10.

We must cherish and cultivate the faith of which prophets and apostles have testified—the faith that lays hold on the promises of God and waits for deliverance in His appointed time and way. The sure word of prophecy will meet its final fulfillment in the glorious advent of our Lord and Saviour Jesus Christ, as King of kings and Lord of lords. The time of waiting may seem long, the soul may be oppressed by discouraging circumstances, many in whom confidence has been placed may fall by the way; but with the prophet who endeavored to encourage Judah in a time of unparalleled apostasy, let us confidently declare, "The Lord is in His holy temple: let all the earth keep silence [388] before Him." Habakkuk 2:20. Let us ever hold in remembrance the cheering message, "The vision is yet for an appointed time, but at the end it shall speak, and not lie: though it tarry, wait for it; because it will surely come, it will not tarry.... The just shall live by his faith." Verses 3, 4.

"O Lord, revive Thy work in the midst of the years, In the midst of the years make known; In wrath remember mercy.

"God came from Teman, And the Holy One from Mount Paran. His glory covered the heavens, And the earth was full of His praise. And His brightness was as the light; He had bright beams out of His side: And there was the hiding of His power. Before Him went the pestilence, And burning coals went forth at His feet. He stood, and measured the earth: He beheld, and drove asunder the nations; And the everlasting mountains were scattered, The perpetual hills did bow: His ways are everlasting."

"Thou wentest forth for the salvation of Thy people, Even for salvation with Thine anointed."

"Although the fig tree shall not blossom, Neither shall fruit be in the vines; The labor of the olive shall fail, And the fields shall yield no meat; The flock shall be cut off from the fold, And there shall be no herd in the stalls: Yet I will rejoice in the Lord, I will joy in the God of my salvation. The Lord God is my strength."

Habakkuk 3:2-6, 13, 17-19, margin. [389]

Habakkuk was not the only one through whom was given a message of bright hope and of future triumph as well as of present judgment. During the reign of Josiah the word of the Lord came to Zephaniah, specifying plainly the results of continued apostasy, and calling the attention of the true church to the glorious prospect beyond. His prophecies of impending judgment upon Judah apply with equal force to the judgments that are to fall upon an impenitent world at the time of the second advent of Christ: [390]

"The great day of the Lord is near, It is near, and hasteth greatly, Even the voice of the day of the Lord: The mighty man shall cry there bitterly.

"That day is a day of wrath, A day of trouble and distress, A day of wasteness and desolation, A day of darkness and gloominess,

"A day of clouds and thick darkness, A day of the trumpet and alarm Against the fenced cities, And against the high towers."

Zephaniah 1:14-16.

"I will bring distress upon men, that they shall walk like blind men, because they have sinned against the Lord: and their blood shall be poured out as dust.... Neither their silver nor their gold shall be able to deliver them in the day of the Lord's wrath: but the whole land shall be devoured by the fire of His jealousy: for He shall make even a speedy riddance of all them that dwell in the land." Verses 17, 18.

"Gather yourselves together, yea, gather together, O nation not desired; Before the decree bring forth, Before the day pass as the chaff, Before the fierce anger of the Lord come upon you, Before the day of the Lord's anger come upon you.

"Seek ye the Lord, all ye meek of the earth, Which have wrought His judgment; Seek righteousness, Seek meekness: It may be ye shall be hid In the day of the Lord's anger."

Zephaniah 2:1-3. [391]

"Behold, at that time I will deal with all them that afflict thee: and I will save her that halteth, and gather her that was driven away; and I will make them a praise and a name, whose shame hath been in all the earth. At that time will I bring you in, and at that time will I gather you: for I will make you a name and a praise among all the peoples of the earth, when I bring again your captivity before your eyes, saith the Lord." Zephaniah 3:19, 20, R.V.

"Sing, O daughter of Zion; shout, O Israel; Be glad and rejoice with all the heart, O daughter of Jerusalem. The Lord hath taken away thy judgments, He hath cast out thine enemy: The King of Israel, even the Lord, Is in the midst of thee: Thou shalt not see evil any more.

"In that day it shall be said to Jerusalem, Fear thou not: And to Zion, Let not thine hands be slack. The Lord thy God in the midst of thee Is mighty; He will save, He will rejoice over thee with joy; He will rest in His love, He will joy over thee with singing."

Verses 14-17. [392]

Chapter 33

The Book of the Law

The silent yet powerful influences set in operation by the messages of the prophets regarding the Babylonian Captivity did much to prepare the way for a reformation that took place in the eighteenth year of Josiah's reign. This reform movement, by which threatened judgments were averted for a season, was brought about in a wholly unexpected manner through the discovery and study of a portion of Holy Scripture that for many years had been strangely misplaced and lost.

Nearly a century before, during the first Passover celebrated by Hezekiah, provision had been made for the daily public reading of the book of the law to the people by teaching priests. It was the observance of the statutes recorded by Moses, especially those given in the book of the covenant, which forms a part of Deuteronomy, that had made the reign of Hezekiah so prosperous. But Manasseh had dared set aside these statutes; and during his reign the temple [393] copy of the book of the law, through careless neglect, had become lost. Thus for many years the people generally were deprived of its instruction.

The long-lost manuscript was found in the temple by Hilkiah, the high priest, while the building was undergoing extensive repairs in harmony with King Josiah's plan for the preservation of the sacred structure. The high priest handed the precious volume to Shaphan, a learned scribe, who read it and then took it to the king with the story of its discovery.

Josiah was deeply stirred as he heard read for the first time the exhortations and warnings recorded in this ancient manuscript. Never before had he realized so fully the plainness with which God had set before Israel "life and death, blessing and cursing" (Deuteronomy 30:19): and how repeatedly they had been urged to choose the way of life, that they might become a praise in the earth, a blessing to all nations. "Be strong and of a good courage, fear not, nor be afraid," Israel had been exhorted through Moses; "for the Lord thy God. He it is that doth go with thee; He will not fail thee, not forsake thee." Deuteronomy 31:6.

The book abounded in assurances of God's willingness to save to the uttermost those who should place their trust fully in Him. As He had wrought in their deliverance from Egyptian bondage, so would He work mightily in establishing them in the Land of Promise and in placing them at the head of the nations of earth.

The encouragements offered as the reward of obedience were accompanied by prophecies of judgments against the disobedient; and as the king heard the inspired words, he [394] recognized, in the picture set before him, conditions that were similar to those actually existing in his kingdom. In connection with these prophetic portrayals of departure from

God, he was startled to find plain statements to the effect that the day of calamity would follow swiftly and that there would be no remedy. The language was plain; there could be no mistaking the meaning of the words. And at the close of the volume, in a summary of God's dealings with Israel and a rehearsal of the events of the future, these matters were made doubly plain. In the hearing of all Israel, Moses had declared:

"Give ear, O ye heavens, and I will speak; And hear, O earth, the words of my mouth. My doctrine shall drop as the rain, My speech shall distil as the dew, As the small rain upon the tender herb, And as the showers upon the grass: Because I will publish the name of the Lord: Ascribe ye greatness unto our God. He is the Rock, His work is perfect: For all His ways are judgment: A God of truth and without iniquity, Just and right is He."

Deuteronomy 32:1-4.

"Remember the days of old, Consider the years of many generations: Ask thy father, and he will show thee; Thy elders, and they will tell thee. When the Most High divided to the nations their inheritance, When He separated the sons of Adam, He set the bounds of the people According to the number of the children of Israel. For the Lord's portion is His people; Jacob is the lot of His inheritance. [395]

He found him in a desert land, And in the waste howling wilderness; He led him about, He instructed him, He kept him as the apple of His eye."

Verses 7-10.

But Israel "forsook God which made him, And lightly esteemed the Rock of his salvation. They provoked Him to jealousy with strange gods, With abominations provoked they Him to anger. They sacrificed unto devils, not to God; To gods whom they knew not, To new gods that came newly up, Whom your fathers feared not. Of the Rock that begat thee thou art unmindful, And hast forgotten God that formed thee.

"And when the Lord saw it, He abhorred them, Because of the provoking of His sons, and of His daughters. And He said, I will hide My face from them, I will see what their end shall be: For they are a very froward generation, Children in whom is no faith. They have moved Me to jealousy with that which is not God; They have provoked Me to anger with their vanities: And I will move them to jealousy with those which are not a people; I will provoke them to anger with a foolish nation."

"I will heap mischiefs upon them; I will spend Mine arrows upon them. They shall be burnt with hunger, and devoured with burning heat, And with bitter destruction."

"For they are a nation void of counsel, Neither is there any understanding in them. O that they were wise, that they understood this, That they would consider their latter end! [396]

How should one chase a thousand, And two put ten thousand to flight, Except their Rock had sold them, And the Lord had shut them up? For their rock is not as our Rock, Even our enemies themselves being judges."

"Is not this laid up in store with Me, And sealed up among My treasures? To Me belongeth vengeance, and recompense; Their foot shall slide in due time: For the day of their calamity is at hand, And the things that shall come upon them make haste."

Verses 15-21, 23, 24, 28-31, 34, 35.

These and similar passages revealed to Josiah God's love for His people and His abhorrence of sin. As the king read the prophecies of swift judgment upon those who should persist in rebellion, he trembled for the future. The perversity of Judah had been great; what was to be the outcome of their continued apostasy?

In former years the king had not been indifferent to the prevailing idolatry. "In the eighth year of his reign, while he was yet young," he had consecrated himself fully to the service of God. Four years later, at the age of twenty, he had made an earnest effort to remove temptation from his subjects by purging "Judah and Jerusalem from the high places, and the groves, and the carved images, and the molten images." "They brake down the altars of Baalim in his presence; and the images, that were on high above them, he cut down; and the groves, and the carved images, and the molten images, he brake in pieces, and made dust of them, and strowed it upon the graves of them that had sacrificed unto them. And he burnt the bones of the priests [397] upon their altars, and cleansed Judah and Jerusalem." 2 Chronicles 34:3-5.

Not content with doing thorough work in the land of Judah, the youthful ruler had extended his efforts to the portions of Palestine formerly occupied by the ten tribes of Israel, only a feeble remnant of which now remained. "So did he," the record reads, "in the cities of Manasseh, and Ephraim, and Simeon, even unto Naphtali." Not until he had traversed the length and breadth of this region of ruined homes, and "had broken down the altars and the [398] groves, and had beaten the graven images into powder, and cut down all the idols throughout all the land of Israel," did he return to Jerusalem. Verses 6, 7.

Thus Josiah, from his earliest manhood, had endeavored to take advantage of his position as king to exalt the principles of God's holy law. And now, while Shaphan the scribe was reading to him out of the book of the law, the king discerned in this volume a treasure of knowledge, a powerful ally, in the work of reform he so much desired to see wrought in the land. He resolved to walk in the light of its counsels, and also to do all in his power to acquaint his people with its teachings and to lead them, if possible, to cultivate reverence and love for the law of heaven.

But was it possible to bring about the needed reform? Israel had almost reached the limit of divine forbearance; soon God would arise to punish those who had brought dishonor upon His name. Already the anger of the Lord was kindled against the people. Overwhelmed with sorrow and dismay, Josiah rent his garments and bowed before God in agony of spirit, seeking pardon for the sins of an impenitent nation.

At that time the prophetess Huldah was living in Jerusalem, near the temple. The mind of the king, filled with anxious foreboding, reverted to her, and he determined to inquire of the Lord through this chosen messenger to learn, if possible, whether by any means within his power he might save erring Judah, now on the verge of ruin.

The gravity of the situation and the respect in which he held the prophetess led him to choose as his messengers to her the first men of the kingdom. "Go ye," he bade them, [399] "inquire of the Lord for me, and for the people, and for all Judah, concerning the words of this book that is found: for great is the wrath of the Lord that is kindled against us, because our fathers have not hearkened unto the words of this book, to do according unto all that which is written concerning us." 2 Kings 22:13.

Through Huldah the Lord sent Josiah word that Jerusalem's ruin could not be averted. Even should the people now humble themselves before God, they could not escape their punishment. So long had their senses been deadened by wrongdoing that, if judgment should not come upon them, they would soon return to the same sinful course. "Tell the man that sent you to me," the prophetess declared, "Thus saith the Lord, Behold, I will bring evil upon this place, and upon the inhabitants thereof, even all the words of the book which the king of Judah hath read: because they have forsaken Me, and have burned incense unto other gods, that they might provoke Me to anger with all the works of their hands; therefore My wrath shall be kindled against this place, and shall not be quenched." Verses 15-17.

But because the king had humbled his heart before God, the Lord would acknowledge his promptness in seeking forgiveness and mercy. To him was sent the message: "Because thine heart was tender, and thou hast humbled thyself before the Lord, when thou heardest what I spake against this place, and against the inhabitants thereof, that they should become a desolation and a curse, and hast rent thy clothes, and wept before Me; I also have heard thee, saith the Lord. Behold therefore, I will gather thee unto thy fathers, and thou shalt be gathered into thy grave in [400] peace; and thine eyes shall not see all the evil which I will bring upon this place." Verses 19, 20.

The king must leave with God the events of the future; he could not alter the eternal decrees of Jehovah. But in announcing the retributive judgments of Heaven, the Lord had not withdrawn opportunity for repentance and reformation; and Josiah, discerning in this a willingness on the part of God to temper His judgments with mercy, determined to do all in his power to bring about decided reforms. He arranged at once for a great convocation, to which were invited the elders and magistrates in Jerusalem and Judah, together with the common people. These, with the priests and Levites, met the king in the court of the temple.

To this vast assembly the king himself read "all the words of the book of the covenant which was found in the house of the Lord." 2 Kings 23:2. The royal reader was deeply affected, and he delivered his message with the pathos of a broken heart. His hearers were profoundly moved. The intensity of feeling revealed in the countenance of the king, the solemnity of the message itself, the warning of judgments impending—all these had their effect, and many determined to join with the king in seeking forgiveness.

Josiah now proposed that those highest in authority unite with the people in solemnly covenanting before God to co-operate with one another in an effort to institute decided changes. "The king stood by a pillar, and made a covenant before the Lord, to walk after the Lord, and to keep His [401] commandments and His testimonies and His statutes with all their heart and all their soul, to perform the words of this covenant that were written in this book." The response was more hearty than the king had dared hope for: "All the people stood to the covenant." Verse 3.

In the reformation that followed, the king turned his attention to the destruction of every vestige of idolatry that remained. So long had the inhabitants of the land followed the customs of the surrounding nations in bowing down to images of wood and stone, that it seemed almost beyond the power of man to remove every trace of these evils. But Josiah persevered in his effort to cleanse the land. Sternly he met idolatry by slaying "all the priests of the high places;" "moreover the workers with familiar spirits, and the wizards, and the images, and the idols, and all the abominations that were spied in the land of Judah and in Jerusalem, did Josiah put away, that he might perform the words of the law which were written in the book that Hilkiah the priest found in the house of the Lord." Verses 20, 24.

In the days of the rending of the kingdom, centuries before, when Jeroboam the son of Nebat, in bold defiance of the God whom Israel had served, was endeavoring to turn the hearts of the people away from the services of the temple in Jerusalem to new forms of worship, he had set up an unconsecrated altar at Bethel. During the dedication of this altar, where many in years to come were to be seduced into idolatrous practices, there had suddenly appeared a man of God from Judea, with words of condemnation for the sacrilegious proceedings. He had "cried against the altar," declaring: [402]

"O altar, altar, thus saith the Lord; Behold, a child shall be born unto the house of David, Josiah by name; and upon thee shall he offer the priests of the high places that burn incense upon thee, and men's bones shall be burnt upon thee." 1 Kings 13:2. This announcement had been accompanied by a sign that the word spoken was of the Lord.

Three centuries had passed. During the reformation wrought by Josiah, the king found himself in Bethel, where stood this ancient altar. The prophecy uttered so many years before in the presence of Jeroboam, was now to be literally fulfilled.

"The altar that was at Bethel, and the high place which Jeroboam the son of Nebat, who made Israel to sin, had made, both that altar and the high place he brake down, and burned the high place, and stamped it small to powder, and burned the grove.

"And as Josiah turned himself, he spied the sepulchers that were there in the mount, and sent, and took the bones out of the sepulchers, and burned them upon the altar, and polluted it, according to the word of the Lord which the man of God proclaimed, who proclaimed these words.

"Then he said, What title is that that I see? And the men of the city told him, It is the sepulcher of the man of God, which came from Judah, and proclaimed these things that thou hast done against the altar of Bethel. And he said, Let him alone; let no man move his bones. So they let his bones alone, with the bones of the prophet that came out of Samaria." 2 Kings 23:15-18.

On the southern slopes of Olivet, opposite the beautiful temple of Jehovah on Mount Moriah, were the shrines and [403] [404] [405] images that had been placed there by Solomon to please his idolatrous wives. See 1 Kings 11:6-8. For upwards of three centuries the great, misshapen images had stood on the "Mount of Offense," mute witnesses to the apostasy of Israel's wisest king. These, too, were removed and destroyed by Josiah.

The king sought further to establish the faith of Judah in the God of their fathers by holding a great Passover feast, in harmony with the provisions made in the book of the law. Preparation was made by those having the sacred services in charge, and on the great day of the feast, offerings were freely made. "There was not holden such a Passover from the days of the judges that judged Israel, nor in all the days of the kings of Israel, nor of the kings of Judah." 2 Kings 23:22. But the zeal of Josiah, acceptable though it was to God, could not atone for the sins of past generations; nor could the piety displayed by the king's followers effect a change of heart in many who stubbornly refused to turn from idolatry to the worship of the true God.

For more than a decade following the celebration of the Passover, Josiah continued to reign. At the age of thirty-nine he met death in battle with the forces of Egypt, "and was buried in one of the sepulchers of his fathers." "All Judah and Jerusalem mourned for Josiah. And Jeremiah lamented for Josiah: and all the singing men and the singing women spake of Josiah in their lamentations to this day, and made them an ordinance in Israel: and, behold, they are written in the lamentations." 2 Chronicles 35:24, 25. Like unto Josiah "was there no king before him, [406] that turned to the Lord with all his heart, and with all his soul, and with all his might, according to all the law of Moses; neither after him arose there any like him. Notwithstanding the Lord turned not from the fierceness of His great wrath, ... because of all the provocations that Manasseh had provoked Him withal." 2 Kings 23:25, 26. The time was rapidly approaching when Jerusalem was to be utterly destroyed and the inhabitants of the land carried captive to Babylon, there to learn the lessons they had refused to learn under circumstances more favorable. [407]

Chapter 34

Jeremiah

Among those who had hoped for a permanent spiritual revival as the result of the reformation under Josiah was Jeremiah, called of God to the prophetic office while still a youth, in the thirteenth year of Josiah's reign. A member of the Levitical priesthood, Jeremiah had been trained from childhood for holy service. In those happy years of preparation he little realized that he had been ordained from birth to be "a prophet unto the nations;" and when the divine call came, he was overwhelmed with a sense of his unworthiness. "Ah, Lord God!" he exclaimed, "behold, I cannot speak: for I am a child." Jeremiah 1:5, 6.

In the youthful Jeremiah, God saw one who would be true to his trust and who would stand for the right against great opposition. In childhood he had proved faithful; and now he was to endure hardness, as a good soldier of the cross. "Say not, I am a child," the Lord bade His chosen messenger; "for thou shalt go to all that I shall send thee, and whatsoever I command thee thou shalt speak. Be not [408] afraid of their faces: for I am with thee to deliver thee." "Gird up thy loins, and arise, and speak unto them all that I command thee: be not dismayed at their faces, lest I confound thee before them. For, behold, I have made thee this day a defensed city, and an iron pillar, and brazen walls against the whole land, against the kings of Judah, against the princes thereof, against the priests thereof, and against the people of the land. And they shall fight against thee; but they shall not prevail against thee; for I am with thee, saith the Lord, to deliver thee." Verses 7, 8, 17-19.

For forty years Jeremiah was to stand before the nation as a witness for truth and righteousness. In a time of unparalleled apostasy he was to exemplify in life and character the worship of the only true God. During the terrible sieges of Jerusalem he was to be the mouthpiece of Jehovah. He was to predict the downfall of the house of David and the destruction of the beautiful temple built by Solomon. And when imprisoned because of his fearless utterances, he was still to speak plainly against sin in high places. Despised, hated, rejected of men, he was finally to witness the literal fulfillment of his own prophecies of impending doom, and share in the sorrow and woe that should follow the destruction of the fated city.

Yet amid the general ruin into which the nation was rapidly passing, Jeremiah was often permitted to look beyond the distressing scenes of the present to the glorious prospects of the future, when God's people should be ransomed from the land of the enemy and planted again in Zion. He foresaw the time when the Lord would renew His covenant relationship with them. "Their soul shall be as a watered [409] garden; and they shall not sorrow any more at all." Jeremiah 31:12.

Of his call to the prophetic mission, Jeremiah himself wrote: "The Lord put forth His hand, and touched my mouth. And the Lord said unto me, Behold, I have put My words in thy mouth. See, I have this day set thee over the nations and over the kingdoms, to root out, and to pull down, and to destroy, and to throw down, to build, and to plant." Jeremiah 1:9, 10.

Thank God for the words, "to build, and to plant." By these words Jeremiah was assured of the Lord's purpose to restore and to heal. Stern were the messages to be borne in the years that were to follow. Prophecies of swift-coming judgments were to be fearlessly delivered. From the plains of Shinar "an evil" was to "break forth upon all the inhabitants of the land." "I will utter My judgments against them," the Lord declared, "touching all their wickedness, who have forsaken Me." Verses 14, 16. Yet the prophet was to accompany these messages with assurances of forgiveness to all who should turn from their evil-doing.

As a wise master builder, Jeremiah at the very beginning of his lifework sought to encourage the men of Judah to lay the foundations of their spiritual life broad and deep, by making thorough work of repentance. Long had they been building with material likened by the apostle Paul to wood, hay, and stubble, and by Jeremiah himself to dross. "Refuse silver shall men call them," he declared of the impenitent nation, "because the Lord hath rejected them." Jeremiah 6:30, margin. Now they were urged to begin building wisely and for eternity, casting aside the rubbish [410] of apostasy and unbelief, and using as foundation material the pure gold, the refined silver, the precious stones—faith and obedience and good works—which alone are acceptable in the sight of a holy God.

Through Jeremiah the word of the Lord to His people was: "Return, thou backsliding Israel, ... and I will not cause Mine anger to fall upon you: for I am merciful, saith the Lord, and I will not keep anger forever. Only acknowledge thine iniquity, that thou hast transgressed against the Lord thy God.... Turn, O backsliding children, saith the Lord; for I am married unto you." "Thou shalt call Me, my Father; and shalt not turn away from Me." "Return, ye backsliding children, and I will heal your backslidings." Jeremiah 3:12-14, 19, 22.

And in addition to these wonderful pleadings, the Lord gave His erring people the very words with which they might turn to Him. They were to say: "Behold, we come unto Thee; for Thou art the Lord our God. Truly in vain is salvation hoped for from the hills, and from the multitude of mountains: truly in the Lord our God is the salvation of Israel.... We lie down in our shame, and our confusion covereth us: for we have sinned against the Lord our God, we and our fathers, from our youth even unto this day, and have not obeyed the voice of the Lord our God." Verses 22-25.

The reformation under Josiah had cleansed the land of the idolatrous shrines, but the hearts of the multitude had not been transformed. The seeds of truth that had sprung up and given promise of an abundant harvest had been choked by thorns. Another such backsliding would be [411] fatal; and the Lord sought to arouse the nation to a realization of their danger. Only as they should prove loyal to Jehovah could they hope for the divine favor and for prosperity.

Jeremiah called their attention repeatedly to the counsels given in Deuteronomy. More than any other of the prophets, he emphasized the teachings of the Mosaic law and showed how these might bring the highest spiritual blessing to the nation and to every individual heart. "Ask for the old paths, where is the good way, and walk therein," he pleaded, "and ye shall find rest for your souls." Jeremiah 6:16.

On one occasion, by command of the Lord, the prophet took his position at one of the principal entrances to the city and there urged the importance of keeping holy the Sabbath day. The inhabitants of Jerusalem were in danger of losing sight of the sanctity of the Sabbath, and they were solemnly warned against following their secular pursuits on that day. A blessing was promised on condition of obedience. "If ye diligently hearken unto Me," the Lord declared, and "hallow the Sabbath day, to do no work therein; then shall there enter into the gates of this city kings and princes sitting upon the throne of David, riding in chariots and on horses, they, and their princes, the men of Judah, and the inhabitants of Jerusalem: and this city shall remain forever." Jeremiah 17:24, 25.

This promise of prosperity as the reward of allegiance was accompanied by a prophecy of the terrible judgments that would befall the city should its inhabitants prove disloyal to God and His law. If the admonitions to obey the [412] Lord God of their fathers and to hallow His Sabbath day were not heeded, the city and its palaces would be utterly destroyed by fire.

Thus the prophet stood firmly for the sound principles of right living so clearly outlined in the book of the law. But the conditions prevailing in the land of Judah were such that only by the most decided measures could a change for the better be brought about; therefore he labored most earnestly in behalf of the impenitent. "Break up your fallow ground," he pleaded, "and sow not among thorns." "O Jerusalem, wash thine heart from wickedness, that thou mayest be saved." Jeremiah 4:3, 14.

But by the great mass of the people the call to repentance and reformation was unheeded. Since the death of good King Josiah, those who ruled the nation had been proving untrue to their trust and had been leading many astray. Jehoahaz, deposed by the interference of the king of Egypt, had been followed by Jehoiakim, an older son of Josiah. From the beginning of Jehoiakim's reign, Jeremiah had little hope of saving his beloved land from destruction and the people from captivity. Yet he was not permitted to remain silent while utter ruin threatened the kingdom. Those who had remained loyal to God must be encouraged to persevere in rightdoing, and sinners must, if possible, be induced to turn from iniquity.

The crisis demanded a public and far-reaching effort. Jeremiah was commanded by the Lord to stand in the court of the temple and speak to all the people of Judah who might pass in and out. From the messages given him he must diminish not a word, that sinners in Zion might have the [413] fullest possible opportunity to hearken and to turn from their evil ways.

The prophet obeyed; he stood in the gate of the Lord's house and there lifted his voice in warning and entreaty. Under the inspiration of the Almighty he declared:

"Hear the word of the Lord, all ye of Judah, that enter in at these gates to worship the Lord. Thus saith the Lord of hosts, the God of Israel, Amend your ways and your doings, and I will cause you to dwell in this place. Trust ye not in lying words, saying, The temple of the Lord, The temple of the Lord, The temple of the Lord, are these. For if ye thoroughly amend your ways and your doings; if ye thoroughly execute judgment between a man and his neighbor; if ye oppress not the stranger, the fatherless, and the widow, and shed not innocent blood in this place, neither walk after other gods to your hurt: then will I cause you to dwell in this place, in the land that I gave to your fathers, forever and ever." Jeremiah 7:2-7.

The unwillingness of the Lord to chastise is here vividly shown. He stays His judgments that He may plead with the impenitent. He who exercises "loving-kindness, judgment, and righteousness, in the earth" yearns over His erring children; in every way possible He seeks to teach them the way of life everlasting. Jeremiah 9:24. He had brought the Israelites out of bondage that they might serve Him, the only true and living God. Though they had wandered long in idolatry and had slighted His warnings, yet He now declares His willingness to defer chastisement and grant yet another opportunity for repentance. He makes plain the fact that only by the most thorough heart reformation could [414] the impending doom be averted. In vain would be the trust they might place in the temple and its services. Rites and ceremonies could not atone for sin. Notwithstanding their claim to be the chosen people of God, reformation of heart and of the life practice alone could save them from the inevitable result of continued transgression.

Thus it was that "in the cities of Judah, and in the streets of Jerusalem" the message of Jeremiah to Judah was, "Hear ye the words of this covenant,"—the plain precepts of Jehovah as recorded in the Sacred Scriptures,—"and do them." Jeremiah 11:6. And this is the message he proclaimed as he stood in the temple courts in the beginning of the reign of Jehoiakim.

Israel's experience from the days of the Exodus was briefly reviewed. God's covenant with them had been, "Obey My voice, and I will be your God, and ye shall be My people: and walk ye in all the ways that I have commanded you, that it may be well unto you." Shamelessly and repeatedly had this covenant been broken. The chosen nation had "walked in the counsels and in the imagination of their evil heart, and went backward, and not forward." Jeremiah 7:23, 24.

"Why," the Lord inquired, "is this people of Jerusalem slidden back by a perpetual backsliding?" Jeremiah 8:5. In the language of the prophet it was because they had obeyed not the voice of the Lord their God and had refused to be corrected. See Jeremiah 5:3. "Truth is perished," he mourned, "and is cut off from their mouth." "The stork in the heaven knoweth her appointed times; and the turtle and the crane and the swallow observe the time of their [415] coming; but My people know not the judgment of the Lord." "Shall I not visit them for these things? saith the Lord: shall not My soul be avenged on such a nation as this?" Jeremiah 7:28; 8:7; Jeremiah 9:9.

The time had come for deep heart searching. While Josiah had been their ruler, the people had had some ground for hope. But no longer could he intercede in their behalf, for he had fallen in battle. The sins of the nation were such that the time for intercession had all but passed by. "Though Moses and Samuel stood before Me," the Lord declared, "yet My mind could not be toward this people: cast them out of My sight, and let them go forth. And it shall come to pass, if they say unto thee, Whither shall we go forth? then thou shalt tell them. Thus saith the Lord; Such as are for death, to death; and such as are for the sword, to the sword; and such as are for the famine, to the famine; and such as are for the captivity, to the captivity." Jeremiah 15:1, 2.

A refusal to heed the invitation of mercy that God was now offering would bring upon the impenitent nation the judgments that had befallen the northern kingdom of Israel over a century before. The message to them now was: "If ye will not hearken to Me, to walk in My law, which I have set before you, to hearken to the words of My servants the prophets, whom I sent unto you, both rising up early, and sending them, but ye have not hearkened; then will I make this house like Shiloh, and will make this city a curse to all the nations of the earth." Jeremiah 26:4-6.

Those who stood in the temple court listening to Jeremiah's discourse understood clearly this reference to Shiloh, [416] and to the time in the days of Eli when the Philistines had overcome Israel and carried away the ark of the testament.

The sin of Eli had consisted in passing lightly over the iniquity of his sons in sacred office, and over the evils prevailing throughout the land. His neglect to correct these evils had brought upon Israel a fearful calamity. His sons had fallen in battle, Eli himself had lost his life, the ark of God had been taken from the land of Israel, thirty thousand of the people had been slain—and all because sin had been allowed to flourish unrebuked and unchecked. Israel had vainly thought that, notwithstanding their sinful practices, the presence of the ark would ensure them victory over the Philistines. In like manner, during the days of Jeremiah, the inhabitants of Judah were prone to believe that a strict observance of the divinely appointed services of the temple would preserve them from a just punishment for their wicked course.

What a lesson is this to men holding positions of responsibility today in the church of God! What a solemn warning to deal faithfully with wrongs that bring dishonor to the cause of truth! Let none who claim to be the depositaries of God's law flatter themselves that the regard they may outwardly show toward the commandments will preserve them from the exercise of divine justice. Let none refuse to be reproved for evil, nor charge the servants of God with being too zealous in endeavoring to cleanse the camp from evil-doing. A sin-hating God calls upon those who claim to keep His law to depart from all iniquity. A neglect to repent and to render willing obedience will bring upon men and women today as serious consequences as came [417] upon ancient Israel. There is a limit beyond which the judgments of Jehovah can no longer be delayed. The desolation of Jerusalem in the days of Jeremiah is a solemn warning to modern Israel, that the counsels and admonitions given them through chosen instrumentalities cannot be disregarded with impunity.

Jeremiah's message to priests and people aroused the antagonism of many. With boisterous denunciation they cried out, "Why hast thou prophesied in the name of the Lord, saying, This house shall be like Shiloh, and this city shall be desolate without an inhabitant? And all the people were gathered against Jeremiah in the house of the Lord." Jeremiah 26:9. Priests, false prophets, and people turned in wrath upon him who would not speak to them smooth things or prophesy deceit. Thus was the message of God despised, and His servant threatened with death.

Tidings of the words of Jeremiah were carried to the princes of Judah, and they hastened from the palace of the king to the temple, to learn for themselves the truth of the matter. "Then spake the priests and the prophets unto the princes and to all the people, saying, This man is worthy to die; for he hath prophesied against this city, as ye have heard with your ears." Verse 11. But Jeremiah stood boldly before the princes and the people, declaring: "The Lord sent me to prophesy against this house and against this city all the words that ye have heard. Therefore now amend your ways and your doings, and obey the voice of the Lord your God; and the Lord will repent Him of the evil that He hath pronounced against you. As for me, behold, I am in your hand: do with me as seemeth good and meet unto [418] you. But know ye for certain, that if ye put me to death, ye shall surely bring innocent blood upon yourselves, and upon this city, and upon the inhabitants thereof: for of a truth the Lord hath sent me unto you to speak all these words in your ears." Verses 12-15.

Had the prophet been intimidated by the threatening attitude of those high in authority, his message would have been without effect, and he would have lost his life; but the courage with which he delivered the solemn warning commanded the respect of the people and turned the princes of Israel in his favor. They reasoned with the priests and false prophets, showing them how unwise would be the extreme measures they advocated, and their words produced a reaction in the minds of the people. Thus God raised up defenders for His servant.

The elders also united in protesting against the decision of the priests regarding the fate of Jeremiah. They cited the case of Micah, who had prophesied judgments upon Jerusalem, saying, "Zion shall be plowed like a field, and Jerusalem shall become heaps, and the mountain of the house as the high places of a forest." And they asked: "Did Hezekiah king of Judah and all Judah put him at all to death? did he not fear the Lord, and besought the Lord, and the Lord repented Him of the evil which He had pronounced against them? Thus might we procure great evil against our souls." Verses 18, 19.

Through the pleading of these men of influence the prophet's life was spared, although many of the priests and false prophets, unable to endure the condemning truths he [419] uttered, would gladly have seen him put to death on the plea of sedition.

From the day of his call to the close of his ministry, Jeremiah stood before Judah as "a tower and a fortress" against which the wrath of man could not prevail. "They shall fight against thee," the Lord had forewarned His servant, "but they shall not prevail against thee: for I am with thee to save thee and to deliver thee, saith the Lord. And I will deliver thee out of the hand of the wicked, and I will redeem thee out of the hand of the terrible." Jeremiah 6:27; 15:20, 21.

Naturally of a timid and shrinking disposition, Jeremiah longed for the peace and quiet of a life of retirement, where [420] he need not witness the continued impenitence of his beloved nation. His heart was wrung with anguish over the ruin wrought by sin. "O that my head were waters, and mine eyes a fountain of tears," he mourned, "that I might weep day and night for the slain of the daughter of my people! O that I had in the wilderness a lodging place of wayfaring men; that I might leave my people, and go from them." Jeremiah 9:1, 2.

Cruel were the mockings he was called upon to endure. His sensitive soul was pierced through and through by the arrows of derision hurled at him by those who despised his messages and made light of his burden for their conversion. "I was a derision to all my people," he declared, "and their song all the day." "I am in derision daily, everyone mocketh me." "All my familiars watched for my halting, saying, Peradventure he will be enticed, and we shall prevail against him, and we shall take our revenge on him." Lamentations 3:14; Jeremiah 20:7, 10.

But the faithful prophet was daily strengthened to endure. "The Lord is with me as a mighty terrible One," he declared in faith; "therefore my persecutors shall stumble, and they shall not prevail: they shall be really ashamed; for they shall not prosper: their everlasting confusion shall never be forgotten." "Sing unto the Lord, praise ye the Lord: for He hath delivered the soul of the poor from the hand of evildoers." Jeremiah 20:11, 13.

The experiences through which Jeremiah passed in the days of his youth and also in the later years of his ministry, taught him the lesson that "the way of man is not in [421] himself: it is not in man that walketh to direct his steps." He learned to pray, "O Lord, correct me, but with judgment; not in Thine anger, lest Thou bring me to nothing." Jeremiah 10:23, 24.

When called to drink of the cup of tribulation and sorrow, and when tempted in his misery to say, "My strength and my hope is perished from the Lord," he recalled the providences of God in his behalf and triumphantly exclaimed, "It is of the Lord's mercies that we are not consumed, because His compassions fail not. They are new every morning: great is Thy faithfulness. The Lord is my portion, saith my soul; therefore will I hope in Him. The Lord is good unto them that wait for Him, to the soul that seeketh Him. It is good that a man should both hope and quietly wait for the salvation of the Lord." Lamentations 3:18, 22-26. [422]

Chapter 35

Approaching Doom

The first years of Jehoiakim's reign were filled with warnings of approaching doom. The word of the Lord spoken by the prophets was about to be fulfilled. The Assyrian power to the northward, long supreme, was no longer to rule the nations. Egypt on the south, in whose power the king of Judah was vainly placing his trust, was soon to receive a decided check. All unexpectedly a new world power, the Babylonian Empire, was rising to the eastward and swiftly overshadowing all other nations.

Within a few short years the king of Babylon was to be used as the instrument of God's wrath upon impenitent Judah. Again and again Jerusalem was to be invested and entered by the besieging armies of Nebuchadnezzar. Company after company—at first a few only, but later on thousands and tens of thousands—were to be taken captive to the land of Shinar, there to dwell in enforced exile. Jehoiakim, Jehoiachin, Zedekiah—all these Jewish kings were in turn to become vassals of the Babylonian [423] ruler, and all in turn were to rebel. Severer and yet more severe chastisements were to be inflicted upon the rebellious nation, until at last the entire land was to become a desolation, Jerusalem was to be laid waste and burned with fire, the temple that Solomon had built was to be destroyed, and the kingdom of Judah was to fall, never again to occupy its former position among the nations of earth.

Those times of change, so fraught with peril to the Israelitish nation, were marked with many messages from Heaven through Jeremiah. Thus the Lord gave the children of Judah ample opportunity of freeing themselves from entangling alliances with Egypt, and of avoiding controversy with the rulers of Babylon. As the threatened danger came closer, he taught the people by means of a series of acted parables, hoping thus to arouse them to a sense of their obligation to God, and also to encourage them to maintain friendly relations with the Babylonian government.

To illustrate the importance of yielding implicit obedience to the requirements of God, Jeremiah gathered some Rechabites into one of the chambers of the temple and set wine before them, inviting them to drink. As was to have been expected, he met with remonstrance and absolute refusal. "We will drink no wine," the Rechabites firmly declared, "for Jonadab the son of Rechab our father commanded us, saying, Ye shall drink no wine, neither ye, nor your sons forever."

"Then came the word of the Lord unto Jeremiah, saying, Thus saith the Lord of hosts, the God of Israel; Go and tell the men of Judah and the inhabitants of Jerusalem, [424] Will ye not receive instruction to hearken to My words? saith the Lord. The words of Jonadab the son of Rechab, that he commanded his sons not to drink wine, are performed; for unto this day they drink none, but obey their father's commandment." Jeremiah 35:6, 12-14.

God sought thus to bring into sharp contrast the obedience of the Rechabites with the disobedience and rebellion of His people. The Rechabites had obeyed the command of their father and now refused to be enticed into transgression. But the men of Judah had hearkened not to the words of the Lord, and were in consequence about to suffer His severest judgments.

"I have spoken unto you, rising early and speaking," the Lord declared, "but ye hearkened not unto Me. I have sent also unto you all My servants the prophets, rising up early and sending them, saying, Return ye now every man from his evil way, and amend your doings, and go not after other gods to serve them, and ye shall dwell in the land which I have given to you and to your fathers: but ye have not inclined your ear, nor hearkened unto Me. Because the sons of Jonadab the son of Rechab have performed the commandment of their father, which he commanded them; but this people hath not hearkened unto Me: therefore thus saith the Lord God of hosts, the God of Israel; Behold, I will bring upon Judah and upon all the inhabitants of Jerusalem all the evil that I have pronounced against them: because I have spoken unto them, but they have not heard; and I have called unto them, but they have not answered." Verses 14-17. [425]

When men's hearts are softened and subdued by the constraining influence of the Holy Spirit, they will give heed to counsel; but when they turn from admonition until their hearts become hardened, the Lord permits them to be led by other influences. Refusing the truth, they accept falsehood, which becomes a snare to their own destruction.

God had pleaded with Judah not to provoke Him to anger, but they had hearkened not. Finally sentence was pronounced against them. They were to be led away captive to Babylon. The Chaldeans were to be used as the instrument by which God would chastise His disobedient people. The sufferings of the men of Judah were to be in proportion to the light they had had and to the warnings they had despised and rejected. Long had God delayed His judgments, but now He would visit His displeasure upon them as a last effort to check them in their evil course.

Upon the house of the Rechabites was pronounced a continued blessing. The prophet declared, "Because ye have obeyed the commandment of Jonadab your father, and kept all his precepts, and done according unto all that he hath commanded you: therefore thus saith the Lord of hosts, the God of Israel; Jonadab the son of Rechab shall not want a man to stand before Me forever." Verses 18, 19. Thus God taught His people that faithfulness and obedience would be reflected back upon Judah in blessing, even as the Rechabites were blessed for obedience to their father's command.

The lesson is for us. If the requirements of a good and wise father, who took the best and most effectual means [426] to secure his posterity against the evils of intemperance, were worthy of strict obedience, surely God's authority should be held in as much greater reverence as He is holier than man. Our Creator and our Commander, infinite in power, terrible in judgment, seeks by every means to bring men to see and repent of their sins. By the mouth of His servants He predicts the dangers of disobedience; He sounds the note of warning and faithfully reproves sin. His people are kept in prosperity only by His mercy, through the vigilant watchcare of chosen instrumentalities. He cannot uphold and guard a people who reject His counsel and despise His reproofs. For a time He may withhold His retributive judgments; yet He cannot always stay His hand.

The children of Judah were numbered among those of whom God had declared, "Ye shall be unto Me a kingdom of priests, and an holy nation." Exodus 19:6. Never did Jeremiah in his ministry lose sight of the vital importance of heart holiness in the varied relationships of life, and especially in the service of the most high God. Plainly he foresaw the downfall of the kingdom and a scattering of the inhabitants of Judah among the nations; but with the eye of faith he looked beyond all this to the times of restoration. Ringing in his ears was the divine promise: "I will gather the remnant of My flock out of all countries whither I have driven them, and will bring them again to their folds.... Behold, the days come, saith the Lord, that I will raise unto David a righteous Branch, and a King shall reign and prosper, and shall execute judgment and justice in the earth. In His days Judah shall be saved, and Israel shall [427] dwell safely: and this is His name whereby He shall be called, The Lord Our Righteousness." Jeremiah 23:3-6.

Thus prophecies of oncoming judgment were mingled with promises of final and glorious deliverance. Those who should choose to make their peace with God and live holy lives amid the prevailing apostasy, would receive strength for every trial and be enabled to witness for Him with mighty power. And in the ages to come the deliverance wrought in their behalf would exceed in fame that wrought for the children of Israel at the time of the Exodus. The days were coming, the Lord declared through His prophet, when "they shall no more say, The Lord liveth, which brought up the children of Israel out of the land of Egypt; but, The Lord liveth, which brought up and which led the seed of the house of Israel out of the north country, and from all countries whither I had driven them; and they shall dwell in their own land." Verses 7, 8. Such were the wonderful prophecies uttered by Jeremiah during the closing years of the history of the kingdom of Judah, when the Babylonians were coming unto universal rule, and were even then bringing their besieging armies against the walls of Zion.

Like sweetest music these promises of deliverance fell upon the ears of those who were steadfast in their worship of Jehovah. In the homes of the high and the lowly, where the counsels of a covenant-keeping God were still held in reverence, the words of the prophet were repeated again and again. Even the children were mightily stirred, and upon their young and receptive minds lasting impressions were made. [428]

It was their conscientious observance of the commands of Holy Scripture, that in the days of Jeremiah's ministry brought to Daniel and his fellows opportunities to exalt the true God before the nations of earth. The instruction these Hebrew children had received in the homes of their parents, made them strong in faith and constant in their service of the living God, the Creator of the heavens and the earth. When, early in the reign of Jehoiakim, Nebuchadnezzar for the first time besieged and captured Jerusalem, and carried away Daniel and his companions, with others specially chosen for service in the court of Babylon, the faith of the Hebrew captives was tried to the utmost. But those who had learned to place their trust in the promises of God found these all-sufficient in every experience through which they were called to pass during their sojourn in a strange land. The Scriptures proved to them a guide and a stay.

As an interpreter of the meaning of the judgments beginning to fall upon Judah, Jeremiah stood nobly in defense of the justice of God and of His merciful designs even in the severest chastisements. Untiringly the prophet labored. Desirous of reaching all classes, he extended the sphere of his influence beyond Jerusalem to the surrounding districts by frequent visits to various parts of the kingdom.

In his testimonies to the church, Jeremiah constantly referred to the teachings of the book of the law that had been so greatly honored and exalted during Josiah's reign. He emphasized anew the importance of maintaining a covenant relationship with the all-merciful and compassionate [429] Being who upon the heights of Sinai had spoken the precepts of the Decalogue. Jeremiah's words of warning and entreaty reached every part of the kingdom, and all had opportunity to know the will of God concerning the nation.

The prophet made plain the fact that our heavenly Father allows His judgments to fall, "that the nations may know themselves to be but men." Psalm 9:20. "If ye walk contrary unto Me, and will not hearken unto Me," the Lord had forewarned His people, "I, even I, ... will scatter you among the heathen, and will draw out a sword after you: and your land shall be desolate, and your cities waste." Leviticus 26:21, 28, 33.

At the very time messages of impending doom were urged upon princes and people, their ruler, Jehoiakim, who should have been a wise spiritual leader, foremost in confession of sin and in reformation and good works, was spending his time in selfish pleasure. "I will build me a wide house and large chambers," he proposed; and this house, "ceiled with cedar, and painted with vermilion" (Jeremiah 22:14), was built with money and labor secured through fraud and oppression.

The wrath of the prophet was aroused, and he was inspired to pronounce judgment upon the faithless ruler. "Woe unto him that buildeth his house by unrighteousness, and his chambers by wrong," he declared; "that useth his neighbor's service without wages, and giveth him not for his work.... Shalt thou reign, because thou closest thyself in cedar? Did not thy father eat and drink, and do judgment and justice, and then it was well with him? He [430] judged the cause of the poor and needy; then it was well with him: was not this to know Me? saith the Lord. But thine eyes and thine heart are not but for thy covetousness, and for to shed innocent blood, and for oppression, and for violence, to do it.

"Therefore thus saith the Lord concerning Jehoiakim the son of Josiah king of Judah; They shall not lament for him, saying, Ah my brother! or, Ah sister! they shall not lament for him, saying, Ah lord! or, Ah his glory! He shall be buried with the burial of an ass, drawn and cast forth beyond the gates of Jerusalem." Verses 13-19.

Within a few years this terrible judgment was to be visited upon Jehoiakim; but first the Lord in mercy informed the impenitent nation of His set purpose. In the fourth year of Jehoiakim's reign "Jeremiah the prophet spake unto all the people of Judah, and to all the inhabitants of Jerusalem," pointing out that for over a score of years, "from the thirteenth year of Josiah, ... even unto this day," he had borne witness of God's desire to save, but that His messages had been despised. Jeremiah 25:2, 3. And now the word of the Lord to them was:

"Thus saith the Lord of hosts; Because ye have not heard My words, behold, I will send and take all the families of the north, saith the Lord, and Nebuchadnezzar the king of Babylon, My servant, and will bring them against this land, and against the inhabitants thereof, and against all these nations round about, and will utterly destroy them, and make them an astonishment, and an hissing, and perpetual desolations. Moreover I will take from them [431] the voice of mirth, and the voice of gladness, the voice of the bridegroom, and the voice of the bride, the sound of the millstones, and the light of the candle. And this whole land shall be a desolation, and an astonishment; and these nations shall serve the king of Babylon seventy years." Verses 8-11.

Although the sentence of doom had been clearly pronounced, its awful import could scarcely be understood by the multitudes who heard. That deeper impressions might be made, the Lord sought to illustrate the meaning of the words spoken. He bade Jeremiah liken the fate of the nation to the draining of a cup filled with the wine of divine wrath. Among the first to drink of this cup of woe was to be "Jerusalem, and the cities of Judah, and the kings thereof." Others were to partake of the same cup—"Pharaoh king of Egypt, and his servants, and his princes, and all his people," and many other nations of earth—until God's purpose should have been fulfilled. See Jeremiah 25.

To illustrate further the nature of the swift-coming judgments, the prophet was bidden to "take of the ancients of the people, and of the ancients of the priests; and go forth unto the valley of the son of Hinnom," and there, after reviewing the apostasy of Judah, he was to dash to pieces "a potter's earthen bottle," and declare in behalf of Jehovah, whose servant he was, "Even so will I break this people and this city, as one breaketh a potter's vessel, that cannot be made whole again."

The prophet did as he was commanded. Then, returning to the city, he stood in the court of the temple and declared [432] in the hearing of all the people, "Thus saith the Lord of hosts, the God of Israel; Behold, I will bring upon this city and upon all her towns all the evil that I have pronounced against it, because they have hardened their necks, that they might not hear My words." See Jeremiah 19.

The prophet's words, instead of leading to confession and repentance, aroused the anger of those high in authority, and as a consequence Jeremiah was deprived of his liberty. Imprisoned, and placed in the stocks, the prophet nevertheless continued to speak the messages of Heaven to those who stood by. His voice could not be silenced by persecution. The word of truth, he declared, "was in mine heart as a burning fire shut up in my bones, and I was weary with forbearing, and I could not stay." Jeremiah 20:9.

It was about this time that the Lord commanded Jeremiah to commit to writing the messages He desired to bear to those for whose salvation His heart of pity was continually yearning. "Take thee a roll of a book," the Lord bade His servant, "and write therein all the words that I have spoken unto thee against Israel, and against Judah, and against all the nations, from the day I spake unto thee, from the days of Josiah, even unto this day. It may be that the house of Judah will hear all the evil which I purpose to do unto them; that they may return every man from his evil way; that I may forgive their iniquity and their sin." Jeremiah 36:2, 3.

In obedience to this command, Jeremiah called to his aid a faithful friend, Baruch the scribe, and dictated "all the words of the Lord, which He had spoken unto him." [433] Verse 4. These were carefully written out on a roll of parchment and constituted a solemn reproof for sin, a warning of the sure result of continual apostasy, and an earnest appeal for the renunciation of all evil.

When the writing was completed, Jeremiah, who was still a prisoner, sent Baruch to read the roll to the multitudes who were assembling at the temple on the occasion of a national fast day, "in the fifth year of Jehoiakim the son of Josiah king of Judah, in the ninth month." "It may be," the prophet said, "they will present their supplication before the Lord, and will return everyone from his evil way: for great is the anger and the fury that the Lord hath pronounced against this people." Verses 9, 7.

Baruch obeyed, and the roll was read before all the people of Judah. Afterward the scribe was summoned before the princes to read the words to them. They listened with great interest and promised to inform the king concerning all they had heard, but counseled the scribe to hide himself, for they feared the king would reject the testimony and seek to slay those who had prepared and delivered the message.

When King Jehoiakim was told by the princes what Baruch had read, he immediately ordered the roll brought before him and read in his hearing. One of the royal attendants, Jehudi by name, fetched the roll and began reading the words of reproof and warning. It was the time of winter, and the king and his companions of state, the princes of Judah, were gathered about an open fire. Only a small portion had been read, when the king, far from trembling [434] at the danger hanging over himself and his people, seized the roll and in a frenzy of rage "cut it with the penknife and cast it into the fire that was on the hearth, until all the roll was consumed." Verse 23.

Neither the king nor his princes were afraid "nor rent their garments." Certain of the princes, however, "had made intercession to the king that he would not burn the roll: but he would not hear them." The writing having been destroyed, the wrath of the wicked king rose against Jeremiah and Baruch, and he forthwith sent for them to be taken; "but the Lord hid them." Verses 24-26. [435]

In bringing to the attention of the temple worshipers, and of the princes and king, the written admonitions contained in the inspired roll, God was graciously seeking to warn the men of Judah for their good. "It may be," He said, "the house of Judah will hear all the evil which I purpose to do unto them; that they may return every man from his evil way; that I may forgive their iniquity and their sin." Verse 3. God pities men struggling in the blindness of perversity; He seeks to enlighten the darkened understanding by sending reproofs and threatenings designed to cause the most exalted to feel their ignorance and to deplore their errors. He endeavors to help the self-complacent to become dissatisfied with their vain attainments and to seek for spiritual blessing through a close connection with heaven.

God's plan is not to send messengers who will please and flatter sinners; He delivers no messages of peace to lull the unsanctified into carnal security. Instead, He lays heavy burdens upon the conscience of the wrongdoer and pierces his soul with sharp arrows of conviction. Ministering angels present to him the fearful judgments of God, to deepen the sense of need and to prompt the agonizing cry, "What must I do to be saved?" Acts 16:30. But the Hand that humbles to the dust, rebukes sin, and puts pride and ambition to shame, is the Hand that lifts up the penitent, stricken one. With deepest sympathy He who permits the chastisement to fall, inquires, "What wilt thou that I shall do unto thee?"

When man has sinned against a holy and merciful God, he can pursue no course so noble as to repent sincerely and [436] confess his errors in tears and bitterness of soul. This God requires of him; He accepts nothing less than a broken heart and a contrite spirit. But King Jehoiakim and his lords, in their arrogance and pride, refused the invitation of God. They would not heed the warning, and repent. The gracious opportunity proffered them at the time of the burning of the sacred roll, was their last. God had declared that if at that time they refused to hear His voice, He would inflict upon them fearful retribution. They did refuse to hear, and He pronounced His final judgments upon Judah, and He would visit with special wrath the man who had proudly lifted himself up against the Almighty.

"Thus saith the Lord of Jehoiakim king of Judah; He shall have none to sit upon the throne of David: and his dead body shall be cast out in the day to the heat, and in the night to the frost. And I will punish him and his seed and his servants for their iniquity; and I will bring upon them, and upon the inhabitants of Jerusalem, and upon the men of Judah, all the evil that I have pronounced against them." Jeremiah 36:30, 31.

The burning of the roll was not the end of the matter. The written words were more easily disposed of than the reproof and warning they contained and the swift-coming punishment God had pronounced against rebellious Israel. But even the written roll was reproduced. "Take thee again another roll," the Lord commanded His servant, "and write in it all the former words that were in the first roll, which Jehoiakim the king of Judah hath burned." The record of the prophecies concerning Judah and Jerusalem had been [437] reduced to ashes; but the words were still living in the heart of Jeremiah, "as a burning fire," and the prophet was permitted to reproduce that which the wrath of man would fain have destroyed.

Taking another roll, Jeremiah gave it to Baruch, "who wrote therein from the mouth of Jeremiah all the words of the book which Jehoiakim king of Judah had burned in the fire: and there were added besides unto them many like words." Verses 28, 32. The wrath of man had sought to prevent the labors of the prophet of God; but the very means by which Jehoiakim had endeavored to limit the influence of the servant of Jehovah, gave further opportunity for making plain the divine requirements.

The spirit of opposition to reproof, that led to the persecution and imprisonment of Jeremiah, exists today. Many refuse to heed repeated warnings, preferring rather to listen to false teachers who flatter their vanity and overlook their evil-doing. In the day of trouble such will have no sure refuge, no help from heaven. God's chosen servants should meet with courage and patience the trials and sufferings that befall them through reproach, neglect, and misrepresentation. They should continue to discharge faithfully the work God has given them to do, ever remembering that the prophets of old and the Saviour of mankind and His apostles also endured abuse and persecution for the Word's sake.

It was God's purpose that Jehoiakim should heed the counsels of Jeremiah and thus win favor in the eyes of Nebuchadnezzar and save himself much sorrow. The youthful [438] king had sworn allegiance to the Babylonian ruler, and had he remained true to his promise he would have commanded the respect of the heathen, and this would have led to precious opportunities for the conversion of souls.

Scorning the unusual privileges granted him, Judah's king willfully followed a way of his own choosing. He violated his word of honor to the Babylonian ruler, and rebelled. This brought him and his kingdom into a very strait place. Against him were sent "bands of the Chaldees, and bands of the Syrians, and bands of the Moabites, and bands of the children of Ammon," and he was powerless to prevent the land from being overrun by these marauders. 2 Kings 24:2. Within a few years he closed his disastrous reign in ignominy, rejected of Heaven, unloved by his people, and despised by the rulers of Babylon whose confidence he had betrayed—and all as the result of his fatal mistake in turning from the purpose of God as revealed through His appointed messenger.

Jehoiachin [also known as Jeconiah, and Coniah], the son of Jehoiakim, occupied the throne only three months and ten days, when he surrendered to the Chaldean armies which, because of the rebellion of Judah's ruler, were once more besieging the fated city. On this occasion Nebuchadnezzar "carried away Jehoiachin to Babylon, and the king's mother, and the king's wives, and his officers, and the mighty of the land," several thousand in number, together with "craftsmen and smiths a thousand." With these the king of Babylon took "all the treasures of the house of the Lord, and the treasures of the king's house." 2 Kings 24:15, 16, 13. [439]

The kingdom of Judah, broken in power and robbed of its strength both in men and in treasure, was nevertheless still permitted to exist as a separate government. At its head Nebuchadnezzar placed Mattaniah, a younger son of Josiah, changing his name to Zedekiah. [440]

Chapter 36

The Last King of Judah

Zedekiah at the beginning of his reign was trusted fully by the king of Babylon and had as a tried counselor the prophet Jeremiah. By pursuing an honorable course toward the Babylonians and by paying heed to the messages from the Lord through Jeremiah, he could have kept the respect of many in high authority and have had opportunity to communicate to them a knowledge of the true God. Thus the captive exiles already in Babylon would have been placed on vantage ground and granted many liberties; the name of God would have been honored far and wide; and those that remained in the land of Judah would have been spared the terrible calamities that finally came upon them.

Through Jeremiah, Zedekiah and all Judah, including those taken to Babylon, were counseled to submit quietly to the temporary rule of their conquerors. It was especially important that those in captivity should seek the peace of the land into which they had been carried. This, however, [441] was contrary to the inclinations of the human heart; and Satan, taking advantage of the circumstances, caused false prophets to arise among the people, both in Jerusalem and in Babylon, who declared that the yoke of bondage would soon be broken and the former prestige of the nation restored.

The heeding of such flattering prophecies would have led to fatal moves on the part of the king and the exiles, and would have frustrated the merciful designs of God in their behalf. Lest an insurrection be incited and great suffering ensue, the Lord commanded Jeremiah to meet the crisis without delay, by warning the king of Judah of the sure consequence of rebellion. The captives also were admonished, by written communications, not to be deluded into believing their deliverance near. "Let not your prophets and your diviners, that be in the midst of you, deceive you," he urged. Jeremiah 29:8. In this connection mention was made of the Lord's purpose to restore Israel at the close of the seventy years of captivity foretold by His messengers.

With what tender compassion did God inform His captive people of His plans for Israel! He knew that should they be persuaded by false prophets to look for a speedy deliverance, their position in Babylon would be made very difficult. Any demonstration or insurrection on their part would awaken the vigilance and severity of the Chaldean authorities and would lead to a further restriction of their liberties. Suffering and disaster would result. He desired them to submit quietly to their fate and make their servitude as pleasant as possible; and His counsel to them was: "Build ye houses, and dwell in them; and plant gardens, [442] and eat the fruit of them; ... and seek the peace of the city whither I have caused you to be carried away captives, and pray unto the Lord for it: for in the peace thereof shall ye have peace." Verses 5-7.

Among the false teachers in Babylon were two men who claimed to be holy, but whose lives were corrupt. Jeremiah had condemned the evil course of these men and had warned them of their danger. Angered by reproof, they sought to oppose the work of the true prophet by stirring up the people to discredit his words and to act contrary to the counsel of God in the matter of subjecting themselves to the king of Babylon. The Lord testified through Jeremiah that these false prophets should be delivered into the hands of Nebuchadnezzar and slain before his eyes. Not long afterward, this prediction was literally fulfilled.

To the end of time, men will arise to create confusion and rebellion among those who claim to be representatives of the true God. Those who prophesy lies will encourage men to look upon sin as a light thing. When the terrible results of their evil deeds are made manifest, they will seek, if possible, to make the one who has faithfully warned them, responsible for their difficulties, even as the Jews charged Jeremiah with their evil fortunes. But as surely as the words of Jehovah through His prophet were vindicated anciently, so surely will the certainty of His messages be established today.

From the first, Jeremiah had followed a consistent course in counseling submission to the Babylonians. This counsel was given not only to Judah, but to many of the surrounding [443] nations. In the earlier portion of Zedekiah's reign, ambassadors from the rulers of Edom, Moab, Tyre, and other nations visited the king of Judah to learn whether in his judgment the time was opportune for a united revolt and whether he would join them in battling against the king of Babylon. While these ambassadors were awaiting a response, the word of the Lord came to Jeremiah, saying, "Make thee bonds and yokes, and put them upon thy neck, and send them to the king of Edom, and to the king of Moab, and to the king of the Ammonites, and to the king of Tyrus, and to the king of Zidon, by the hand of the messengers which come to Jerusalem unto Zedekiah king of Judah." Jeremiah 27:2, 3.

Jeremiah was commanded to instruct the ambassadors to inform their rulers that God had given them all into the hand of Nebuchadnezzar, the king of Babylon, and that they were to "serve him, and his son, and his son's son, until the very time of his land come." Verse 7.

The ambassadors were further instructed to declare to their rulers that if they refused to serve the Babylonian king they should be punished "with the sword, and with the famine, and with the pestilence" till they were consumed. Especially were they to turn from the teaching of false prophets who might counsel otherwise. "Hearken not ye to your prophets," the Lord declared, "nor to your diviners, nor to your dreamers, nor to your enchanters, nor to your sorcerers, which speak unto you, saying, Ye shall not serve the king of Babylon: for they prophesy a lie unto you, to remove you far from your land; and that I should [444] drive you out, and ye should perish. But the nations that bring their neck under the yoke of the king of Babylon, and serve him, those will I let remain still in their own land, saith the Lord; and they shall till it, and dwell therein." Verses 8-11. The lightest punishment that a merciful God could inflict upon so rebellious a people was submission to the rule of Babylon, but if they warred against this decree of servitude they were to feel the full vigor of His chastisement.

The amazement of the assembled council of nations knew no bounds when Jeremiah, carrying the yoke of subjection about his neck, made known to them the will of God.

Against determined opposition Jeremiah stood firmly for the policy of submission. Prominent among those who presumed to gainsay the counsel of the Lord was Hananiah, [445] one of the false prophets against whom the people had been warned. Thinking to gain the favor of the king and of the royal court, he lifted his voice in protest, declaring that God had given him words of encouragement for the Jews. Said he: "Thus speaketh the Lord of hosts, the God of Israel, saying, I have broken the yoke of the king of Babylon. Within two full years will I bring again into this place all the vessels of the Lord's house, that Nebuchadnezzar king of Babylon took away from this place, and carried them to Babylon: and I will bring again to this place Jeconiah the son of Jehoiakim king of Judah, with all the captives of Judah, that went into Babylon, saith the Lord: for I will break the yoke of the king of Babylon." Jeremiah 28:2-4.

Jeremiah, in the presence of the priests and people, earnestly entreated them to submit to the king of Babylon for the time the Lord had specified. He cited the men of Judah to the prophecies of Hosea, Habakkuk, Zephaniah, and others whose messages of reproof and warning had been similar to his own. He referred them to events which had taken place in fulfillment of prophecies of retribution for unrepented sin. In the past the judgments of God had been visited upon the impenitent in exact fulfillment of His purpose as revealed through His messengers.

"The prophet which prophesieth of peace," Jeremiah proposed in conclusion, "when the word of the prophet shall come to pass, then shall the prophet be known, that the Lord hath truly sent him." Verse 9. If Israel chose to run the risk, future developments would effectually decide which was the true prophet. [446]

The words of Jeremiah counseling submission aroused Hananiah to a daring challenge of the reliability of the message delivered. Taking the symbolic yoke from Jeremiah's neck, Hananiah broke it, saying, "Thus saith the Lord; Even so will I break the yoke of Nebuchadnezzar king of Babylon from the neck of all nations within the space of two full years.

"And the prophet Jeremiah went his way." Verse 11. Apparently he could do nothing more than to retire from the scene of conflict. But Jeremiah was given another message. "Go and tell Hananiah," he was bidden, "Thus saith the Lord; Thou hast broken the yokes of wood; but thou shalt make for them yokes of iron. For thus saith the Lord of hosts, the God of Israel; I have put a yoke of iron upon the neck of all these nations, that they may serve Nebuchadnezzar king of Babylon; and they shall serve him...."

"Then said the prophet Jeremiah unto Hananiah the prophet, Hear now, Hananiah; The Lord hath not sent thee; but thou makest this people to trust in a lie. Therefore thus saith the Lord; Behold, I will cast thee from off the face of the earth: this year thou shalt die, because thou hast taught rebellion against the Lord. So Hananiah the prophet died the same year in the seventh month." Verses 13-17.

The false prophet had strengthened the unbelief of the people in Jeremiah and his message. He had wickedly declared himself the Lord's messenger, and he suffered death in consequence. In the fifth month Jeremiah prophesied the death of Hananiah, and in the seventh month his words were proved true by their fulfillment. [447]

The unrest caused by the representations of the false prophets brought Zedekiah under suspicion of treason, and only by quick and decisive action on his part was he permitted to continue reigning as a vassal. Opportunity for such action was taken advantage of shortly after the return of the ambassadors from Jerusalem to the surrounding nations, when the king of Judah accompanied Seraiah, "a quiet prince," on an important mission to Babylon. Jeremiah 51:59. During this visit to the Chaldean court, Zedekiah renewed his oath of allegiance to Nebuchadnezzar.

Through Daniel and others of the Hebrew captives, the Babylonian monarch had been made acquainted with the power and supreme authority of the true God; and when Zedekiah once more solemnly promised to remain loyal, Nebuchadnezzar required him to swear to this promise in the name of the Lord God of Israel. Had Zedekiah respected this renewal of his covenant oath, his loyalty would have had a profound influence on the minds of many who were watching the conduct of those who claimed to reverence the name and to cherish the honor of the God of the Hebrews.

But Judah's king lost sight of his high privilege of bringing honor to the name of the living God. Of Zedekiah it is recorded: "He did that which was evil in the sight of the Lord his God, and humbled not himself before Jeremiah the prophet speaking from the mouth of the Lord. And he also rebelled against King Nebuchadnezzar, who had made him swear by God: but he stiffened his neck, and hardened his heart from turning unto the Lord God of Israel." 2 Chronicles 36:12, 13. [448]

While Jeremiah continued to bear his testimony in the land of Judah, the prophet Ezekiel was raised up from among the captives in Babylon, to warn and to comfort the exiles, and also to confirm the word of the Lord that was being spoken through Jeremiah. During the years that remained of Zedekiah's reign, Ezekiel made very plain the folly of trusting to the false predictions of those who were causing the captives to hope for an early return to Jerusalem. He was also instructed to foretell, by means of a variety of symbols and solemn messages, the siege and utter destruction of Jerusalem.

In the sixth year of the reign of Zedekiah, the Lord revealed to Ezekiel in vision some of the abominations that were being practiced in Jerusalem, and within the gate of the Lord's house, and even in the inner court. The chambers of images, and the pictured idols, "every form of creeping things, and abominable beasts, and all the idols of the house of Israel"—all these in rapid succession passed before the astonished gaze of the prophet. Ezekiel 8:10.

Those who should have been spiritual leaders among the people, "the ancients of the house of Israel," to the number of seventy, were seen offering incense before the idolatrous representations that had been introduced into hidden chambers within the sacred precincts of the temple court. "The Lord seeth us not," the men of Judah flattered themselves as they engaged in their heathenish practices; "the Lord hath forsaken the earth," they blasphemously declared. Verses 11, 12.

There were still "greater abominations" for the prophet to behold. At a gate leading from the outer to the inner [449] court he was shown "women weeping for Tammuz," and within "the inner court of the Lord's house, ... at the door of the temple of the Lord, between the porch and the altar, were about five and twenty men, with their backs toward the temple of the Lord, and their faces toward the east; and they worshiped the sun toward the east." Verses 13-16.

And now the glorious Being who accompanied Ezekiel throughout this astonishing vision of wickedness in high places in the land of Judah, inquired of the prophet: "Hast thou seen this, O son of man? Is it a light thing to the house of Judah that they commit the abominations which they commit here? for they have filled the land with violence, and have returned to provoke Me to anger: and, lo, they put the branch to their nose. Therefore will I also deal in fury: Mine eye shall not spare, neither will I have pity: and though they cry in Mine ears with a loud voice, yet will I not hear them." Verses 17, 18.

Through Jeremiah the Lord had declared of the wicked men who presumptuously dared to stand before the people in His name: "Both prophet and priest are profane; yea, in My house have I found their wickedness." Jeremiah 23:11. In the terrible arraignment of Judah as recorded in the closing narrative of the chronicler of Zedekiah's reign, this charge of violating the sanctity of the temple was repeated. "Moreover," the sacred writer declared, "all the chief of the priests, and the people, transgressed very much after all the abominations of the heathen; and polluted the house of the Lord which He had hallowed in Jerusalem." 2 Chronicles 36:14. [450]

The day of doom for the kingdom of Judah was fast approaching. No longer could the Lord set before them the hope of averting the severest of His judgments. "Should ye be utterly unpunished?" He inquired. "Ye shall not be unpunished." Jeremiah 25:29.

Even these words were received with mocking derision. "The days are prolonged, and every vision faileth," declared the impenitent. But through Ezekiel this denial of the sure word of prophecy was sternly rebuked. "Tell them," the Lord declared, "I will make this proverb to cease, and they shall no more use it as a proverb in Israel; but say unto them, The days are at hand, and the effect of every vision. For there shall be no more any vain vision nor flattering divination within the house of Israel. For I am the Lord: I will speak, and the word that I shall speak shall come to pass; it shall be no more prolonged: for in your days, O rebellious house, will I say the word, and will perform it, saith the Lord God.

"Again," testifies Ezekiel, "the word of the Lord came to me, saying, Son of man, behold, they of the house of Israel say, The vision that he seeth is for many days to come, and he prophesieth of the times that are far off. Therefore say unto them, Thus saith the Lord God; There shall none of My words be prolonged any more, but the word which I have spoken shall be done, saith the Lord God." Ezekiel 12:22-28.

Foremost among those who were rapidly leading the nation to ruin was Zedekiah their king. Forsaking utterly the counsels of the Lord as given through the prophets, forgetting the debt of gratitude he owed Nebuchadnezzar, [451] violating his solemn oath of allegiance taken in the name of the Lord God of Israel, Judah's king rebelled against the prophets, against his benefactor, and against his God. In the vanity of his own wisdom he turned for help to the ancient enemy of Israel's prosperity, "sending his ambassadors into Egypt, that they might give him horses and much people."

"Shall he prosper?" the Lord inquired concerning the one who had thus basely betrayed every sacred trust; "shall he escape that doeth such things? or shall he break the covenant, and be delivered? As I live, saith the Lord God, surely in the place where the king dwelleth that made him king, whose oath he despised, and whose covenant he brake, even with him in the midst of Babylon he shall die. Neither shall Pharaoh with his mighty army and great company make for him in the war: ... seeing he despised the oath by breaking the covenant, when, lo, he had given his hand, and hath done all these things, he shall not escape." Ezekiel 17:15-18.

To the "profane wicked prince" had come the day of final reckoning. "Remove the diadem," the Lord decreed, "and take off the crown." Not until Christ Himself should set up His kingdom was Judah again to be permitted to have a king. "I will overturn, overturn, overturn, it," was the divine edict concerning the throne of the house of David; "and it shall be no more, until He come whose right it is; and I will give it Him." Ezekiel 21:25-27. [452]

Chapter 37

Carried Captive Into Babylon

In the ninth year of Zedekiah's reign "Nebuchadnezzar king of Babylon came, he, and all his host, against Jerusalem," to besiege the city. 2 Kings 25:1. The outlook for Judah was hopeless. "Behold, I am against thee," the Lord Himself declared through Ezekiel. "I the Lord have drawn forth My sword out of his sheath" it shall not return any more.... Every heart shall melt, and all hands shall be feeble, and every spirit shall faint, and all knees shall be weak as water." "I will pour out Mine indignation upon thee, I will blow against thee in the fire of My wrath, and deliver thee into the hand of brutish men, and skillful to destroy." Ezekiel 21:3, 5-7, 31.

The Egyptians endeavored to come to the rescue of the beleaguered city; and the Chaldeans, in order to keep them back, abandoned for a time their siege of the Judean capital. Hope sprang up in the heart of Zedekiah, and he sent a [453] messenger to Jeremiah, asking him to pray to God in behalf of the Hebrew nation.

The prophet's fearful answer was that the Chaldeans would return and destroy the city. The fiat had gone forth; no longer could the impenitent nation avert the divine judgments. "Deceive not yourselves," the Lord warned His people. "The Chaldeans ... shall not depart. For though ye had smitten the whole army of the Chaldeans that fight against you, and there remained but wounded men among them, yet should they rise up every man in his tent, and burn this city with fire." Jeremiah 37:9, 10. The remnant of Judah were to go into captivity, to learn through adversity the lessons they had refused to learn under circumstances more favorable. From this decree of the holy Watcher there could be no appeal.

Among the righteous still in Jerusalem, to whom had been made plain the divine purpose, were some who determined to place beyond the reach of ruthless hands the sacred ark containing the tables of stone on which had been traced the precepts of the Decalogue. This they did. With mourning and sadness they secreted the ark in a cave, where it was to be hidden from the people of Israel and Judah because of their sins, and was to be no more restored to them. That sacred ark is yet hidden. It has never been disturbed since it was secreted.

For many years Jeremiah had stood before the people as a faithful witness for God; and now, as the fated city was about to pass into the hands of the heathen, he considered his work done and attempted to leave, but was prevented by a son of one of the false prophets, who reported [454] that Jeremiah was about to join the Babylonians, to whom he had repeatedly urged the men of Judah to submit. The prophet denied the lying charge, but nevertheless "the princes were wroth with Jeremiah, and smote him, and put him in prison." Verse 15.

The hopes that had sprung up in the hearts of princes and people when the armies of Nebuchadnezzar turned south to meet the Egyptians, were soon dashed to the ground. The word of the Lord had been, "Behold, I am against thee, Pharaoh king of Egypt." The might of Egypt was but a broken reed. "All the inhabitants of Egypt," Inspiration had declared, "shall know that I am the Lord, because they have been a staff of reed to the house of Israel." "I will strengthen the arms of the king of Babylon, and the arms of Pharaoh shall fall down; and they shall know that I am the Lord, when I shall put My sword into the hand of the king of Babylon, and he shall stretch it out upon the land of Egypt." Ezekiel 29:3, 6; 30:25.

While the princes of Judah were still vainly looking toward Egypt for help, King Zedekiah with anxious foreboding was thinking of the prophet of God that had been thrust into prison. After many days the king sent for him and asked him secretly, "Is there any word from the Lord?" Jeremiah answered, "There is: for, said He, thou shalt be delivered into the hand of the king of Babylon.

"Moreover Jeremiah said unto King Zedekiah, What have I offended against thee, or against thy servants, or against this people, that ye have put me in prison? Where are now your prophets which prophesied unto you, saying, [455] The king of Babylon shall not come against you, nor against this land? Therefore hear now, I pray thee, O my lord the king: let my supplication, I pray thee, be accepted before thee; that thou cause me not to return to the house of Jonathan the scribe, lest I die there." Jeremiah 37:17-20.

At this Zedekiah commanded that they "commit Jeremiah into the court of the prison, and that they should give him daily a piece of bread out of the bakers' street, until all the bread in the city were spent. Thus Jeremiah remained in the court of the prison." Verse 21.

The king dared not openly manifest any faith in Jeremiah. Though his fear drove him to seek information of him privately, yet he was too weak to brave the disapprobation of his princes and of the people by submitting to the will of God as declared by the prophet.

From the court of the prison Jeremiah continued to advise submission to the Babylonian rule. To offer resistance would be to invite sure death. The message of the Lord to Judah was: "He that remaineth in this city shall die by the sword, by the famine, and by the pestilence: but he that goeth forth to the Chaldeans shall live; for he shall have his life for a prey, and shall live." Plain and positive were the words spoken. In the name of the Lord the prophet boldly declared, "This city shall surely be given into the hand of the king of Babylon's army, which shall take it." Jeremiah 38:2, 3.

At last the princes, enraged over the repeated counsels of Jeremiah, which were contrary to their set policy of resistance, made a vigorous protest before the king, urging [456] that the prophet was an enemy to the nation, and that his words had weakened the hands of the people and brought misfortune upon them; therefore he should be put to death.

The cowardly king knew that the charges were false; but in order to propitiate those who occupied high and influential positions in the nation, he feigned to believe their falsehoods and gave Jeremiah into their hands to do with him as they pleased. The prophet was cast "into the dungeon of Malchiah the son of Hammelech, that was in the court of the prison: and they let down Jeremiah with cords. And in the dungeon there was no water, but mire: so Jeremiah sunk in the mire." Verse 6. But God raised up friends for him, who besought the king in his behalf, and had him again removed to the court of the prison.

Once more the king sent privately for Jeremiah, and bade him faithfully relate the purpose of God toward Jerusalem. In response, Jeremiah inquired, "If I declare it unto thee, wilt thou not surely put me to death? and if I give thee counsel, wilt thou not hearken unto me?" The king entered into a secret compact with the prophet. "As the Lord liveth, that made us this soul," Zedekiah promised, "I will not put thee to death, neither will I give thee into the hand of these men that seek thy life." Verses 15, 16.

There was still opportunity for the king to reveal a willingness to heed the warnings of Jehovah, and thus to temper with mercy the judgments even now falling on city and nation. "If thou wilt assuredly go forth unto the king of Babylon's princes," was the message given the king, "then thy soul shall live, and this city shall not be burned with [457] fire; and thou shalt live, and thine house: but if thou wilt not go forth to the king of Babylon's princes, then shall this city be given into the hand of the Chaldeans, and they shall burn it with fire, and thou shalt not escape out of their hand."

"I am afraid of the Jews that are fallen to the Chaldeans," the king replied, "lest they deliver me into their hand, and they mock me." But the prophet promised, "They shall not deliver thee." And he added the earnest entreaty, "Obey, I beseech thee, the voice of the Lord, which I speak unto thee: so it shall be well unto thee, and thy soul shall live." Verses 17-20.

Thus even to the last hour, God made plain His willingness to show mercy to those who would choose to submit to His just requirements. Had the king chosen to obey, the lives of the people might have been spared, and the city saved from conflagration; but he thought he had gone too far to retrace his steps. He was afraid of the Jews, afraid of ridicule, afraid for his life. After years of rebellion against God, Zedekiah thought it too humiliating to say to his people, I accept the word of the Lord, as spoken through the prophet Jeremiah; I dare not venture to war against the enemy in the face of all these warnings.

With tears Jeremiah entreated Zedekiah to save himself and his people. With anguish of spirit he assured him that unless he should heed the counsel of God, he could not escape with his life, and all his possessions would fall to the Babylonians. But the king had started on the wrong course, and he would not retrace his steps. He decided to [458] follow the counsel of the false prophets, and of the men whom he really despised, and who ridiculed his weakness in yielding so readily to their wishes. He sacrificed the noble freedom of his manhood and became a cringing slave to public opinion. With no fixed purpose to do evil, he was also without resolution to stand boldly for the right. Convicted though he was of the value of the counsel given by Jeremiah, he had not the moral stamina to obey; and as a consequence he advanced steadily in the wrong direction.

The king was even too weak to be willing that his courtiers and people should know that he had held a conference with Jeremiah, so fully had the fear of man taken possession of his soul. If Zedekiah had stood up bravely and declared that he believed the words of the prophet, already half fulfilled, what desolation might have been averted! He should have said, I will obey the Lord, and save the city from utter ruin. I dare not disregard the commands of God because of the fear or favor of man. I love the truth, I hate sin, and I will follow the counsel of the Mighty One of Israel.

Then the people would have respected his courageous spirit, and those who were wavering between faith and unbelief would have taken a firm stand for the right. The very fearlessness and justice of this course would have inspired his subjects with admiration and loyalty. He would have had ample support, and Judah would have been spared the untold woe of carnage and famine and fire.

The weakness of Zedekiah was a sin for which he paid a fearful penalty. The enemy swept down like a resistless avalanche and devastated the city. The Hebrew armies [459] were beaten back in confusion. The nation was conquered. Zedekiah was taken prisoner, and his sons were slain before his eyes. The king was led away from Jerusalem a captive, his eyes were put out, and after arriving in Babylon he perished miserably. The beautiful temple that for more than four centuries had crowned the summit of Mount Zion was not spared by the Chaldeans. "They burnt the house of God, and brake down the wall of Jerusalem, and burnt all the palaces thereof with fire, and destroyed all the goodly vessels thereof." 2 Chronicles 36:19.

At the time of the final overthrow of Jerusalem by Nebuchadnezzar, many had escaped the horrors of the long siege, only to perish by the sword. Of those who still remained, some, notably the chief of the priests and officers [460] and the princes of the realm, were taken to Babylon and there executed as traitors. Others were carried captive, to live in servitude to Nebuchadnezzar and to his sons "until the reign of the kingdom of Persia: to fulfill the word of the Lord by the mouth of Jeremiah." Verses 20, 21.

Of Jeremiah himself it is recorded: "Nebuchadnezzar king of Babylon gave charge concerning Jeremiah to Nebuchadnezzar-adan the captain of the guard, saying, Take him, and look well to him, and do him no harm; but do unto him even as he shall say unto thee." Jeremiah 39:11, 12.

Released from prison by the Babylonian officers, the prophet chose to cast in his lot with the feeble remnant, certain "poor of the land" left by the Chaldeans to be "vinedressers and husbandmen." Over these the Babylonians set Gedaliah as governor. Only a few months passed before the newly appointed governor was treacherously slain. The poor people, after passing through many trials, were finally persuaded by their leaders to take refuge in the land of Egypt. Against this move, Jeremiah lifted his voice in protest. "Go ye not into Egypt," he pleaded. But the inspired counsel was not heeded, and "all the remnant of Judah, ... even men, and women, and children," took flight into Egypt. "They obeyed not the voice of the Lord: thus came they even to Tahpanhes." Jeremiah 43:5-7.

The prophecies of doom pronounced by Jeremiah upon the remnant that had rebelled against Nebuchadnezzar by fleeing to Egypt were mingled with promises of pardon to those who should repent of their folly and stand ready to return. While the Lord would not spare those who turned [461] from His counsel to the seductive influences of Egyptian idolatry, yet He would show mercy to those who should prove loyal and true. "A small number that escape the sword shall return out of the land of Egypt into the land of Judah," He declared; "and all the remnant of Judah, that are gone into the land of Egypt to sojourn there, shall know whose words shall stand, Mine, or theirs." Jeremiah 44:28.

The sorrow of the prophet over the utter perversity of those who would have been the spiritual light of the world, his sorrow over the fate of Zion and of the people carried captive to Babylon, is revealed in the lamentations he has left on record as a memorial of the folly of turning from the counsels of Jehovah to human wisdom. Amid the ruin wrought, Jeremiah could still declare, "It is of the Lord's mercies that we are not consumed;" and his constant prayer was, "Let us search and try our ways, and turn again to the Lord." Lamentations 3:22, 40. While Judah was still a kingdom among the nations, he had inquired of his God, "Hast Thou utterly rejected Judah? hath Thy soul loathed Zion?" and he had made bold to plead, "Do not abhor us, for Thy name's sake." Jeremiah 14:19, 21. The prophet's absolute faith in God's eternal purpose to bring order out of confusion, and to demonstrate to the nations of earth and to the entire universe His attributes of justice and love, now led him to plead confidently in behalf of those who might turn from evil to righteousness.

But now Zion was utterly destroyed; the people of God were in their captivity. Overwhelmed with grief, the [462] prophet exclaimed: "How doth the city sit solitary, that was full of people! how is she become as a widow! she that was great among the nations, and princess among the provinces, how is she become tributary! She weepeth sore in the night, and her tears are on her cheeks: among all her lovers she hath none to comfort her: all her friends have dealt treacherously with her, they are become her enemies.

"Judah is gone into captivity because of affliction, and because of great servitude: she dwelleth among the heathen, she findeth no rest: all her persecutors overtook her between the straits. The ways of Zion do mourn, because none come to the solemn feasts: all her gates are desolate: her priests sigh, her virgins are afflicted, and she is in bitterness. Her adversaries are the chief, her enemies prosper; for the Lord hath afflicted her for the multitude of her transgressions: her children are gone into captivity before the enemy."

"How hath the Lord covered the daughter of Zion with a cloud in His anger, and cast down from heaven unto the earth the beauty of Israel, and remembered not His footstool in the day of His anger! The Lord hath swallowed up all the habitations of Jacob, and hath not pitied: He hath thrown down in His wrath the strongholds of the daughter of Judah; He hath brought them down to the ground: He hath polluted the kingdom and the princes thereof. He hath cut off in His fierce anger all the horn of Israel: He hath drawn back His right hand from before the enemy, and He burned against Jacob like a flaming fire, which devoureth round about. He hath bent His bow like an enemy: He stood with His right hand as an adversary, and slew all [463] that were pleasant to the eye in the tabernacle of the daughter of Zion: He poured out His fury like fire."

"What thing shall I take to witness for thee? what thing shall I liken to thee, O daughter of Jerusalem? what shall I equal to thee, that I may comfort thee, O virgin daughter of Zion? for thy breach is great like the sea: who can heal thee?"

"Remember, O Lord, what is come upon us: consider, and behold our reproach. Our inheritance is turned to strangers, our houses to aliens. We are orphans and fatherless, our mothers are as widows.... Our fathers have sinned, and are not; and we have borne their iniquities. Servants have ruled over us: there is none that doth deliver us out of their hand.... For this our heart is faint; for these things our eyes are dim."

"Thou, O Lord, remainest forever; Thy throne from generation to generation. Wherefore dost Thou forget us forever, and forsake us so long time? Turn Thou us unto Thee, O Lord, and we shall be turned; renew our days as of old." Lamentations 1:1-5; 2:1-4, 13; Lamentations 5:1-3, 7, 8, 17, 19-21. [464]

Chapter 38

Light Through Darkness

The dark years of destruction and death marking the end of the kingdom of Judah would have brought despair to the stoutest heart had it not been for the encouragements in the prophetic utterances of God's messengers. Through Jeremiah in Jerusalem, through Daniel in the court of Babylon, through Ezekiel on the banks of the Chebar, the Lord in mercy made clear His eternal purpose and gave assurance of His willingness to fulfill to His chosen people the promises recorded in the writings of Moses. That which He had said He would do for those who should prove true to Him, He would surely bring to pass. "The word of God ... liveth and abideth forever." 1 Peter 1:23.

In the days of the wilderness wandering the Lord had made abundant provision for His children to keep in remembrance the words of His law. After the settlement in Canaan the divine precepts were to be repeated daily in every home; they were to be written plainly upon the doorposts and [465] gates, and spread upon memorial tablets. They were to be set to music and chanted by young and old. Priests were to teach these holy precepts in public assemblies, and the rulers of the land were to make them their daily study. "Meditate therein day and night," the Lord commanded Joshua concerning the book of the law, "that thou mayest observe to do according to all that is written therein: for then thou shalt make thy way prosperous, and then thou shalt have good success." Joshua 1:8.

The writings of Moses were taught by Joshua to all Israel. "There was not a word of all that Moses commanded, which Joshua read not before all the congregation of Israel, with the women, and the little ones, and the strangers that were conversant among them." Joshua 8:35. This was in harmony with the express command of Jehovah providing for a public rehearsal of the words of the book of the law every seven years, during the Feast of Tabernacles. "Gather the people together, men, and women, and children, and thy stranger that is within thy gates," the spiritual leaders of Israel had been instructed, "that they may hear, and that they may learn, and fear the Lord your God, and observe to do all the words of this law: and that their children, which have not known anything, may hear, and learn to fear the Lord your God, as long as ye live in the land whither ye go over Jordan to possess it." Deuteronomy 31:12, 13.

Had this counsel been heeded through the centuries that followed, how different would have been Israel's history! Only as a reverence for God's Holy Word was cherished in the hearts of the people, could they hope to fulfill the divine [466] purpose. It was regard for the law of God that gave Israel strength during the reign of David and the earlier years of Solomon's rule; it was through faith in the living word that reformation was wrought in the days of Elijah and of Josiah. And it was to these same Scriptures of truth, Israel's richest heritage, that Jeremiah appealed in his efforts toward reform. Wherever he ministered he met the people with the earnest plea, "Hear ye the words of this covenant," words which would bring them a full understanding of God's purpose to extend to all nations a knowledge of saving truth. Jeremiah 11:2.

In the closing years of Judah's apostasy the exhortations of the prophets were seemingly of but little avail; and as the armies of the Chaldeans came for the third and last time to besiege Jerusalem, hope fled from every heart. Jeremiah predicted utter ruin; and it was because of his insistence on surrender that he had finally been thrown into prison. But God left not to hopeless despair the faithful remnant who were still in the city. Even while Jeremiah was kept under close surveillance by those who scorned his messages, there came to him fresh revelations concerning Heaven's willingness to forgive and to save, which have been an unfailing source of comfort to the church of God from that day to this.

Laying fast hold on the promises of God, Jeremiah, by means of an acted parable, illustrated before the inhabitants of the fated city his strong faith in the ultimate fulfillment of God's purpose for His people. In the presence of witnesses, and with careful observance of all necessary legal forms, he purchased for seventeen shekels of silver an [467] [468] [469] ancestral field situated in the neighboring village of Anathoth.

From every human point of view this purchase of land in territory already under the control of the Babylonians, appeared to be an act of folly. The prophet himself had been foretelling the destruction of Jerusalem, the desolation of Judea, and the utter ruin of the kingdom. He had been prophesying a long period of captivity in faraway Babylon. Already advanced in years, he could never hope to receive personal benefit from the purchase he had made. However, his study of the prophecies that were recorded in the Scriptures had created within his heart a firm conviction that the Lord purposed to restore to the children of the captivity their ancient possession of the Land of Promise. With the eye of faith Jeremiah saw the exiles returning at the end of the years of affliction and reoccupying the land of their fathers. Through the purchase of the Anathoth estate he would do what he could to inspire others with the hope that brought so much comfort to his own heart.

Having signed the deeds of transfer and secured the countersignatures of witnesses, Jeremiah charged Baruch his secretary: "Take these evidences, this evidence of the purchase, both which is sealed, and this evidence which is open; and put them in an earthen vessel, that they may continue many days. For thus saith the Lord of hosts, the God of Israel; Houses and fields and vineyards shall be possessed again in this land." Jeremiah 32:14, 15.

So discouraging was the outlook for Judah at the time of this extraordinary transaction that immediately after perfecting the details of the purchase and arranging for [470] the preservation of the written records, the faith of Jeremiah, unshaken though it had been, was now sorely tried. Had he, in his endeavor to encourage Judah, acted presumptuously? In his desire to establish confidence in the promises of God's word, had he given ground for false hope? Those who had entered into covenant relationship with God had long since scorned the provisions made in their behalf. Could the promises to the chosen nation ever meet with complete fulfillment?

Perplexed in spirit, bowed down with sorrow over the sufferings of those who had refused to repent of their sins, the prophet appealed to God for further enlightenment concerning the divine purpose for mankind.

"Ah Lord God!" he prayed, "behold, Thou hast made the heaven and the earth by Thy great power and stretched-out arm, and there is nothing too hard for Thee: Thou showest loving-kindness unto thousands, and recompensest the iniquity of the fathers into the bosom of their children after them: the great, the mighty God, the Lord of hosts, is His name, great in counsel, and mighty in work: for Thine eyes are open upon all the ways of the sons of men: to give everyone according to his ways, and according to the fruit of his doings: which hast set signs and wonders in the land of Egypt, even unto this day, and in Israel, and among other men; and hast made Thee a name, as at this day; and hast brought forth Thy people Israel out of the land of Egypt with signs, and with wonders, and with a strong hand, and with a stretched-out arm, and with great terror; and hast given them this land, which Thou didst swear to their fathers to give them, a land flowing with milk and [471] honey; and they came in, and possessed it; but they obeyed not Thy voice, neither walked in Thy law; they have done nothing of all that Thou commandedst them to do: therefore Thou hast caused all this evil to come upon them." Verses 17-23.

Nebuchadnezzar's armies were about to take the walls of Zion by storm. Thousands were perishing in a last desperate defense of the city. Many thousands more were dying of hunger and disease. The fate of Jerusalem was already sealed. The besieging towers of the enemy's forces were already overlooking the walls. "Behold the mounts," the prophet continued in his prayer to God; "they are come unto the city to take it; and the city is given into the hand of the Chaldeans, that fight against it, because of the sword, and of the famine, and of the pestilence: and what Thou hast spoken is come to pass; and, behold, Thou seest it. And Thou hast said unto me, O Lord God, Buy thee the field for money, and take witnesses; for the city is given into the hand of the Chaldeans." Verses 24, 25.

The prayer of the prophet was graciously answered. "The word of the Lord unto Jeremiah" in that hour of distress, when the faith of the messenger of truth was being tried as by fire, was: "Behold, I am the Lord, the God of all flesh: is there anything too hard for Me?" Verses 26, 27. The city was soon to fall into the hand of the Chaldeans; its gates and palaces were to be set on fire and burned; but, notwithstanding the fact that destruction was imminent and the inhabitants of Jerusalem were to be carried away captive, nevertheless the eternal purpose of Jehovah for Israel was yet to be fulfilled. In further answer to the prayer [472] of His servant, the Lord declared concerning those upon whom His chastisements were falling:

"Behold, I will gather them out of all countries, whither I have driven them in Mine anger, and in My fury, and in great wrath; and I will bring them again unto this place, and I will cause them to dwell safely: and they shall be My people, and I will be their God: and I will give them one heart, and one way, that they may fear Me forever, for the good of them, and of their children after them: and I will make an everlasting covenant with them, that I will not turn away from them, to do them good; but I will put My fear in their hearts, that they shall not depart from Me. Yea, I will rejoice over them to do them good, and I will plant them in this land assuredly with My whole heart and with My whole soul.

"For thus saith the Lord; Like as I have brought all this great evil upon this people, so will I bring upon them all the good that I have promised them. And fields shall be bought in this land, whereof ye say, It is desolate without man or beast; it is given into the hand of the Chaldeans. Men shall buy fields for money, and subscribe evidences, and seal them, and take witnesses in the land of Benjamin, and in the places about Jerusalem, and in the cities of Judah, and in the cities of the mountains, and in the cities of the valley, and in the cities of the south: for I will cause their captivity to return, saith the Lord." Verses 37-44.

In confirmation of these assurances of deliverance and restoration, "the word of the Lord came unto Jeremiah the second time, while he was yet shut up in the court of the prison, saying, [473]

"Thus saith the Lord the Maker thereof, the Lord that formed it, to establish it; the Lord is His name; Call unto Me, and I will answer thee, and show thee great and mighty things, which thou knowest not. For thus saith the Lord, the God of Israel, concerning the houses of this city, and concerning the houses of the kings of Judah, which are thrown down by the mounts, and by the sword; ... Behold, I will bring it health and cure, and I will cure them, and will reveal unto them the abundance of peace and truth. And I will cause the captivity of Judah and the captivity of Israel to return, and will build them, as at the first. And I will cleanse them from all their iniquity, whereby they have sinned against Me; and I will pardon all their iniquities.... And it shall be to Me a name of joy, a praise and an honor before all the nations of the earth, which shall hear all the good that I do unto them: and they shall fear and tremble for all the goodness and for all the prosperity that I procure unto it.

"Thus saith the Lord; Again there shall be heard in this place, which ye say shall be desolate without man and without beast, even in the cities of Judah, and in the streets of Jerusalem, ... the voice of joy, and the voice of gladness, the voice of the bridegroom, and the voice of the bride, the voice of them that shall say, Praise the Lord of hosts: for the Lord is good; for His mercy endureth forever: and of them that shall bring the sacrifice of praise into the house of the Lord. For I will cause to return the captivity of the land, as at the first, saith the Lord.

"Thus saith the Lord of hosts; Again in this place, which is desolate without man and without beast, and in all the [474] cities thereof, shall be an habitation of shepherds causing their flocks to lie down. In the cities of the mountains, and in the cities of the vale, and in the cities of the south, and in the land of Benjamin, and in the places about Jerusalem, and in the cities of Judah, shall the flocks pass again under the hands of him that telleth them, saith the Lord.

"Behold, the days come, saith the Lord, that I will perform that good thing which I have promised unto the house of Israel and to the house of Judah." Jeremiah 33:1-14.

Thus was the church of God comforted in one of the darkest hours of her long conflict with the forces of evil. Satan had seemingly triumphed in his efforts to destroy Israel; but the Lord was overruling the events of the present, and during the years that were to follow, His people were to have opportunity to redeem the past. His message to the church was:

"Fear thou not, O My servant Jacob; ... neither be dismayed, O Israel: for, lo, I will save thee from afar, and thy seed from the land of their captivity; and Jacob shall return, and shall be in rest, and be quiet, and none shall make him afraid. For I am with thee, saith the Lord, to save thee." "I will restore health unto thee, and I will heal thee of thy wounds." Jeremiah 30:10, 11, 17.

In the glad day of restoration the tribes of divided Israel were to be reunited as one people. The Lord was to be acknowledged as ruler over "all the families of Israel." "They shall be My people." He declared. "Sing with gladness for Jacob, and shout among the chief of the nations: publish ye, praise ye, and say, O Lord, save Thy people, [475] the remnant of Israel. Behold, I will bring them from the north country, and gather them from the coasts of the earth, and with them the blind and the lame; ... they shall come with weeping, and with supplications will I lead them: I will cause them to walk by the rivers of waters in a straight way, wherein they shall not stumble: for I am a Father to Israel, and Ephraim is My first-born." Jeremiah 31:1, 7-9.

Humbled in the sight of the nations, those who once had been recognized as favored of Heaven above all other peoples of the earth were to learn in exile the lesson of obedience so necessary for their future happiness. Until they had learned this lesson, God could not do for them all that He desired to do. "I will correct thee in measure, and will not leave thee altogether unpunished," He declared in explanation of His purpose to chastise them for their spiritual good. Jeremiah 30:11. Yet those who had been the object of His tender love were not forever set aside; before all the nations of earth He would demonstrate His plan to bring victory out of apparent defeat, to save rather than to destroy. To the prophet was given the message:

"He that scattered Israel will gather him, and keep him, as a shepherd doth his flock. For the Lord hath redeemed Jacob, and ransomed him from the hand of him that was stronger than he. Therefore they shall come and sing in the height of Zion, and shall flow together to the goodness of the Lord, for wheat, and for wine, and for oil, and for the young of the flock and of the herd: and their soul shall be as a watered garden; and they shall not sorrow any [476] more at all.... I will turn their mourning into joy, and will comfort them, and make them rejoice from their sorrow. And I will satiate the soul of the priests with fatness, and My people shall be satisfied with My goodness, saith the Lord."

"Thus saith the Lord of hosts, the God of Israel; As yet they shall use this speech in the land of Judah and in the cities thereof, when I shall bring again their captivity; The Lord bless thee, O habitation of justice, and mountain of holiness. And there shall dwell in Judah itself, and in all the cities thereof together, husbandmen, and they that go forth with flocks. For I have satiated the weary soul, and I have replenished every sorrowful soul."

"Behold, the days come, saith the Lord, that I will make a new covenant with the house of Israel, and with the house of Judah: not according to the covenant that I made with their fathers in the day that I took them by the hand to bring them out of the land of Egypt; which My covenant they brake, although I was an husband unto them, saith the Lord: but this shall be the covenant that I will make with the house of Israel; After those days, saith the Lord, I will put My law in their inward parts, and write it in their hearts; and will be their God, and they shall be My people. And they shall teach no more every man his neighbor, and every man his brother, saying, Know the Lord: for they shall all know Me, from the least of them unto the greatest of them, saith the Lord: for I will forgive their iniquity, and I will remember their sin no more." Jeremiah 31:10-14, 23-25, 31-34. [477]

Chapter 39

In the Court of Babylon

Beginning of Section 5 — In the Lands of the Heathen. This chapter is based on Daniel 1.

Among the children of Israel who were carried captive to Babylon at the beginning of the seventy years' captivity were Christian patriots, men who were as true as steel to principle, who would not be corrupted by selfishness, but who would honor God at the loss of all things. In the land of their captivity these men were to carry out God's purpose by giving to heathen nations the blessings that come through a knowledge of Jehovah. They were to be His representatives. Never were they to compromise with idolaters; their faith and their name as worshipers of the living God they were to bear as a high honor. And this they did. In prosperity and adversity they honored God, and God honored them.

The fact that these men, worshipers of Jehovah, were captives in Babylon, and that the vessels of God's house had been placed in the Temple of the Babylonish gods, was boastfully cited by the victors as evidence that their religion [480] and customs were superior to the religion and customs of the Hebrews. Yet through the very humiliations that Israel's departure from Him had invited, God gave Babylon evidence of His supremacy, of the holiness of His requirements, and of the sure results of obedience. And this testimony He gave, as alone it could be given, through those who were loyal to Him.

Among those who maintained their allegiance to God were Daniel and his three companions—illustrious examples of what men may become who unite with the God of wisdom and power. From the comparative simplicity of their Jewish home, these youth of royal line were taken to the most magnificent of cities and into the court of the world's greatest monarch. Nebuchadnezzar "spake unto Ashpenaz the master of his eunuchs, that he should bring certain of the children of Israel, and of the king's seed, and of the princes; children in whom was no blemish, but well favored, and skillful in all wisdom, and cunning in knowledge, and understanding science, and such as had ability in them to stand in the king's palace...."

"Now among these were of the children of Judah, Daniel, Hananiah, Mishael, and Azariah." Seeing in these youth the promise of remarkable ability, Nebuchadnezzar determined that they should be trained to fill important positions in his kingdom. That they might be fully qualified for their lifework, he arranged for them to learn the language of the Chaldeans and for three years to be granted the unusual educational advantages afforded princes of the realm.

The names of Daniel and his companions were changed [481] to names representing Chaldean deities. Great significance was attached to the names given by Hebrew parents to their children. Often these stood for traits of character that the parent desired to see developed in the child. The prince in whose charge the captive youth were placed, "gave unto Daniel the name of Belteshazzar; and to Hananiah, of Shadrach; and to Mishael, of Meshach; and to Azariah, of Abednego."

The king did not compel the Hebrew youth to renounce their faith in favor of idolatry, but he hoped to bring this about gradually. By giving them names significant of idolatry, by bringing them daily into close association with idolatrous customs, and under the influence of the seductive rites of heathen worship, he hoped to induce them to renounce the religion of their nation and to unite with the worship of the Babylonians.

At the very outset of their career there came to them a decisive test of character. It was provided that they should eat of the food and drink of the wine that came from the king's table. In this the king thought to give them an expression of his favor and of his solicitude for their welfare. But a portion having been offered to idols, the food from the king's table was consecrated to idolatry; and one partaking of it would be regarded as offering homage to the gods of Babylon. In such homage, loyalty to Jehovah forbade Daniel and his companions to join. Even a mere pretense of eating the food or drinking the wine would be a denial of their faith. To do this would be to array themselves with heathenism and to dishonor the principles of the law of God. [482]

Nor dared they risk the enervating effect of luxury and dissipation on physical, mental, and spiritual development. They were acquainted with the history of Nadab and Abihu, the record of whose intemperance and its results had been preserved in the parchments of the Pentateuch; and they knew that their own physical and mental power would be injuriously affected by the use of wine.

Daniel and his associates had been trained by their parents to habits of strict temperance. They had been taught that God would hold them accountable for their capabilities, and that they must never dwarf or enfeeble their powers. This education was to Daniel and his companions the means of their preservation amidst the demoralizing influences of the court of Babylon. Strong were the temptations surrounding them in that corrupt and luxurious court, but they remained uncontaminated. No power, no influence, could sway them from the principles they had learned in early life by a study of the word and works of God.

Had Daniel so desired, he might have found in his surroundings a plausible excuse for departing from strictly temperate habits. He might have argued that, dependent as he was on the king's favor and subject to his power, there was no other course for him to pursue than to eat of the king's food and drink of his wine; for should he adhere to the divine teaching, he would offend the king and probably lose his position and his life. Should he disregard the commandment of the Lord he would retain the favor of the king and secure for himself intellectual advantages and flattering worldly prospects. [483]

But Daniel did not hesitate. The approval of God was dearer to him than the favor of the most powerful earthly potentate—dearer than life itself. He determined to stand firm in his integrity, let the result be what it might. He "purposed in his heart that he would not defile himself with the portion of the king's meat, nor with the wine which he drank." And in this resolve he was supported by his three companions.

In reaching this decision, the Hebrew youth did not act presumptuously but in firm reliance upon God. They did not choose to be singular, but they would be so rather than dishonor God. Should they compromise with wrong in this instance by yielding to the pressure of circumstances, their departure from principle would weaken their sense of right and their abhorrence of wrong. The first wrong step would lead to others, until, their connection with Heaven severed, they would be swept away by temptation.

"God had brought Daniel into favor and tender love with the prince of the eunuchs," and the request that he might not defile himself was received with respect. Yet the prince hesitated to grant it. "I fear my lord the king, who hath appointed your meat and your drink," he explained to Daniel; "for why should he see your faces worse liking than the children which are of your sort? then shall ye make me endanger my head to the king."

Daniel then appealed to Melzar, the officer in special charge of the Hebrew youth, requesting that they might be excused from eating the king's meat and drinking his wine. He asked that the matter be tested by a ten days' trial, the [484] Hebrew youth during this time being supplied with simple food, while their companions ate of the king's dainties.

Melzar, though fearful that by complying with this request he would incur the displeasure of the king, nevertheless consented; and Daniel knew that his case was won. At the end of the ten days' trial the result was found to be the opposite of the prince's fears. "Their countenances appeared fairer and fatter in flesh than all the children which did eat the portion of the king's meat." In personal appearance the Hebrew youth showed a marked superiority over their companions. As a result, Daniel and his associates were permitted to continue their simple diet during their entire course of training.

For three years the Hebrew youth studied to acquire "the learning and the tongue of the Chaldeans." During this time they held fast their allegiance to God and depended constantly upon His power. With their habits of self-denial they united earnestness of purpose, diligence, and steadfastness. It was not pride or ambition that had brought them into the king's court, into companionship with those who neither knew nor feared God; they were captives in a strange land, placed there by Infinite Wisdom. Separated from home influences and sacred associations, they sought to acquit themselves creditably, for the honor of their down-trodden people, and for the glory of Him whose servants they were.

The Lord regarded with approval the firmness and self-denial of the Hebrew youth, and their purity of motive; and His blessing attended them. He "gave them knowledge and skill in all learning and wisdom: and Daniel had understanding [485] in all visions and dreams." The promise was fulfilled, "Them that honor Me I will honor." 1 Samuel 2:30. As Daniel clung to God with unwavering trust, the spirit of prophetic power came upon him. While receiving instruction from man in the duties of court life, he was being taught by God to read the mysteries of the future and to record for coming generations, through figures and symbols, events covering the history of this world till the close of time.

When the time came for the youth in training to be tested, the Hebrews were examined, with other candidates, for the service of the kingdom. But "among them all was found none like Daniel, Hananiah, Mishael, and Azariah." Their keen comprehension, their wide knowledge, their choice and exact language, testified to the unimpaired strength and vigor of their mental powers. "In all matters of wisdom and understanding, that the king inquired of them, he found them ten times better than all the magicians and astrologers that were in all his realm;" "therefore stood they before the king."

At the court of Babylon were gathered representatives from all lands, men of the highest talent, men the most richly endowed with natural gifts, and possessed of the broadest culture that the world could bestow; yet among them all, the Hebrew youth were without a peer. In physical strength and beauty, in mental vigor and literary attainment, they stood unrivaled. The erect form, the firm, elastic step, the fair countenance, the undimmed senses, the untainted breath—all were so many certificates of good habits, insignia of the nobility with which nature honors those who are obedient to her laws. [486]

In acquiring the wisdom of the Babylonians, Daniel and his companions were far more successful than their fellow students; but their learning did not come by chance. They obtained their knowledge by the faithful use of their powers, under the guidance of the Holy Spirit. They placed themselves in connection with the Source of all wisdom, making the knowledge of God the foundation of their education. In faith they prayed for wisdom, and they lived their prayers. They placed themselves where God could bless them. They avoided that which would weaken their powers, and improved every opportunity to become intelligent in all lines of learning. They followed the rules of life that could not fail to give them strength of intellect. They sought to acquire knowledge for one purpose—that they might honor God. They realized that in order to stand as representatives of true religion amid the false religions of heathenism they must have clearness of intellect and must perfect a Christian character. And God Himself was their teacher. Constantly praying, conscientiously studying, keeping in touch with the Unseen, they walked with God as did Enoch.

True success in any line of work is not the result of chance or accident or destiny. It is the outworking of God's providences, the reward of faith and discretion, of virtue and perseverance. Fine mental qualities and a high moral tone are not the result of accident. God gives opportunities; success depends upon the use made of them.

While God was working in Daniel and his companions "to will and to do of His good pleasure," they were working out their own salvation. Philippians 2:13. Herein is revealed [487] the outworking of the divine principle of co-operation, without which no true success can be attained. Human effort avails nothing without divine power; and without human endeavor, divine effort is with many of no avail. To make God's grace our own, we must act our part. His grace is given to work in us to will and to do, but never as a substitute for our effort.

As the Lord co-operated with Daniel and his fellows, so He will co-operate with all who strive to do His will. And by the impartation of His Spirit He will strengthen every true purpose, every noble resolution. Those who walk in the path of obedience will encounter many hindrances. Strong, subtle influences may bind them to the world; but the Lord is able to render futile every agency that works for the defeat of His chosen ones; in His strength they may overcome every temptation, conquer every difficulty.

God brought Daniel and his associates into connection with the great men of Babylon, that in the midst of a nation of idolaters they might represent His character. How did they become fitted for a position of so great trust and honor? It was faithfulness in little things that gave complexion to their whole life. They honored God in the smallest duties, as well as in the larger responsibilities.

As God called Daniel to witness for Him in Babylon, so He calls us to be His witnesses in the world today. In the smallest as well as the largest affairs of life, He desires us to reveal to men the principles of His kingdom. Many are waiting for some great work to be brought to them, while daily they lose opportunities for revealing faithfulness to [488] God. Daily they fail of discharging with wholeheartedness the little duties of life. While they wait for some large work in which they may exercise supposedly great talents, and thus satisfy their ambitious longings, their days pass away.

In the life of the true Christian there are no nonessentials; in the sight of Omnipotence every duty is important. The Lord measures with exactness every possibility for service. The unused capabilities are just as much brought into account as those that are used. We shall be judged by what we ought to have done, but did not accomplish because we did not use our powers to glorify God.

A noble character is not the result of accident; it is not due to special favors or endowments of Providence. It is the result of self-discipline, of subjection of the lower to the higher nature, of the surrender of self to the service of God and man.

Through the fidelity to the principles of temperance shown by the Hebrew youth God is speaking to the youth of today. There is need of men who like Daniel will do and dare for the cause of right. Pure hearts, strong hands, fearless courage, are needed; for the warfare between vice and virtue calls for ceaseless vigilance. To every soul Satan comes with temptation in many alluring forms on the point of indulgence of appetite.

The body is a most important medium through which the mind and the soul are developed for the upbuilding of character. Hence it is that the adversary of souls directs his temptations to the enfeebling and degrading of the physical powers. His success here often means the surrender of the [489] whole being to evil. The tendencies of the physical nature, unless under the dominion of a higher power, will surely work ruin and death. The body is to be brought into subjection to the higher powers of the being. The passions are to be controlled by the will, which is itself to be under the control of God. The kingly power of reason, sanctified by divine grace, is to bear sway in the life. Intellectual power, physical stamina, and the length of life depend upon immutable laws. Through obedience to these laws, man may stand conqueror of himself, conqueror of his own inclinations, conqueror of principalities and powers, of "the rulers of the darkness of this world," and of "spiritual wickedness in high places." Ephesians 6:12.

In that ancient ritual which is the gospel in symbol, no blemished offering could be brought to God's altar. The sacrifice that was to represent Christ must be spotless. The word of God points to this as an illustration of what His children are to be—"a living sacrifice," "holy and without blemish." Romans 12:1; Ephesians 5:27.

The Hebrew worthies were men of like passions with ourselves; yet, notwithstanding the seductive influences of the court of Babylon, they stood firm, because they depended upon a strength that is infinite. In them a heathen nation beheld an illustration of the goodness and beneficence of God, and of the love of Christ. And in their experience we have an instance of the triumph of principle over temptation, of purity over depravity, of devotion and loyalty over atheism and idolatry.

The spirit that possessed Daniel, the youth of today may have; they may draw from the same source of strength, [490] possess the same power of self-control, and reveal the same grace in their lives, even under circumstances as unfavorable. Though surrounded by temptations to self-indulgence, especially in our large cities, where every form of sensual gratification is made easy and inviting, yet by divine grace their purpose to honor God may remain firm. Through strong resolution and vigilant watchfulness they may withstand every temptation that assails the soul. But only by him who determines to do right because it is right will the victory be gained.

What a lifework was that of these noble Hebrews! As they bade farewell to their childhood home, little did they dream what a high destiny was to be theirs. Faithful and steadfast, they yielded to the divine guiding, so that through them God could fulfill His purpose.

The same mighty truths that were revealed through these men, God desires to reveal through the youth and children today. The life of Daniel and his fellows is a demonstration of what He will do for those who yield themselves to Him and with the whole heart seek to accomplish His purpose. [491]

Chapter 40

Nebuchadnezzar's Dream

This chapter is based on Daniel 2.

Soon after Daniel and his companions entered the service of the king of Babylon, events occurred that revealed to an idolatrous nation the power and faithfulness of the God of Israel. Nebuchadnezzar had a remarkable dream, by which "his spirit was troubled, and his sleep brake from him." But although the king's mind was deeply impressed, he found it impossible, when he awoke, to recall the particulars.

In his perplexity, Nebuchadnezzar assembled his wise men—"the magicians, and the astrologers, and the sorcerers"—and besought their help. "I have dreamed a dream," he said, "and my spirit was troubled to know the dream." With this statement of his perplexity he requested them to reveal to him that which would bring relief to his mind.

To this the wise men responded, "O king, live forever: tell thy servants the dream, and we will show the interpretation." [492]

Dissatisfied with their evasive answer, and suspicious because, despite their pretentious claims to reveal the secrets of men, they nevertheless seemed unwilling to grant him help, the king commanded his wise men, with promises of wealth and honor on the one hand, and threats of death on the other, to tell him not only the interpretation of the dream, but the dream itself. "The thing is gone from me," he said; "if ye will not make known unto me the dream, with the interpretation thereof, ye shall be cut in pieces, and your houses shall be made a dunghill. But if ye show the dream, and the interpretation thereof, ye shall receive of me gifts and rewards and great honor."

Still the wise men returned the answer, "Let the king tell his servants the dream, and we will show the interpretation of it."

Nebuchadnezzar, now thoroughly aroused and angered by the apparent perfidy of those in whom he had trusted, declared: "I know of certainty that ye would gain the time, because ye see the thing is gone from me. But if ye will not make known unto me the dream, there is but one decree for you: for ye have prepared lying and corrupt words to speak before me, till the time be changed: therefore tell me the dream, and I shall know that ye can show me the interpretation thereof."

Filled with fear for the consequences of their failure, the magicians endeavored to show the king that his request was unreasonable and his test beyond that which had ever been required of any man. "There is not a man upon the earth," they remonstrated, "that can show the king's matter: therefore there is no king, lord, nor ruler, that asked such things [493] at any magician, or astrologer, or Chaldean. And it is a rare thing that the king requireth, and there is none other that can show it before the king, except the gods, whose dwelling is not with flesh."

Then "the king was angry and very furious, and commanded to destroy all the wise men of Babylon."

Among those sought for by the officers who were preparing to fulfill the provisions of the royal decree, were Daniel and his friends. When told that according to the decree they also must die, "with counsel and wisdom" Daniel inquired of Arioch, the captain of the king's guard, "Why is the decree so hasty from the king?" Arioch told him the story of the king's perplexity over his remarkable dream, and of his failure to secure help from those in whom he had hitherto placed fullest confidence. Upon hearing this, Daniel, taking his life in his hands, ventured into the king's presence and begged that time be granted, that he might petition his God to reveal to him the dream and its interpretation.

To this request the monarch acceded. "Then Daniel went to his house, and made the thing known to Hananiah, Mishael, and Azariah, his companions." Together they sought for wisdom from the Source of light and knowledge. Their faith was strong in the consciousness that God had placed them where they were, that they were doing His work and meeting the demands of duty. In times of perplexity and danger they had always turned to Him for guidance and protection, and He had proved an ever-present help. Now with contrition of heart they submitted themselves anew to the Judge of the earth, pleading that He would [494] grant them deliverance in this their time of special need. And they did not plead in vain. The God whom they had honored, now honored them. The Spirit of the Lord rested upon them, and to Daniel, "in a night vision," was revealed the king's dream and its meaning.

Daniel's first act was to thank God for the revelation given him. "Blessed be the name of God forever and ever," he exclaimed; "for wisdom and might are His: and He changeth the times and the seasons: He removeth kings, and setteth up kings: He giveth wisdom unto the wise, and knowledge to them that know understanding: He revealeth the deep and secret things: He knoweth what is in the darkness, and the light dwelleth with Him. I thank Thee, and praise Thee, O Thou God of my fathers, who hast given me wisdom and might, and hast made known unto me now what we desired of Thee: for Thou hast now made known unto us the king's matter."

Going immediately to Arioch, whom the king had commanded to destroy the wise men, Daniel said, "Destroy not the wise men of Babylon: bring me in before the king, and I will show unto the king the interpretation." Quickly the officer ushered Daniel in before the king, with the words, "I have found a man of the captives of Judah, that will make known unto the king the interpretation."

Behold the Jewish captive, calm and self-possessed, in the presence of the monarch of the world's most powerful empire. In his first words he disclaimed honor for himself and exalted God as the source of all wisdom. To the anxious inquiry of the king, "Art thou able to make known unto me the dream which I have seen, and the interpretation [495] [496] [497] thereof?" he replied: "The secret which the king hath demanded cannot the wise men, the astrologers, the magicians, the soothsayers, show unto the king; but there is a God in heaven that revealeth secrets, and maketh known to the king Nebuchadnezzar what shall be in the latter days.

"Thy dream," Daniel declared, "and the visions of thy head upon thy bed, are these; As for thee, O king, thy thoughts came into thy mind upon thy bed, what should come to pass hereafter: and He that revealeth secrets maketh known to thee what shall come to pass. But as for me, this secret is not revealed to me for any wisdom that I have more than any living, but for their sakes that shall make known the interpretation to the king, and that thou mightest know the thoughts of thy heart.

"Thou, O king, sawest, and behold a great image. This great image, whose brightness was excellent, stood before thee; and the form thereof was terrible. This image's head was of fine gold, his breast and his arms of silver, his belly and his thighs of brass, his legs of iron, his feet part of iron and part of clay.

"Thou sawest till that a stone was cut out without hands, which smote the image upon his feet that were of iron and clay, and brake them to pieces. Then was the iron, the clay, the brass, the silver, and the gold, broken to pieces together, and became like the chaff of the summer threshing floors; and the wind carried them away, that no place was found for them: and the stone that smote the image became a great mountain, and filled the whole earth.

"This is the dream," confidently declared Daniel; and the king, listening with closest attention to every particular, [498] knew it was the very dream over which he had been so troubled. Thus his mind was prepared to receive with favor the interpretation. The King of kings was about to communicate great truth to the Babylonian monarch. God would reveal that He has power over the kingdoms of the world, power to enthrone and to dethrone kings. Nebuchadnezzar's mind was to be awakened, if possible, to a sense of his responsibility to Heaven. The events of the future, reaching down to the end of time, were to be opened before him.

"Thou, O king, art a king of kings," Daniel continued, "for the God of heaven hath given thee a kingdom, power, and strength, and glory. And wheresoever the children of men dwell, the beasts of the field and fowls of the heaven hath He given into thine hand, and hath made thee ruler over them all. Thou art this head of gold.

"And after thee shall arise another kingdom inferior to thee, and another third kingdom of brass, which shall bear rule over all the earth.

"And the fourth kingdom shall be strong as iron: forasmuch as iron breaketh in pieces and subdueth all things: and as iron that breaketh all these, shall it break in pieces and bruise.

"And whereas thou sawest the feet and toes, part of potters' clay, and part of iron, the kingdom shall be divided; but there shall be in it of the strength of the iron, forasmuch as thou sawest the iron mixed with miry clay. And as the toes of the feet were part of iron, and part of clay, so the kingdom shall be partly strong, and partly broken. And whereas thou sawest iron mixed with miry clay, they shall [499] mingle themselves with the seed of men: but they shall not cleave one to another, even as iron is not mixed with clay."

"In the days of these kings shall the God of heaven set up a kingdom, which shall never be destroyed: and the kingdom shall not be left to other people, but it shall break in pieces and consume all these kingdoms, and it shall stand forever. Forasmuch as thou sawest that the stone was cut out of the mountain without hands, and that it brake in pieces the iron, the brass, the clay, the silver, and the gold; the great God hath made known to the king what shall come to pass hereafter: and the dream is certain, and the interpretation thereof sure."

The king was convinced of the truth of the interpretation, and in humility and awe he "fell upon his face, and worshiped," saying, "Of a truth it is, that your God is a God of gods, and a Lord of kings, and a revealer of secrets, seeing thou couldest reveal this secret."

Nebuchadnezzar revoked the decree for the destruction of the wise men. Their lives were spared because of Daniel's connection with the Revealer of secrets. And "the king made Daniel a great man, and gave him many great gifts, and made him ruler over the whole province of Babylon, and chief of the governors over all the wise men of Babylon. Then Daniel requested of the king, and he set Shadrach, Meshach, and Abednego, over the affairs of the province of Babylon: but Daniel sat in the gate of the king."

In the annals of human history, the growth of nations, the rise and fall of empires, appear as if dependent on the will and prowess of man; the shaping of events seems, to [500] a great degree, to be determined by his power, ambition, or caprice. But in the word of God the curtain is drawn aside, and we behold, above, behind, and through all the play and counterplay of human interest and power and passions, the agencies of the All-merciful One, silently, patiently working out the counsels of His own will.

In words of matchless beauty and tenderness, the apostle Paul set before the sages of Athens the divine purpose in the creation and distribution of races and nations. "God that made the world and all things therein," declared the apostle, "hath made of one blood all nations of men for to dwell on all the face of the earth, and hath determined the times before appointed, and the bounds of their habitation; that they should seek the Lord, if haply they might feel after Him, and find Him." Acts 17:24-27.

God has made plain that whosoever will, may come "into the bond of the covenant." Ezekiel 20:37. In the creation it was His purpose that the earth should be inhabited by beings whose existence would be a blessing to themselves and to one another, and an honor to their Creator. All who will may identify themselves with this purpose. Of them it is spoken, "This people have I formed for Myself; they shall show forth My praise." Isaiah 43:21.

In His law God has made known the principles that underlie all true prosperity, both of nations and of individuals. To the Israelites Moses declared of this law: "This is your wisdom and your understanding." "It is not a vain thing for you; because it is your life." Deuteronomy 4:6; 32:47. The blessings thus assured to Israel are, on the same [501] conditions and in the same degree, assured to every nation and to every individual under the broad heavens.

Hundreds of years before certain nations came upon the stage of action, the Omniscient One looked down the ages and predicted the rise and fall of the universal kingdoms. God declared to Nebuchadnezzar that the kingdom of Babylon should fall, and a second kingdom would arise, which also would have its period of trial. Failing to exalt the true God, its glory would fade, and a third kingdom would occupy its place. This also would pass away; and a fourth, strong as iron, would subdue the nations of the world.

Had the rulers of Babylon—that richest of all earthly kingdoms—kept always before them the fear of Jehovah, they would have been given wisdom and power which would have bound them to Him and kept them strong. But they made God their refuge only when harassed and perplexed. At such times, failing to find help in their great men, they sought it from men like Daniel—men who they knew honored the living God and were honored by Him. To these men they appealed to unravel the mysteries of Providence; for though the rulers of proud Babylon were men of the highest intellect, they had separated themselves so far from God by transgression that they could not understand the revelations and the warnings given them concerning the future.

In the history of nations the student of God's word may behold the literal fulfillment of divine prophecy. Babylon, shattered and broken at last, passed away because in prosperity its rulers had regarded themselves as independent of [502] God, and had ascribed the glory of their kingdom to human achievement. The Medo-Persian realm was visited by the wrath of Heaven because in it God's law had been trampled underfoot. The fear of the Lord had found no place in the hearts of the vast majority of the people. Wickedness, blasphemy, and corruption prevailed. The kingdoms that followed were even more base and corrupt; and these sank lower and still lower in the scale of moral worth.

The power exercised by every ruler on the earth is Heaven-imparted; and upon his use of the power thus bestowed, his success depends. To each the word of the divine Watcher is, "I girded thee, though thou hast not known Me." Isaiah 45:5. And to each the words spoken to Nebuchadnezzar of old are the lesson of life: "Break off thy sins by righteousness, and thine iniquities by showing mercy to the poor: if it may be a lengthening of thy tranquillity." Daniel 4:27.

To understand these things,—to understand that "righteousness exalteth a nation;" that "the throne is established by righteousness," and "upholden by mercy;" to recognize the outworking of these principles in the manifestation of His power who "removeth kings, and setteth up kings,"—this is to understand the philosophy of history. Proverbs 14:34; 16:12; Proverbs 20:28; Daniel 2:21.

In the word of God only is this clearly set forth. Here it is shown that the strength of nations, as of individuals, is not found in the opportunities or facilities that appear to make them invincible; it is not found in their boasted greatness. It is measured by the fidelity with which they fulfill God's purpose. [503]

Chapter 41

The Fiery Furnace

This chapter is based on Daniel 3.

The dream of the great image, opening before Nebuchadnezzar events reaching to the close of time, had been given that he might understand the part he was to act in the world's history, and the relation that his kingdom should sustain to the kingdom of heaven. In the interpretation of the dream, he had been plainly instructed regarding the establishment of God's everlasting kingdom. "In the days of these kings," Daniel had declared, "shall the God of heaven set up a kingdom, which shall never be destroyed: and the kingdom shall not be left to other people, but it shall break in pieces and consume all these kingdoms, and it shall stand forever.... The dream is certain, and the interpretation thereof sure." Daniel 2:44, 45.

The king had acknowledged the power of God, saying to Daniel, "Of a truth it is, that your God is a God of gods, ... and a revealer of secrets." Verse 47. For a time afterward, Nebuchadnezzar was influenced by the fear of God; [504] but his heart was not yet cleansed from worldly ambition and a desire for self-exaltation. The prosperity attending his reign filled him with pride. In time he ceased to honor God, and resumed his idol worship with increased zeal and bigotry.

The words, "Thou art this head of gold," had made a deep impression upon the ruler's mind. Verse 38. The wise men of his realm, taking advantage of this and of his return to idolatry, proposed that he make an image similar to the one seen in his dream, and set it up where all might behold the head of gold, which had been interpreted as representing his kingdom.

Pleased with the flattering suggestion, he determined to carry it out, and to go even farther. Instead of reproducing the image as he had seen it, he would excel the original. His image should not deteriorate in value from the head to the feet, but should be entirely of gold—symbolic throughout of Babylon as an eternal, indestructible, all-powerful kingdom, which should break in pieces all other kingdoms and stand forever.

The thought of establishing the empire and a dynasty that should endure forever, appealed very strongly to the mighty ruler before whose arms the nations of earth had been unable to stand. With an enthusiasm born of boundless ambition and selfish pride, he entered into counsel with his wise men as to how to bring this about. Forgetting the remarkable providences connected with the dream of the great image; forgetting also that the God of Israel through His servant Daniel had made plain the significance of the image, and that in connection with this interpretation the [505] great men of the realm had been saved an ignominious death; forgetting all except their desire to establish their own power and supremacy, the king and his counselors of state determined that by every means possible they would endeavor to exalt Babylon as supreme, and worthy of universal allegiance.

The symbolic representation by which God had revealed to king and people His purpose for the nations of earth, was now to be made to serve for the glorification of human power. Daniel's interpretation was to be rejected and forgotten; truth was to be misinterpreted and misapplied. The symbol designed of Heaven to unfold to the minds of men important events of the future, was to be used to hinder the spread of the knowledge that God desired the world to receive. Thus through the devisings of ambitious men, Satan was seeking to thwart the divine purpose for the human race. The enemy of mankind knew that truth unmixed with error is a power mighty to save; but that when used to exalt self and to further the projects of men, it becomes a power for evil.

From his rich store of treasure, Nebuchadnezzar caused to be made a great golden image, similar in its general features to that which had been seen in vision, save in the one particular of the material of which it was composed. Accustomed as they were to magnificent representations of their heathen deities, the Chaldeans had never before produced anything so imposing and majestic as this resplendent statue, threescore cubits in height and six cubits in breadth. And it is not surprising that in a land where idol worship was of universal prevalence, the beautiful and priceless [506] image in the plain of Dura, representing the glory of Babylon and its magnificence and power, should be consecrated as an object of worship. This was accordingly provided for, and a decree went forth that on the day of the dedication all should show their supreme loyalty to the Babylonian power by bowing before the image.

The appointed day came, and a vast concourse from all "people, nations, and languages," assembled on the plain of Dura. In harmony with the king's command, when the sound of music was heard, the whole company "fell down and worshipped the golden image." On that eventful day the powers of darkness seemed to be gaining a signal triumph; the worship of the golden image bade fair to become connected permanently with the established forms of idolatry recognized as the state religion of the land. Satan hoped thereby to defeat God's purpose of making the presence of captive Israel in Babylon a means of blessing to all the nations of heathendom.

But God decreed otherwise. Not all had bowed the knee to the idolatrous symbol of human power. In the midst of the worshipping multitude there were three men who were firmly resolved not thus to dishonor the God of heaven. Their God was King of kings and Lord of lords; they would bow to none other.

To Nebuchadnezzar, flushed with triumph, was brought the word that among his subjects there were some who dared disobey his mandate. Certain of the wise men, jealous of the honors that had been bestowed upon the faithful companions of Daniel, now reported to the king their flagrant [507] violation of his wishes. "O king, live forever," they exclaimed. "There are certain Jews whom thou hast set over the affairs of the province of Babylon, Shadrach, Meshach, and Abednego; these men, O king, have not regarded thee: they serve not thy gods, nor worship the golden image which thou hast set up."

The king commanded that the men be brought before him. "Is it true," he inquired, "do not ye serve my gods, nor worship the golden image which I have set up?" He endeavored by threats to induce them to unite with the multitude. Pointing to the fiery furnace, he reminded them of the punishment awaiting them if they should persist in their refusal to obey his will. But firmly the Hebrews testified to their allegiance to the God of heaven, and their faith in His power to deliver. The act of bowing to the image was understood by all to be an act of worship. Such homage they could render to God alone.

As the three Hebrews stood before the king, he was convinced that they possessed something the other wise men of his kingdom did not have. They had been faithful in the performance of every duty. He would give them another trial. If only they would signify their willingness to unite with the multitude in worshiping the image, all would be well with them; "but if ye worship not," he added, "ye shall be cast the same hour into the midst of a burning fiery furnace." Then with his hand stretched upward in defiance, he demanded, "Who is that God that shall deliver you out of my hands?"

In vain were the king's threats. He could not turn the [508] men from their allegiance to the Ruler of the universe. From the history of their fathers they had learned that disobedience to God results in dishonor, disaster, and death; and that the fear of the Lord is the beginning of wisdom, the foundation of all true prosperity. Calmly facing the furnace, they said, "O Nebuchadnezzar, we are not careful to answer thee in this matter. If it be so [if this is your decision], our God whom we serve is able to deliver us from the burning fiery furnace, and He will deliver us out of thine hand, O king." Their faith strengthened as they declared that God would be glorified by delivering them, and with triumphant assurance born of implicit trust in God, they added, "But if not, be it known unto thee, O king, that we will not serve thy gods, nor worship the golden image which thou hast set up."

The king's wrath knew no bounds. "Full of fury," "the form of his visage was changed against Shadrach, Meshach, and Abednego," representatives of a despised and captive race. Directing that the furnace be heated seven times hotter than its wont, he commanded the mighty men of his army to bind the worshipers of Israel's God, preparatory to summary execution.

"Then these men were bound in their coats, their hosen, and their hats, and their other garments, and were cast into the midst of the burning fiery furnace. Therefore because the king's commandment was urgent, and the furnace exceeding hot, the flame of the fire slew those men that took up Shadrach, Meshach, and Abednego."

But the Lord did not forget His own. As His witnesses were cast into the furnace, the Saviour revealed Himself to [509] them in person, and together they walked in the midst of the fire. In the presence of the Lord of heat and cold, the flames lost their power to consume.

From his royal seat the king looked on, expecting to see the men who had defied him utterly destroyed. But his feelings of triumph suddenly changed. The nobles standing near saw his face grow pale as he started from the throne and looked intently into the glowing flames. In alarm the king, turning to his lords, asked, "Did not we cast three men bound into the midst of the fire? ... Lo, I see four men loose, walking in the midst of the fire, and they have no hurt; and the form of the fourth is like the Son of God."

How did that heathen king know what the Son of God was like? The Hebrew captives filling positions of trust in Babylon had in life and character represented before him the truth. When asked for a reason of their faith, they had given it without hesitation. Plainly and simply they had presented the principles of righteousness, thus teaching those around them of the God whom they worshiped. They had told of Christ, the Redeemer to come; and in the form of the fourth in the midst of the fire the king recognized the Son of God.

And now, his own greatness and dignity forgotten, Nebuchadnezzar descended from his throne and, going to the mouth of the furnace, cried out, "Ye servants of the most high God, come forth, and come hither."

Then Shadrach, Meshach, and Abednego came forth before the vast multitude, showing themselves unhurt. The presence of their Saviour had guarded them from harm, and only their fetters had been burned. "And the princes, governors, [510] and captains, and the king's counselors, being gathered together, saw these men, upon whose bodies the fire had no power, nor was an hair of their head singed, neither were their coats changed, nor the smell of fire had passed on them."

Forgotten was the great golden image, set up with such pomp. In the presence of the living God, men feared and trembled. "Blessed be the God of Shadrach, Meshach, and Abednego," the humbled king was constrained to acknowledge, "who hath sent His angel, and delivered His servants that trusted in Him, and have changed the king's word, and yielded their bodies, that they might not serve nor worship any god, except their own God."

The experiences of that day led Nebuchadnezzar to issue a decree, "that every people, nation, and language, which speak anything amiss against the God of Shadrach, Meshach, and Abednego, shall be cut in pieces, and their houses shall be made a dunghill." "There is no other god," he urged as the reason for the decree, "that can deliver after this sort."

In these and like words the king of Babylon endeavored to spread abroad before all the peoples of earth his conviction that the power and authority of the God of the Hebrews was worthy of supreme adoration. And God was pleased with the effort of the king to show Him reverence, and to make the royal confession of allegiance as widespread as was the Babylonian realm.

It was right for the king to make public confession, and to seek to exalt the God of heaven above all other gods; but in endeavoring to force his subjects to make a similar confession [511] of faith and to show similar reverence, Nebuchadnezzar was exceeding his right as a temporal sovereign. He had no more right, either civil or moral, to threaten men with death for not worshiping God, than he had to make the decree consigning to the flames all who refused to worship the golden image. God never compels the obedience of man. He leaves all free to choose whom they will serve.

By the deliverance of His faithful servants, the Lord declared that He takes His stand with the oppressed, and rebukes all earthly powers that rebel against the authority [512] of Heaven. The three Hebrews declared to the whole nation of Babylon their faith in Him whom they worshiped. They relied on God. In the hour of their trial they remembered the promise, "When thou passest through the waters, I will be with thee; and through the rivers, they shall not overflow thee: when thou walkest through the fire, thou shalt not be burned; neither shall the flame kindle upon thee." Isaiah 43:2. And in a marvelous manner their faith in the living Word had been honored in the sight of all. The tidings of their wonderful deliverance were carried to many countries by the representatives of the different nations that had been invited by Nebuchadnezzar to the dedication. Through the faithfulness of His children, God was glorified in all the earth.

Important are the lessons to be learned from the experience of the Hebrew youth on the plain of Dura. In this our day, many of God's servants, though innocent of wrongdoing, will be given over to suffer humiliation and abuse at the hands of those who, inspired by Satan, are filled with envy and religious bigotry. Especially will the wrath of man be aroused against those who hallow the Sabbath of the fourth commandment; and at last a universal decree will denounce these as deserving of death.

The season of distress before God's people will call for a faith that will not falter. His children must make it manifest that He is the only object of their worship, and that no consideration, not even that of life itself, can induce them to make the least concession to false worship. To the loyal heart the commands of sinful, finite men will sink into [513] insignificance beside the word of the eternal God. Truth will be obeyed though the result be imprisonment or exile or death.

As in the days of Shadrach, Meshach, and Abednego, so in the closing period of earth's history the Lord will work mightily in behalf of those who stand steadfastly for the right. He who walked with the Hebrew worthies in the fiery furnace will be with His followers wherever they are. His abiding presence will comfort and sustain. In the midst of the time of trouble—trouble such as has not been since there was a nation—His chosen ones will stand unmoved. Satan with all the hosts of evil cannot destroy the weakest of God's saints. Angels that excel in strength will protect them, and in their behalf Jehovah will reveal Himself as a "God of gods," able to save to the uttermost those who have put their trust in Him. [514]

Chapter 42

True Greatness

This chapter is based on Daniel 4.

Exalted to the pinnacle of worldly honor, and acknowledged even by Inspiration as "a king of kings" (Ezekiel 26:7). Nebuchadnezzar nevertheless at times had ascribed to the favor of Jehovah the glory of his kingdom and the splendor of his reign. Such had been the case after his dream of the great image. His mind had been profoundly influenced by this vision and by the thought that the Babylonian Empire, universal though it was, was finally to fall, and other kingdoms were to bear sway, until at last all earthly powers were to be superseded by a kingdom set up by the God of heaven, which kingdom was never to be destroyed.

Nebuchadnezzar's noble conception of God's purpose concerning the nations was lost sight of later in his experience; yet when his proud spirit was humbled before the multitude on the plain of Dura, he once more had acknowledged that God's kingdom is "an everlasting kingdom, and His dominion is from generation to generation." An idolater [515] by birth and training, and at the head of an idolatrous people, he had nevertheless an innate sense of justice and right, and God was able to use him as an instrument for the punishment of the rebellious and for the fulfillment of the divine purpose. "The terrible of the nations" (Ezekiel 28:7), it was given Nebuchadnezzar, after years of patient and wearing labor, to conquer Tyre; Egypt also fell a prey to his victorious armies; and as he added nation after nation to the Babylonian realm, he added more and more to his fame as the greatest ruler of the age.

It is not surprising that the successful monarch, so ambitious and so proud-spirited, should be tempted to turn aside from the path of humility, which alone leads to true greatness. In the intervals between his wars of conquest he gave much thought to the strengthening and beautifying of his capital, until at length the city of Babylon became the chief glory of his kingdom, "the golden city," "the praise of the whole earth." His passion as a builder, and his signal success in making Babylon one of the wonders of the world, ministered to his pride, until he was in grave danger of spoiling his record as a wise ruler whom God could continue to use as an instrument for the carrying out of the divine purpose.

In mercy God gave the king another dream, to warn him of his peril and of the snare that had been laid for his ruin. In a vision of the night, Nebuchadnezzar saw a great tree growing in the midst of the earth, its top towering to the heavens and its branches stretching to the ends of the earth. Flocks and herds from the mountains and hills enjoyed shelter beneath its shadow, and the birds of [516] the air built their nests in its boughs. "The leaves thereof were fair, and the fruit thereof much, and in it was meat for all: ... and all flesh was fed of it."

As the king gazed upon the lofty tree, he beheld "a Watcher," even "an Holy One," who approached the tree and in a loud voice cried:

"Hew down the tree, and cut off his branches, shake off his leaves, and scatter his fruit: let the beasts get away from under it, and the fowls from his branches: nevertheless leave the stump of his roots in the earth, even with a band of iron and brass, in the tender grass of the field; and let it be wet with the dew of heaven, and let his portion be with the beasts in the grass of the earth: let his heart be changed from man's, and let a beast's heart be given unto him; and let seven times pass over him. This matter is by the decree of the watchers, and the demand by the word of the holy ones: to the intent that the living may know that the Most High ruleth in the kingdom of men, and giveth it to whomsoever He will, and setteth up over it the basest of men."

Greatly troubled by the dream, which was evidently a prediction of adversity, the king repeated it to "the magicians, the astrologers, the Chaldeans, and the soothsayers;" but although the dream was very explicit, none of the wise men could interpret it.

Once more in this idolatrous nation, testimony was to be borne to the fact that only those who love and fear God can understand the mysteries of the kingdom of heaven. The king in his perplexity sent for his servant Daniel, a man esteemed for his integrity and constancy and for his unrivaled wisdom. [517]

When Daniel, in response to the royal summons, stood in the king's presence, Nebuchadnezzar said, "O Belteshazzar, master of the magicians, because I know that the spirit of the holy gods is in thee, and no secret troubleth thee, tell me the visions of my dream that I have seen, and the interpretation thereof." After relating the dream, Nebuchadnezzar said: "O Belteshazzar, declare the interpretation thereof, forasmuch as all the wise men of my kingdom are not able to make known unto me the interpretation: but thou art able; for the spirit of the holy gods is in thee."

To Daniel the meaning of the dream was plain, and its significance startled him. He "was astonied for one hour, and his thoughts troubled him." Seeing Daniel's hesitation and distress, the king expressed sympathy for his servant. "Belteshazzar," he said, "let not the dream, or the interpretation thereof, trouble thee."

"My lord," Daniel answered, "the dream be to them that hate thee, and the interpretation thereof to thine enemies." The prophet realized that upon him God had laid the solemn duty of revealing to Nebuchadnezzar the judgment that was about to fall upon him because of his pride and arrogance. Daniel must interpret the dream in language the king could understand; and although its dreadful import had made him hesitate in dumb amazement, yet he must state the truth, whatever the consequences to himself.

Then Daniel made known the mandate of the Almighty. "The tree that thou sawest," he said, "which grew, and was strong, whose height reached unto the heaven, and the sight thereof to all the earth; whose leaves were fair, and [518] the fruit thereof much, and in it was meat for all; under which the beast of the field dwelt, and upon whose branches the fowls of the heaven had their habitation: it is thou, O king, that art grown and become strong: for thy greatness is grown, and reacheth unto heaven, and thy dominion to the end of the earth.

"And whereas the king saw a Watcher and an Holy One coming down from heaven, and saying, Hew the tree down, and destroy it; yet leave the stump of the roots thereof in the earth, even with a band of iron and brass, in the tender grass of the field; and let it be wet with the dew of heaven, and let his portion be with the beasts of the field, till seven times pass over him; this is the interpretation, O king, and this is the decree of the Most High, which is come upon my lord the king: that they shall drive thee from men, and thy dwelling shall be with the beasts of the field, and they shall make thee to eat grass as oxen, and they shall wet thee with the dew of heaven, and seven times shall pass over thee, till thou know that the Most High ruleth in the kingdom of men, and giveth it to whomsoever He will. And whereas they commanded to leave the stump of the tree roots; thy kingdom shall be sure unto thee, after that thou shalt have known that the Heavens do rule."

Having faithfully interpreted the dream, Daniel urged the proud monarch to repent and turn to God, that by rightdoing he might avert the threatened calamity. "O king," the prophet pleaded, "let my counsel be acceptable unto thee, and break off thy sins by righteousness, and thine iniquities [519] by showing mercy to the poor; if it may be a lengthening of thy tranquillity."

For a time the impression of the warning and the counsel of the prophet was strong upon Nebuchadnezzar; but the heart that is not transformed by the grace of God soon loses the impressions of the Holy Spirit. Self-indulgence and ambition had not yet been eradicated from the king's heart, and later on these traits reappeared. Notwithstanding the instruction so graciously given him, and the warnings of past experience, Nebuchadnezzar again allowed himself to be controlled by a spirit of jealousy against the kingdoms that were to follow. His rule, which heretofore had been to a great degree just and merciful, became oppressive. Hardening his heart, he used his God-given talents for self-glorification, exalting himself above the God who had given him life and power.

For months the judgment of God lingered. But instead of being led to repentance by this forbearance, the king indulged his pride until he lost confidence in the interpretation of the dream, and jested at his former fears.

A year from the time he had received the warning, Nebuchadnezzar, walking in his palace and thinking with pride of his power as a ruler and of his success as a builder, exclaimed, "Is not this great Babylon, that I have built for the house of the kingdom by the might of my power, and for the honor of my majesty?"

While the proud boast was yet on the king's lips, a voice from heaven announced that God's appointed time of judgment [520] had come. Upon his ears fell the mandate of Jehovah: "O King Nebuchadnezzar, to thee it is spoken; The kingdom is departed from thee. And they shall drive thee from men, and thy dwelling shall be with the beasts of the field: they shall make thee to eat grass as oxen, and seven times shall pass over thee, until thou know that the Most High ruleth in the kingdom of men, and giveth it to whomsoever He will."

In a moment the reason that God had given him was taken away; the judgment that the king thought perfect, the wisdom on which he prided himself, was removed, and the once mighty ruler was a maniac. His hand could no longer sway the scepter. The messages of warning had been unheeded; now, stripped of the power his Creator had given him, and driven from men, Nebuchadnezzar "did eat grass as oxen, and his body was wet with the dew of heaven, till his hairs were grown like eagles' feathers, and his nails like birds' claws."

For seven years Nebuchadnezzar was an astonishment to all his subjects; for seven years he was humbled before all the world. Then his reason was restored and, looking up in humility to the God of heaven, he recognized the divine hand in his chastisement. In a public proclamation he acknowledged his guilt and the great mercy of God in his restoration. "At the end of the days," he said, "I Nebuchadnezzar lifted up mine eyes unto heaven, and mine understanding returned unto me, and I blessed the Most High, and I praised and honored Him that liveth forever, whose dominion is an everlasting dominion, and His kingdom [521] is from generation to generation: and all the inhabitants of the earth are reputed as nothing: and He doeth according to His will in the army of heaven, and among the inhabitants of the earth: and none can stay His hand, or say unto Him, What doest Thou?

"At the same time my reason returned unto me; and for the glory of my kingdom, mine honor and brightness returned unto me; and my counselors and my lords sought unto me; and I was established in my kingdom, and excellent majesty was added unto me."

The once proud monarch had become a humble child of God; the tyrannical, overbearing ruler, a wise and compassionate king. He who had defied and blasphemed the God of heaven, now acknowledged the power of the Most High and earnestly sought to promote the fear of Jehovah and the happiness of his subjects. Under the rebuke of Him who is King of kings and Lord of lords, Nebuchadnezzar had learned at last the lesson which all rulers need to learn—that true greatness consists in true goodness. He acknowledged Jehovah as the living God, saying, "I Nebuchadnezzar praise and extol and honor the King of heaven, all whose works are truth, and His ways judgment: and those that walk in pride He is able to abase."

God's purpose that the greatest kingdom in the world should show forth His praise was now fulfilled. This public proclamation, in which Nebuchadnezzar acknowledged the mercy and goodness and authority of God, was the last act of his life recorded in sacred history. [522]

Chapter 43

The Unseen Watcher

This chapter is based on Daniel 5.

Toward the close of Daniel's life great changes were taking place in the land to which, over threescore years before, he and his Hebrew companions had been carried captive. Nebuchadnezzar, "the terrible of the nations" (Ezekiel 28:7), had died, and Babylon, "the praise of the whole earth" (Jeremiah 51:41), had passed under the unwise rule of his successors, and gradual but sure dissolution was resulting.

Through the folly and weakness of Belshazzar, the grandson of Nebuchadnezzar, proud Babylon was soon to fall. Admitted in his youth to a share in kingly authority, Belshazzar gloried in his power and lifted up his heart against the God of heaven. Many had been his opportunities to know the divine will and to understand his responsibility of rendering obedience thereto. He had known of his grandfather's banishment, by the decree of God, from the society of men; and he was familiar with Nebuchadnezzar's conversion and miraculous restoration. But Belshazzar [523] allowed the love of pleasure and self-glorification to efface the lessons that he should never have forgotten. He wasted the opportunities graciously granted him, and neglected to use the means within his reach for becoming more fully acquainted with truth. That which Nebuchadnezzar had finally gained at the cost of untold suffering and humiliation, Belshazzar passed by with indifference.

It was not long before reverses came. Babylon was besieged by Cyrus, nephew of Darius the Mede, and commanding general of the combined armies of the Medes and Persians. But within the seemingly impregnable fortress, with its massive walls and its gates of brass, protected by the river Euphrates, and stocked with provision in abundance, the voluptuous monarch felt safe and passed his time in mirth and revelry.

In his pride and arrogancy, with a reckless feeling of security Belshazzar "made a great feast to a thousand of his lords, and drank wine before the thousand." All the attractions that wealth and power could command, added splendor to the scene. Beautiful women with their enchantments were among the guests in attendance at the royal banquet. Men of genius and education were there. Princes and statesmen drank wine like water and reveled under its maddening influence.

With reason dethroned through shameless intoxication, and with lower impulses and passions now in the ascendancy, the king himself took the lead in the riotous orgy. As the feast progressed, he "commanded to bring the golden and silver vessels which ... Nebuchadnezzar had taken out of [524] the temple which was in Jerusalem; that the king, and his princes, his wives, and his concubines, might drink therein." The king would prove that nothing was too sacred for his hands to handle. "They brought the golden vessels; ... and the king, and his princes, his wives, and his concubines, drank in them. They drank wine, and praised the gods of gold, and of silver, of brass, of iron, of wood, and of stone."

Little did Belshazzar think that there was a heavenly Witness to his idolatrous revelry; that a divine Watcher, unrecognized, looked upon the scene of profanation, heard the sacrilegious mirth, beheld the idolatry. But soon the uninvited Guest made His presence felt. When the revelry was at its height a bloodless hand came forth and traced upon the walls of the palace characters that gleamed like fire—words which, though unknown to the vast throng, were a portent of doom to the now conscience-stricken king and his guests.

Hushed was the boisterous mirth, while men and women, seized with nameless terror, watched the hand slowly tracing the mysterious characters. Before them passed, as in panoramic view, the deeds of their evil lives; they seemed to be arraigned before the judgment bar of the eternal God, whose power they had just defied. Where but a few moments before had been hilarity and blasphemous witticism, were pallid faces and cries of fear. When God makes men fear, they cannot hide the intensity of their terror.

Belshazzar was the most terrified of them all. He it was who above all others had been responsible for the rebellion against God which that night had reached its height in the Babylonian realm. In the presence of the [525] [526] [527] unseen Watcher, the representative of Him whose power had been challenged and whose name had been blasphemed, the king was paralyzed with fear. Conscience was awakened. "The joints of his loins were loosed, and his knees smote one against another." Belshazzar had impiously lifted himself up against the God of heaven and had trusted in his own might, not supposing that any would dare say, "Why doest thou thus?" but now he realized that he must render an account of the stewardship entrusted him, and that for his wasted opportunities and his defiant attitude he could offer no excuse.

In vain the king tried to read the burning letters. But here was a secret he could not fathom, a power he could neither understand nor gainsay. In despair he turned to the wise men of his realm for help. His wild cry rang out in the assembly, calling upon the astrologers, the Chaldeans, and the soothsayers to read the writing. "Whosoever shall read this writing," he promised, "and show me the interpretation thereof, shall be clothed with scarlet, and have a chain of gold about his neck, and shall be the third ruler in the kingdom." But of no avail was his appeal to his trusted advisers, with offers of rich awards. Heavenly wisdom cannot be bought or sold. "All the king's wise men ... could not read the writing, nor make known to the king the interpretation thereof." They were no more able to read the mysterious characters than had been the wise men of a former generation to interpret the dreams of Nebuchadnezzar.

Then the queen mother remembered Daniel, who, over half a century before, had made known to King Nebuchadnezzar [528] the dream of the great image and its interpretation. "O king, live forever," she said. "Let not thy thoughts trouble thee, nor let thy countenance be changed: there is a man in thy kingdom, in whom is the spirit of the holy gods; and in the days of thy father light and understanding and wisdom, like the wisdom of the gods, was found in him; whom the king Nebuchadnezzar ... made master of the magicians, astrologers, Chaldeans, and soothsayers; forasmuch as an excellent spirit, and knowledge, and understanding, interpreting of dreams, and showing of hard sentences, and dissolving of doubts, were found in the same Daniel, whom the king named Belteshazzar: now let Daniel be called, and he will show the interpretation."

"Then was Daniel brought in before the king." Making an effort to regain his composure, Belshazzar said to the prophet: "Art thou that Daniel, which art of the children of the captivity of Judah, whom the king my father brought out of Jewry? I have even heard of thee, that the spirit of the gods is in thee, and that light and understanding and excellent wisdom is found in thee. And now the wise men, the astrologers, have been brought in before me, that they should read this writing, and make known unto me the interpretation thereof: but they could not show the interpretation of the thing: and I have heard of thee, that thou canst make interpretations, and dissolve doubts: now if thou canst read the writing, and make known to me the interpretation thereof, thou shalt be clothed with scarlet, and have a chain of gold about thy neck, and shalt be the third ruler in the kingdom." [529]

Before that terror-stricken throng, Daniel, unmoved by the promises of the king, stood in the quiet dignity of a servant of the Most High, not to speak words of flattery, but to interpret a message of doom. "Let thy gifts be to thyself," he said, "and give thy rewards to another; yet I will read the writing unto the king, and make known to him the interpretation."

The prophet first reminded Belshazzar of matters with which he was familiar, but which had not taught him the lesson of humility that might have saved him. He spoke of Nebuchadnezzar's sin and fall, and of the Lord's dealings with him—the dominion and glory bestowed upon him, the divine judgment for his pride, and his subsequent acknowledgment of the power and mercy of the God of Israel; and then in bold and emphatic words he rebuked Belshazzar for his great wickedness. He held the king's sin up before him, showing him the lessons he might have learned but did not. Belshazzar had not read aright the experience of his grandfather, nor heeded the warning of events so significant to himself. The opportunity of knowing and obeying the true God had been given him, but had not been taken to heart, and he was about to reap the consequence of his rebellion.

"Thou, ... O Belshazzar," the prophet declared, "hast not humbled thine heart, though thou knewest all this; but hast lifted up thyself against the Lord of heaven; and they have brought the vessels of His house before thee, and thou, and thy lords, thy wives, and thy concubines, have drunk wine in them; and thou hast praised the gods of silver, and gold, of brass, iron, wood, and stone, which see not, nor hear, nor know: and the God in whose hand thy breath is, and whose [530] are all thy ways, hast thou not glorified: then was the part of the hand set from Him; and this writing was written."

Turning to the Heaven-sent message on the wall, the prophet read, "Mene, Mene, Tekel, Upharsin." The hand that had traced the characters was no longer visible, but these four words were still gleaming forth with terrible distinctness; and now with bated breath the people listened while the aged prophet declared:

"This is the interpretation of the thing: Mene; God hath numbered thy kingdom, and finished it. Tekel; Thou art weighed in the balances, and art found wanting. Peres; Thy kingdom is divided, and given to the Medes and Persians."

In that last night of mad folly, Belshazzar and his lords had filled up the measure of their guilt and the guilt of the Chaldean kingdom. No longer could God's restraining hand ward off the impending evil. Through manifold providences, God had sought to teach them reverence for His law. "We would have healed Babylon," He declared of those whose judgment was now reaching unto heaven, "but she is not healed." Jeremiah 51:9. Because of the strange perversity of the human heart, God had at last found it necessary to pass the irrevocable sentence. Belshazzar was to fall, and his kingdom was to pass into other hands.

As the prophet ceased speaking, the king commanded that he be awarded the promised honors; and in harmony with this, "they clothed Daniel with scarlet, and put a chain of gold about his neck, and made a proclamation concerning him, that he should be the third ruler in the kingdom." [531]

More than a century before, Inspiration had foretold that "the night of ... pleasure" during which king and counselors would vie with one another in blasphemy against God, would suddenly be changed into a season of fear and destruction. And now, in rapid succession, momentous events followed one another exactly as had been portrayed in the prophetic scriptures years before the principals in the drama had been born.

While still in the festal hall, surrounded by those whose doom has been sealed, the king is informed by a messenger that "his city is taken" by the enemy against whose devices he had felt so secure; "that the passages are stopped, ... and the men of war are affrighted." Verses 31, 32. Even while he and his nobles were drinking from the sacred vessels of Jehovah, and praising their gods of silver and of gold, the Medes and the Persians, having turned the Euphrates out of its channel, were marching into the heart of the unguarded city. The army of Cyrus now stood under the walls of the palace; the city was filled with the soldiers of the enemy, "as with caterpillars" (verse 14); and their triumphant shouts could be heard above the despairing cries of the astonished revelers.

"In that night was Belshazzar the king of the Chaldeans slain," and an alien monarch sat upon the throne.

Clearly had the Hebrew prophets spoken concerning the manner in which Babylon should fall. As in vision God had revealed to them the events of the future, they had exclaimed: "How is Sheshach taken! and how is the praise of the whole earth surprised! how is Babylon become an astonishment among the nations!" "How is the hammer of the whole [532] earth cut asunder and broken! how is Babylon become a desolation among the nations!" "At the noise of the taking of Babylon the earth is moved, and the cry is heard among the nations."

"Babylon is suddenly fallen and destroyed." "The spoiler is come upon her, even upon Babylon, and her mighty men are taken, every one of their bows is broken: for the Lord God of recompenses shall surely requite. And I will make drunk her princes, and her wise men, her captains, and her rulers, and her mighty men: and they shall sleep a perpetual sleep, and not wake, saith the King, whose name is the Lord of hosts."

"I have laid a snare for thee, and thou art also taken, O Babylon, and thou wast not aware: thou art found, and also caught, because thou hast striven against the Lord. The Lord hath opened His armory, and hath brought forth the weapons of His indignation: for this is the work of the Lord God of hosts in the land of the Chaldeans."

"Thus saith the Lord of hosts; The children of Israel and the children of Judah were oppressed together: and all that took them captives held them fast; they refused to let them go. Their Redeemer is strong; the Lord of hosts is His name: He shall throughly plead their cause, that He may give rest to the land, and disquiet the inhabitants of Babylon." Jeremiah 51:41; 50:23, 46; Jeremiah 51:8, 56, 57; 50:24, 25, 33, 34.

Thus "the broad walls of Babylon" became "utterly broken, and her high gates ... burned with fire." Thus did Jehovah of hosts "cause the arrogancy of the proud to cease," and lay low "the haughtiness of the terrible." Thus [533] did "Babylon, the glory of kingdoms, the beauty of the Chaldees' excellency," become as Sodom and Gomorrah—a place forever accursed. "It shall never be inhabited," Inspiration has declared, "neither shall it be dwelt in from generation to generation: neither shall the Arabian pitch tent there; neither shall the shepherds make their fold there. But wild beasts of the desert shall lie there; and their houses shall be full of doleful creatures; and owls shall dwell there, and satyrs shall dance there. And the wild beasts of the islands shall cry in their desolate houses, and dragons in their pleasant palaces." "I will also make it a possession for the bittern, and pools of water: and I will sweep it with the besom of destruction, saith the Lord of hosts." Jeremiah 51:58; Isaiah 13:11, 19-22; 14:23.

To the last ruler of Babylon, as in type to its first, had come the sentence of the divine Watcher: "O king, ... to thee it is spoken; The kingdom is departed from thee." Daniel 4:31.

"Come down, and sit in the dust, O virgin daughter of Babylon, Sit on the ground: there is no throne.... Sit thou silent, And get thee into darkness, O daughter of the Chaldeans: For thou shalt no more be called, The lady of kingdoms.

"I was wroth with My people, I have polluted Mine inheritance, and given them into thine hand: Thou didst show them no mercy; ...

"And thou saidst, I shall be a lady forever: So that thou didst not lay these things to thy heart, Neither didst remember the latter end of it. [534]

"Therefore hear now this, Thou that art given to pleasures That dwellest carelessly, That sayest in thine heart, I am, and none else beside me; I shall not sit as a widow, Neither shall I know the loss of children: ...

"These two things shall come to thee in a moment in one day, The loss of children, and widowhood: They shall come upon thee in their perfection for the multitude of thy sorceries, and for the great abundance of thine enchantments. For thou hast trusted in thy wickedness: Thou hast said, None seeth me.

"Thy wisdom and thy knowledge, it hath perverted thee; And thou hast said in thine heart, I am, and none else beside me. Therefore shall evil come upon thee; Thou shalt not know from whence it riseth: And mischief shall fall upon thee; Thou shalt not be able to put it off: And desolation shall come upon thee suddenly, which thou shalt not know.

"Stand now with thine enchantments, and with the multitude of thy sorceries, wherein thou hast labored from thy youth; If so be thou shalt be able to profit, If so be thou mayest prevail.

"Thou art wearied in the multitude of thy counsels. Let now the astrologers, the stargazers, the monthly prognosticators, Stand up, and save thee from these things that shall come upon thee. Behold, they shall be as stubble; ... They shall not deliver themselves from the power of the flame: ... None shall save thee." Isaiah 47:1-15. [535]

Every nation that has come upon the stage of action has been permitted to occupy its place on the earth, that the fact might be determined whether it would fulfill the purposes of the Watcher and the Holy One. Prophecy has traced the rise and progress of the world's great empires—Babylon, Medo-Persia, Greece, and Rome. With each of these, as with the nations of less power, history has repeated itself. Each has had its period of test; each has failed, its glory faded, its power departed.

While nations have rejected God's principles, and in this rejection have wrought their own ruin, yet a divine, overruling purpose has manifestly been at work throughout the ages. It was this that the prophet Ezekiel saw in the wonderful representation given him during his exile in the land of the Chaldeans, when before his astonished gaze were portrayed the symbols that revealed an overruling Power that has to do with the affairs of earthly rulers.

Upon the banks of the river Chebar, Ezekiel beheld a whirlwind seeming to come from the north, "a great cloud, and a fire infolding itself, and a brightness was about it, and out of the midst thereof as the color of amber." A number of wheels intersecting one another were moved by four living beings. High above all these "was the likeness of a throne, as the appearance of a sapphire stone: and upon the likeness of the throne was the likeness as the appearance of a man above upon it." "And there appeared in the cherubims the form of a man's hand under their wings." Ezekiel 1:4, 26; 10:8. The wheels were so complicated in arrangement that at first sight they appeared to be in confusion; yet they moved in perfect harmony. Heavenly beings, [536] sustained and guided by the hand beneath the wings of the cherubim, were impelling those wheels; above them, upon the sapphire throne, was the Eternal One; and round about the throne was a rainbow, the emblem of divine mercy.

As the wheellike complications were under the guidance of the hand beneath the wings of the cherubim, so the complicated play of human events is under divine control. Amidst the strife and tumult of nations He that sitteth above the cherubim still guides the affairs of this earth.

The history of nations speaks to us today. To every nation and to every individual God has assigned a place in His great plan. Today men and nations are being tested by the plummet in the hand of Him who makes no mistake. All are by their own choice deciding their destiny, and God is overruling all for the accomplishment of His purposes.

The prophecies which the great I AM has given in His word, uniting link after link in the chain of events, from eternity in the past to eternity in the future, tell us where we are today in the procession of the ages and what may be expected in the time to come. All that prophecy has foretold as coming to pass, until the present time, has been traced on the pages of history, and we may be assured that all which is yet to come will be fulfilled in its order.

Today the signs of the times declare that we are standing on the threshold of great and solemn events. Everything in our world is in agitation. Before our eyes is fulfilling the Saviour's prophecy of the events to precede His coming: "Ye shall hear of wars and rumors of wars.... Nation shall rise against nation, and kingdom against kingdom: [537] and there shall be famines, and pestilences, and earthquakes, in divers places." Matthew 24:6, 7.

The present is a time of overwhelming interest to all living. Rulers and statesmen, men who occupy positions of trust and authority, thinking men and women of all classes, have their attention fixed upon the events taking place about us. They are watching the relations that exist among the nations. They observe the intensity that is taking possession of every earthly element, and they recognize that something great and decisive is about to take place—that the world is on the verge of a stupendous crisis.

The Bible, and the Bible only, gives a correct view of these things. Here are revealed the great final scenes in the history of our world, events that already are casting their shadows before, the sound of their approach causing the earth to tremble and men's hearts to fail them for fear.

"Behold, the Lord maketh the earth empty, and maketh it waste, and turneth it upside down, and scattereth abroad the inhabitants thereof; ... because they have transgressed the laws, changed the ordinance, broken the everlasting covenant. Therefore hath the curse devoured the earth, and they that dwell therein are desolate." Isaiah 24:1-6.

"Alas for the day! for the day of the Lord is at hand, and as a destruction from the Almighty shall it come.... The seed is rotten under their clods, the garners are laid desolate, the barns are broken down; for the corn is withered. How do the beasts groan! the herds of cattle are perplexed, because they have no pasture; yea, the flocks of sheep are made desolate." "The vine is dried up, and the fig tree languisheth; [538] the pomegranate tree, the palm tree also, and the apple tree, even all the trees of the field, are withered: because joy is withered away from the sons of men." Joel 1:15-18, 12.

"I am pained at my very heart; ... I cannot hold my peace, because thou hast heard, O my soul, the sound of the trumpet, the alarm of war. Destruction upon destruction is cried; for the whole land is spoiled." Jeremiah 4:19, 20.

"Alas! for that day is great, so that none is like it: it is even the time of Jacob's trouble; but he shall be saved out of it." Jeremiah 30:7.

"Because thou hast made the Lord, which is my refuge, Even the Most High, thy habitation; There shall no evil befall thee, Neither shall any plague come nigh thy dwelling."
Psalm 91:9, 10.

"O daughter of Zion, ... the Lord shall redeem thee from the hand of thine enemies. Now also many nations are gathered against thee, that say, Let her be defiled, and let our eye look upon Zion. But they know not the thoughts of the Lord, neither understand they His counsel." Micah 4:10-12. God will not fail His church in the hour of her greatest peril. He has promised deliverance. "I will bring again the captivity of Jacob's tents," He has declared, "and have mercy on His dwelling places." Jeremiah 30:18.

Then will the purpose of God be fulfilled; the principles of His kingdom will be honored by all beneath the sun. [539]

Chapter 44

In the Lions' Den

This chapter is based on Daniel 6.

When Darius the Median took the throne formerly occupied by the Babylonian rulers, he at once proceeded to reorganize the government. He "set over the kingdom an hundred and twenty princes; ... and over these three presidents; of whom Daniel was first: that the princes might give accounts unto them, and the king should have no damage. Then this Daniel was preferred above the presidents and princes, because an excellent spirit was in him; and the king thought to set him over the whole realm."

The honors bestowed upon Daniel excited the jealousy of the leading men of the kingdom, and they sought for occasion of complaint against him. But they could find none, "forasmuch as he was faithful, neither was there any error or fault found in him."

Daniel's blameless conduct excited still further the jealousy of his enemies. "We shall not find any occasion against this Daniel," they were constrained to acknowledge, "except [540] we find it against him concerning the law of his God."

Thereupon the presidents and princes, counseling together, devised a scheme whereby they hoped to accomplish the prophet's destruction. They determined to ask the king to sign a decree which they should prepare, forbidding any person in the realm to ask anything of God or man, except of Darius the king, for the space of thirty days. A violation of this decree should be punished by casting the offender into a den of lions.

Accordingly, the princes prepared such a decree, and presented it to Darius for his signature. Appealing to his vanity, they persuaded him that the carrying out of this edict would add greatly to his honor and authority. Ignorant of the subtle purpose of the princes, the king did not discern their animosity as revealed in the decree, and, yielding to their flattery, he signed it.

The enemies of Daniel left the presence of Darius, rejoicing over the snare now securely laid for the servant of Jehovah. In the conspiracy thus formed, Satan had played an important part. The prophet was high in command in the kingdom, and evil angels feared that his influence would weaken their control over its rulers. It was these satanic agencies who had stirred the princes to envy and jealousy; it was they who had inspired the plan for Daniel's destruction; and the princes, yielding themselves as instruments of evil, carried it into effect.

The prophet's enemies counted on Daniel's firm adherence to principle for the success of their plan. And they were not mistaken in their estimate of his character. He quickly [541] read their malignant purpose in framing the decree, but he did not change his course in a single particular. Why should he cease to pray now, when he most needed to pray? Rather would he relinquish life itself, than his hope of help in God. With calmness he performed his duties as chief of the princes; and at the hour of prayer he went to his chamber, and with his windows open toward Jerusalem, in accordance with his usual custom, he offered his petition to the God of [542] heaven. He did not try to conceal his act. Although he knew full well the consequences of his fidelity to God, his spirit faltered not. Before those who were plotting his ruin, he would not allow it even to appear that his connection with Heaven was severed. In all cases where the king had a right to command, Daniel would obey; but neither the king nor his decree could make him swerve from allegiance to the King of kings.

Thus the prophet boldly yet quietly and humbly declared that no earthly power has a right to interpose between the soul and God. Surrounded by idolaters, he was a faithful witness to this truth. His dauntless adherence to right was a bright light in the moral darkness of that heathen court. Daniel stands before the world today a worthy example of Christian fearlessness and fidelity.

For an entire day the princes watched Daniel. Three times they saw him go to his chamber, and three times they heard his voice lifted in earnest intercession to God. The next morning they laid their complaint before the king. Daniel, his most honored and faithful statesman, had set the royal decree at defiance. "Hast thou not signed a decree," they reminded him, "that every man that shall ask a petition of any god or man within thirty days, save of thee, O king, shall be cast into the den of lions?"

"The thing is true," the king answered, "according to the law of the Medes and Persians, which altereth not."

Exultantly they now informed Darius of the conduct of his most trusted adviser. "That Daniel, which is of the children of the captivity of Judah," they exclaimed, "regardeth [543] not thee, O king, nor the decree that thou hast signed, but maketh his petition three times a day."

When the monarch heard these words, he saw at once the snare that had been set for his faithful servant. He saw that it was not zeal for kingly glory and honor, but jealousy against Daniel, that had led to the proposal for a royal decree. "Sore displeased with himself" for his part in the evil that had been wrought, he "labored till the going down of the sun" to deliver his friend. The princes, anticipating this effort on the part of the king, came to him with the words, "Know, O king, that the law of the Medes and Persians is, that no decree nor statute which the king establisheth may be changed." The decree, though rashly made, was unalterable and must be carried into effect.

"Then the king commanded, and they brought Daniel, and cast him into the den of lions. Now the king spake and said unto Daniel, Thy God whom thou servest continually, He will deliver thee." A stone was laid on the mouth of the den, and the king himself "sealed it with his own signet, and with the signet of his lords; that the purpose might not be changed concerning Daniel. Then the king went to his palace, and passed the night fasting: neither were instruments of music brought before him: and his sleep went from him."

God did not prevent Daniel's enemies from casting him into the lions' den; He permitted evil angels and wicked men thus far to accomplish their purpose; but it was that He might make the deliverance of His servant more marked, and the defeat of the enemies of truth and righteousness [544] more complete. "Surely the wrath of man shall praise Thee" (Psalm 76:10), the psalmist has testified. Through the courage of this one man who chose to follow right rather than policy, Satan was to be defeated, and the name of God was to be exalted and honored.

Early the next morning King Darius hastened to the den and "cried with a lamentable voice," "O Daniel, servant of the living God, is thy God, whom thou servest continually, able to deliver thee from the lions?"

The voice of the prophet replied: "O king, live forever. My God hath sent His angel, and hath shut the lions' mouths, that they have not hurt me: forasmuch as before Him innocency was found in me; and also before thee, O king, have I done no hurt."

"Then was the king exceeding glad for him, and commanded that they should take Daniel up out of the den. So Daniel was taken up out of the den, and no manner of hurt was found upon him, because he believed in his God.

"And the king commanded, and they brought those men which had accused Daniel, and they cast them into the den of lions, them, their children, and their wives; and the lions had the mastery of them, and brake all their bones in pieces or ever they came at the bottom of the den."

Once more a proclamation was issued by a heathen ruler, exalting the God of Daniel as the true God. "King Darius wrote unto all people, nations, and languages, that dwell in all the earth; Peace be multiplied unto you. I make a decree, that in every dominion of my kingdom men tremble and fear before the God of Daniel: for He is the living God, and steadfast forever, and His kingdom that which shall not [545] be destroyed, and His dominion shall be even unto the end. He delivereth and rescueth, and He worketh signs and wonders in heaven and in earth, who hath delivered Daniel from the power of the lions."

The wicked opposition to God's servant was now completely broken. "Daniel prospered in the reign of Darius, and in the reign of Cyrus the Persian." And through association with him, these heathen monarchs were constrained to acknowledge his God as "the living God, and steadfast forever, and His kingdom that which shall not be destroyed."

From the story of Daniel's deliverance we may learn that in seasons of trial and gloom God's children should be just what they were when their prospects were bright with hope and their surroundings all that they could desire. Daniel in the lions' den was the same Daniel who stood before the king as chief among the ministers of state and as a prophet of the Most High. A man whose heart is stayed upon God will be the same in the hour of his greatest trial as he is in prosperity, when the light and favor of God and of man beam upon him. Faith reaches to the unseen, and grasps eternal realities.

Heaven is very near those who suffer for righteousness' sake. Christ identifies His interests with the interests of His faithful people; He suffers in the person of His saints, and whoever touches His chosen ones touches Him. The power that is near to deliver from physical harm or distress is also near to save from the greater evil, making it possible for the servant of God to maintain his integrity under all circumstances, and to triumph through divine grace. [546]

The experience of Daniel as a statesman in the kingdoms of Babylon and Medo-Persia reveals the truth that a businessman is not necessarily a designing, policy man, but that he may be a man instructed by God at every step. Daniel, the prime minister of the greatest of earthly kingdoms, was at the same time a prophet of God, receiving the light of heavenly inspiration. A man of like passions as ourselves, the pen of inspiration describes him as without fault. His business transactions, when subjected to the closest scrutiny of his enemies, were found to be without one flaw. He was an example of what every businessman may become when his heart is converted and consecrated, and when his motives are right in the sight of God.

Strict compliance with the requirements of Heaven brings temporal as well as spiritual blessings. Unwavering in his allegiance to God, unyielding in his mastery of self, Daniel, by his noble dignity and unswerving integrity, while yet a young man, won the "favor and tender love" of the heathen officer in whose charge he had been placed. Daniel 1:9. The same characteristics marked his afterlife. He rose speedily to the position of prime minister of the kingdom of Babylon. Through the reign of successive monarchs, the downfall of the nation, and the establishment of another world empire, such were his wisdom and statesmanship, so perfect his tact, his courtesy, his genuine goodness of heart, his fidelity to principle, that even his enemies were forced to the confession that "they could find none occasion nor fault; forasmuch as he was faithful." [547]

Honored by men with the responsibilities of state and with the secrets of kingdoms bearing universal sway, Daniel was honored by God as His ambassador, and was given many revelations of the mysteries of ages to come. His wonderful prophecies, as recorded by him in chapters 7 to 12 of the book bearing his name, were not fully understood even by the prophet himself; but before his life labors closed, he was given the blessed assurance that "at the end of the days"—in the closing period of this world's history—he would again be permitted to stand in his lot and place. It was not given him to understand all that God had revealed of the divine purpose. "Shut up the words, and seal the book," he was directed concerning his prophetic writings; these were to be sealed "even to the time of the end." "Go thy way, Daniel," the angel once more directed the faithful messenger of Jehovah; "for the words are closed up and sealed till the time of the end.... Go thou thy way till the end be: for thou shalt rest, and stand in thy lot at the end of the days." Daniel 12:4, 9, 13.

As we near the close of this world's history, the prophecies recorded by Daniel demand our special attention, as they relate to the very time in which we are living. With them should be linked the teachings of the last book of the New Testament Scriptures. Satan has led many to believe that the prophetic portions of the writings of Daniel and of John the revelator cannot be understood. But the promise is plain that special blessing will accompany the study of these prophecies. "The wise shall understand" (verse 10), was spoken of the visions of Daniel that were to be unsealed [548] in the latter days; and of the revelation that Christ gave to His servant John for the guidance of God's people all through the centuries, the promise is, "Blessed is he that readeth, and they that hear the words of this prophecy, and keep those things which are written therein." Revelation 1:3.

From the rise and fall of nations as made plain in the books of Daniel and the Revelation, we need to learn how worthless is mere outward and worldly glory. Babylon, with all its power and magnificence, the like of which our world has never since beheld,—power and magnificence which to the people of that day seemed so stable and enduring,—how completely has it passed away! As "the flower of the grass," it has perished. James 1:10. So perished the Medo-Persian kingdom, and the kingdoms of Grecia and Rome. And so perishes all that has not God for its foundation. Only that which is bound up with His purpose, and expresses His character, can endure. His principles are the only steadfast things our world knows.

A careful study of the working out of God's purpose in the history of nations and in the revelation of things to come, will help us to estimate at their true value things seen and things unseen, and to learn what is the true aim of life. Thus, viewing the things of time in the light of eternity, we may, like Daniel and his fellows, live for that which is true and noble and enduring. And learning in this life the principles of the kingdom of our Lord and Saviour, that blessed kingdom which is to endure for ever and ever, we may be prepared at His coming to enter with Him into its possession. [549]

Chapter 45

The Return of the Exiles

Beginning of Section 6 — After the Exile

The advent of the army of Cyrus before the walls of Babylon was to the Jews a sign that their deliverance from captivity was drawing nigh. More than a century before the birth of Cyrus, Inspiration had mentioned him by name, and had caused a record to be made of the actual work he should do in taking the city of Babylon unawares, and in preparing the way for the release of the children of the captivity. Through Isaiah the word had been spoken:

"Thus saith the Lord to His anointed, to Cyrus, whose right hand I have holden, to subdue nations before him; ... to open before him the two-leaved gates; and the gates shall not be shut; I will go before thee, and make the crooked places straight: I will break in pieces the gates of brass, and cut in sunder the bars of iron: and I will give thee the treasures of darkness, and hidden riches of secret places, that thou mayest know that I, the Lord, which call thee by thy name, am the God of Israel." Isaiah 45:1-3. [552]

In the unexpected entry of the army of the Persian conqueror into the heart of the Babylonian capital by way of the channel of the river whose waters had been turned aside, and through the inner gates that in careless security had been left open and unprotected, the Jews had abundant evidence of the literal fulfillment of Isaiah's prophecy concerning the sudden overthrow of their oppressors. And this should have been to them an unmistakable sign that God was shaping the affairs of nations in their behalf; for inseparably linked with the prophecy outlining the manner of Babylon's capture and fall were the words:

"Cyrus, he is My shepherd, and shall perform all My pleasure: even saying to Jerusalem, Thou shalt be built; and to the temple, Thy foundation shall be laid." "I have raised him up in righteousness, and I will direct all his ways: he shall build My city, and he shall let go My captives, not for price nor reward, saith the Lord of hosts." Isaiah 44:28; 45:13.

Nor were these the only prophecies upon which the exiles had opportunity to base their hope of speedy deliverance. The writings of Jeremiah were within their reach, and in these was plainly set forth the length of time that should elapse before the restoration of Israel from Babylon. "When seventy years are accomplished," the Lord had foretold through His messenger, "I will punish the king of Babylon, and that nation, saith the Lord, for their iniquity, and the land of the Chaldeans, and will make it perpetual desolations." Jeremiah 25:12. Favor would be shown the remnant of Judah, in answer to fervent prayer. "I will be [553] found of you, saith the Lord: and I will turn away your captivity, and I will gather you from all the nations, and from all the places whither I have driven you, saith the Lord; and I will bring you again into the place whence I caused you to be carried away captive." Jeremiah 29:14.

Often had Daniel and his companions gone over these and similar prophecies outlining God's purpose for His people. And now, as the rapid course of events betokened the mighty hand of God at work among the nations, Daniel gave special thought to the promises made to Israel. His faith in the prophetic word led him to enter into experiences foretold by the sacred writers. "After seventy years be accomplished at Babylon," the Lord had declared, "I will visit you, and perform My good word toward you, in causing you to return.... I know the thoughts that I think toward you, saith the Lord, thoughts of peace, and not of evil, to give you an expected end. Then shall ye call upon Me, and ye shall go and pray unto Me, and I will hearken unto you. And ye shall seek Me, and find Me, when ye shall search for Me with all your heart." Verses 10-13.

Shortly before the fall of Babylon, when Daniel was meditating on these prophecies and seeking God for an understanding of the times, a series of visions was given him concerning the rise and fall of kingdoms. With the first vision, as recorded in the seventh chapter of the book of Daniel, an interpretation was given; yet not all was made clear to the prophet. "My cogitations much troubled me," he wrote of his experience at the time, "and my countenance [554] changed in me: but I kept the matter in my heart." Daniel 7:28.

Through another vision further light was thrown upon the events of the future; and it was at the close of this vision that Daniel heard "one saint speaking, and another saint said unto that certain saint which spake, How long shall be the vision?" Daniel 8:13. The answer that was given, "Unto two thousand and three hundred days; then shall the sanctuary be cleansed" (verse 14), filled him with perplexity. Earnestly he sought for the meaning of the vision. He could not understand the relation sustained by the seventy years' captivity, as foretold through Jeremiah, to the twenty-three hundred years that in vision he heard the heavenly visitant declare should elapse before the cleansing of God's sanctuary. The angel Gabriel gave him a partial interpretation; yet when the prophet heard the words, "The vision ... shall be for many days," he fainted away. "I Daniel fainted," he records of his experience, "and was sick certain days; afterward I rose up, and did the king's business; and I was astonished at the vision, but none understood it." Verses 26, 27.

Still burdened in behalf of Israel, Daniel studied anew the prophecies of Jeremiah. They were very plain—so plain that he understood by these testimonies recorded in books "the number of the years, whereof the word of the Lord came to Jeremiah the prophet, that He would accomplish seventy years in the desolations of Jerusalem." Daniel 9:2.

With faith founded on the sure word of prophecy, Daniel pleaded with the Lord for the speedy fulfillment of these [555] promises. He pleaded for the honor of God to be preserved. In his petition he identified himself fully with those who had fallen short of the divine purpose, confessing their sins as his own.

"I set my face unto the Lord God," the prophet declared, "to seek by prayer and supplications, with fasting, and sackcloth, and ashes: and I prayed unto the Lord my God, and made my confession." Verses 3, 4. Though Daniel had long been in the service of God, and had been spoken of by heaven as "greatly beloved," yet he now appeared before God as a sinner, urging the great need of the people he loved. His prayer was eloquent in its simplicity, and intensely earnest. Hear him pleading:

"O Lord, the great and dreadful God, keeping the covenant and mercy to them that love Him, and to them that keep His commandments; we have sinned, and have committed iniquity, and have done wickedly, and have rebelled, even by departing from Thy precepts and from Thy judgments; neither have we hearkened unto Thy servants the prophets, which spake in Thy name to our kings, our princes, and our fathers, and to all the people of the land.

"O Lord, righteousness belongeth unto Thee, but unto us confusion of faces, as at this day; to the men of Judah, and to the inhabitants of Jerusalem, and unto all Israel, that are near, and that are far off, through all the countries whither Thou hast driven them, because of their trespass that they have trespassed against Thee....

"To the Lord our God belong mercies and forgiveness, though we have rebelled against Him." "O Lord, according to all Thy righteousness, I beseech Thee, let Thine anger [556] and Thy fury be turned away from Thy city Jerusalem, Thy holy mountain: because for our sins, and for the iniquities of our fathers, Jerusalem and Thy people are become a reproach to all that are about us.

"Now therefore, O our God, hear the prayer of Thy servant, and his supplications, and cause Thy face to shine upon Thy sanctuary that is desolate, for the Lord's sake. O my God, incline Thine ear, and hear; open Thine eyes, and behold our desolations, and the city which is called by Thy name: for we do not present our supplications before Thee for our righteousness, but for Thy great mercies.

"O Lord, hear; O Lord, forgive; O Lord, hearken and do; defer not, for Thine own sake, O my God: for Thy city and Thy people are called by Thy name." Verses 4-9, 16-19.

Heaven was bending low to hear the earnest supplication of the prophet. Even before he had finished his plea for pardon and restoration, the mighty Gabriel again appeared to him, and called his attention to the vision he had seen prior to the fall of Babylon and the death of Belshazzar. And then the angel outlined before him in detail the period of the seventy weeks, which was to begin at the time of "the going forth of the commandment to restore and to build Jerusalem." Verse 25.

Daniel's prayer had been offered "in the first year of Darius" (verse 1), the Median monarch whose general, Cyrus, had wrested from Babylonia the scepter of universal rule. The reign of Darius was honored of God. To him was sent the angel Gabriel, "to confirm and to strengthen him." Daniel 11:1. Upon his death, within about two years [557] of the fall of Babylon, Cyrus succeeded to the throne, and the beginning of his reign marked the completion of the seventy years since the first company of Hebrews had been taken by Nebuchadnezzar from their Judean home to Babylon.

The deliverance of Daniel from the den of lions had been used of God to create a favorable impression upon the mind of Cyrus the Great. The sterling qualities of the man of God as a statesman of farseeing ability led the Persian ruler to show him marked respect and to honor his judgment. And now, just at the time God had said He would cause His temple at Jerusalem to be rebuilt, He moved upon Cyrus as His agent to discern the prophecies concerning himself, with which Daniel was so familiar, and to grant the Jewish people their liberty.

As the king saw the words foretelling, more than a hundred years before his birth, the manner in which Babylon should be taken; as he read the message addressed to him by the Ruler of the universe, "I girded thee, though thou hast not known Me: that they may know from the rising of the sun, and from the west, that there is none beside Me;" as he saw before his eyes the declaration of the eternal God, "For Jacob My servant's sake, and Israel Mine elect, I have even called thee by thy name: I have surnamed thee, though thou hast not known Me;" as he traced the inspired record, "I have raised him up in righteousness, and I will direct all his ways: he shall build My city, and he shall let go My captives, not for price nor reward," his heart was profoundly moved, and he determined to fulfill his divinely appointed mission. Isaiah 45:5, 6, 4, 13. He would let the Judean [558] captives go free; he would help them restore the temple of Jehovah.

In a written proclamation published "throughout all his kingdom," Cyrus made known his desire to provide for the return of the Hebrews and for the rebuilding of their temple. "The Lord God of heaven hath given me all the kingdoms of the earth," the king gratefully acknowledged in this public proclamation; "and He hath charged me to build Him an house at Jerusalem, which is in Judah. Who is there among you of all His people? His God be with him, and let him go up to Jerusalem, ... and build the house of the Lord God of Israel, (He is the God,) which is in Jerusalem. And whosoever remaineth in any place where he sojourneth, let the men of his place help him with silver, and with gold, and with goods, and with beasts, beside the freewill offering." Ezra 1:1-4.

"Let the house be builded," he further directed regarding the temple structure, "the place where they offered sacrifices, and let the foundations thereof be strongly laid; the height thereof threescore cubits, and the breadth thereof threescore cubits; with three rows of great stones, and a row of new timber: and let the expenses be given out of the king's house: and also let the golden and silver vessels of the house of God, which Nebuchadnezzar took forth out of the temple which is at Jerusalem, and brought unto Babylon, be restored, and brought again unto the temple which is at Jerusalem." Ezra 6:3-5.

Tidings of this decree reached the farthermost provinces of the king's realm, and everywhere among the children of the dispersion there was great rejoicing. Many, like Daniel, [559] had been studying the prophecies, and had been seeking God for His promised intervention in behalf of Zion. And now their prayers were being answered; and with heartfelt joy they could unite in singing:

"When the Lord turned again the captivity of Zion, We were like them that dream. Then was our mouth filled with laughter, And our tongue with singing: Then said they among the heathen, The Lord hath done great things for them. The Lord hath done great things for us; Whereof we are glad."

Psalm 126:1-3.

"The chief of the fathers of Judah and Benjamin, and the priests, and the Levites, with all them whose spirit God had raised"—these were the goodly remnant, about fifty thousand strong, from among the Jews in the lands of exile, who determined to take advantage of the wonderful opportunity offered them "to go up to build the house of the Lord which is in Jerusalem." Their friends did not permit them to go empty-handed. "All they that were about them strengthened their hands with vessels of silver, with gold, with goods, and with beasts, and with precious things." And to these and many other voluntary offerings were added "the vessels of the house of the Lord, which Nebuchadnezzar had brought forth out of Jerusalem; ... even those did Cyrus king of Persia bring forth by the hand of Mithredath the treasurer, ... five thousand and four hundred" in number, for use in the temple that was to be rebuilt. Ezra 1:5-11.

Upon Zerubbabel (known also as Sheshbazzar), a descendant of King David, Cyrus placed the responsibility of [560] acting as governor of the company returning to Judea; and with him was associated Joshua the high priest. The long journey across the desert wastes was accomplished in safety, and the happy company, grateful to God for His many mercies, at once undertook the work of re-establishing that which had been broken down and destroyed. "The chief of the fathers" led out in offering of their substance to help defray the expense of rebuilding the temple; and the people, following their example, gave freely of their meager store. See Ezra 2:64-70.

As speedily as possible, an altar was erected on the site of the ancient altar in the temple court. To the exercises connected with the dedication of this altar, the people had "gathered themselves together as one man;" and there they united in re-establishing the sacred services that had been interrupted at the time of the destruction of Jerusalem by Nebuchadnezzar. Before separating to dwell in the homes they were endeavoring to restore, "they kept also the Feast of Tabernacles." Ezra 3:1-6.

The setting up of the altar of daily burnt offerings greatly cheered the faithful remnant. Heartily they entered into the preparations necessary for the rebuilding of the temple, gathering courage as these preparations advanced from month to month. They had for many years been deprived of the visible tokens of God's presence. And now, surrounded as they were by many sad reminders of the apostasy of their fathers, they longed for some abiding token of divine forgiveness and favor. Above the regaining of personal property and ancient privileges, they valued the approval of God. Wonderfully had He wrought in their [561] [562] [563] behalf, and they felt the assurance of His presence with them; yet they desired greater blessings still. With joyous anticipation they looked forward to the time when, with temple rebuilt, they might behold the shining forth of His glory from within.

The workmen engaged in the preparation of the building material, found among the ruins some of the immense stones brought to the temple site in the days of Solomon. These were made ready for use, and much new material was provided; and soon the work was advanced to the point where the foundation stone must be laid. This was done in the presence of many thousands who had assembled to witness the progress of the work and to give expression to their joy in having a part in it. While the cornerstone was being set in position, the people, accompanied by the trumpets of the priests and the cymbals of the sons of Asaph, "sang together by course in praising and giving thanks unto the Lord; because He is good, for His mercy endureth forever toward Israel." Verse 11.

The house that was about to be rebuilt had been the subject of many prophecies concerning the favor that God desired to show Zion, and all who were present at the laying of the cornerstone should have entered heartily into the spirit of the occasion. Yet mingled with the music and the shouts of praise that were heard on that glad day, was a discordant note. "Many of the priests and Levites and chief of the fathers, who were ancient men, that had seen the first house, when the foundation of this house was laid before their eyes, wept with a loud voice." Verse 12. [564]

It was natural that sadness should fill the hearts of these aged men, as they thought of the results of long-continued impenitence. Had they and their generation obeyed God, and carried out His purpose for Israel, the temple built by Solomon would not have been destroyed and the captivity would not have been necessary. But because of ingratitude and disloyalty they had been scattered among the heathen.

Conditions were now changed. In tender mercy the Lord had again visited His people and allowed them to return to their own land. Sadness because of the mistakes of the past should have given way to feelings of great joy. God had moved upon the heart of Cyrus to aid them in rebuilding the temple, and this should have called forth expressions of profound gratitude. But some failed of discerning God's opening providences. Instead of rejoicing, they cherished thoughts of discontent and discouragement. They had seen the glory of Solomon's temple, and they lamented because of the inferiority of the building now to be erected.

The murmuring and complaining, and the unfavorable comparisons made, had a depressing influence on the minds of many and weakened the hands of the builders. The workmen were led to question whether they should proceed with the erection of a building that at the beginning was so freely criticized and was the cause of so much lamentation.

There were many in the congregation, however, whose larger faith and broader vision did not lead them to view this lesser glory with such dissatisfaction. "Many shouted aloud for joy: so that the people could not discern the noise [565] of the shout of joy from the noise of the weeping of the people: for the people shouted with a loud shout, and the noise was heard afar off." Verses 12, 13.

Could those who failed to rejoice at the laying of the foundation stone of the temple have foreseen the results of their lack of faith on that day, they would have been appalled. Little did they realize the weight of their words of disapproval and disappointment; little did they know how much their expressed dissatisfaction would delay the completion of the Lord's house.

The magnificence of the first temple, and the imposing rites of its religious services, had been a source of pride to Israel before their captivity; but their worship had ofttimes been lacking in those qualities which God regards as most essential. The glory of the first temple, the splendor of its service, could not recommend them to God; for that which is alone of value in His sight, they did not offer. They did not bring Him the sacrifice of a humble and contrite spirit.

It is when the vital principles of the kingdom of God are lost sight of, that ceremonies become multitudinous and extravagant. It is when the character building is neglected, when the adornment of the soul is lacking, when the simplicity of godliness is despised, that pride and love of display demand magnificent church edifices, splendid adornings, and imposing ceremonials. But in all this God is not honored. He values His church, not for its external advantages, but for the sincere piety which distinguishes it from the world. He estimates it according to the growth of its members in the knowledge of Christ, according to their progress in [566] spiritual experience. He looks for the principles of love and goodness. Not all the beauty of art can bear comparison with the beauty of temper and character to be revealed in those who are Christ's representatives.

A congregation may be the poorest in the land. It may be without the attractions of any outward show; but if the members possess the principles of the character of Christ, angels will unite with them in their worship. The praise and thanksgiving from grateful hearts will ascend to God as a sweet oblation.

"Give thanks unto the Lord, for He is good: For His mercy endureth forever. Let the redeemed of the Lord say so, Whom He hath redeemed from the hand of the enemy."

"Sing unto Him, sing psalms unto Him: Talk ye of all His wondrous works. Glory ye in His holy name: Let the heart of them rejoice that seek the Lord."

"For He satisfieth the longing soul, And filleth the hungry soul with goodness."

Psalm 107:1, 2; 105:2, 3; Psalm 107:9. [567]

Chapter 46

"The Prophets of God Helping Them"

Close by the Israelites who had set themselves to the task of rebuilding the temple, dwelt the Samaritans, a mixed race that had sprung up through the intermarriage of heathen colonists from the provinces of Assyria with the remnant of the ten tribes which had been left in Samaria and Galilee. In later years the Samaritans claimed to worship the true God, but in heart and practice they were idolaters. It is true, they held that their idols were but to remind them of the living God, the Ruler of the universe; nevertheless the people were prone to reverence graven images.

During the period of the restoration, these Samaritans came to be known as "the adversaries of Judah and Benjamin." Hearing that "the children of the captivity builded the temple unto the Lord God of Israel," "they came to Zerubbabel, and to the chief of the fathers," and expressed a desire to unite with them in its erection. "Let us build with you," they proposed; "for we seek your God, as ye do; [568] and we do sacrifice unto Him since the days of Esarhaddon king of Assur, which brought us up hither." But the privilege they asked was refused them. "Ye have nothing to do with us to build an house unto our God," the leaders of the Israelites declared; "but we ourselves together will build unto the Lord God of Israel, as King Cyrus the king of Persia hath commanded us." Ezra 4:1-3.

Only a remnant had chosen to return from Babylon; and now, as they undertake a work seemingly beyond their strength, their nearest neighbors come with an offer of help. The Samaritans refer to their worship of the true God, and express a desire to share the privileges and blessings connected with the temple service. "We seek your God, as ye do," they declare. "Let us build with you." But had the Jewish leaders accepted this offer of assistance, they would have opened a door for the entrance of idolatry. They discerned the insincerity of the Samaritans. They realized that help gained through an alliance with these men would be as nothing in comparison with the blessing they might expect to receive by following the plain commands of Jehovah.

Regarding the relation that Israel should sustain to surrounding peoples, the Lord had declared through Moses: "Thou shalt make no covenant with them, nor show mercy unto them: neither shalt thou make marriages with them; ... for they will turn away thy son from following Me, that they may serve other gods: so will the anger of the Lord be kindled against you, and destroy thee suddenly." "Thou art an holy people unto the Lord thy God, and the Lord hath [569] chosen thee to be a peculiar people unto Himself, above all the nations that are upon the earth." Deuteronomy 7:2-4; 14:2.

The result that would follow an entrance into covenant relation with surrounding nations was plainly foretold. "The Lord shall scatter thee among all people, from the one end of the earth even unto the other," Moses had declared; "and there thou shalt serve other gods, which neither thou nor thy fathers have known, even wood and stone. And among these nations shalt thou find no ease, neither shall the sole of thy foot have rest: but the Lord shall give thee there a trembling heart, and failing of eyes, and sorrow of mind: and thy life shall hang in doubt before thee; and thou shalt fear day and night, and shalt have none assurance of thy life: in the morning thou shalt say, Would God it were even! and at even thou shalt say, Would God it were morning! for the fear of thine heart wherewith thou shalt fear, and for the sight of thine eyes which thou shalt see." Deuteronomy 28:64-67. "But if from thence thou shalt seek the Lord thy God," the promise had been, "thou shalt find Him, if thou seek Him with all thy heart and with all thy soul." Deuteronomy 4:29.

Zerubbabel and his associates were familiar with these and many like scriptures; and in the recent captivity they had evidence after evidence of their fulfillment. And now, having repented of the evils that had brought upon them and their fathers the judgments foretold so plainly through Moses; having turned with all the heart to God, and renewed their covenant relationship with Him, they had been [570] permitted to return to Judea, that they might restore that which had been destroyed. Should they, at the very beginning of their undertaking, enter into a covenant with idolaters?

"Thou shalt make no covenant with them," God had said; and those who had recently rededicated themselves to the Lord at the altar set up before the ruins of His temple, realized that the line of demarcation between His people and the world is ever to be kept unmistakably distinct. They refused to enter into alliance with those who, though familiar with the requirements of God's law, would not yield to its claims.

The principles set forth in Deuteronomy for the instruction of Israel are to be followed by God's people to the end of time. True prosperity is dependent on the continuance of our covenant relationship with God. Never can we afford to compromise principle by entering into alliance with those who do not fear Him.

There is constant danger that professing Christians will come to think that in order to have influence with worldlings, they must to a certain extent conform to the world. But though such a course may appear to afford great advantages, it always ends in spiritual loss. Against every subtle influence that seeks entrance by means of flattering inducements from the enemies of truth, God's people must strictly guard. They are pilgrims and strangers in this world, traveling a path beset with danger. To the ingenious subterfuges and alluring inducements held out to tempt from allegiance, they must give no heed.

It is not the open and avowed enemies of the cause of [571] God that are most to be feared. Those who, like the adversaries of Judah and Benjamin, come with smooth words and fair speeches, apparently seeking for friendly alliance with God's children, have greater power to deceive. Against such every soul should be on the alert, lest some carefully concealed and masterly snare take him unaware. And especially today, while earth's history is closing, the Lord requires of His children a vigilance that knows no relaxation. But though the conflict is a ceaseless one, none are left to struggle alone. Angels help and protect those who walk humbly before God. Never will our Lord betray one who trusts in Him. As His children draw near to Him for protection from evil, in pity and love He lifts up for them a standard against the enemy. Touch them not, He says; for they are Mine. I have graven them upon the palms of My hands.

Untiring in their opposition, the Samaritans "weakened the hands of the people of Judah, and troubled them in building, and hired counselors against them, to frustrate their purpose, all the days of Cyrus king of Persia, even until the reign of Darius." Ezra 4:4, 5. By false reports they aroused suspicion in minds easily led to suspect. But for many years the powers of evil were held in check, and the people in Judea had liberty to continue their work.

While Satan was striving to influence the highest powers in the kingdom of Medo-Persia to show disfavor to God's people, angels worked in behalf of the exiles. The controversy was one in which all heaven was interested. Through the prophet Daniel we are given a glimpse of this mighty struggle between the forces of good and the forces of evil. [572] For three weeks Gabriel wrestled with the powers of darkness, seeking to counteract the influences at work on the mind of Cyrus; and before the contest closed, Christ Himself came to Gabriel's aid. "The prince of the kingdom of Persia withstood me one and twenty days," Gabriel declares; "but, lo, Michael, one of the chief princes, came to help me; and I remained there with the kings of Persia." Daniel 10:13. All that heaven could do in behalf of the people of God was done. The victory was finally gained; the forces of the enemy were held in check all the days of Cyrus, and all the days of his son Cambyses, who reigned about seven and a half years.

This was a time of wonderful opportunity for the Jews. The highest agencies of heaven were working on the hearts of kings, and it was for the people of God to labor with the utmost activity to carry out the decree of Cyrus. They should have spared no effort to restore the temple and its services, and to re-establish themselves in their Judean homes. But in the day of God's power many proved unwilling. The opposition of their enemies was strong and determined, and gradually the builders lost heart. Some could not forget the scene at the laying of the cornerstone, when many had given expression to their lack of confidence in the enterprise. And as the Samaritans grew more bold, many of the Jews questioned whether, after all, the time had come to rebuild. The feeling soon became widespread. Many of the workmen, discouraged and disheartened, returned to their homes to take up the ordinary pursuits of life.

During the reign of Cambyses the work on the temple progressed slowly. And during the reign of the false Smerdis [573] (called Artaxerxes in Ezra 4:7) the Samaritans induced the unscrupulous impostor to issue a decree forbidding the Jews to rebuild their temple and city.

For over a year the temple was neglected and well-nigh forsaken. The people dwelt in their homes and strove to attain temporal prosperity, but their situation was deplorable. Work as they might they did not prosper. The very elements of nature seemed to conspire against them. Because they had let the temple lie waste, the Lord sent upon their substance a wasting drought. God had bestowed upon them the fruits of field and garden, the corn and the wine and the oil, as a token of His favor; but because they had used these bountiful gifts so selfishly, the blessings were removed.

Such were the conditions existing during the early part of the reign of Darius Hystaspes. Spiritually as well as temporally, the Israelites were in a pitiable state. So long had they murmured and doubted; so long had they chosen to make personal interests first, while viewing with apathy the Lord's temple in ruins, that many had lost sight of God's purpose in restoring them to Judea; and these were saying, "The time is not come, the time that the Lord's house should be built." Haggai 1:2.

But even this dark hour was not without hope for those whose trust was in God. The prophets Haggai and Zechariah were raised up to meet the crisis. In stirring testimonies these appointed messengers revealed to the people the cause of their troubles. The lack of temporal prosperity was the result of a neglect to put God's interests first, the prophets declared. Had the Israelites honored God, had they shown Him due respect and courtesy, by making the building of [574] His house their first work, they would have invited His presence and blessing.

To those who had become discouraged, Haggai addressed the searching inquiry, "Is it time for you, O ye, to dwell in your ceiled houses, and this house lie waste? Now therefore thus saith the Lord of hosts; Consider your ways." Why have you done so little? Why do you feel concern for your own buildings and unconcern for the Lord's building? Where is the zeal you once felt for the restoration of the Lord's house? What have you gained by serving self? The desire to escape poverty has led you to neglect the temple, but this neglect has brought upon you that which you feared. "Ye have sown much, and bring in little; ye eat, but ye have not enough; ye drink, but ye are not filled with drink; ye clothe you, but there is none warm; and he that earneth wages earneth wages to put it into a bag with holes." Verses 4-6.

And then, in words that they could not fail to understand, the Lord revealed the cause that had brought them to want: "Ye looked for much, and, lo, it came to little; and when ye brought it home, I did blow upon it. Why? saith the Lord of hosts. Because of Mine house that is waste, and ye run every man unto his own house. Therefore the heaven over you is stayed from dew, and the earth is stayed from her fruit. And I called for a drought upon the land, and upon the mountains, and upon the corn, and upon the new wine, and upon the oil, and upon that which the ground bringeth forth, and upon men, and upon cattle, and upon all the labor of the hands." Verses 9-11. [575]

"Consider your ways," the Lord urged. "Go up to the mountain, and bring wood, and build the house; and I will take pleasure in it, and I will be glorified." Verses 7, 8.

The message of counsel and reproof given through Haggai was taken to heart by the leaders and people of Israel. They felt that God was in earnest with them. They dared not disregard the repeated instruction sent them—that their prosperity, both temporal and spiritual, was dependent on faithful obedience to God's commands. Aroused by the warnings of the prophet, Zerubbabel and Joshua, "with all the remnant of the people, obeyed the voice of the Lord their God, and the words of Haggai the prophet." Verse 12.

As soon as Israel decided to obey, the words of reproof were followed by a message of encouragement. "Then spake Haggai ... unto the people, saying, I am with you, saith the Lord. And the Lord stirred up the spirit of Zerubbabel" and of Joshua, and "of all the remnant of the people; and they came and did work in the house of the Lord of hosts, their God." Verses 13, 14.

In less than a month after the work on the temple was resumed, the builders received another comforting message. "Be strong, O Zerubbabel," the Lord Himself urged through His prophet; "be strong, O Joshua; ... and be strong, all ye people of the land, saith the Lord, and work: for I am with you, saith the Lord of hosts." Haggai 2:4.

To Israel encamped before Mount Sinai the Lord had declared: "I will dwell among the children of Israel, and will be their God. And they shall know that I am the Lord [576] their God, that brought them forth out of the land of Egypt, that I may dwell among them: I am the Lord their God." Exodus 29:45, 46. And now, notwithstanding the fact that they had repeatedly "rebelled, and vexed His Holy Spirit" (Isaiah 63:10), God once more, through the messages of His prophet, was stretching out His hand to save. As a recognition of their co-operation with His purpose, He was renewing His covenant that His Spirit should remain among them; and He bade them, "Fear not."

To His children today the Lord declares, "Be strong, ... and work: for I am with you." The Christian always has a strong helper in the Lord. The way of the Lord's helping we may not know; but this we do know: He will never fail those who put their trust in Him. Could Christians realize how many times the Lord has ordered their way, that the purposes of the enemy concerning them might not be accomplished, they would not stumble along complainingly. Their faith would be stayed on God, and no trial would have power to move them. They would acknowledge Him as their wisdom and efficiency, and He would bring to pass that which He desires to work out through them.

The earnest pleadings and the encouragements given through Haggai were emphasized and added to by Zechariah, whom God raised up to stand by his side in urging Israel to carry out the command to arise and build. Zechariah's first message was an assurance that God's word never fails and a promise of blessing to those who would hearken to the sure word of prophecy. [577]

With fields lying waste, with their scant store of provisions rapidly failing, and surrounded as they were by unfriendly peoples, the Israelites nevertheless moved forward by faith in response to the call of God's messengers, and labored diligently to restore the ruined temple. It was a work requiring firm reliance upon God. As the people endeavored to do their part, and sought for a renewal of God's grace in heart and life, message after message was given them through Haggai and Zechariah, with assurances that their faith would be richly rewarded and that the word of God concerning the future glory of the temple whose walls they were rearing would not fail. In this very building would appear, in the fullness of time, the Desire of all nations as the Teacher and Saviour of mankind.

Thus the builders were not left to struggle alone; "with them were the prophets of God helping them;" and the Lord of hosts Himself had declared, "Be strong, ... and work: for I am with you." Ezra 5:2; Haggai 2:4.

With heartfelt repentance and a willingness to advance by faith, came the promise of temporal prosperity. "From this day," the Lord declared, "will I bless you." Verse 19.

To Zerubbabel their leader—he who, through all the years since their return from Babylon, had been so sorely tried—was given a most precious message. The day was coming, the

Lord declared, when all the enemies of His chosen people would be cast down. "In that day, saith the Lord of hosts, will I take thee, O Zerubbabel, My servant, ... and will make thee as a signet: for I have chosen thee." Verse 23. Now the governor of Israel could see the meaning [578] of the providence that had led him through discouragement and perplexity; he could discern God's purpose in it all.

This personal word to Zerubbabel has been left on record for the encouragement of God's children in every age. God has a purpose in sending trial to His children. He never leads them otherwise than they would choose to be led if they could see the end from the beginning, and discern the glory of the purpose that they are fulfilling. All that He brings upon them in test and trial comes that they may be strong to do and to suffer for Him.

The messages delivered by Haggai and Zechariah roused the people to put forth every possible effort for the rebuilding of the temple; but, as they worked, they were sadly harassed by the Samaritans and others who devised many hindrances. On one occasion the provincial officers of the Medo-Persian realm visited Jerusalem and requested the name of the one who had authorized the restoration of the building. If at that time the Jews had not been trusting in the Lord for guidance, this inquiry might have resulted disastrously to them. "But the eye of their God was upon the elders of the Jews, that they could not cause them to cease, till the matter came to Darius." Ezra 5:5. The officers were answered so wisely that they decided to write a letter to Darius Hystaspes, then the ruler of Medo-Persia, directing his attention to the original decree made by Cyrus, which commanded that the house of God at Jerusalem be rebuilt, and that the expenses for the same be paid from the king's treasury. [579]

Darius searched for this decree, and found it; whereupon he directed those who had made the inquiry to allow the rebuilding of the temple to proceed. "Let the work of this house of God alone," he commanded; "let the governor of the Jews and the elders of the Jews build this house of God in his place.

"Moreover," Darius continued, "I make a decree what ye shall do to the elders of these Jews for the building of this house of God: that of the king's goods, even of the tribute beyond the river, forthwith expenses be given unto these men, that they be not hindered. And that which they have need of, both young bullocks, and rams, and lambs, for the burnt offerings of the God of heaven, wheat, salt, wine, and oil, according to the appointment of the priests which are at Jerusalem, let it be given them day by day without fail: that they may offer sacrifices of sweet savors unto the God of heaven, and pray for the life of the king, and of his sons." Ezra 6:7-10.

The king further decreed that severe penalties be meted out to those who should in any wise alter the decree; and he closed with the remarkable statement: "The God that hath caused His name to dwell there destroy all kings and people, that shall put to their hand to alter and to destroy this house of God which is at Jerusalem. I Darius have made a decree; let it be done with the speed." Verse 12. Thus the Lord prepared the way for the completion of the temple.

For months before this decree was made, the Israelites had kept on working by faith, the prophets of God still helping them by means of timely messages, through which [580] the divine purpose for Israel was kept before the workers. Two months after Haggai's last recorded message was delivered, Zechariah had a series of visions regarding the work of God in the earth. These messages, given in the form of parables and symbols, came at a time of great uncertainty and anxiety, and were of peculiar significance to the men who were advancing in the name of the God of Israel. It seemed to the leaders as if the permission granted the Jews to rebuild was about to be withdrawn; the future appeared very dark. God saw that His people were in need of being sustained and cheered by a revelation of His infinite compassion and love.

In vision Zechariah heard the angel of the Lord inquiring, "O Lord of hosts, how long wilt Thou not have mercy on Jerusalem and on the cities of Judah, against which Thou hast had indignation these threescore and ten years? And the Lord answered the angel that talked with me," Zechariah declared, "with good words and comfortable words.

"So the angel that communed with me said unto me, Cry thou, saying, Thus saith the Lord of hosts; I am jealous for Jerusalem and for Zion with a great jealousy. And I am very sore displeased with the heathen that are at ease: for I was but a little displeased, and they helped forward the affliction. Therefore thus saith the Lord; I am returned to Jerusalem with mercies: My house shall be built in it, ... and a line shall be stretched forth upon Jerusalem." Zechariah 1:12-16.

The prophet was now directed to predict, "Thus saith the [581] Lord of hosts; My cities through prosperity shall yet be spread abroad; and the Lord shall yet comfort Zion, and shall yet choose Jerusalem." Verse 17.

Zechariah then saw the powers that had "scattered Judah, Israel, and Jerusalem," symbolized by four horns. Immediately afterward he saw four carpenters, representing the agencies used by the Lord in restoring His people and the house of His worship. See verses 18-21.

"I lifted up mine eyes again," Zechariah said, "and looked, and behold a man with a measuring line in his hand. Then said I, Whither goest thou? And he said unto me, To measure Jerusalem, to see what is the breadth thereof, and what is the length thereof. And, behold, the angel that talked with me went forth, and another angel went out to meet him, and said unto him, Run, speak to this young man, saying, Jerusalem shall be inhabited as towns without walls for the multitude of men and cattle therein: for I, saith the Lord, will be unto her a wall of fire round about, and will be the glory in the midst of her." Zechariah 2:1-5.

God had commanded that Jerusalem be rebuilt; the vision of the measuring of the city was an assurance that He would give comfort and strength to His afflicted ones, and fulfill to them the promises of His everlasting covenant. His protecting care, He declared, would be like "a wall of fire round about;" and through them His glory would be revealed to all the sons of men. That which He was accomplishing for His people was to be known in all the earth. "Cry out and shout, thou inhabitant of Zion: for great is the Holy One of Israel in the midst of thee." Isaiah 12:6. [582]

Chapter 47

Joshua and the Angel

The steady advancement made by the builders of the temple greatly discomfited and alarmed the hosts of evil. Satan determined to put forth still further effort to weaken and discourage God's people by holding before them their imperfections of character. If those who had long suffered because of transgression could again be induced to disregard God's commandments, they would be brought once more under the bondage of sin.

Because Israel had been chosen to preserve the knowledge of God in the earth, they had ever been the special objects of Satan's enmity; he was determined to cause their destruction. While they were obedient, he could do them no harm; therefore he had bent all his power and cunning to entice them into sin. Ensnared by his temptations, they had transgressed the law of God and had been left to become the prey of their enemies.

Yet though they were carried as captives to Babylon, God did not forsake them. He sent His prophets to them with [583] reproofs and warnings, and aroused them to see their guilt. When they humbled themselves before God and returned to Him with true repentance, He sent them messages of encouragement, declaring that He would deliver them from captivity, restore them to His favor, and once more establish them in their own land. And now that this work of restoration had begun, and a remnant of Israel had already returned to Judea, Satan was determined to frustrate the carrying out of the divine purpose, and to this end he was seeking to move upon the heathen nations to destroy them utterly.

But in this crisis the Lord strengthened His people "with good words and comfortable words." Zechariah 1:13. Through an impressive illustration of the work of Satan and the work of Christ, He showed the power of their Mediator to vanquish the accuser of His people.

In vision the prophet beholds "Joshua the high priest," "clothed with filthy garments" (Zechariah 3:1, 3), standing before the Angel of the Lord, entreating God's mercy in behalf of His afflicted people. As he pleads for the fulfillment of God's promises, Satan stands up boldly to resist him. He points to the transgressions of Israel as a reason why they should not be restored to the favor of God. He claims them as his prey, and demands that they be given into his hands.

The high priest cannot defend himself or his people from Satan's accusations. He does not claim that Israel is free from fault. In filthy garments, symbolizing the sins of the people, which he bears as their representative, he stands before the Angel, confessing their guilt, yet pointing to their [584] repentance and humiliation, and relying upon the mercy of a sin-pardoning Redeemer. In faith he claims the promises of God.

Then the Angel, who is Christ Himself, the Saviour of sinners, puts to silence the accuser of His people, declaring, "The Lord rebuke thee, O Satan; even the Lord that hath chosen Jerusalem rebuke thee: is not this a brand plucked out of the fire?" Verse 2. Long had Israel remained in the furnace of affliction. Because of their sins they had been well-nigh consumed in the flame kindled by Satan and his agents for their destruction, but God had now set His hand to bring them forth.

As the intercession of Joshua is accepted, the command is given, "Take away the filthy garments from him;" and to Joshua the Angel says, "Behold, I have caused thine iniquity to pass from thee, and I will clothe thee with change of raiment." "So they set a fair miter upon his head, and clothed him with garments." Verses 4, 5. His own sins and those of his people were pardoned. Israel was clothed with "change of raiment"—the righteousness of Christ imputed to them. The miter placed upon Joshua's head was such as was worn by the priests, and bore the inscription, "Holiness to the Lord" (Exodus 28:36), signifying that notwithstanding his former transgressions, he was now qualified to minister before God in His sanctuary.

The Angel now declared to Joshua: "Thus saith the Lord of hosts; If thou wilt walk in My ways, and if thou wilt keep My charge, then thou shalt also judge My house, and shalt also keep My courts, and I will give thee places [585] to walk among these that stand by." Zechariah 3:7. If obedient, he should be honored as the judge, or ruler, over the temple and all its services; he should walk among attending angels, even in this life; and at last he should join the glorified throng around the throne of God.

"Hear now, O Joshua the high priest, thou, and thy fellows that sit before thee: for they are men wondered at: for, behold, I will bring forth My Servant the Branch." Verse 8. In the Branch, the Deliverer to come, lay the hope of Israel. It was by faith in the coming Saviour that Joshua and his people had received pardon. Through faith in Christ they had been restored to God's favor. By virtue of His merits, if they walked in His ways and kept His statutes, they would be "men wondered at," honored as the chosen of Heaven among the nations of the earth.

As Satan accused Joshua and his people, so in all ages he accuses those who seek the mercy and favor of God. He is "the accuser of our brethren, ... which accused them before our God day and night." Revelation 12:10. Over every soul that is rescued from the power of evil, and whose name is registered in the Lamb's book of life, the controversy is repeated. Never is one received into the family of God without exciting the determined resistance of the enemy. But He who was the hope of Israel then, their defense, their justification and redemption, is the hope of the church today.

Satan's accusations against those who seek the Lord are not prompted by displeasure at their sins. He exults in their defective characters; for he knows that only through their transgression of God's law can he obtain power over them. [586] His accusations arise solely from his enmity to Christ. Through the plan of salvation, Jesus is breaking Satan's hold upon the human family and rescuing souls from his power. All the hatred and malignity of the archrebel is stirred as he beholds the evidences of Christ's supremacy; and with fiendish power and cunning he works to wrest from Him the children of men who have accepted salvation. He leads men into skepticism, causing them to lose confidence in God and to separate from His love; he tempts them to break the law and then claims them as his captives, contesting Christ's right to take them from him.

Satan knows that those who ask God for pardon and grace will obtain it; therefore he presents their sins before them to discourage them. Against those who are trying to obey God, he is constantly seeking occasion for complaint. Even their best and most acceptable service he seeks to make appear corrupt. By countless devices, the most subtle and the most cruel, he endeavors to secure their condemnation.

In his own strength, man cannot meet the charges of the enemy. In sin-stained garments, confessing his guilt, he stands before God. But Jesus, our Advocate, presents an effectual plea in behalf of all who by repentance and faith have committed the keeping of their souls to Him. He pleads their cause, and by the mighty arguments of Calvary, vanquishes their accuser. His perfect obedience to God's law has given Him all power in heaven and in earth, and He claims from His Father mercy and reconciliation for guilty man. To the accuser of His people He declares: [587] "The Lord rebuke thee, O Satan. These are the purchase of My blood, brands plucked from the burning." And to those who rely on Him in faith, He gives the assurance, "Behold, I have caused thine iniquity to pass from thee, and I will clothe thee with change of raiment." Zechariah 3:4.

All who have put on the robe of Christ's righteousness will stand before Him as chosen and faithful and true. Satan has no power to pluck them out of the hand of the Saviour. Not one soul who in penitence and faith has claimed His protection will Christ permit to pass under the enemy's power. His word is pledged: "Let him take hold of My strength, that he may make peace with Me; and he shall make peace with Me." Isaiah 27:5. The promise given to Joshua is given to all: "If thou wilt keep My charge, ... I will give thee places to walk among these that stand by." Zechariah 3:7. Angels of God will walk on either side of them, even in this world, and they will stand at last among the angels that surround the throne of God.

Zechariah's vision of Joshua and the Angel applies with peculiar force to the experience of God's people in the closing scenes of the great day of atonement. The remnant church will then be brought into great trial and distress. Those who keep the commandments of God and the faith of Jesus will feel the ire of the dragon and his hosts. Satan numbers the world as his subjects; he has gained control even of many professing Christians. But here is a little company who are resisting his supremacy. If he could blot them from the earth, his triumph would be complete. As he influenced [588] the heathen nations to destroy Israel, so in the near future he will stir up the wicked powers of earth to destroy the people of God. Men will be required to render obedience to human edicts in violation of the divine law.

Those who are true to God will be menaced, denounced, proscribed. They will be "betrayed both by parents, and brethren, and kinsfolks, and friends," even unto death. Luke 21:16. Their only hope is in the mercy of God; their only defense will be prayer. As Joshua pleaded before the Angel, so the remnant church, with brokenness of heart and unfaltering faith, will plead for pardon and deliverance through Jesus, their Advocate. They are fully conscious of the sinfulness of their lives, they see their weakness and unworthiness; and they are ready to despair.

The tempter stands by to accuse them, as he stood by to resist Joshua. He points to their filthy garments, their defective characters. He presents their weakness and folly, their sins of ingratitude, their unlikeness to Christ, which has dishonored their Redeemer. He endeavors to affright them with the thought that their case is hopeless, that the stain of their defilement will never be washed away. He hopes so to destroy their faith that they will yield to his temptations, and turn from their allegiance to God.

Satan has an accurate knowledge of the sins that he has tempted God's people to commit, and he urges his accusations against them, declaring, that by their sins they have forfeited divine protection, and claiming that he has the right to destroy them. He pronounces them just as deserving as himself of exclusion from the favor of God. "Are [589] these," he says, "the people who are to take my place in heaven, and the place of the angels who united with me? They profess to obey the law of God; but have they kept its precepts? Have they not been lovers of self more than lovers of God? Have they not placed their own interests above His service? Have they not loved the things of the world? Look at the sins that have marked their lives. Behold their selfishness, their malice, their hatred of one another. Will God banish me and my angels from His presence, and yet reward those who have been guilty of the same sins? Thou canst not do this, O Lord, in justice. Justice demands that sentence be pronounced against them."

But while the followers of Christ have sinned, they have not given themselves up to be controlled by the satanic agencies. They have repented of their sins and have sought the Lord in humility and contrition, and the divine Advocate pleads in their behalf. He who has been most abused by their ingratitude, who knows their sin and also their penitence, declares: "The Lord rebuke thee, O Satan. I gave My life for these souls. They are graven upon the palms of My hands. They may have imperfections of character; they may have failed in their endeavors; but they have repented, and I have forgiven and accepted them."

The assaults of Satan are strong, his delusions are subtle; but the Lord's eye is upon His people. Their affliction is great, the flames of the furnace seem about to consume them; but Jesus will bring them forth as gold tried in the fire. Their earthliness will be removed, that through them the image of Christ may be perfectly revealed. [590]

At times the Lord may seem to have forgotten the perils of His church and the injury done her by her enemies. But God has not forgotten. Nothing in this world is so dear to the heart of God as His church. It is not His will that worldly policy shall corrupt her record. He does not leave His people to be overcome by Satan's temptations. He will punish those who misrepresent Him, but He will be gracious to all who sincerely repent. To those who call upon Him for strength for the development of Christian character, He will give all needed help.

In the time of the end the people of God will sigh and cry for the abominations done in the land. With tears they will warn the wicked of their danger in trampling upon the divine law, and with unutterable sorrow they will humble themselves before the Lord in penitence. The wicked will mock their sorrow and ridicule their solemn appeals. But the anguish and humiliation of God's people is unmistakable evidence that they are regaining the strength and nobility of character lost in consequence of sin. It is because they are drawing nearer to Christ, because their eyes are fixed on His perfect purity, that they discern so clearly the exceeding sinfulness of sin. Meekness and lowliness are the conditions of success and victory. A crown of glory awaits those who bow at the foot of the cross.

God's faithful, praying ones are, as it were, shut in with Him. They themselves know not how securely they are shielded. Urged on by Satan, the rulers of this world are seeking to destroy them; but could the eyes of God's children be opened as were the eyes of Elisha's servant at [591] Dothan, they would see angels of God encamped about them, holding in check the hosts of darkness.

As the people of God afflict their souls before Him, pleading for purity of heart, the command is given, "Take away the filthy garments," and the encouraging words are spoken, "Behold, I have caused thine iniquity to pass from thee, and I will clothe thee with change of raiment." Zechariah 3:4. The spotless robe of Christ's righteousness is placed upon the tried, tempted, faithful children of God. The despised remnant are clothed in glorious apparel, nevermore to be defiled by the corruptions of the world. Their names are retained in the Lamb's book of life, enrolled among the faithful of all ages. They have resisted the wiles of the deceiver; they have not been turned from their loyalty by the dragon's roar. Now they are eternally secure from the tempter's devices. Their sins are transferred to the originator of sin. A "fair miter" is set upon their heads.

While Satan has been urging his accusations, holy angels, unseen, have been passing to and fro, placing upon the faithful ones the seal of the living God. These are they that stand upon Mount Zion with the Lamb, having the Father's name written in their foreheads. They sing the new song before the throne, that song which no man can learn save the hundred and forty and four thousand which were redeemed from the earth. "These are they which follow the Lamb whithersoever He goeth. These were redeemed from among men, being the first fruits unto God and to the Lamb. And in their mouth was found no guile: for they are without fault before the throne of God." Revelation 14:4, 5. [592]

Now is reached the complete fulfillment of the words of the Angel: "Hear now, O Joshua the high priest, thou, and thy fellows that sit before thee: for they are men wondered at: for, behold, I will bring forth My Servant the Branch." Zechariah 3:8. Christ is revealed as the Redeemer and Deliverer of His people. Now indeed are the remnant "men wondered at," as the tears and humiliation of their pilgrimage give place to joy and honor in the presence of God and the Lamb. "In that day shall the branch of the Lord be beautiful and glorious, and the fruit of the earth shall be excellent and comely for them that are escaped of Israel. And it shall come to pass, that he that is left in Zion, and he that remaineth in Jerusalem, shall be called holy, even everyone that is written among the living in Jerusalem." Isaiah 4:2, 3. [593]

Chapter 48

"Not by Might, nor by Power"

Immediately after Zechariah's vision of Joshua and the Angel, the prophet received a message regarding the work of Zerubbabel. "The Angel that talked with me," Zechariah declares, "came again, and waked me, as a man that is wakened out of his sleep, and said unto me, What seest thou? And I said, I have looked, and behold a candlestick all of gold, with a bowl upon the top of it, and his seven lamps thereon, and seven pipes to the seven lamps, which are upon the top thereof: and two olive trees by it, one upon the right side of the bowl, and the other upon the left side thereof.

"So I answered and spake to the Angel that talked with me, saying, What are these, my Lord? ... Then He answered and spake unto me, saying, This is the word of the Lord unto Zerubbabel, saying, Not by might, nor by power, but by my Spirit, saith the Lord of hosts."

"Then answered I, and said unto Him, What are these two olive trees upon the right side of the candlestick and [594] upon the left side thereof? And I answered again, and said unto Him, What be these two olive branches which through the two golden pipes empty the golden oil out of themselves? ... Then said He, These are the two anointed ones, that stand by the Lord of the whole earth." Zechariah 4:1-6, 11-14.

In this vision the two olive trees which stand before God are represented as emptying the golden oil out of themselves through golden tubes into the bowl of the candlestick. From this the lamps of the sanctuary are fed, that they may give a bright, continuous light. So from the anointed ones that stand in God's presence the fullness of divine light and love and power is imparted to His people, that they may impart to others light and joy and refreshing. Those who are thus enriched are to enrich others with the treasure of God's love.

In rebuilding the house of the Lord, Zerubbabel had labored in the face of manifold difficulties. From the beginning, adversaries had "weakened the hands of the people of Judah, and troubled them in building," "and made them to cease by force and power." Ezra 4:4, 23. But the Lord had interposed in behalf of the builders, and now He spoke through His prophet to Zerubbabel, saying, "Who art thou, O great mountain? before Zerubbabel thou shalt become a plain: and he shall bring forth the headstone thereof with shoutings, crying, Grace, grace unto it." Zechariah 4:7.

Throughout the history of God's people great mountains of difficulty, apparently insurmountable, have loomed up before those who were trying to carry out the purposes of [595] Heaven. Such obstacles are permitted by the Lord as a test of faith. When we are hedged about on every side, this is the time above all others to trust in God and in the power of His Spirit. The exercise of a living faith means an increase of spiritual strength and the development of an unfaltering trust. It is thus that the soul becomes a conquering power. Before the demand of faith, the obstacles placed by Satan across the pathway of the Christian will disappear; for the powers of heaven will come to his aid. "Nothing shall be impossible unto you." Matthew 17:20.

The way of the world is to begin with pomp and boasting. God's way is to make the day of small things the beginning of the glorious triumph of truth and righteousness. Sometimes He trains His workers by bringing to them disappointment and apparent failure. It is His purpose that they shall learn to master difficulties.

Often men are tempted to falter before the perplexities and obstacles that confront them. But if they will hold the beginning of their confidence steadfast unto the end, God will make the way clear. Success will come to them as they struggle against difficulties. Before the intrepid spirit and unwavering faith of a Zerubbabel, great mountains of difficulty will become a plain; and he whose hands have laid the foundation, even "his hands shall also finish it." "He shall bring forth the headstone thereof with shoutings, crying, Grace, grace unto it." Zechariah 4:9, 7.

Human power and human might did not establish the church of God, and neither can they destroy it. Not on the rock of human strength, but on Christ Jesus, the Rock [596] of Ages, was the church founded, "and the gates of hell shall not prevail against it." Matthew 16:18. The presence of God gives stability to His cause. "Put not your trust in princes, nor in the son of man," is the word that comes to us. Psalm 146:3. "In quietness and in confidence shall be your strength." Isaiah 30:15. God's glorious work, founded on the eternal principles of right, will never come to nought. It will go on from strength to strength, "not by might, nor by power, but by My Spirit, saith the Lord of hosts." Zechariah 4:6.

The promise, "The hands of Zerubbabel have laid the foundation of this house; his hands shall also finish it," was literally fulfilled. Verse 9. "The elders of the Jews builded, and they prospered through the prophesying of Haggai the prophet and Zechariah the son of Iddo. And they builded, and finished it, according to the commandment of the God of Israel, and according to the commandment of Cyrus, and Darius, and Artaxerxes king of Persia. And this house was finished on the third day of the month Adar [the twelfth month], which was in the sixth year of the reign of Darius the king." Ezra 6:14, 15.

Shortly afterward the restored temple was dedicated. "The children of Israel, the priests, and the Levites, and the rest of the children of the captivity, kept the dedication of this house of God with joy;" and "upon the fourteenth day of the first month" they "kept the Passover." Verses 16, 17, 19.

The second temple did not equal the first in magnificence, nor was it hallowed by those visible tokens of the divine presence which pertained to the first temple. There was [597] no manifestation of supernatural power to mark its dedication. No cloud of glory was seen to fill the newly erected sanctuary. No fire from heaven descended to consume the sacrifice upon its altar. The Shekinah no longer abode between the cherubim in the most holy place; the ark, the mercy seat, and the tables of testimony were not found there. No sign from heaven made known to the inquiring priest the will of Jehovah.

And yet this was the building concerning which the Lord had declared by the prophet Haggai: "The glory of this latter house shall be greater than of the former." "I will shake all nations, and the Desire of all nations shall come: and I will fill this house with glory, saith the Lord of hosts." Haggai 2:9, 7. For centuries learned men have endeavored to show wherein the promise of God, given to Haggai, has been fulfilled; yet in the advent of Jesus of Nazareth, the Desire of all nations, who by His personal presence hallowed the precincts of the temple, many have steadfastly refused to see any special significance. Pride and unbelief have blinded their minds to the true meaning of the prophet's words.

The second temple was honored, not with the cloud of Jehovah's glory, but with the presence of the One in whom dwelt "all the fullness of the Godhead bodily"—God Himself "manifest in the flesh." Colossians 2:9; 1 Timothy 3:16. In being honored with the personal presence of Christ during His earthly ministry, and in this alone, did the second temple exceed the first in glory. The "Desire of all nations" had indeed come to His temple, when the Man of Nazareth taught and healed in the sacred courts. [598]

Chapter 49

In the Days of Queen Esther

Under the favor shown them by Cyrus, nearly fifty thousand of the children of the captivity had taken advantage of the decree permitting their return. These, however, in comparison with the hundreds of thousands scattered throughout the provinces of Medo-Persia, were but a mere remnant. The great majority of the Israelites had chosen to remain in the land of their exile rather than undergo the hardships of the return journey and the re-establishment of their desolated cities and homes.

A score or more of years passed by, when a second decree, quite as favorable as the first, was issued by Darius Hystaspes, the monarch then ruling. Thus did God in mercy provide another opportunity for the Jews in the Medo-Persian realm to return to the land of their fathers. The Lord foresaw the troublous times that were to follow during the reign of Xerxes,—the Ahasuerus of the book of Esther,—and He not only wrought a change of feeling in the hearts of men [599] in authority, but also inspired Zechariah to plead with the exiles to return.

"Ho, ho, come forth, and flee from the land of the north," was the message given the scattered tribes of Israel who had become settled in many lands far from their former home. "I have spread you abroad as the four winds of the heaven, saith the Lord. Deliver thyself, O Zion, that dwellest with the daughter of Babylon. For thus saith the Lord of hosts; After the glory hath He sent me unto the nations which spoiled you: for he that toucheth you toucheth the apple of His eye. For, behold, I will shake mine hand upon them, and they shall be a spoil to their servants: and ye shall know that the Lord of hosts hath sent me." Zechariah 2:6-9.

It was still the Lord's purpose, as it had been from the beginning, that His people should be a praise in the earth, to the glory of His name. During the long years of their exile He had given them many opportunities to return to their allegiance to Him. Some had chosen to listen and to learn; some had found salvation in the midst of affliction. Many of these were to be numbered among the remnant that should return. They were likened by Inspiration to "the highest branch of the high cedar," which was to be planted "upon an high mountain and eminent: in the mountain of the height of Israel." Ezekiel 17:22, 23.

It was those "whose spirit God had raised" (Ezra 1:5) who had returned under the decree of Cyrus. But God ceased not to plead with those who voluntarily remained in the land of their exile, and through manifold agencies He made [600] it possible for them also to return. The large number, however, of those who failed to respond to the decree of Cyrus, remained unimpressible to later influences; and even when Zechariah warned them to flee from Babylon without further delay, they did not heed the invitation.

Meanwhile conditions in the Medo-Persian realm were rapidly changing. Darius Hystaspes, under whose reign the Jews had been shown marked favor, was succeeded by Xerxes the Great. It was during his reign that those of the Jews who had failed of heeding the message to flee were called upon to face a terrible crisis. Having refused to take advantage of the way of escape God had provided, now they were brought face to face with death.

Through Haman the Agagite, an unscrupulous man high in authority in Medo-Persia, Satan worked at this time to counterwork the purposes of God. Haman cherished bitter malice against Mordecai, a Jew. Mordecai had done Haman no harm, but had simply refused to show him worshipful reverence. Scorning to "lay hands on Mordecai alone," Haman plotted "to destroy all the Jews that were throughout the whole kingdom of Ahasuerus, even the people of Mordecai." Esther 3:6.

Misled by the false statements of Haman, Xerxes was induced to issue a decree providing for the massacre of all the Jews "scattered abroad and dispersed among the people in all the provinces" of the Medo-Persian kingdom. Verse 8. A certain day was appointed on which the Jews were to be destroyed and their property confiscated. Little did the king realize the far-reaching results that would have [601] accompanied the complete carrying out of this decree. Satan himself, the hidden instigator of the scheme, was trying to rid the earth of those who preserved the knowledge of the true God.

"In every province, whithersoever the king's commandment and his decree came, there was great mourning among the Jews, and fasting, and weeping, and wailing; and many lay in sackcloth and ashes." Esther 4:3. The decree of the Medes and Persians could not be revoked; apparently there was no hope; all the Israelites were doomed to destruction.

But the plots of the enemy were defeated by a Power that reigns among the children of men. In the providence of God, Esther, a Jewess who feared the Most High, had been made queen of the Medo-Persian kingdom. Mordecai was a near relative of hers. In their extremity they decided to appeal to Xerxes in behalf of their people. Esther was to venture into his presence as an intercessor. "Who knoweth," said Mordecai, "whether thou art come to the kingdom for such a time as this?" Verse 14.

The crisis that Esther faced demanded quick, earnest action; but both she and Mordecai realized that unless God should work mightily in their behalf, their own efforts would be unavailing. So Esther took time for communion with God, the source of her strength. "Go," she directed Mordecai, "gather together all the Jews that are present in Shushan, and fast ye for me, and neither eat nor drink three days, night or day: I also and my maidens will fast likewise; and so will I go in unto the king, which is not according to the law: and if I perish, I perish." Verse 16. [602]

The events that followed in rapid succession,—the appearance of Esther before the king, the marked favor shown her, the banquets of the king and queen with Haman as the only guest, the troubled sleep of the king, the public honor shown Mordecai, and the humiliation and fall of Haman upon the discovery of his wicked plot,—all these are parts of a familiar story. God wrought marvelously for His penitent people; and a counter decree issued by the king, allowing them to fight for their lives, was rapidly communicated to every part of the realm by mounted couriers, who were "hastened and pressed on by the king's commandment." "And in every province, and in every city, whithersoever the king's commandment and his decree came, the Jews had joy and gladness, a feast and a good day. And many of the people of the land became Jews; for the fear of the Jews fell upon them." Esther 8:14, 17.

On the day appointed for their destruction, "the Jews gathered themselves together in their cities throughout all the provinces of the king Ahasuerus, to lay hand on such as sought their hurt: and no man could withstand them; for the fear of them fell upon all people." Angels that excel in strength had been commissioned by God to protect His people while they "stood for their lives." Esther 9:2, 16.

Mordecai was given the position of honor formerly occupied by Haman. He "was next unto King Ahasuerus, and great among the Jews, and accepted of the multitude of his brethren" (Esther 10:3); and he sought to promote the welfare of Israel. Thus did God bring His chosen people once more into favor at the Medo-Persian court, [603] [604] [605] making possible the carrying out of His purpose to restore them to their own land. But it was not until several years later, in the seventh year of Artaxerxes I, the successor of Xerxes the Great, that any considerable number returned to Jerusalem, under Ezra.

The trying experiences that came to God's people in the days of Esther were not peculiar to that age alone. The revelator, looking down the ages to the close of time, has declared, "The dragon was wroth with the woman, and went to make war with the remnant of her seed, which keep the commandments of God, and have the testimony of Jesus Christ." Revelation 12:17. Some who today are living on the earth will see these words fulfilled. The same spirit that in ages past led men to persecute the true church, will in the future lead to the pursuance of a similar course toward those who maintain their loyalty to God. Even now preparations are being made for this last great conflict.

The decree that will finally go forth against the remnant people of God will be very similar to that issued by Ahasuerus against the Jews. Today the enemies of the true church see in the little company keeping the Sabbath commandment, a Mordecai at the gate. The reverence of God's people for His law is a constant rebuke to those who have cast off the fear of the Lord and are trampling on His Sabbath.

Satan will arouse indignation against the minority who refuse to accept popular customs and traditions. Men of position and reputation will join with the lawless and the vile to take counsel against the people of God. Wealth, genius, education, will combine to cover them with contempt. [606] Persecuting rulers, ministers, and church members will conspire against them. With voice and pen, by boasts, threats, and ridicule, they will seek to overthrow their faith. By false representations and angry appeals, men will stir up the passions of the people. Not having a "Thus saith the Scriptures" to bring against the advocates of the Bible Sabbath, they will resort to oppressive enactments to supply the lack. To secure popularity and patronage, legislators will yield to the demand for Sunday laws. But those who fear God, cannot accept an institution that violates a precept of the Decalogue. On this battlefield will be fought the last great conflict in the controversy between truth and error. And we are not left in doubt as to the issue. Today, as in the days of Esther and Mordecai, the Lord will vindicate His truth and His people. [607]

Chapter 50

Ezra, the Priest and Scribe

About seventy years after the return of the first company of exiles under Zerubbabel and Joshua, Artaxerxes Longimanus came to the throne of Medo-Persia. The name of this king is connected with sacred history by a series of remarkable providences. It was during his reign that Ezra and Nehemiah lived and labored. He is the one who in 457 B.C. issued the third and final decree for the restoration of Jerusalem. His reign saw the return of a company of Jews under Ezra, the completion of the walls of Jerusalem by Nehemiah and his associates, the reorganization of the temple services, and the great religious reformations instituted by Ezra and Nehemiah. During his long rule he often showed favor to God's people, and in his trusted and well-beloved Jewish friends, Ezra and Nehemiah, he recognized men of God's appointment, raised up for a special work.

The experience of Ezra while living among the Jews who remained in Babylon was so unusual that it attracted the favorable notice of King Artaxerxes, with whom he [608] talked freely regarding the power of the God of heaven, and the divine purpose in restoring the Jews to Jerusalem.

Born of the sons of Aaron, Ezra had been given a priestly training; and in addition to this he had acquired a familiarity with the writings of the magicians, the astrologers, and the wise men of the Medo-Persian realm. But he was not satisfied with his spiritual condition. He longed to be in full harmony with God; he longed for wisdom to carry out the divine will. And so he "prepared his heart to seek the law of the Lord, and to do it." Ezra 7:10. This led him to apply himself diligently to a study of the history of God's people, as recorded in the writings of prophets and kings. He searched the historical and poetical books of the Bible to learn why the Lord had permitted Jerusalem to be destroyed and His people carried captive into a heathen land.

To the experiences of Israel from the time the promise was made to Abraham, Ezra gave special thought. He studied the instruction given at Mount Sinai and through the long period of wilderness wandering. As he learned more and still more concerning God's dealings with His children, and comprehended the sacredness of the law given at Sinai, Ezra's heart was stirred. He experienced a new and thorough conversion and determined to master the records of sacred history, that he might use this knowledge to bring blessing and light to his people.

Ezra endeavored to gain a heart preparation for the work he believed was before him. He sought God earnestly, that he might be a wise teacher in Israel. As he learned to yield mind and will to divine control, there were brought [609] into his life the principles of true sanctification, which, in later years, had a molding influence, not only upon the youth who sought his instruction, but upon all others associated with him.

God chose Ezra to be an instrument of good to Israel, that He might put honor upon the priesthood, the glory of which had been greatly eclipsed during the captivity. Ezra developed into a man of extraordinary learning and became "a ready scribe in the law of Moses." Verse 6. These qualifications made him an eminent man in the Medo-Persian kingdom.

Ezra became a mouthpiece for God, educating those about him in the principles that govern heaven. During the remaining years of his life, whether near the court of the king of Medo-Persia or at Jerusalem, his principal work was that of a teacher. As he communicated to others the truths he learned, his capacity for labor increased. He became a man of piety and zeal. He was the Lord's witness to the world of the power of Bible truth to ennoble the daily life.

The efforts of Ezra to revive an interest in the study of the Scriptures were given permanency by his painstaking, lifelong work of preserving and multiplying the Sacred Writings. He gathered all the copies of the law that he could find and had these transcribed and distributed. The pure word, thus multiplied and placed in the hands of many people, gave knowledge that was of inestimable value.

Ezra's faith that God would do a mighty work for His people, led him to tell Artaxerxes of his desire to return to Jerusalem to revive an interest in the study of God's [610] word and to assist his brethren in restoring the Holy City. As Ezra declared his perfect trust in the God of Israel as one abundantly able to protect and care for His people, the king was deeply impressed. He well understood that the Israelites were returning to Jerusalem that they might serve Jehovah; yet so great was the king's confidence in the integrity of Ezra that he showed him marked favor, granting his request and bestowing on him rich gifts for the temple service. He made him a special representative of the Medo-Persian kingdom and conferred on him extensive powers for the carrying out of the purposes that were in his heart.

The decree of Artaxerxes Longimanus for the restoring and building of Jerusalem, the third issued since the close of the seventy years' captivity, is remarkable for its expressions regarding the God of heaven, for its recognition of the attainments of Ezra, and for the liberality of the grants made to the remnant people of God. Artaxerxes refers to Ezra as "the priest, the scribe, even a scribe of the words of the commandments of the Lord, and of His statutes to Israel;" "a scribe of the law of the God of heaven." The king united with his counselors in offering freely "unto the God of Israel, whose habitation is in Jerusalem;" and in addition he made provision for meeting many heavy expenses by ordering that they be paid "out of the king's treasure house." Verses 11, 12, 15, 20.

"Thou art sent of the king, and of his seven counselors," Artaxerxes declared to Ezra, "to inquire concerning Judah and Jerusalem, according to the law of thy God which is in thine hand." And he further decreed: "Whatsoever is [611] commanded by the God of heaven, let it be diligently done for the house of the God of heaven: for why should there be wrath against the realm of the king and his sons?" Verses 14, 23.

In giving permission to the Israelites to return, Artaxerxes arranged for the restoration of the members of the priesthood to their ancient rites and privileges. "We certify you," he declared, "that touching any of the priests and Levites, singers, porters, Nethinims, or ministers of this house of God, it shall not be lawful to impose toll, tribute, or custom, upon them." He also arranged for the appointment of civil officers to govern the people justly in accordance with the Jewish code of laws. "Thou, Ezra, after the wisdom of thy God, that is in thine hand," he directed, "set magistrates and judges, which may judge all the people that are beyond the river, all such as know the laws of thy God; and teach ye them that know them not. And whosoever will not do the law of thy God, and the law of the king, let judgment be executed speedily upon him, whether it be unto death, or to banishment, or to confiscation of goods, or to imprisonment." Verses 24-26.

Thus, "according to the good hand of his God upon him," Ezra had persuaded the king to make abundant provision for the return of all the people of Israel and of the priests and Levites in the Medo-Persian realm, who were minded "of their own free will to go up to Jerusalem." Verses 9, 13. Thus again the children of the dispersion were given opportunity to return to the land with the possession of which were linked the promises to the house of Israel. [612] This decree brought great rejoicing to those who had been uniting with Ezra in a study of God's purposes concerning His people. "Blessed be the Lord God of our fathers," Ezra exclaimed, "which hath put such a thing as this in the king's heart, to beautify the house of the Lord which is in Jerusalem: and hath extended mercy unto me before the king, and his counselors, and before all the king's mighty princes." Verses 27, 28.

In the issuing of this decree by Artaxerxes, God's providence was manifest. Some discerned this and gladly took advantage of the privilege of returning under circumstances so favorable. A general place of meeting was named, and at the appointed time those who were desirous of going to Jerusalem assembled for the long journey. "I gathered them together to the river that runneth to Ahava," Ezra says, "and there abode we in tents three days." Ezra 8:15.

Ezra had expected that a large number would return to Jerusalem, but the number who responded to the call was disappointingly small. Many who had acquired houses and lands had no desire to sacrifice these possessions. They loved ease and comfort and were well satisfied to remain. Their example proved a hindrance to others who otherwise might have chosen to cast in their lot with those who were advancing by faith.

As Ezra looked over the company assembled, he was surprised to find none of the sons of Levi. Where were the members of the tribe that had been set apart for the sacred service of the temple? To the call, Who is on the Lord's side? the Levites should have been the first to respond. [613] During the captivity, and afterward, they had been granted many privileges. They had enjoyed the fullest liberty to minister to the spiritual needs of their brethren in exile. Synagogues had been built, in which the priests conducted the worship of God and instructed the people. The observance of the Sabbath, and the performance of the sacred rites peculiar to the Jewish faith, had been freely allowed.

But with the passing of the years after the close of the captivity, conditions changed, and many new responsibilities [614] rested upon the leaders in Israel. The temple at Jerusalem had been rebuilt and dedicated, and more priests were needed to carry on its services. There was pressing need of men of God to act as teachers of the people. And besides, the Jews remaining in Babylon were in danger of having their religious liberty restricted. Through the prophet Zechariah, as well as by their recent experience during the troublous times of Esther and Mordecai, the Jews in Medo-Persia had been plainly warned to return to their own land. The time had come when it was perilous for them to dwell longer in the midst of heathen influences. In view of these changed conditions, the priests in Babylon should have been quick to discern in the issuance of the decree a special call to them to return to Jerusalem.

The king and his princes had done more than their part in opening the way for the return. They had provided abundant means, but where were the men? The sons of Levi failed at a time when the influence of a decision to accompany their brethren would have led others to follow their example. Their strange indifference is a sad revelation of the attitude of the Israelites in Babylon toward God's purpose for His people.

Once more Ezra appealed to the Levites, sending them an urgent invitation to unite with his company. To emphasize the importance of quick action, he sent with his written plea several of his "chief men" and "men of understanding." Ezra 7:28; 8:16.

While the travelers tarried with Ezra, these trusted messengers hastened back with the plea, "Bring unto us ministers [615] for the house of our God." Ezra 8:17. The appeal was heeded; some who had been halting, made final decision to return. In all, about forty priests and two hundred and twenty Nethinim—men upon whom Ezra could rely as wise ministers and good teachers and helpers—were brought to the camp.

All were now ready to set forth. Before them was a journey that would occupy several months. The men were taking with them their wives and children, and their substance, besides large treasure for the temple and its service. Ezra was aware that enemies lay in wait by the way, ready to plunder and destroy him and his company; yet he had asked from the king no armed force for protection. "I was ashamed," he has explained, "to require of the king a band of soldiers and horsemen to help us against the enemy in the way: because we had spoken unto the king, saying, The hand of our God is upon all them for good that seek Him; but His power and His wrath is against all them that forsake Him." Verse 22.

In this matter, Ezra and his companions saw an opportunity to magnify the name of God before the heathen. Faith in the power of the living God would be strengthened if the Israelites themselves should now reveal implicit faith in their divine Leader. They therefore determined to put their trust wholly in Him. They would ask for no guard of soldiers. They would give the heathen no occasion to ascribe to the strength of man the glory that belongs to God alone. They could not afford to arouse in the minds of their heathen friends one doubt as to the sincerity of their dependence on [616] God as His people. Strength would be gained, not through wealth, not through the power and influence of idolatrous men, but through the favor of God. Only by keeping the law of the Lord before them, and striving to obey it, would they be protected.

This knowledge of the conditions under which they would continue to enjoy the prospering hand of God, lent more than ordinary solemnity to the consecration service that was held by Ezra and his company of faithful souls just before their departure. "I proclaimed a fast there, at the river of Ahava," Ezra has declared of this experience, "that we might afflict ourselves before our God, to seek of Him a right way for us, and for our little ones, and for all our substance." "So we fasted and besought our God for this: and He was entreated of us." Verses 21, 23.

The blessing of God, however, did not make unnecessary the exercise of prudence and forethought. As a special precaution in safeguarding the treasure, Ezra "separated twelve of the chief of the priests"—men whose faithfulness and fidelity had been proved—"and weighed unto them the silver, and the gold, and the vessels, even the offering of the house of our God, which the king, and his counselors, and his lords, and all Israel there present, had offered." These men were solemnly charged to act as vigilant stewards over the treasure entrusted to their care. "Ye are holy unto the Lord," Ezra declared; "the vessels are holy also; and the silver and the gold are a freewill offering unto the Lord God of your fathers. Watch ye, and keep them, until ye weigh them before the chief of the priests and the Levites, [617] and chief of the fathers of Israel, at Jerusalem, in the chambers of the house of the Lord." Verses 24, 25, 28, 29.

The care exercised by Ezra in providing for the transportation and safety of the Lord's treasure, teaches a lesson worthy of thoughtful study. Only those whose trustworthiness had been proved were chosen, and they were instructed plainly regarding the responsibility resting on them. In the appointment of faithful officers to act as treasurers of the Lord's goods, Ezra recognized the necessity and value of order and organization in connection with the work of God.

During the few days that the Israelites tarried at the river, every provision was completed for the long journey. "We departed," Ezra writes, "on the twelfth day of the first month, to go unto Jerusalem: and the hand of our God was upon us, and He delivered us from the hand of the enemy, and of such as lay in wait by the way." Verse 31. About four months were occupied on the journey, the multitude that accompanied Ezra, several thousand in all, including women and children, necessitating slow progress. But all were preserved in safety. Their enemies were restrained from harming them. Their journey was a prosperous one, and on the first day of the fifth month, in the seventh year of Artaxerxes, they reached Jerusalem. [618]

Chapter 51

A Spiritual Revival

Ezra's arrival in Jerusalem was opportune. There was great need of the influence of his presence. His coming brought courage and hope to the hearts of many who had long labored under difficulties. Since the return of the first company of exiles under the leadership of Zerubbabel and Joshua, over seventy years before, much had been accomplished. The temple had been finished, and the walls of the city had been partially repaired. Yet much remained undone.

Among those who had returned to Jerusalem in former years, there were many who had remained true to God as long as they lived; but a considerable number of the children and the children's children lost sight of the sacredness of God's law. Even some of the men entrusted with responsibilities were living in open sin. Their course was largely neutralizing the efforts made by others to advance the cause of God; for so long as flagrant violations of the law [619] were allowed to go unrebuked, the blessing of Heaven could not rest upon the people.

It was in the providence of God that those who returned with Ezra had had special seasons of seeking the Lord. The experiences through which they had just passed, on their journey from Babylon, unprotected as they had been by any human power, had taught them rich spiritual lessons. Many had grown strong in faith; and as these mingled with the discouraged and the indifferent in Jerusalem, their influence was a powerful factor in the reform soon afterward instituted.

On the fourth day after the arrival, the treasures of silver and gold, with the vessels for the service of the sanctuary, were delivered by the treasurers into the hands of the temple officers, in the presence of witnesses, and with the utmost exactitude. Every article was examined "by number and by weight." Ezra 8:34.

The children of the captivity who had returned with Ezra "offered burnt offerings unto the God of Israel" for a sin offering and as a token of their gratitude and thanksgiving for the protection of holy angels during the journey. "And they delivered the king's commissions unto the king's lieutenants, and to the governors on this side the river: and they furthered the people, and the house of God." Verses 35, 36.

Very soon thereafter a few of the chief men of Israel approached Ezra with a serious complaint. Some of "the people of Israel, and the priests, and the Levites" had so far disregarded the holy commands of Jehovah as to intermarry [620] with the surrounding peoples. "They have taken of their daughters for themselves, and for their sons," Ezra was told, "so that the holy seed have mingled themselves with the people" of heathen lands; "yea, the hand of the princes and rulers hath been chief in this trespass." Ezra 9:1, 2.

In his study of the causes leading to the Babylonish captivity, Ezra had learned that Israel's apostasy was largely traceable to their mingling with heathen nations. He had seen that if they had obeyed God's command to keep separate from the nations surrounding them, they would have been spared many sad and humiliating experiences. Now when he learned that notwithstanding the lessons of the past, men of prominence had dared transgress the laws given as a safeguard against apostasy, his heart was stirred within him. He thought of God's goodness in again giving His people a foothold in their native land, and he was overwhelmed with righteous indignation and with grief at their ingratitude. "When I heard this thing," he says, "I rent my garment and my mantle, and plucked off the hair of my head and of my beard, and sat down astonied.

"Then were assembled unto me everyone that trembled at the words of God of Israel, because of the transgression of those that had been carried away; and I sat astonied until the evening sacrifice." Verses 3, 4.

At the time of the evening sacrifice Ezra rose, and, once more rending his garment and his mantle, he fell upon his knees and unburdened his soul in supplication to Heaven. Spreading out his hands unto the Lord, he exclaimed, "O my God, I am ashamed and blush to lift up my face to [621] Thee, my God: for our iniquities are increased over our head, and our trespass is grown up unto the heavens.

"Since the days of our fathers," the suppliant continued, "have we been in a great trespass unto this day; and for our iniquities have we, our kings, and our priests, been delivered into the hand of the kings of the lands, to the sword, to captivity, and to a spoil, and to confusion of face, as it is this day. And now for a little space grace hath been showed from the Lord our God, to leave us a remnant to escape, and to give us a nail in His holy place, that our God may lighten our eyes, and give us a little reviving in our bondage. For we were bondmen; yet our God hath not forsaken us in our bondage, but hath extended mercy unto us in the sight of the kings of Persia, to give us a reviving, to set up the house of our God, and to repair the desolations thereof, and to give us a wall in Judah and in Jerusalem.

"And now, O our God, what shall we say after this? for we have forsaken Thy commandments, which Thou hast commanded by Thy servants the prophets.... And after all that is come upon us for our evil deeds, and for our great trespass, seeing that Thou our God hast punished us less than our iniquities deserve, and hast given us such deliverance as this; should we again break Thy commandments, and join in affinity with the people of these abominations? wouldest not Thou be angry with us till Thou hadst consumed us, so that there should be no remnant nor escaping? O Lord God of Israel, Thou art righteous: for we remain yet escaped, as it is this day: behold, we are before Thee in our trespasses: for we cannot stand before Thee because of this." Verses 6-15. [622]

The sorrow of Ezra and his associates over the evils that had insidiously crept into the very heart of the Lord's work, wrought repentance. Many of those who had sinned were deeply affected. "The people wept very sore." Ezra 10:1. In a limited degree they began to realize the heinousness of sin and the horror with which God regards it. They saw the sacredness of the law spoken at Sinai, and many trembled at the thought of their transgressions.

One of those present, Shechaniah by name, acknowledged as true all the words spoken by Ezra. "We have trespassed against our God," he confessed, "and have taken strange wives of the people of the land: yet now there is hope in Israel concerning this thing." Shechaniah proposed that all who had transgressed should make a covenant with God to forsake their sin and to be adjudged "according to the law." "Arise," he bade Ezra; "for this matter belongeth unto thee: we also will be with thee: be of good courage." "Then arose Ezra, and made the chief priests, the Levites, and all Israel, to swear that they should do according to this word." Verses 2-5.

This was the beginning of a wonderful reformation. With infinite patience and tact, and with a careful consideration for the rights and welfare of every individual concerned, Ezra and his associates strove to lead the penitent of Israel into the right way. Above all else, Ezra was a teacher of the law; and as he gave personal attention to the examination of every case, he sought to impress the people with the holiness of this law and the blessings to be gained through obedience. [623]

Wherever Ezra labored, there sprang up a revival in the study of the Holy Scriptures. Teachers were appointed to instruct the people; the law of the Lord was exalted and made honorable. The books of the prophets were searched, and the passages foretelling the coming of the Messiah brought hope and comfort to many a sad and weary heart.

More than two thousand years have passed since Ezra "prepared his heart to seek the law of the Lord, and to do it" (Ezra 7:10), yet the lapse of time has not lessened the influence of his pious example. Through the centuries the record of his life of consecration has inspired many with the determination "to seek the law of the Lord, and to do it."

Ezra's motives were high and holy; in all that he did he was actuated by a deep love for souls. The compassion and tenderness that he revealed toward those who had sinned, either willfully or through ignorance, should be an object lesson to all who seek to bring about reforms. The servants of God are to be as firm as a rock where right principles are involved; and yet, withal, they are to manifest sympathy and forbearance. Like Ezra, they are to teach transgressors the way of life by calculating principles that are the foundation of all rightdoing.

In this age of the world, when Satan is seeking, through manifold agencies, to blind the eyes of men and women to the binding claims of the law of God, there is need of men who can cause many to "tremble at the commandment of our God." Ezra 10:3. There is need of true reformers, who will point transgressors to the great Lawgiver and teach them that "the law of the Lord is perfect, converting [624] the soul." Psalm 19:7. There is need of men mighty in the Scriptures, men whose every word and act exalts the statutes of Jehovah, men who seek to strengthen faith. Teachers are needed, oh, so much, who will inspire hearts with reverence and love for the Scriptures.

The widespread iniquity prevalent today may in a great degree be attributed to a failure to study and obey the Scriptures, for when the word of God is set aside, its power to restrain the evil passions of the natural heart is rejected. Men sow to the flesh and of the flesh reap corruption.

With the setting aside of the Bible has come a turning away from God's law. The doctrine that men are released from obedience to the divine precepts, has weakened the force of moral obligation and opened the floodgates of iniquity upon the world. Lawlessness, dissipation, and corruption are sweeping in like an overwhelming flood. Everywhere are seen envy, evil surmising, hypocrisy, estrangement, emulation, strife, betrayal of sacred trusts, indulgence of lust. The whole system of religious principles and doctrines, which should form the foundation and framework of social life, seems to be a tottering mass, ready to fall in ruins.

In the last days of this earth's history the voice that spoke from Sinai is still declaring, "Thou shalt have no other gods before Me." Exodus 20:3. Man has set his will against the will of God, but he cannot silence the word of command. The human mind cannot evade its obligation to a higher power. Theories and speculations may abound; men may try to set science in opposition to revelation, and thus do [625] away with God's law; but stronger and still stronger comes the command, "Thou shalt worship the Lord thy God, and Him only shalt thou serve." Matthew 4:10.

There is no such thing as weakening or strengthening the law of Jehovah. As it has been, so it is. It always has been, and always will be, holy, just, and good, complete in itself. It cannot be repealed or changed. To "honor" or "dishonor" it is but the speech of men.

Between the laws of men and the precepts of Jehovah will come the last great conflict of the controversy between truth and error. Upon this battle we are now entering—a battle not between rival churches contending for the supremacy, but between the religion of the Bible and the religions of fable and tradition. The agencies which have united against truth are now actively at work. God's Holy Word, which has been handed down to us at so great a cost of suffering and bloodshed, is little valued. There are few who really accept it as the rule of life. Infidelity prevails to an alarming extent, not in the world only, but in the church. Many have come to deny doctrines which are the very pillars of the Christian faith. The great facts of creation as presented by the inspired writers, the fall of man, the atonement, the perpetuity of the law—these all are practically rejected by a large share of the professedly Christian world. Thousands who pride themselves on their knowledge regard it as an evidence of weakness to place implicit confidence in the Bible, and a proof of learning to cavil at the Scriptures and to spiritualize and explain away their most important truths. [626]

Christians should be preparing for what is soon to break upon the world as an overwhelming surprise, and this preparation they should make by diligently studying the word of God and striving to conform their lives to its precepts. The tremendous issues of eternity demand of us something besides an imaginary religion, a religion of words and forms, where truth is kept in the outer court. God calls for a revival and a reformation. The words of the Bible and the Bible alone, should be heard from the pulpit. But the Bible has been robbed of its power, and the result is seen in a lowering of the tone of spiritual life. In many sermons of today there is not that divine manifestation which awakens the conscience and brings life to the soul. The hearers cannot say, "Did not our heart burn within us, while He talked with us by the way, and while He opened to us the Scriptures?" Luke 24:32. There are many who are crying out for the living God, longing for the divine presence. Let the word of God speak to the heart. Let those who have heard only tradition and human theories and maxims, hear the voice of Him who can renew the soul unto eternal life.

Great light shone forth from patriarchs and prophets. Glorious things were spoken of Zion, the City of God. Thus the Lord designs that the light shall shine forth through His followers today. If the saints of the Old Testament bore so bright a testimony of loyalty, should not those upon whom is shining the accumulated light of centuries, bear a still more signal witness to the power of truth? The glory of the prophecies sheds their light upon our pathway. [627] Type has met antitype in the death of God's Son. Christ has risen from the dead, proclaiming over the rent sepulcher, "I am the resurrection, and the life." John 11:25. He has sent His Spirit into the world to bring all things to our remembrance. By a miracle of power He has preserved His written word through the ages.

The Reformers whose protest has given us the name of Protestant, felt that God had called them to give the light of the gospel to the world; and in the effort to do this they were ready to sacrifice their possessions, their liberty, even life itself. In the face of persecution and death the gospel was proclaimed far and near. The word of God was carried to the people; and all classes, high and low, rich and poor, learned and ignorant, eagerly studied it for themselves. Are we, in this last conflict of the great controversy, as faithful to our trust as the early Reformers were to theirs?

"Blow the trumpet in Zion, sanctify a fast, call a solemn assembly: gather the people, sanctify the congregation, assemble the elders, gather the children: ... let the priests, the ministers of the Lord, weep between the porch and the altar, and let them say, Spare Thy people, O Lord, and give not Thine heritage to reproach." "Turn ye even to Me with all your hearts, and with fasting, and with weeping, and with mourning: and rend your heart, and not your garments, and turn unto the Lord your God: for He is gracious and merciful, slow to anger, and of great kindness, and repenteth Him of the evil. Who knoweth if He will return and repent, and leave a blessing behind Him?" Joel 2:15-17, 12-14. [628]

Chapter 52

A Man of Opportunity

This chapter is based on Nehemiah 1; 2.

Nehemiah, one of the Hebrew exiles, occupied a position of influence and honor in the Persian court. As cupbearer to the king he was admitted freely to the royal presence. By virtue of his position, and because of his abilities and fidelity, he had become the monarch's friend and counselor. The recipient of royal favor, however, though surrounded by pomp and splendor, did not forget his God nor his people. With deepest interest his heart turned toward Jerusalem; his hopes and joys were bound up with her prosperity. Through this man, prepared by his residence in the Persian court for the work to which he was to be called, God purposed to bring blessing to His people in the land of their fathers.

By messengers from Judea the Hebrew patriot learned that days of trial had come to Jerusalem, the chosen city. The returned exiles were suffering affliction and reproach. The temple and portions of the city had been rebuilt; but [629] the work of restoration was hindered, the temple services were disturbed, and the people kept in constant alarm by the fact that the walls of the city were still largely in ruins.

Overwhelmed with sorrow, Nehemiah could neither eat nor drink; he "wept, and mourned certain days, and fasted." In his grief he turned to the divine Helper. "I ... prayed," he said, "before the God of heaven." Faithfully he made confession of his sins and the sins of his people. He pleaded that God would maintain the cause of Israel, restore their courage and strength, and help them to build up the waste places of Judah.

As Nehemiah prayed, his faith and courage grew strong. His mouth was filled with holy arguments. He pointed to the dishonor that would be cast upon God, if His people, now that they had returned to Him, should be left in weakness and oppression; and he urged the Lord to bring to pass His promise: "If ye turn unto Me, and keep My Commandments, and do them; though there were of you cast out unto the uttermost part of the heaven, yet will I gather them from thence, and will bring them unto the place that I have chosen to set My name there." See Deuteronomy 4:29-31. This promise had been given to Israel through Moses before they had entered Canaan, and during the centuries it had stood unchanged. God's people had now returned to Him in penitence and faith, and His promise would not fail.

Nehemiah had often poured out his soul in behalf of his people. But now as he prayed a holy purpose formed in his mind. He resolved that if he could obtain the consent of the king, and the necessary aid in procuring implements [630] and material, he would himself undertake the task of rebuilding the walls of Jerusalem and restoring Israel's national strength. And he asked the Lord to grant him favor in the sight of the king, that this plan might be carried out. "Prosper, I pray Thee, Thy servant this day," he entreated, "and grant him mercy in the sight of this man."

Four months Nehemiah waited for a favorable opportunity to present his request to the king. During this time, though his heart was heavy with grief, he endeavored to bear himself with cheerfulness in the royal presence. In those halls of luxury and splendor all must appear light-hearted and happy. Distress must not cast its shadow over the countenance of any attendant of royalty. But in Nehemiah's seasons of retirement, concealed from human sight, many were the prayers, the confessions, the tears, heard and witnessed by God and angels.

At length the sorrow that burdened the patriot's heart could no longer be concealed. Sleepless nights and care-filled days left their trace upon his countenance. The king, jealous for his own safety, was accustomed to read countenances and to penetrate disguises, and he saw that some secret trouble was preying upon his cupbearer. "Why is thy countenance sad," he inquired, "seeing thou art not sick? this is nothing else but sorrow of heart."

The question filled Nehemiah with apprehension. Would not the king be angry to hear that while outwardly engaged in his service, the courtier's thoughts had been far away with his afflicted people? Would not the offender's life be forfeited? His cherished plan for restoring the strength of [631] Jerusalem—was it about to be overthrown? "Then," he writes, "I was very sore afraid." With trembling lips and tearful eyes he revealed the cause of his sorrow. "Let the king live forever," he answered. "Why should not my countenance be sad, when the city, the place of my fathers' sepulchers, lieth waste, and the gates thereof are consumed with fire?"

The recital of the condition of Jerusalem awakened the sympathy of the monarch without arousing his prejudices. Another question gave the opportunity for which Nehemiah had long waited: "For what dost thou make request?" But the man of God did not venture to reply till he had sought direction from One higher than Artaxerxes. He had a sacred trust to fulfill, in which he required help from the king; and he realized that much depended upon his presenting the matter in such a way as to win his approval and enlist his aid. "I prayed," he said, "to the God of heaven." In that brief prayer Nehemiah pressed into the presence of the King of kings and won to his side a power that can turn hearts as the rivers of waters are turned.

To pray as Nehemiah prayed in his hour of need is a resource at the command of the Christian under circumstances when other forms of prayer may be impossible. Toilers in the busy walks of life, crowded and almost overwhelmed with perplexity, can send up a petition to God for divine guidance. Travelers by sea and land, when threatened with some great danger, can thus commit themselves to Heaven's protection. In times of sudden difficulty or peril the heart may send up its cry for help to One who [632] has pledged Himself to come to the aid of His faithful, believing ones whenever they call upon Him. In every circumstance, under every condition, the soul weighed down with grief and care, or fiercely assailed by temptation, may find assurance, support, and succor in the unfailing love and power of a covenant-keeping God.

Nehemiah, in that brief moment of prayer to the King of kings, gathered courage to tell Artaxerxes of his desire to be released for a time from his duties at the court, and he asked for authority to build up the waste places of Jerusalem [633] and to make it once more a strong and defensed city. Momentous results to the Jewish nation hung upon this request. "And," Nehemiah declares, "the king granted me, according to the good hand of my God upon me."

Having secured the help he sought, Nehemiah with prudence and forethought proceeded to make the arrangements necessary to ensure the success of the enterprise. He neglected no precaution that would tend to its accomplishment. Not even to his own countrymen did he reveal his purpose. While he knew that many would rejoice in his success, he feared that some, by acts of indiscretion, might arouse the jealousy of their enemies and perhaps bring about the defeat of the undertaking.

His request to the king had been so favorably received that Nehemiah was encouraged to ask for still further assistance. To give dignity and authority to his mission, as well as to provide protection on the journey, he asked for and secured a military escort. He obtained royal letters to the governors of the provinces beyond the Euphrates, the territory through which he must pass on his way to Judea; and he obtained, also, a letter to the keeper of the king's forest in the mountains of Lebanon, directing him to furnish such timber as would be needed. That there might be no occasion for complaint that he had exceeded his commission, Nehemiah was careful to have the authority and privileges accorded him, clearly defined.

This example of wise forethought and resolute action should be a lesson to all Christians. God's children are not only to pray in faith, but to work with diligent and provident [634] care. They encounter many difficulties and often hinder the working of Providence in their behalf, because they regard prudence and painstaking effort as having little to do with religion. Nehemiah did not regard his duty done when he had wept and prayed before the Lord. He united his petitions with holy endeavor, putting forth earnest, prayerful efforts for the success of the enterprise in which he was engaged. Careful consideration and well-matured plans are as essential to the carrying forward of sacred enterprises today as in the time of the rebuilding of Jerusalem's walls.

Nehemiah did not depend upon uncertainty. The means that he lacked he solicited from those who were able to bestow. And the Lord is still willing to move upon the hearts of those in possession of His goods, in behalf of the cause of truth. Those who labor for Him are to avail themselves of the help that He prompts men to give. These gifts may open ways by which the light of truth shall go to many benighted lands. The donors may have no faith in Christ, no acquaintance with His word; but their gifts are not on this account to be refused. [635]

Chapter 53

The Builders on the Wall

This chapter is based on Nehemiah 2; 3; and 4.

Nehemiah's journey to Jerusalem was accomplished in safety. The royal letters to the governors of the provinces along his route secured him honorable reception and prompt assistance. No enemy dared molest the official who was guarded by the power of the Persian king and treated with marked consideration by the provincial rulers. His arrival in Jerusalem, however, with a military escort, showing that he had come on some important mission, excited the jealousy of the heathen tribes living near the city, who had so often indulged their enmity against the Jews by heaping upon them injury and insult. Foremost in this evil work were certain chiefs of these tribes, Sanballat the Horonite, Tobiah the Ammonite, and Geshem the Arabian. From the first these leaders watched with critical eyes the movements of Nehemiah and endeavored by every means in their power to thwart his plans and hinder his work. [636]

Nehemiah continued to exercise the same caution and prudence that had hitherto marked his course. Knowing that bitter and determined enemies stood ready to oppose him, he concealed the nature of his mission from them until a study of the situation should enable him to form his plans. Thus he hoped to secure the co-operation of the people and set them at work before the opposition of his enemies should be aroused.

Choosing a few men whom he knew to be worthy of confidence, Nehemiah told them of the circumstances that had led him to come to Jerusalem, the object that he wished to accomplish, and the plans he proposed to follow. Their interest in his undertaking was at once enlisted and their assistance secured.

On the third night after his arrival Nehemiah rose at midnight and with a few trusted companions went out to view for himself the desolation of Jerusalem. Mounted on his mule, he passed from one part of the city to another, surveying the broken-down walls and gates of the city of his fathers. Painful reflections filled the mind of the Jewish patriot as with sorrow-stricken heart he gazed upon the ruined defenses of his beloved Jerusalem. Memories of Israel's past greatness stood out in sharp contrast with the evidences of her humiliation.

In secrecy and silence Nehemiah completed his circuit of the walls. "The rulers knew not whither I went," he declares, "or what I did; neither had I as yet told it to the Jews, nor to the priests, nor to the nobles, nor to the rulers, nor to the rest that did the work." The remainder of the [637] night he spent in prayer; for he knew that the morning would call for earnest effort to arouse and unite his dispirited and divided countrymen.

Nehemiah bore a royal commission requiring the inhabitants to co-operate with him in rebuilding the walls of the city, but he did not depend upon the exercise of authority. He sought rather to gain the confidence and sympathy of the people, knowing that a union of hearts as well as of hands was essential in the great work before him. When on the morrow he called the people together he presented such arguments as were calculated to arouse their dormant energies and unite their scattered numbers.

Nehemiah's hearers did not know, neither did he tell them, of his midnight circuit of the night before. But the fact that he had made this circuit contributed greatly to his success; for he was able to speak of the condition of the city with an accuracy and a minuteness that astonished his hearers. The impression made upon him as he had looked upon the weakness and degradation of Jerusalem, gave earnestness and power to his words.

Nehemiah presented before the people their reproach among the heathen—their religion dishonored, their God blasphemed. He told them that in a distant land he had heard of their affliction, that he had entreated the favor of Heaven in their behalf, and that, as he was praying, he had determined to ask permission from the king to come to their assistance. He had asked God that the king might not only grant this permission, but might also invest him with the authority and give him the help needed for the [638] work; and his prayer had been answered in such a way as to show that the plan was of the Lord.

All this he related, and then, having shown that he was sustained by the combined authority of the God of Israel and the Persian king, Nehemiah asked the people directly whether they would take advantage of this opportunity and arise and build the wall.

The appeal went straight to their hearts. The thought of how Heaven's favor had been manifested toward them put their fears to shame, and with new courage they said with one voice, "Let us rise up and build." "So they strengthened their hands for this good work."

Nehemiah's whole soul was in the enterprise he had undertaken. His hope, his energy, his enthusiasm, his determination, were contagious, inspiring others with the same high courage and lofty purpose. Each man became a Nehemiah in his turn and helped to make stronger the heart and hand of his neighbor.

When the enemies of Israel heard what the Jews were hoping to accomplish, they laughed them to scorn, saying, "What is this thing that ye do? will ye rebel against the king?" But Nehemiah answered, "The God of heaven, He will prosper us; therefore we His servants will arise and build: but ye have no portion, nor right, nor memorial, in Jerusalem."

Among the first to catch Nehemiah's spirit of zeal and earnestness were the priests. Because of their influential position, these men could do much to advance or hinder the work; and their ready co-operation, at the very outset, contributed not a little to its success. The majority of the [639] princes and rulers of Israel came up nobly to their duty, and these faithful men have honorable mention in the book of God. There were a few, the Tekoite nobles, who "put not their necks to the work of their Lord." The memory of these slothful servants is branded with shame and has been handed down as a warning to all future generations.

In every religious movement there are some who, while they cannot deny that the cause is God's, still hold themselves aloof, refusing to make any effort to help. It were well for such ones to remember the record kept on high—that book in which there are no omissions, no mistakes, and out of which they will be judged. There every neglected opportunity to do service for God is recorded; and there, too, every deed of faith and love is held in everlasting remembrance.

Against the inspiring influence of Nehemiah's presence the example of the Tekoite nobles had little weight. The people in general were animated by patriotism and zeal. Men of ability and influence organized the various classes of citizens into companies, each leader making himself responsible for the erection of a certain part of the wall. And of some it is written that they builded "everyone over against his house."

Nor did Nehemiah's energy abate, now that the work was actually begun. With tireless vigilance he superintended the building, directing the workmen, noting the hindrances, and providing for emergencies. Along the whole extent of that three miles of wall his influence was constantly felt. With timely words he encouraged the fearful, aroused the laggard, and approved the diligent. And ever he watched [640] the movements of their enemies, who from time to time collected at a distance and engaged in conversation, as if plotting mischief, and then, drawing nearer the workmen, attempted to divert their attention.

In his many activities Nehemiah did not forget the source of his strength. His heart was constantly uplifted to God, the great Overseer of all. "The God of heaven," he exclaimed, "He will prosper us;" and the words, echoed and re-echoed, thrilled the hearts of all the workers on the wall. [641]

But the restoration of the defenses of Jerusalem did not go forward unhindered. Satan was working to stir up opposition and bring discouragement. Sanballat, Tobiah, and Geshem, his principal agents in this movement, now set themselves to hinder the work of rebuilding. They endeavored to cause division among the workmen. They ridiculed the efforts of the builders, declaring the enterprise an impossibility and predicting failure.

"What do these feeble Jews?" exclaimed Sanballat mockingly; "will they fortify themselves? ... will they revive the stones out of the heaps of the rubbish which are burned?" [642] Tobiah, still more contemptuous, added, "Even that which they build, if a fox go up, he shall even break down their stone wall."

The builders were soon beset by more active opposition. They were compelled to guard continually against the plots of their adversaries, who, professing friendliness, sought in various ways to cause confusion and perplexity, and to arouse distrust. They endeavored to destroy the courage of the Jews; they formed conspiracies to draw Nehemiah into their toils; and falsehearted Jews were found ready to aid the treacherous undertaking. The report was spread that Nehemiah was plotting against the Persian monarch, intending to exalt himself as a king over Israel, and that all who aided him were traitors.

But Nehemiah continued to look to God for guidance and support, and "the people had a mind to work." The enterprise went forward until the gaps were filled and the entire wall built up to half its intended height.

As the enemies of Israel saw how unavailing were their efforts, they were filled with rage. Hitherto they had not dared employ violent measures, for they knew that Nehemiah and his companions were acting under the king's commission, and they feared that active opposition against him might bring upon them the monarch's displeasure. But now in their anger they themselves became guilty of the crime of which they had accused Nehemiah. Assembling for counsel, they "conspired all of them together to come and to fight against Jerusalem."

At the same time that the Samaritans were plotting against Nehemiah and his work, some of the leading men [643] among the Jews, becoming disaffected, sought to discourage him by exaggerating the difficulties attending the enterprise. "The strength of the bearers of burdens is decayed," they said, "and there is much rubbish; so that we are not able to build the wall."

Discouragement came from still another source. "The Jews which dwelt by," those who were taking no part in the work, gathered up the statements and reports of their enemies and used these to weaken courage and create disaffection.

But taunts and ridicule, opposition and threats, seemed only to inspire Nehemiah with firmer determination and to arouse him to greater watchfulness. He recognized the dangers that must be met in this warfare with their enemies, but his courage was undaunted. "We made our prayer unto our God," he declares, "and set a watch against them day and night." "Therefore set I in the lower places behind the wall, and on the higher places, I even set the people after their families with their swords, their spears, and their bows. And I looked, and rose up, and said unto the nobles, and to the rulers, and to the rest of the people, Be not ye afraid of them: remember the Lord, which is great and terrible, and fight for your brethren, your sons, and your daughters, your wives, and your houses.

"And it came to pass, when our enemies heard that it was known unto us, and God had brought their counsel to nought, that we returned all of us to the wall, everyone unto his work. And it came to pass from that time forth, that the half of my servants wrought in the work, and the other half of them held both the spears, the shields, and [644] the bows, and the habergeons.... They which builded on the wall, and they that bare burdens, with those that laded, everyone with one of his hands wrought in the work, and with the other hand held a weapon. For the builders, everyone had his sword girded by his side, and so builded."

Beside Nehemiah stood a trumpeter, and on different parts of the wall were stationed priests bearing the sacred trumpets. The people were scattered in their labors, but on the approach of danger at any point a signal was given for them to repair thither without delay. "So we labored in the work," Nehemiah says, "and half of them held the spears from the rising of the morning till the stars appeared."

Those who had been living in towns and villages outside Jerusalem were now required to lodge within the walls, both to guard the work and to be ready for duty in the morning. This would prevent unnecessary delay, and would cut off the opportunity which the enemy would otherwise improve, of attacking the workmen as they went to and from their homes. Nehemiah and his companions did not shrink from hardship or trying service. Neither by day nor night, not even during the short time given to sleep, did they put off their clothing or lay aside their armor.

The opposition and discouragement that the builders in Nehemiah's day met from open enemies and pretended friends is typical of the experience that those today will have who work for God. Christians are tried, not only by the anger, contempt, and cruelty of enemies, but by the indolence, inconsistency, lukewarmness, and treachery of avowed friends and helpers. Derision and reproach are [645] hurled at them. And the same enemy that leads to contempt, at a favorable opportunity uses more cruel and violent measures.

Satan takes advantage of every unconsecrated element for the accomplishment of his purposes. Among those who profess to be the supporters of God's cause there are those who unite with His enemies and thus lay His cause open to the attacks of His bitterest foes. Even some who desire the work of God to prosper will yet weaken the hands of His servants by hearing, reporting, and half believing the slanders, boasts, and menaces of His adversaries. Satan works with marvelous success through his agents, and all who yield to their influence are subject to a bewitching power that destroys the wisdom of the wise and the understanding of the prudent. But, like Nehemiah, God's people are neither to fear nor to despise their enemies. Putting their trust in God, they are to go steadily forward, doing His work with unselfishness, and committing to His providence the cause for which they stand.

Amidst great discouragement, Nehemiah made God his trust, his sure defense. And He who was the support of His servant then has been the dependence of His people in every age. In every crisis His people may confidently declare, "If God be for us, who can be against us?" Romans 8:31. However craftily the plots of Satan and his agents may be laid, God can detect them, and bring to nought all their counsels. The response of faith today will be the response made by Nehemiah, "Our God shall fight for us;" for God is in the work, and no man can prevent its ultimate success. [646]

Chapter 54

A Rebuke Against Extortion

This chapter is based on Nehemiah 5.

The wall of Jerusalem had not yet been completed when Nehemiah's attention was called to the unhappy condition of the poorer classes of the people. In the unsettled state of the country, tillage had been to some extent neglected. Furthermore, because of the selfish course pursued by some who had returned to Judea, the Lord's blessing was not resting upon their land, and there was a scarcity of grain.

In order to obtain food for their families, the poor were obliged to buy on credit and at exorbitant prices. They were also compelled to raise money by borrowing on interest to pay the heavy taxes imposed upon them by the kings of Persia. To add to the distress of the poor, the more wealthy among the Jews had taken advantage of their necessities, thus enriching themselves.

The Lord had commanded Israel, through Moses, that every third year a tithe be raised for the benefit of the poor; [647] and a further provision had been made in the suspension of agricultural labor every seventh year, the land lying fallow, its spontaneous products being left to those in need. Faithfulness in devoting these offerings to the relief of the poor and to other benevolent uses would have tended to keep fresh before the people the truth of God's ownership of all, and their opportunity to be channels of blessing. It was Jehovah's purpose that the Israelites should have a training that would eradicate selfishness, and develop breadth and nobility of character.

God had also instructed through Moses: "If thou lend money to any of My people that is poor by thee, thou shalt not be to him as an usurer." "Thou shalt not lend upon usury to thy brother; usury of money, usury of victuals, usury of anything that is lent upon usury." Exodus 22:25; Deuteronomy 23:19. Again He had said, "If there be among you a poor man of one of thy brethren within any of thy gates in thy land which the Lord thy God giveth thee, thou shalt not harden thine heart, nor shut thine hand from thy poor brother: but thou shalt open thine hand wide unto him, and shalt surely lend him sufficient for his need, in that which he wanteth." "For the poor shall never cease out of the land: therefore I command thee, saying, Thou shalt open thine hand wide unto thy brother, to thy poor, and to thy needy, in thy land." Deuteronomy 15:7, 8, 11.

At times following the return of the exiles from Babylon, the wealthy Jews had gone directly contrary to these commands. When the poor were obliged to borrow to pay tribute to the king, the wealthy had lent them money, but [648] had exacted a high rate of interest. By taking mortgages on the lands of the poor, they had gradually reduced the unfortunate debtors to the deepest poverty. Many had been forced to sell their sons and daughters into servitude; and there seemed no hope of improving their condition, no way to redeem either their children or their lands, no prospect before them but ever-increasing distress, with perpetual want and bondage. Yet they were of the same nation, children of the same covenant, as their more favored brethren.

At length the people presented their condition before Nehemiah. "Lo," they said, "we bring into bondage our sons and our daughters to be servants, and some of our daughters are brought into bondage already: neither is it in our power to redeem them; for other men have our lands and vineyards."

As Nehemiah heard of this cruel oppression, his soul was filled with indignation. "I was very angry," he says, "when I heard their cry and these words." He saw that if he succeeded in breaking up the oppressive custom of exaction he must take a decided stand for justice. With characteristic energy and determination he went to work to bring relief to his brethren.

The fact that the oppressors were men of wealth, whose support was greatly needed in the work of restoring the city, did not for a moment influence Nehemiah. He sharply rebuked the nobles and rulers, and when he had gathered a great assembly of the people he set before them the requirements of God touching the case.

He called their attention to events that had occurred in [649] the reign of King Ahaz. He repeated the message which God had at the time sent to Israel to rebuke their cruelty and oppression. The children of Judah, because of their idolatry, had been delivered into the hands of their still more idolatrous brethren, the people of Israel. The latter had indulged their enmity by slaying in battle many thousands of the men of Judah and had seized all the women and children, intending to keep them as slaves or to sell them into bondage to the heathen.

Because of the sins of Judah, the Lord had not interposed to prevent the battle; but by the prophet Oded He rebuked the cruel design of the victorious army: "Ye purpose to keep under the children of Judah and Jerusalem for bondmen and bondwomen unto you: but are there not with you, even with you, sins against the Lord your God?" 2 Chronicles 28:10. Oded warned the people of Israel that the anger of the Lord was kindled against them, and that their course of injustice and oppression would call down His judgments. Upon hearing these words, the armed men left the captives and the spoil before the princes and all the congregation. Then certain leading men of the tribe of Ephraim "took the captives, and with the spoil clothed all that were naked among them, and arrayed them, and shod them, and gave them to eat and to drink, and anointed them, and carried all the feeble of them upon asses, and brought them to Jericho, the city of palm trees, to their brethren." Verse 15.

Nehemiah and others had ransomed certain of the Jews who had been sold to the heathen, and he now placed this course in contrast with the conduct of those who for the [650] sake of worldly gain were enslaving their brethren. "It is not good that ye do," he said; "ought ye not to walk in the fear of our God because of the reproach of the heathen our enemies?"

Nehemiah showed them that he himself, being invested with authority from the Persian king, might have demanded large contributions for his personal benefit. But instead of this he had not taken even that which justly belonged to him, but had given liberally to relieve the poor in their need. He urged those among the Jewish rulers who had been guilty of extortion, to cease this iniquitous work; to restore the lands of the poor, and also the increase of money which they had exacted from them; and to lend to them without security or usury.

These words were spoken in the presence of the whole congregation. Had the rulers chosen to justify themselves, they had opportunity to do so. But they offered no excuse. "We will restore them," they declared, "and will require nothing of them; so will we do as thou sayest." At this, Nehemiah in the presence of the priests "took an oath of them, that they should do according to this promise." "And all the congregation said, Amen, and praised the Lord. And the people did according to this promise."

This record teaches an important lesson. "The love of money is the root of all evil." 1 Timothy 6:10. In this generation the desire for gain is the absorbing passion. Wealth is often obtained by fraud. There are multitudes struggling with poverty, compelled to labor hard for small wages, unable to secure even the barest necessities of life. Toil and deprivation, with no hope of better things, make [651] their burden heavy. Careworn and oppressed, they know not where to turn for relief. And all this that the rich may support their extravagance or indulge their desire to hoard!

Love of money and love of display have made this world as a den of thieves and robbers. The Scriptures picture the greed and oppression that will prevail just before Christ's second coming. "Go to now, ye rich men," James writes; "ye have heaped treasure together for the last days. Behold, the hire of the laborers who have reaped down your fields, which is of you kept back by fraud, crieth: and the cries of them which have reaped are entered into the ears of the Lord of Sabaoth. Ye have lived in pleasure on the earth, and been wanton; ye have nourished your hearts, as in a day of slaughter. Ye have condemned and killed the just; and he doth not resist you." James 5:1, 3-6.

Even among those who profess to be walking in the fear of the Lord, there are some who are acting over again the course pursued by the nobles of Israel. Because it is in their power to do so, they exact more than is just, and thus become oppressors. And because avarice and treachery are seen in the lives of those who have named the name of Christ, because the church retains on her books the names of those who have gained their possessions by injustice, the religion of Christ is held in contempt. Extravagance, overreaching, extortion, are corrupting the faith of many and destroying their spirituality. The church is in a great degree responsible for the sins of her members. She gives countenance to evil if she fails to lift her voice against it.

The customs of the world are no criterion for the Christian. He is not to imitate its sharp practices, its overreaching, [652] its extortion. Every unjust act toward a fellow being is a violation of the golden rule. Every wrong done to the children of God is done to Christ Himself in the person of His saints. Every attempt to take advantage of the ignorance, weakness, or misfortune of another is registered as fraud in the ledger of heaven. He who truly fears God, would rather toil day and night, and eat the bread of poverty, than to indulge the passion for gain that oppresses the widow and fatherless or turns the stranger from his right.

The slightest departure from rectitude breaks down the barriers and prepares the heart to do greater injustice. Just to that extent that a man would gain advantage for himself at the disadvantage of another, will his soul become insensible to the influence of the Spirit of God. Gain obtained at such a cost is a fearful loss.

We were all debtors to divine justice, but we had nothing with which to pay the debt. Then the Son of God, who pitied us, paid the price of our redemption. He became poor that through His poverty we might be rich. By deeds of liberality toward His poor we may prove the sincerity of our gratitude for the mercy extended to us. "Let us do good unto all men," the apostle Paul enjoins, "especially unto them who are of the household of faith." Galatians 6:10. And his words accord with those of the Saviour: "Ye have the poor with you always, and whensoever ye will ye may do them good." "Whatsoever ye would that men should do to you, do ye even so to them: for this is the law and the prophets." Mark 14:7; Matthew 7:12. [653]

Chapter 55

Heathen Plots

This chapter is based on Nehemiah 6.

Sanballat and his confederates dared not make open war upon the Jews; but with increasing malice they continued their secret efforts to discourage, perplex, and injure them. The wall about Jerusalem was rapidly approaching completion. When it should be finished and its gates set up, these enemies of Israel could not hope to force an entrance into the city. They were the more eager, therefore, to stop the work without further delay. At last they devised a plan by which they hoped to draw Nehemiah from his station, and while they had him in their power, to kill or imprison him.

Pretending to desire a compromise of the opposing parties, they sought a conference with Nehemiah, and invited him to meet them in a village on the plain of Ono. But enlightened by the Holy Spirit as to their real purpose, he refused. "I sent messengers unto them," he writes, "saying, I am [654] doing a great work, so that I cannot come down: why should the work cease, whilst I leave it, and come down to you?" But the tempters were persistent. Four times they sent a message of similar import, and each time they received the same answer.

Finding this scheme unsuccessful, they resorted to a more daring stratagem. Sanballat sent Nehemiah a messenger bearing an open letter which said: "It is reported among the heathen, and Gashmu saith it, that thou and the Jews think to rebel: for which cause thou buildest the wall, that thou mayest be their king.... And thou hast also appointed prophets to preach of thee at Jerusalem, saying, There is a king in Judah: and now shall it be reported to the king according to these words. Come now therefore, and let us take counsel together."

Had the reports mentioned been actually circulated, there would have been cause for apprehension; for they would soon have been carried to the king, whom a slight suspicion might provoke to the severest measures. But Nehemiah was convinced that the letter was wholly false, written to arouse his fears and draw him into a snare. This conclusion was strengthened by the fact that the letter was sent open, evidently that the people might read the contents, and become alarmed and intimidated.

He promptly returned the answer. "There are no such things done as thou sayest, but thou feignest them out of thine own heart." Nehemiah was not ignorant of Satan's devices. He knew that these attempts were made in order to weaken the hands of the builders and thus frustrate their efforts. [655]

Again and again had Satan been defeated; and now, with deeper malice and cunning, he laid a still more subtle and dangerous snare for the servant of God. Sanballat and his companions hired men who professed to be the friends of Nehemiah, to give him evil counsel as the word of the Lord. The chief one engaged in this iniquitous work was Shemaiah, a man previously held in good repute by Nehemiah. This man shut himself up in a chamber near the sanctuary as if fearing that his life was in danger. The temple was at this time protected by walls and gates, but the gates of the city were not yet set up. Professing great concern for Nehemiah's safety, Shemaiah advised him to seek shelter in the temple. "Let us meet together in the house of God, within the temple," he proposed, "and let us shut the doors of the temple: for they will come to slay thee; yea, in the night will they come to slay thee."

Had Nehemiah followed this treacherous counsel, he would have sacrificed his faith in God, and in the eyes of the people he would have appeared cowardly and contemptible. In view of the important work that he had undertaken, and the confidence that he professed to have in the power of God, it would have been altogether inconsistent for him to hide as if in fear. The alarm would have spread among the people, each would have sought his own safety, and the city would have been left unprotected, to fall a prey to its enemies. That one unwise move on the part of Nehemiah would have been a virtual surrender of all that had been gained.

Nehemiah was not long in penetrating the true character and object of his counselor. "I perceived that God had [656] not sent him," he says, "but that he pronounced this prophecy against me: for Tobiah and Sanballat had hired him. Therefore was he hired, that I should be afraid, and do so, and sin, and that they might have matter for an evil report, that they might reproach me."

The infamous counsel given by Shemaiah was seconded by more than one man of high reputation, who, while professing to be Nehemiah's friends, were secretly in league with his enemies. But it was to no avail that they laid their snare. Nehemiah's fearless answer was: "Should such a man as I flee? and who is there, that, being as I am, would go into the temple to save his life? I will not go in." [657]

Notwithstanding the plots of enemies, open and secret, the work of building went steadily forward, and in less than two months from the time of Nehemiah's arrival in Jerusalem the city was girded with its defenses and the builders could walk upon the walls and look down upon their defeated and astonished foes. "When all our enemies heard thereof, and all the heathen that were about us saw these things," Nehemiah writes, "they were much cast down in their own eyes: for they perceived that this work was wrought of our God."

Yet even this evidence of the Lord's controlling hand was not sufficient to restrain discontent, rebellion, and treachery among the Israelites. "The nobles of Judah sent many letters unto Tobiah, and the letters of Tobiah came unto them. For there were many in Judah sworn unto him, because he was the son-in-law of Shechaniah." Here are seen the evil results of intermarriage with idolaters. A family of Judah had become connected with the enemies of God, and the relation had proved a snare. Many others had done the same. These, like the mixed multitude that came up with Israel from Egypt, were a source of constant trouble. They were not wholehearted in His service; and when God's work demanded a sacrifice, they were ready to violate their solemn oath of co-operation and support.

Some who had been foremost in plotting mischief against the Jews, now professed a desire to be on friendly terms with them. The nobles of Judah who had become entangled in idolatrous marriages, and who had held traitorous correspondence with Tobiah and taken oath to serve him, now [658] represented him as a man of ability and foresight, an alliance with whom would be greatly to the advantage of the Jews. At the same time they betrayed to him Nehemiah's plans and movements. Thus the work of God's people was laid open to the attacks of their enemies, and opportunity was given to misconstrue Nehemiah's words and acts, and to hinder his work.

When the poor and oppressed had appealed to Nehemiah for redress of their wrongs, he had stood boldly in their defense and had caused the wrongdoers to remove the reproach that rested on them. But the authority that he had exercised in behalf of his downtrodden countrymen he did not now exercise in his own behalf. His efforts had been met by some with ingratitude and treachery, but he did not use his power to bring the traitors to punishment. Calmly and unselfishly he went forward in his service for the people, never slackening his efforts or allowing his interest to grow less.

Satan's assaults have ever been directed against those who have sought to advance the work and cause of God. Though often baffled, he as often renews his attacks with fresh vigor, using means hitherto untried. But it is his secret working through those who avow themselves the friends of God's work, that is most to be feared. Open opposition may be fierce and cruel, but it is fraught with far less peril to God's cause than is the secret enmity of those who, while professing to serve God, are at heart the servants of Satan. These have it in their power to place every advantage in the hands of those who will use their knowledge to hinder the work of God and injure His servants. [659]

Every device that the prince of darkness can suggest will be employed to induce God's servants to form a confederacy with the agents of Satan. Repeated solicitations will come to call them from duty; but, like Nehemiah, they should steadfastly reply, "I am doing a great work, so that I cannot come down." God's workers may safely keep on with their work, letting their efforts refute the falsehoods that malice may coin for their injury. Like the builders on the walls of Jerusalem they must refuse to be diverted from their work by threats or mockery or falsehood. Not for one moment are they to relax their watchfulness or vigilance, for enemies are continually on their track. Ever they must make their prayer to God "and set a watch against them day and night." Nehemiah 4:9.

As the time of the end draws near, Satan's temptations will be brought to bear with greater power upon God's workers. He will employ human agents to mock and revile those who "build the wall." But should the builders come down to meet the attacks of their foes, this would but retard the work. They should endeavor to defeat the purposes of their adversaries, but they should not allow anything to call them from their work. Truth is stronger than error, and right will prevail over wrong.

Neither should they allow their enemies to gain their friendship and sympathy, and thus lure them from their post of duty. He who by any unguarded act exposes the cause of God to reproach, or weakens the hands of his fellow workers, brings upon his own character a stain not easily removed, and places a serious obstacle in the way of his future usefulness. [660]

"They that forsake the law praise the wicked." Proverbs 28:4. When those who are uniting with the world, yet claiming great purity, plead for union with those who have ever been the opposers of the cause of truth, we should fear and shun them as decidedly as did Nehemiah.

Such counsel is prompted by the enemy of all good. It is the speech of timeservers, and should be resisted as resolutely today as then. Whatever influence would tend to unsettle the faith of God's people in His guiding power, should be steadfastly withstood.

In Nehemiah's firm devotion to the work of God, and his equally firm reliance on God, lay the reason of the failure of his enemies to draw him into their power. The soul that is indolent falls an easy prey to temptation; but in the life that has a noble aim, an absorbing purpose, evil finds little foothold. The faith of him who is constantly advancing does not weaken; for above, beneath, beyond, he recognizes Infinite Love, working out all things to accomplish His good purpose. God's true servants work with a determination that will not fail because the throne of grace is their constant dependence.

God has provided divine assistance for all the emergencies to which our human resources are unequal. He gives the Holy Spirit to help in every strait, to strengthen our hope and assurance, to illuminate our minds and purify our hearts. He provides opportunities and opens channels of working. If His people are watching the indications of His providence, and are ready to co-operate with Him, they will see mighty results. [661]

Chapter 56

Instructed in the Law of God

This chapter is based on Nehemiah 8; 9; and 10.

It was the time of the Feast of Trumpets. Many were gathered at Jerusalem. The scene was one of mournful interest. The wall of Jerusalem had been rebuilt and the gates set up, but a large part of the city was still in ruins.

On a platform of wood, erected in one of the broadest streets, and surrounded on every hand by the sad reminders of Judah's departed glory, stood Ezra, now an aged man. At his right and left were gathered his brother Levites. Looking down from the platform, their eyes swept over a sea of heads. From all the surrounding country the children of the covenant had assembled. "And Ezra blessed the Lord, the great God. And all the people answered, Amen: ... and they bowed their heads, and worshiped the Lord with their faces to the ground."

Yet even here was evidence of the sin of Israel. Through the intermarriage of the people with other nations, the [662] Hebrew language had become corrupted, and great care was necessary on the part of the speakers to explain the law in the language of the people, that it might be understood by all. Certain of the priests and Levites united with Ezra in explaining the principles of the law. "They read in the book in the law of God distinctly, and gave the sense, and caused them to understand the reading."

"And the ears of all the people were attentive unto the book of the law." They listened, intent and reverent, to the words of the Most High. As the law was explained, they were convinced of their guilt, and they mourned because of their transgressions. But this day was a festival, a day of rejoicing, a holy convocation, a day which the Lord had commanded the people to keep with joy and gladness; and in view of this they were bidden to restrain their grief and to rejoice because of God's great mercy toward them. "This day is holy unto the Lord your God," Nehemiah said. "Mourn not, nor weep.... Go your way, eat the fat, and drink the sweet, and send portions unto them for whom nothing is prepared: for this day is holy unto our Lord: neither be ye sorry; for the joy of the Lord is your strength."

The earlier part of the day was devoted to religious exercises, and the people spent the remainder of the time in gratefully recounting the blessings of God and in enjoying the bounties that He had provided. Portions were also sent to the poor, who had nothing to prepare. There was great rejoicing because the words of the law had been read and understood. [663] [664] [665]

On the following day the reading and explaining of the law were continued. And at the time appointed—on the tenth day of the seventh month—the solemn services of the Day of Atonement were performed according to the command of God.

From the fifteenth to the twenty-second of the same month the people and their rulers kept once more the Feast of Tabernacles. It was proclaimed "in all their cities, and in Jerusalem, saying, Go forth unto the mount, and fetch olive branches, and pine branches, and myrtle branches, and palm branches, and branches of thick trees, to make booths, as it is written. So the people went forth, and brought them, and made themselves booths, everyone upon the roof of his house, and in their courts, and in the courts of the house of God.... And there was very great gladness. Also day by day, from the first day unto the last day, he [Ezra] read in the book of the law of God."

As they had listened from day to day to the words of the law, the people had been convicted of their transgressions, and of the sins of their nation in past generations. They saw that it was because of a departure from God that His protecting care had been withdrawn and that the children of Abraham had been scattered in foreign lands, and they determined to seek His mercy and to pledge themselves to walk in His commandments. Before entering upon this solemn service, held on the second day after the close of the Feast of Tabernacles, they separated themselves from the heathen among them.

As the people prostrated themselves before the Lord, [666] confessing their sins and pleading for pardon, their leaders encouraged them to believe that God, according to His promise, heard their prayers. They must not only mourn and weep, and repent, but they must believe that God pardoned them. They must show their faith by recounting His mercies and praising Him for His goodness. "Stand up," said these teachers, "and bless the Lord your God for ever and ever."

Then from the assembled throng, as they stood with outstretched hands toward heaven, there arose the song:

"Blessed be Thy glorious name, Which is exalted above all blessing and praise. Thou, even Thou, art Lord alone; Thou hast made heaven, the heaven of heavens, with all their host, The earth, and all things that are therein, The seas, and all that is therein, And Thou preservest them all; And the host of heaven worshippeth Thee."

The song of praise ended, the leaders of the congregation related the history of Israel, showing how great had been God's goodness toward them, and how great their ingratitude. Then the whole congregation entered into a covenant to keep all the commandments of God. They had suffered punishment for their sins; now they acknowledged the justice of God's dealings with them and pledged themselves to obey His law. And that this might be "a sure covenant," and be preserved in permanent form, as a memorial of the obligation they had taken upon themselves, it was written out, and the priests, Levites, and princes signed it. It was [667] to serve as a reminder of duty and a barrier against temptation. The people took a solemn oath "to walk in God's law, which was given by Moses the servant of God, and to observe and do all the commandments of the Lord our Lord, and His judgments and His statutes." The oath taken at this time included a promise not to intermarry with the people of the land.

Before the day of fasting ended, the people still further manifested their determination to return to the Lord, by pledging themselves to cease from desecrating the Sabbath. Nehemiah did not at this time, as at a later date, exercise his authority to prevent heathen traders from coming into Jerusalem; but in an effort to save the people from yielding to temptation, he bound them, by a solemn covenant, not to transgress the Sabbath law by purchasing from these venders, hoping that this would discourage the traders and put an end to the traffic.

Provision was also made to support the public worship of God. In addition to the tithe the congregation pledged themselves to contribute yearly a stated sum for the service of the sanctuary. "We cast the lots," Nehemiah writes, "to bring the first fruits of our ground, and the first fruits of all fruit of all trees, year by year, unto the house of the Lord: also the first-born of our sons, and of our cattle, as it is written in the law, and the firstlings of our herds and of our flocks."

Israel had returned to God with deep sorrow for backsliding. They had made confession with mourning and lamentation. They had acknowledged the righteousness of [668] God's dealings with them, and had covenanted to obey His law. Now they must manifest faith in His promises. God had accepted their repentance; they were now to rejoice in the assurance of sins forgiven and their restoration to divine favor.

Nehemiah's efforts to restore the worship of the true God had been crowned with success. As long as the people were true to the oath they had taken, as long as they were obedient to God's word, so long would the Lord fulfill His promise by pouring rich blessings upon them.

For those who are convicted of sin and weighed down with a sense of their unworthiness, there are lessons of faith and encouragement in this record. The Bible faithfully presents the result of Israel's apostasy; but it portrays also the deep humiliation and repentance, the earnest devotion and generous sacrifice, that marked their seasons of return to the Lord.

Every true turning to the Lord brings abiding joy into the life. When a sinner yields to the influence of the Holy Spirit, he sees his own guilt and defilement in contrast with the holiness of the great Searcher of hearts. He sees himself condemned as a transgressor. But he is not, because of this, to give way to despair; for his pardon has already been secured. He may rejoice in the sense of sins forgiven, in the love of a pardoning heavenly Father. It is God's glory to encircle sinful, repentant human beings in the arms of His love, to bind up their wounds, to cleanse them from sin, and to clothe them with the garments of salvation. [669]

Chapter 57

Reformation

This chapter is based on Nehemiah 13.

Solemnly and publicly the people of Judah had pledged themselves to obey the law of God. But when the influence of Ezra and Nehemiah was for a time withdrawn, there were many who departed from the Lord. Nehemiah had returned to Persia. During his absence from Jerusalem, evils crept in that threatened to pervert the nation. Idolaters not only gained a foothold in the city, but contaminated by their presence the very precincts of the temple. Through intermarriage, a friendship had been brought about between Eliashib the high priest and Tobiah the Ammonite, Israel's bitter enemy. As a result of this unhallowed alliance, Eliashib had permitted Tobiah to occupy an apartment connected with the temple, which heretofore had been used as a storeroom for tithes and offerings of the people.

Because of the cruelty and treachery of the Ammonites and Moabites toward Israel, God had declared through [670] Moses that they should be forever shut out from the congregation of His people. See Deuteronomy 23:3-6. In defiance of this word, the high priest had cast out the offerings stored in the chamber of God's house, to make a place for this representative of a proscribed race. Greater contempt for God could not have been shown than to confer such a favor on this enemy of God and His truth.

On returning from Persia, Nehemiah learned of the bold profanation and took prompt measures to expel the intruder. "It grieved me sore," he declares; "therefore I cast forth all the household stuff of Tobiah out of the chamber. Then I commanded, and they cleansed the chambers: and thither brought I again the vessels of the house of God, with the meat offering and the frankincense."

Not only had the temple been profaned, but the offerings had been misapplied. This had tended to discourage the liberalities of the people. They had lost their zeal and fervor, and were reluctant to pay their tithes. The treasuries of the Lord's house were poorly supplied; many of the singers and others employed in the temple service, not receiving sufficient support, had left the work of God to labor elsewhere.

Nehemiah set to work to correct these abuses. He gathered together those who had left the service of the Lord's house, "and set them in their place." This inspired the people with confidence, and all Judah brought "the tithe of the corn and the new wine and the oil." Men who "were counted faithful" were made "treasurers over the treasuries," "and their office was to distribute unto their brethren." [671]

Another result of intercourse with idolaters was a disregard of the Sabbath, the sign distinguishing the Israelites from all other nations as worshipers of the true God. Nehemiah found that heathen merchants and traders from the surrounding country, coming to Jerusalem, had induced many among the Israelites to engage in traffic on the Sabbath. There were some who could not be persuaded to sacrifice principle, but others transgressed and joined with the heathen in their efforts to overcome the scruples of the more conscientious. Many dared openly to violate the Sabbath. "In those days," Nehemiah writes, "saw I in Judah some treading wine presses on the Sabbath, and bringing in sheaves, and lading asses; as also wine, grapes, and figs, and all manner of burdens, which they brought into Jerusalem on the Sabbath day.... There dwelt men of Tyre also therein, which brought fish, and all manner of ware, and sold on the Sabbath unto the children of Judah."

This state of things might have been prevented had the rulers exercised their authority; but a desire to advance their own interests had led them to favor the ungodly. Nehemiah fearlessly rebuked them for their neglect of duty. "What evil thing is this that ye do, and profane the Sabbath day?" he sternly demanded. "Did not your fathers thus, and did not our God bring all this evil upon us, and upon this city? yet ye bring more wrath upon Israel by profaning the Sabbath." He then gave command that "when the gates of Jerusalem began to be dark before the Sabbath," they should be shut, and not opened again till the Sabbath was past; and having more confidence in his own servants [672] than in those that the magistrates of Jerusalem might appoint, he stationed them at the gates to see that his orders were enforced.

Not inclined to abandon their purpose, "the merchants and sellers of all kind of ware lodged without Jerusalem once or twice," hoping to find opportunity for traffic, with either the citizens or the country people. Nehemiah warned them that they would be punished if they continued this practice. "Why lodge ye about the wall?" he demanded; [673] "if ye do so again, I will lay hands on you." "From that time forth came they no more on the Sabbath." He also directed the Levites to guard the gates, knowing that they would command greater respect than the common people, while from their close connection with the service of God it was reasonable to expect that they would be more zealous in enforcing obedience to His law.

And now Nehemiah turned his attention to the danger that again threatened Israel from intermarriage and association with idolaters. "In those days," he writes, "saw I Jews that had married wives of Ashdod, of Ammon, and of Moab: and their children spake half in the speech of Ashdod, and could not speak in the Jews' language, but according to the language of each people."

These unlawful alliances were causing great confusion in Israel; for some who entered into them were men in high position, rulers to whom the people had a right to look for counsel and a safe example. Foreseeing the ruin before the nation if this evil were allowed to continue, Nehemiah reasoned earnestly with the wrongdoers. Pointing to the case of Solomon, he reminded them that among all the nations there had risen no king like this man, to whom God had given great wisdom; yet idolatrous women had turned his heart from God, and his example had corrupted Israel. "Shall we then hearken unto you," Nehemiah sternly demanded, "to do all this great evil?" "Ye shall not give your daughters unto their sons, nor take their daughters unto your sons, or for yourselves."

As he set before them God's commands and threatenings, and the fearful judgments visited on Israel in the [674] past for this very sin, their consciences were aroused, and a work of reformation was begun that turned away God's threatened anger and brought His approval and blessing.

There were some in sacred office who pleaded for their heathen wives, declaring that they could not bring themselves to separate from them. But no distinction was made; no respect was shown for rank or position. Whoever among the priests or rulers refused to sever his connection with idolaters was immediately separated from the service of the Lord. A grandson of the high priest, having married a daughter of the notorious Sanballat, was not only removed from office, but promptly banished from Israel. "Remember them, O my God," Nehemiah prayed, "because they have defiled the priesthood, and the covenant of the priesthood, and of the Levites."

How much anguish of soul this needed severity cost the faithful worker for God the judgment alone will reveal. There was a constant struggle with opposing elements, and only by fasting, humiliation, and prayer was advancement made.

Many who had married idolaters chose to go with them into exile, and these, with those who had been expelled from the congregation, joined the Samaritans. Hither some who had occupied high positions in the work of God found their way and after a time cast in their lot fully with them. Desiring to strengthen this alliance, the Samaritans promised to adopt more fully the Jewish faith and customs, and the apostates, determined to outdo their former brethren, erected a temple on Mount Gerizim in opposition to the house of God at Jerusalem. Their religion continued to be [675] a mixture of Judaism and heathenism, and their claim to be the people of God was the source of schism, emulation, and enmity between the two nations, from generation to generation.

In the work of reform to be carried forward today, there is need of men who, like Ezra and Nehemiah, will not palliate or excuse sin, nor shrink from vindicating the honor of God. Those upon whom rests the burden of this work will not hold their peace when wrong is done, neither will they cover evil with a cloak of false charity. They will remember that God is no respecter of persons, and that severity to a few may prove mercy to many. They will remember also that in the one who rebukes evil the spirit of Christ should ever be revealed.

In their work, Ezra and Nehemiah humbled themselves before God, confessing their sins and the sins of their people, and entreating pardon as if they themselves were the offenders. Patiently they toiled and prayed and suffered. That which made their work most difficult was not the open hostility of the heathen, but the secret opposition of pretended friends, who, by lending their influence to the service of evil, increased tenfold the burden of God's servants. These traitors furnished the Lord's enemies with material to use in their warfare upon His people. Their evil passions and rebellious wills were ever at war with the plain requirements of God.

The success attending Nehemiah's efforts shows what prayer, faith, and wise, energetic action will accomplish. Nehemiah was not a priest; he was not a prophet; he made no pretension to high title. He was a reformer raised up [676] for an important time. It was his aim to set his people right with God. Inspired with a great purpose, he bent every energy of his being to its accomplishment. High, unbending integrity marked his efforts. As he came into contact with evil and opposition to right he took so determined a stand that the people were roused to labor with fresh zeal and courage. They could not but recognize his loyalty, his patriotism, and his deep love for God; and, seeing this, they were willing to follow where he led.

Industry in a God-appointed duty is an important part of true religion. Men should seize circumstances as God's instruments with which to work His will. Prompt and decisive action at the right time will gain glorious triumphs, while delay and neglect result in failure and dishonor to God. If the leaders in the cause of truth show no zeal, if they are indifferent and purposeless, the church will be careless, indolent, and pleasure-loving; but if they are filled with a holy purpose to serve God and Him alone, the people will be united, hopeful, eager.

The word of God abounds in sharp and striking contrasts. Sin and holiness are placed side by side, that, beholding, we may shun the one and accept the other. The pages that describe the hatred, falsehood, and treachery of Sanballat and Tobiah, describe also the nobility, devotion, and self-sacrifice of Ezra and Nehemiah. We are left free to copy either, as we choose. The fearful results of transgressing God's commands are placed over against the blessings resulting from obedience. We ourselves must decide whether we will suffer the one or enjoy the other. [677]

The work of restoration and reform carried on by the returned exiles, under the leadership of Zerubbabel, Ezra, and Nehemiah, presents a picture of a work of spiritual restoration that is to be wrought in the closing days of this earth's history. The remnant of Israel were a feeble people, exposed to the ravages of their enemies; but through them God purposed to preserve in the earth a knowledge of Himself and of His law. They were the guardians of the true worship, the keepers of the holy oracles. Varied were the experiences that came to them as they rebuilt the temple and the wall of Jerusalem; strong was the opposition that they had to meet. Heavy were the burdens borne by the leaders in this work; but these men moved forward in unwavering confidence, in humility of spirit, and in firm reliance upon God, believing that He would cause His truth to triumph. Like King Hezekiah, Nehemiah "clave to the Lord, and departed not from following Him, but kept His commandments.... And the Lord was with him." 2 Kings 18:6, 7.

The spiritual restoration of which the work carried forward in Nehemiah's day was a symbol, is outlined in the words of Isaiah: "They shall build the old wastes, they shall raise up the former desolations, and they shall repair the waste cities." "They that shall be of thee shall build the old waste places: thou shalt raise up the foundations of many generations; and thou shalt be called, The repairer of the breach, The restorer of paths to dwell in." Isaiah 61:4; 58:12.

The prophet here describes a people who, in a time of general departure from truth and righteousness, are seeking [678] to restore the principles that are the foundation of the kingdom of God. They are repairers of a breach that has been made in God's law—the wall that He has placed around His chosen ones for their protection, and obedience to whose precepts of justice, truth, and purity is to be their perpetual safeguard.

In words of unmistakable meaning the prophet points out the specific work of this remnant people who build the wall. "If thou turn away thy foot from the Sabbath, from doing thy pleasure on My holy day; and call the Sabbath a delight, the holy of the Lord, honorable; and shalt honor Him, not doing thine own ways, nor finding thine own pleasure, nor speaking thine own words: then shalt thou delight thyself in the Lord; and I will cause thee to ride upon the high places of the earth, and feed thee with the heritage of Jacob thy father: for the mouth of the Lord hath spoken it." Isaiah 58:13, 14.

In the time of the end every divine institution is to be restored. The breach made in the law at the time the Sabbath was changed by man, is to be repaired. God's remnant people, standing before the world as reformers, are to show that the law of God is the foundation of all enduring reform and that the Sabbath of the fourth commandment is to stand as a memorial of creation, a constant reminder of the power of God. In clear, distinct lines they are to present the necessity of obedience to all the precepts of the Decalogue. Constrained by the love of Christ, they are to co-operate with Him in building up the waste places. They are to be repairers of the breach, restorers of paths to dwell in. See verse 12. [679]

Chapter 58

The Coming of a Deliverer

Beginning of Section 7—Light at Eventide

Through the long centuries of "trouble and darkness" and "dimness of anguish" (Isaiah 8:22) marking the history of mankind from the day our first parents lost their Eden home, to the time the Son of God appeared as the Saviour of sinners, the hope of the fallen race was centered in the coming of a Deliverer to free men and women from the bondage of sin and the grave.

The first intimation of such a hope was given to Adam and Eve in the sentence pronounced upon the serpent in Eden when the Lord declared to Satan in their hearing, "I will put enmity between thee and the woman, and between thy seed and her seed; it shall bruise thy head, and thou shalt bruise His heel." Genesis 3:15.

As the guilty pair listened to these words, they were inspired with hope; for in the prophecy concerning the breaking of Satan's power they discerned a promise of [682] deliverance from the ruin wrought through transgression. Though they must suffer from the power of their adversary because they had fallen under his seductive influence and had chosen to disobey the plain command of Jehovah, yet they need not yield to utter despair. The Son of God was offering to atone with His own lifeblood for their transgression. To them was to be granted a period of probation, during which, through faith in the power of Christ to save, they might become once more the children of God.

Satan, by means of his success in turning man aside from the path of obedience, became "the god of this world." 2 Corinthians 4:4. The dominion that once was Adam's passed to the usurper. But the Son of God proposed to come to this earth to pay the penalty of sin, and thus not only redeem man, but recover the dominion forfeited. It is of this restoration that Micah prophesied when he said, "O Tower of the flock, the stronghold of the daughter of Zion, unto Thee shall it come, even the first dominion." Micah 4:8. The apostle Paul has referred to it as "the redemption of the purchased possession." Ephesians 1:14. And the psalmist had in mind the same final restoration of man's original inheritance when he declared, "The righteous shall inherit the land, and dwell therein forever." Psalm 37:29.

This hope of redemption through the advent of the Son of God as Saviour and King, has never become extinct in the hearts of men. From the beginning there have been some whose faith has reached out beyond the shadows of the present to the realities of the future. Adam, Seth, Enoch, Methuselah, Noah, Shem, Abraham, Isaac, and Jacob— [683] through these and other worthies the Lord has preserved the precious revealings of His will. And it was thus that to the children of Israel, the chosen people through whom was to be given to the world the promised Messiah, God imparted a knowledge of the requirements of His law, and of the salvation to be accomplished through the atoning sacrifice of His beloved Son.

The hope of Israel was embodied in the promise made at the time of the call of Abraham, and afterward repeated again and again to his posterity, "In thee shall all families of the earth be blessed." Genesis 12:3. As the purpose of God for the redemption of the race was unfolded to Abraham, the Sun of Righteousness shone upon his heart, and his darkness was scattered. And when, at last, the Saviour Himself walked and talked among the sons of men, He bore witness to the Jews of the patriarch's bright hope of deliverance through the coming of a Redeemer. "Your father Abraham rejoiced to see My day," Christ declared; "and he saw it, and was glad." John 8:56.

This same blessed hope was foreshadowed in the benediction pronounced by the dying patriarch Jacob upon his son Judah:

"Judah, thou art he whom thy brethren shall praise: Thy hand shall be in the neck of thine enemies; Thy father's children shall bow down before thee.... The scepter shall not depart from Judah, Nor a lawgiver from between his feet, Until Shiloh come; And unto Him shall the gathering of the people be."

Genesis 49:8-10. [684]

Again, on the borders of the Promised Land, the coming of the world's Redeemer was foretold in the prophecy uttered by Balaam:

"I shall see Him, but not now: I shall behold Him, but not nigh: There shall come a Star out of Jacob, and a Scepter shall rise out of Israel, And shall smite the corners of Moab, and destroy all the children of Sheth."

Numbers 24:17.

Through Moses, God's purpose to send His Son as the Redeemer of the fallen race, was kept before Israel. On one occasion, shortly before his death, Moses declared, "The Lord thy God will raise up unto thee a Prophet from the midst of thee, of thy brethren, like unto me; unto Him ye shall hearken." Plainly had Moses been instructed for Israel concerning the work of the Messiah to come. "I will raise them up a Prophet from among their brethren, like unto thee," was the word of Jehovah to His servant; "and will put My words in His mouth; and He shall speak unto them all that I shall command Him." Deuteronomy 18:15, 18.

In patriarchal times the sacrificial offerings connected with divine worship constituted a perpetual reminder of the coming of a Saviour, and thus it was with the entire ritual of the sanctuary services throughout Israel's history. In the ministration of the tabernacle, and of the temple that afterward took its place, the people were taught each day, by means of types and shadows, the great truths relative to the advent of Christ as Redeemer, Priest, and King; and [685] once each year their minds were carried forward to the closing events of the great controversy between Christ and Satan, the final purification of the universe from sin and sinners. The sacrifices and offerings of the Mosaic ritual were ever pointing toward a better service, even a heavenly. The earthly sanctuary was "a figure for the time then present," in which were offered both gifts and sacrifices; its two holy places were "patterns of things in the heavens;" for Christ, our great High Priest, is today "a minister of the sanctuary, and of the true tabernacle, which the Lord pitched, and not man." Hebrews 9:9, 23; 8:2.

From the day the Lord declared to the serpent in Eden, "I will put enmity between thee and the woman, and between thy seed and her seed" (Genesis 3:15), Satan has known that he can never hold absolute sway over the inhabitants of this world. When Adam and his sons began to offer the ceremonial sacrifices ordained by God as a type of the coming Redeemer, Satan discerned in these a symbol of communion between earth and heaven. During the long centuries that have followed, it has been his constant effort to intercept this communion. Untiringly has he sought to misrepresent God and to misinterpret the rites pointing to the Saviour, and with a great majority of the members of the human family he has been successful.

While God has desired to teach men that from His own love comes the Gift which reconciles them to Himself, the archenemy of mankind has endeavored to represent God as one who delights in their destruction. Thus the sacrifices and the ordinances designed of Heaven to reveal divine [686] love have been perverted to serve as means whereby sinners have vainly hoped to propitiate, with gifts and good works, the wrath of an offended God. At the same time, Satan has sought to arouse and strengthen the evil passions of men in order that through repeated transgression multitudes might be led on and on, far from God, and hopelessly bound with the fetters of sin.

When God's written word was given through the Hebrew prophets, Satan studied with diligence the messages concerning the Messiah. Carefully he traced the words that outlined with unmistakable clearness Christ's work among men as a suffering sacrifice and as a conquering king. In the parchment rolls of the Old Testament Scriptures he read that the One who was to appear was to be "brought as a lamb to the slaughter," "His visage ... so marred more than any man, and His form more than the sons of men." Isaiah 53:7; 52:14. The promised Saviour of humanity was to be "despised and rejected of men; a man of sorrows, and acquainted with grief; ... smitten of God, and afflicted;" yet He was also to exercise His mighty power in order to "judge the poor of the people." He was to "save the children of the needy," and "break in pieces the oppressor." Isaiah 53:3, 4; Psalm 72:4. These prophecies caused Satan to fear and tremble; yet he relinquished not his purpose to thwart, if possible, the merciful provisions of Jehovah for the redemption of the lost race. He determined to blind the eyes of the people, so far as might be possible, to the real significance of the Messianic prophecies, [687] in order to prepare the way for the rejection of Christ at His coming.

During the centuries immediately preceding the Flood, success had attended Satan's efforts to bring about a worldwide prevalence of rebellion against God. And even the lessons of the Deluge were not long held in remembrance. With artful insinuations Satan again led the children of men step by step into bold rebellion. Again he seemed about to triumph, but God's purpose for fallen man was not thus to be set aside. Through the posterity of faithful Abraham, of the line of Shem, a knowledge of Jehovah's beneficent designs was to be preserved for the benefit of future generations. From time to time divinely appointed messengers of truth were to be raised up to call attention to the meaning of the sacrificial ceremonies, and especially to the promise of Jehovah concerning the advent of the One toward whom all the ordinances of the sacrificial system pointed. Thus the world was to be kept from universal apostasy.

Not without the most determined opposition was the divine purpose carried out. In every way possible the enemy of truth and righteousness worked to cause the descendants of Abraham to forget their high and holy calling, and to turn aside to the worship of false gods. And often his efforts were all but successful. For centuries preceding Christ's first advent, darkness covered the earth, and gross darkness the people. Satan was throwing his hellish shadow athwart the pathway of men, that he might prevent them from gaining a knowledge of God and of the future world. [688] Multitudes were sitting in the shadow of death. Their only hope was for this gloom to be lifted, that God might be revealed.

With prophetic vision David, the anointed of God, had foreseen that the coming of Christ should be "as the light of the morning, when the sun riseth, even a morning without clouds." 2 Samuel 23:4. And Hosea testified, "His going forth is prepared as the morning." Hosea 6:3. Quietly and gently the daylight breaks upon the earth, dispelling the shadow of darkness and waking the earth to life. So was the Sun of Righteousness to arise, "with healing in His wings." Malachi 4:2. The multitudes dwelling "in the land of the shadow of death" were to see "a great light." Isaiah 9:2.

The prophet Isaiah, looking with rapture upon this glorious deliverance, exclaimed:

"Unto us a Child is born, Unto us a Son is given: And the government shall be upon His shoulder: And His name shall be called Wonderful, Counselor, The mighty God, The everlasting Father, The Prince of Peace. Of the increase of His government and peace there shall be no end, Upon the throne of David, And upon His kingdom, To order it, and to establish it With judgment and with justice From henceforth even forever. The zeal of the Lord of hosts will perform this."

Verses 6, 7.

In the later centuries of Israel's history prior to the first advent it was generally understood that the coming of the [689] Messiah was referred to in the prophecy, "It is a light thing that Thou shouldest be My servant to raise up the tribes of Jacob, and to restore the preserved of Israel: I will also give Thee for a light to the Gentiles, that Thou mayest be My salvation unto the end of the earth." "The glory of the Lord shall be revealed," the prophet had foretold, "and all flesh shall see it together." Isaiah 49:6; 40:5. It was of this light of men that John the Baptist afterward testified so boldly, when he proclaimed, "I am the voice of one crying in the wilderness, Make straight the way of the Lord, as said the prophet Esaias." John 1:23.

It was to Christ that the prophetic promise was given: "Thus saith the Lord, the Redeemer of Israel, and His Holy One, to Him whom man despiseth, to Him whom the nation abhorreth, ... thus saith the Lord, ... I will preserve Thee, and give Thee for a covenant of the people, to establish the earth, to cause to inherit the desolate heritages; that Thou mayest say to the prisoners, Go forth; to them that are in darkness, Show yourselves.... They shall not hunger nor thirst; neither shall the heat nor sun smite them: for He that hath mercy on them shall lead them, even by the springs of water shall He guide them." Isaiah 49:7-10.

The steadfast among the Jewish nation, descendants of that holy line through whom a knowledge of God had been preserved, strengthened their faith by dwelling on these and similar passages. With exceeding joy they read how the Lord would anoint One "to preach good tidings unto the meek," "to bind up the brokenhearted, to proclaim [690] liberty to the captives," and to declare "the acceptable year of the Lord." Isaiah 61:1, 2. Yet their hearts were filled with sadness as they thought of the sufferings He must endure in order to fulfill the divine purpose. With deep humiliation of soul they traced the words in the prophetic roll:

"Who hath believed our report? And to whom is the arm of the Lord revealed?

"For He shall grow up before Him as a tender plant, And as a root out of a dry ground: He hath no form nor comeliness; And when we shall see Him, There is no beauty that we should desire Him.

"He is despised and rejected of men; A Man of Sorrows, and acquainted with grief: And we hid as it were our faces from Him; He was despised, and we esteemed Him not.

"Surely He hath borne our griefs, And carried our sorrows: Yet we did esteem Him stricken, Smitten of God, and afflicted.

"But He was wounded for our transgressions, He was bruised for our iniquities: The chastisement of our peace was upon Him; And with His stripes we are healed.

"All we like sheep have gone astray; We have turned everyone to his own way; And the Lord hath laid on Him The iniquity of us all.

"He was oppressed, and He was afflicted, Yet He opened not His mouth: He is brought as a lamb to the slaughter, And as a sheep before her shearers is dumb, So He openeth not His mouth. [691]

"He was taken from prison and from judgment: And who shall declare His generation? For He was cut off out of the land of the living: For the transgression of My people was He stricken.

"And He made His grave with the wicked, And with the rich in His death; Because He had done no violence, Neither was any deceit in His mouth."

Isaiah 53:1-9.

Of the suffering Saviour Jehovah Himself declared through Zechariah, "Awake, O sword, against My Shepherd, and against the Man that is My Fellow." Zechariah 13:7. As the substitute and surety for sinful man, Christ was to suffer under divine justice. He was to understand what justice meant. He was to know what it means for sinners to stand before God without an intercessor.

Through the psalmist the Redeemer had prophesied of Himself:

"Reproach hath broken My heart; And I am full of heaviness: And I looked for some to take pity, But there was none; And for comforters, But I found none. They gave Me also gall for My meat; And in My thirst they gave Me vinegar to drink."

Psalm 69:20, 21.

Of the treatment He was to receive, He prophesied, "Dogs have compassed Me: the assembly of the wicked have enclosed Me: they pierced My hands and My feet. I may tell all My bones: they look and stare upon Me. They part My garments among them, and cast lots upon My vesture." Psalm 22:16-18. [692]

These portrayals of the bitter suffering and cruel death of the Promised One, sad though they were, were rich in promise; for of Him whom "it pleased the Lord to bruise" and to put to grief, in order that He might become "an offering for sin," Jehovah declared:

"He shall see His seed, He shall prolong His days, And the pleasure of the Lord shall prosper in His hand. He shall see of the travail of His soul, and shall be satisfied:

"By His knowledge shall My righteous Servant justify many; For He shall bear their iniquities. Therefore will I divide Him a portion with the great, And He shall divide the spoil with the strong; Because He hath poured out His soul unto death: And He was numbered with the transgressors; And He bare the sin of many, And made intercession for the transgressors."

Isaiah 53:10-12.

It was love for sinners that led Christ to pay the price of redemption. "He saw that there was no man, and wondered that there was no intercessor," none other could ransom men and women from the power of the enemy; "therefore His arm brought salvation unto Him; and His righteousness, it sustained Him." Isaiah 59:16.

"Behold My Servant, whom I uphold; Mine Elect, in whom My soul delighteth; I have put My Spirit upon Him: He shall bring forth judgment to the Gentiles."

Isaiah 42:1.

In His life no self-assertion was to be mingled. The homage which the world gives to position, to wealth, and to talent, was to be foreign to the Son of God. None of the means that men employ to win allegiance or to command [693] homage, was the Messiah to use. His utter renunciation of self was foreshadowed in the words:

"He shall not cry, Nor lift up, Nor cause His voice to be heard in the street. A bruised reed shall He not break, And the smoking flax shall He not quench."

Verses 2, 3.

In marked contrast to the teachers of His day was the Saviour to conduct Himself among men. In His life no noisy disputation, no ostentatious worship, no act to gain applause, was ever to be witnessed. The Messiah was to be hid in God, and God was to be revealed in the character of His Son. Without a knowledge of God, humanity would be eternally lost. Without divine help, men and women would sink lower and lower. Life and power must be imparted by Him who made the world. Man's necessities could be met in no other way.

It was further prophesied of the Messiah: "He shall not fail nor be discouraged, till He have set judgment in the earth: and the isles shall wait for His law." The Son of God was to "magnify the law, and make it honorable." Verses 4, 21. He was not to lessen its importance and binding claims; He was rather to exalt it. At the same time He was to free the divine precepts from those burdensome exactions placed upon them by man, whereby many were brought to discouragement in their efforts to serve God acceptably.

Of the mission of the Saviour the word of Jehovah was: "I the Lord have called Thee in righteousness, and will hold Thine hand, and will keep Thee, and give Thee for [694] a covenant of the people, for a light of the Gentiles; to open the blind eyes, to bring out the prisoners from the prison, and them that sit in darkness out of the prison house. I am the Lord: that is My name: and My glory will I not give to another, neither My praise to graven images. Behold, the former things are come to pass, and new things do I declare: before they spring forth I tell you of them." Verses 6-9. [695]

Through the promised Seed, the God of Israel was to bring deliverance to Zion. "There shall come forth a Rod out of the stem of Jesse, and a Branch shall grow out of his roots." "Behold, a virgin shall conceive, and bear a Son, and shall call His name Immanuel. Butter and honey shall He eat, that He may know to refuse the evil, and choose the good." Isaiah 11:1; 7:14, 15.

"And the Spirit of the Lord shall rest upon Him, the Spirit of wisdom and understanding, the Spirit of counsel and might, the Spirit of knowledge and of the fear of the Lord; and shall make Him of quick understanding in the fear of the Lord: and He shall not judge after the sight of His eyes, neither reprove after the hearing of His ears: but with righteousness shall He judge the poor, and reprove with equity for the meek of the earth: and He shall smite the earth with the rod of His mouth, and with the breath of His lips shall He slay the wicked. And righteousness shall be the girdle of His loins, and faithfulness the girdle of His reins." "And in that day there shall be a Root of Jesse, which shall stand for an ensign of the people; to it shall the Gentiles seek: and His rest shall be glorious." Isaiah 11:2-5, 10.

"Behold the Man whose name is the Branch; ... He shall build the temple of the Lord; and He shall bear the glory, and shall sit and rule upon His throne; and He shall be a priest upon His throne." Zechariah 6:12, 13.

A fountain was to be opened "for sin and for uncleanness" (Zechariah 13:1); the sons of men were to hear the blessed invitation: [696]

"Ho, everyone that thirsteth, come ye to the waters, And he that hath no money; come ye, buy, and eat; Yea, come, buy wine and milk Without money and without price.

"Wherefore do ye spend money for that which is not bread? And your labor for that which satisfieth not? Hearken diligently unto Me, and eat ye that which is good, And let your soul delight itself in fatness.

"Incline your ear, and come unto Me: Hear, and your soul shall live; And I will make an everlasting covenant with you, Even the sure mercies of David."

Isaiah 55:1-3.

To Israel the promise was made: "Behold, I have given Him for a witness to the people, a leader and commander to the people. Behold, thou shalt call a nation that thou knowest not, and nations that knew not thee shall run unto thee because of the Lord thy God, and for the Holy One of Israel; for He hath glorified thee." Verses 4, 5.

"I bring near My righteousness; it shall not be far off, and My salvation shall not tarry: and I will place salvation in Zion for Israel My glory." Isaiah 46:13.

In word and in deed the Messiah, during His earthly ministry, was to reveal to mankind the glory of God the Father. Every act of His life, every word spoken, every miracle wrought, was to make known to fallen humanity the infinite love of God.

"O Zion, that bringest good tidings, Get thee up into the high mountain; O Jerusalem, that bringest good tidings, Lift up thy voice with strength; Lift it up, be not afraid; Say unto the cities of Judah, Behold your God! [697]

"Behold, the Lord God will come with strong hand, And His arm shall rule for Him: Behold, His reward is with Him, And His work before Him. He shall feed His flock like a shepherd: He shall gather the lambs with His arm, And carry them in His bosom, And shall gently lead those that are with young."

Isaiah 40:9-11.

"And in that day shall the deaf hear the words of the Book, And the eyes of the blind shall see out of obscurity, and out of darkness. The meek also shall increase their joy in the Lord, And the poor among men shall rejoice in the Holy One of Israel."

"They also that erred in spirit shall come to understanding, And they that murmured shall learn doctrine."

Isaiah 29:18, 19, 24.

Thus, through patriarchs and prophets, as well as through types and symbols, God spoke to the world concerning the coming of a Deliverer from sin. A long line of inspired prophecy pointed to the advent of "the Desire of all nations." Haggai 2:7. Even the very place of His birth and the time of His appearance were minutely specified.

The Son of David must be born in David's city. Out of Bethlehem, said the prophet, "shall He come forth ... that is to be ruler in Israel; whose goings forth have been from of old, from the days of eternity." Micah 5:2, margin.

"And thou Bethlehem, land of Judah, Art in no wise least among the princes of Judah: For out of thee shall come forth a Governor, Which shall be Shepherd of My people Israel."

Matthew 2:6, R.V. [698]

The time of the first advent and of some of the chief events clustering about the Saviour's lifework was made known by the angel Gabriel to Daniel. "Seventy weeks," said the angel, "are determined upon thy people and upon thy holy city, to finish the transgression, and to make an end of sins, and to make reconciliation for iniquity, and to bring in everlasting righteousness, and to seal up the vision and prophecy, and to anoint the most holy." Daniel 9:24. A day in prophecy stands for a year. See Numbers 14:34; Ezekiel 4:6. The seventy weeks, or four hundred and ninety days, represent four hundred and ninety years. A starting point for this period is given: "Know therefore and understand, that from the going forth of the commandment to restore and to build Jerusalem unto the Messiah the Prince shall be seven weeks, and threescore and two weeks" (Daniel 9:25), sixty-nine weeks, or four hundred and eighty-three years. The commandment to restore and build [699] Jerusalem, as completed by the decree of Artaxerxes Longimanus, went into effect in the autumn of 457 B.C. See Ezra 6:14; 7:1, 9. From this time four hundred and eighty-three years extend to the autumn of A.D. 27. According to the prophecy, this period was to reach to the Messiah, the Anointed One. In A.D. 27, Jesus at His baptism received the anointing of the Holy Spirit and soon afterward began His ministry. Then the message was proclaimed, "The time is fulfilled." Mark 1:15.

Then, said the angel, "He shall confirm the covenant with many for one week [seven years]." For seven years after the Saviour entered on His ministry, the gospel was to be preached especially to the Jews; for three and a half years by Christ Himself, and afterward by the apostles. "In the midst of the week He shall cause the sacrifice and the oblation to cease." Daniel 9:27. In the spring of A.D. 31, Christ, the true Sacrifice, was offered on Calvary. Then the veil of the temple was rent in twain, showing that the sacredness and significance of the sacrificial service had departed. The time had come for the earthly sacrifice and oblation to cease.

The one week—seven years—ended in A.D. 34. Then by the stoning of Stephen the Jews finally sealed their rejection of the gospel; the disciples who were scattered abroad by persecution "went everywhere preaching the word" (Acts 8:4); and shortly after, Saul the persecutor was converted and became Paul the apostle to the Gentiles.

The many prophecies concerning the Saviour's advent led the Hebrews to live in an attitude of constant expectancy. [700] Many died in the faith, not having received the promises. But having seen them afar off, they believed and confessed that they were strangers and pilgrims on the earth. From the days of Enoch the promises repeated through patriarchs and prophets had kept alive the hope of His appearing.

Not at first had God revealed the exact time of the first advent; and even when the prophecy of Daniel made this known, not all rightly interpreted the message.

Century after century passed away; finally the voices of the prophets ceased. The hand of the oppressor was heavy upon Israel. As the Jews departed from God, faith grew dim, and hope well-nigh ceased to illuminate the future. The words of the prophets were uncomprehended by many; and those whose faith should have continued strong were ready to exclaim, "The days are prolonged, and every vision faileth." Ezekiel 12:22. But in heaven's council the hour for the coming of Christ had been determined; and "when the fullness of the time was come, God sent forth His Son, ... to redeem them that were under the law, that we might receive the adoption of sons." Galatians 4:4, 5.

Lessons must be given to humanity in the language of humanity. The Messenger of the covenant must speak. His voice must be heard in His own temple. He, the author of truth, must separate truth from the chaff of man's utterance, which had made it of no effect. The principles of God's government and the plan of redemption must be clearly defined. The lessons of the Old Testament must be fully set before men. [701]

When the Saviour finally appeared "in the likeness of men" (Philippians 2:7), and began His ministry of grace, Satan could but bruise the heel, while by every act of humiliation or suffering Christ was bruising the head of His adversary. The anguish that sin has brought was poured into the bosom of the Sinless; yet while Christ endured the contradiction of sinners against Himself, He was paying the debt for sinful man and breaking the bondage in which humanity had been held. Every pang of anguish, every insult, was working out the deliverance of the race.

Could Satan have induced Christ to yield to a single temptation, could he have led Him by one act or even thought to stain His perfect purity, the prince of darkness would have triumphed over man's Surety and would have gained the whole human family to himself. But while Satan could distress, he could not contaminate. He could cause agony, but not defilement. He made the life of Christ one long scene of conflict and trial, yet with every attack he was losing his hold upon humanity.

In the wilderness of temptation, in the Garden of Gethsemane, and on the cross, our Saviour measured weapons with the prince of darkness. His wounds became the trophies of His victory in behalf of the race. When Christ hung in agony upon the cross, while evil spirits rejoiced and evil men reviled, then indeed His heel was bruised by Satan. But that very act was crushing the serpent's head. Through death He destroyed "him that had the power of death, that is, the devil." Hebrews 2:14. This act decided the destiny of the rebel chief, and made forever sure the plan of [702] salvation. In death He gained the victory over its power; in rising again, He opened the gates of the grave to all His followers. In that last great contest we see fulfilled the prophecy, "It shall bruise thy head, and thou shall bruise His heel." Genesis 3:15.

"Beloved, now are we the sons of God, and it doth not yet appear what we shall be: but we know that, when He shall appear, we shall be like Him; for we shall see Him as He is." 1 John 3:2. Our Redeemer has opened the way, so that the most sinful, the most needy, the most oppressed and despised, may find access to the Father.

"O Lord, Thou art my God; I will exalt Thee, I will praise Thy name; For Thou hast done wonderful things; Thy counsels of old are faithfulness and truth."

Isaiah 25:1. [703]

Chapter 59

"The House of Israel"

In proclaiming the truths of the everlasting gospel to every nation, kindred, tongue, and people, God's church on earth today is fulfilling the ancient prophecy, "Israel shall blossom and bud, and fill the face of the world with fruit." Isaiah 27:6. The followers of Jesus, in co-operation with heavenly intelligences, are rapidly occupying the waste places of the earth; and, as the result of their labors, an abundant fruitage of precious souls is developing. Today, as never before, the dissemination of Bible truth by means of a consecrated church is bringing to the sons of men the benefits foreshadowed centuries ago in the promise to Abraham and to all Israel,—to God's church on earth in every age,—"I will bless thee, ... and thou shalt be a blessing." Genesis 12:2.

This promise of blessing should have met fulfillment in large measure during the centuries following the return of the Israelites from the lands of their captivity. It was God's [704] design that the whole earth be prepared for the first advent of Christ, even as today the way is preparing for His second coming. At the end of the years of humiliating exile, God graciously gave to His people Israel, through Zechariah, the assurance: "I am returned unto Zion, and will dwell in the midst of Jerusalem: and Jerusalem shall be called a city of truth; and the mountain of the Lord of hosts the holy mountain." And of His people He said, "Behold, ... I will be their God, in truth and in righteousness." Zechariah 8:3, 7, 8.

These promises were conditional on obedience. The sins that had characterized the Israelites prior to the captivity, were not to be repeated. "Execute true judgment," the Lord exhorted those who were engaged in rebuilding; "and show mercy and compassions every man to his brother: and oppress not the widow, nor the fatherless, the stranger, nor the poor; and let none of you imagine evil against his brother." "Speak ye every man the truth to his neighbor; execute the judgment of truth and peace in your gates." Zechariah 7:9, 10; 8:16.

Rich were the rewards, both temporal and spiritual, promised those who should put into practice these principles of righteousness. "The seed shall be prosperous," the Lord declared; "the vine shall give her fruit, and the ground shall give her increase, and the heavens shall give their dew; and I will cause the remnant of this people to possess all these things. And it shall come to pass, that as ye were a curse among the heathen, O house of Judah, and house of Israel; so I will save you, and ye shall be a blessing." Zechariah 8:12, 13. [705]

By the Babylonish captivity the Israelites were effectually cured of the worship of graven images. After their return, they gave much attention to religious instruction and to the study of that which had been written in the book of the law and in the prophets concerning the worship of the true God. The restoration of the temple enabled them to carry out fully the ritual services of the sanctuary. Under the leadership of Zerubbabel, of Ezra, and of Nehemiah they repeatedly covenanted to keep all the commandments and ordinances of Jehovah. The seasons of prosperity that followed gave ample evidence of God's willingness to accept and forgive, and yet with fatal shortsightedness they turned again and again from their glorious destiny and selfishly appropriated to themselves that which would have brought healing and spiritual life to countless multitudes.

This failure to fulfill the divine purpose was very apparent in Malachi's day. Sternly the Lord's messenger dealt with the evils that were robbing Israel of temporal prosperity and spiritual power. In his rebuke against transgressors the prophet spared neither priests nor people. "The burden of the word of the Lord to Israel" through Malachi was that the lessons of the past be not forgotten and that the covenant made by Jehovah with the house of Israel be kept with fidelity. Only by heartfelt repentance could the blessing of God be realized. "I pray you," the prophet pleaded, "beseech God that He will be gracious unto us." Malachi 1:1, 9.

Not by any temporary failure of Israel, however, was the plan of the ages for the redemption of mankind to be [706] frustrated. Those to whom the prophet was speaking might not heed the message given, but the purposes of Jehovah were nevertheless to move steadily forward to their complete fulfillment. "From the rising of the sun even unto the going down of the same," the Lord declared through His messenger, "My name shall be great among the Gentiles; and in every place incense shall be offered unto My name, and a pure offering: for My name shall be great among the heathen." Malachi 1:11.

The covenant of "life and peace" God had made with the sons of Levi—the covenant which, if kept, would have brought untold blessing—the Lord now offered to renew with those who once had been spiritual leaders, but who through transgression had become "contemptible and base before all the people." Malachi 2:5, 9.

Solemnly evildoers were warned of the day of judgment to come and of Jehovah's purpose to visit with swift destruction every transgressor. Yet none were left without hope; Malachi's prophecies of judgment were accompanied by invitations to the impenitent to make their peace with God. "Return unto Me," the Lord urged; "and I will return unto you." Malachi 3:7.

It seems as if every heart must respond to such an invitation. The God of heaven is pleading with His erring children to return to Him, that they may again co-operate with Him in carrying forward His work in the earth. The Lord holds out His hand to take the hand of Israel and to help them to the narrow path of self-denial and [707] self-sacrifice, to share with Him the heirship as sons of God. Will they be entreated? Will they discern their only hope?

How sad the record, that in Malachi's day the Israelites hesitated to yield their proud hearts in prompt and loving obedience and hearty co-operation! Self-vindication is apparent in their response, "Wherein shall we return?"

The Lord reveals to His people one of their special sins. "Will a man rob God?" He asks. "Yet ye have robbed Me." Still unconvicted of sin, the disobedient inquire, "Wherein have we robbed Thee?"

Definite indeed is the Lord's answer: "In tithes and offerings. Ye are cursed with a curse: for ye have robbed Me, even this whole nation. Bring ye all the tithes into the store-house, that there may be meat in Mine house, and prove Me now herewith, saith the Lord of hosts, if I will not open you the windows of heaven, and pour you out a blessing, that there shall not be room enough to receive it. And I will rebuke the devourer for your sakes, and he shall not destroy the fruits of your ground; neither shall your vine cast her fruit before the time in the field, saith the Lord of hosts. And all nations shall call you blessed: for ye shall be a delightsome land, saith the Lord of hosts." Verses 7-12.

God blesses the work of men's hands, that they may return to Him His portion. He gives them the sunshine and the rain; He causes vegetation to flourish; He gives health and ability to acquire means. Every blessing comes from His bountiful hand, and He desires men and women to show their gratitude by returning Him a portion in tithes [708] and offerings—in thank offerings, in freewill offerings, in trespass offerings. They are to devote their means to His service, that His vineyard may not remain a barren waste. They are to study what the Lord would do were He in their place. They are to take all difficult matters to Him in prayer. They are to reveal an unselfish interest in the building up of His work in all parts of the world.

Through messages such as those borne by Malachi, the last of the Old Testament prophets, as well as through oppression from heathen foes, the Israelites finally learned the lesson that true prosperity depends upon obedience to the law of God. But with many of the people, obedience was not the outflow of faith and love. Their motives were selfish. Outward service was rendered as a means of attaining to national greatness. The chosen people did not become the light of the world, but shut themselves away from the world as a safeguard against being seduced into idolatry. The restrictions which God had given, forbidding intermarriage between His people and the heathen, and prohibiting Israel from joining in the idolatrous practices of surrounding nations, were so perverted as to build up a wall of partition between the Israelites and all other peoples, thus shutting from others the very blessings which God had commissioned Israel to give to the world.

At the same time the Jews were, by their sins, separating themselves from God. They were unable to discern the deep spiritual significance of their symbolic service. In their self-righteousness they trusted to their own works, to the sacrifices and ordinances themselves, instead of relying upon [709] the merits of Him to whom all these things pointed. Thus "going about to establish their own righteousness" (Romans 10:3), they built themselves up in a self-sufficient formalism. Wanting the Spirit and grace of God, they tried to make up for the lack by a rigorous observance of religious ceremonies and rites. Not content with the ordinances which God Himself had appointed, they encumbered the divine commands with countless exactions of their own devising. The greater their distance from God, the more rigorous they were in the observance of these forms.

With all these minute and burdensome exactions it was a practical impossibility for the people to keep the law. The great principles of righteousness set forth in the Decalogue, and the glorious truths shadowed in the symbolic service, were alike obscured, buried under a mass of human tradition and enactment. Those who were really desirous of serving God, and who tried to observe the whole law as enjoined by the priests and rulers, groaned under a heavy burden.

As a nation, the people of Israel, while desiring the advent of the Messiah, were so far separated from God in heart and life that they could have no true conception of the character or mission of the promised Redeemer. Instead of desiring redemption from sin, and the glory and peace of holiness, their hearts were fixed upon deliverance from their national foes, and restoration to worldly power. They looked for Messiah to come as a conqueror, to break every yoke, and exalt Israel to dominion over all nations. Thus Satan had succeeded in preparing the hearts of the people to [710] reject the Saviour when He should appear. Their own pride of heart, and their false conceptions of His character and mission, would prevent them from honestly weighing the evidences of His Messiahship.

For more than a thousand years the Jewish people had waited the coming of the promised Saviour. Their brightest hopes had rested upon this event. For a thousand years, in song and prophecy, in temple rite and household prayer, His name had been enshrined; and yet when He came, they did not recognize Him as the Messiah for whom they had so long waited. "He came unto His own, and His own received Him not." John 1:11. To their world-loving hearts the Beloved of heaven was "as a root out of a dry ground." In their eyes He had "no form nor comeliness;" they discerned in Him no beauty that they should desire Him. Isaiah 53:2.

The whole life of Jesus of Nazareth among the Jewish people was a reproof to their selfishness, as revealed in their unwillingness to recognize the just claims of the Owner of the vineyard over which they had been placed as husbandmen. They hated His example of truthfulness and piety; and when the final test came, the test which meant obedience unto eternal life or disobedience unto eternal death, they rejected the Holy One of Israel and became responsible for His crucifixion on Calvary's cross.

In the parable of the vineyard, Christ near the close of His earthly ministry called the attention of the Jewish teachers to the rich blessings bestowed upon Israel, and in these showed God's claim to their obedience. Plainly He set [711] before them the glory of God's purpose, which through obedience they might have fulfilled. Withdrawing the veil from the future, He showed how, by failure to fulfill His purpose, the whole nation was forfeiting His blessing and bringing ruin upon itself.

"There was a certain householder," Christ said, "which planted a vineyard, and hedged it round about, and digged a wine press in it, and built a tower, and let it out to husbandmen, and went into a far country." Matthew 21:33.

Thus the Saviour referred to "the vineyard of the Lord of hosts," which the prophet Isaiah centuries before had declared to be "the house of Israel." Isaiah 5:7.

"And when the time of the fruit drew near," Christ continued, the owner of the vineyard "sent his servants to the husbandmen, that they might receive the fruits of it. And the husbandmen took his servants, and beat one, and killed another, and stoned another. Again, he sent other servants more than the first: and they did unto them likewise. But last of all he sent unto them his son, saying, They will reverence my son. But when the husbandmen saw the son, they said among themselves, This is the heir; come, let us kill him, and let us seize on his inheritance. And they caught him, and cast him out of the vineyard, and slew him."

Having portrayed before the priests their crowning act of wickedness, Christ now put to them the question, "When the lord therefore of the vineyard cometh, what will he do unto those husbandmen?" The priests had been following the narrative with deep interest; and without considering the relation of the subject to themselves, they joined [712] with the people in answering, "He will miserably destroy those wicked men, and will let out his vineyard unto other husbandmen, which shall render him the fruits in their seasons."

Unwittingly they had pronounced their own doom. Jesus looked upon them, and under His searching gaze they knew that He read the secrets of their hearts. His divinity flashed out before them with unmistakable power. They saw in the husbandmen a picture of themselves, and they involuntarily exclaimed, "God forbid!"

Solemnly and regretfully Christ asked: "Did ye never read in the Scriptures, The stone which the builders rejected, the same is become the head of the corner: this is the Lord's doing, and it is marvelous in our eyes? Therefore say I unto you, The kingdom of God shall be taken from you, and given to a nation bringing forth the fruits thereof. And whosoever shall fall on this stone shall be broken: but on whomsoever it shall fall, it will grind him to powder." Matthew 21:34-44.

Christ would have averted the doom of the Jewish nation if the people had received Him. But envy and jealousy made them implacable. They determined that they would not receive Jesus of Nazareth as the Messiah. They rejected the Light of the world, and henceforth their lives were surrounded with darkness as the darkness of midnight. The doom foretold came upon the Jewish nation. Their own fierce passions, uncontrolled, wrought their ruin. In their blind rage they destroyed one another. Their rebellious, stubborn pride brought upon them the wrath of their Roman [713] conquerors. Jerusalem was destroyed, the temple laid in ruins, and its site plowed like a field. The children of Judah perished by the most horrible forms of death. Millions were sold to serve as bondmen in heathen lands.

That which God purposed to do for the world through Israel, the chosen nation, He will finally accomplish through His church on earth today. He has "let out His vineyard [714] unto other husbandmen," even to His covenant-keeping people, who faithfully "render Him the fruits in their seasons." Never has the Lord been without true representatives on this earth who have made His interests their own. These witnesses for God are numbered among the spiritual Israel, and to them will be fulfilled all the covenant promises made by Jehovah to His ancient people.

Today the church of God is free to carry forward to completion the divine plan for the salvation of a lost race. For many centuries God's people suffered a restriction of their liberties. The preaching of the gospel in its purity was prohibited, and the severest of penalties were visited upon those who dared disobey the mandates of men. As a consequence, the Lord's great moral vineyard was almost wholly unoccupied. The people were deprived of the light of God's word. The darkness of error and superstition threatened to blot out a knowledge of true religion. God's church on earth was as verily in captivity during this long period of relentless persecution as were the children of Israel held captive in Babylon during the period of the exile.

But, thank God, His church is no longer in bondage. To spiritual Israel have been restored the privileges accorded the people of God at the time of their deliverance from Babylon. In every part of the earth, men and women are responding to the Heaven-sent message which John the revelator prophesied would be proclaimed prior to the second coming of Christ: "Fear God, and give glory to Him; for the hour of His judgment is come." Revelation 14:7. [715]

No longer have the hosts of evil power to keep the church captive; for "Babylon is fallen, is fallen, that great city," which hath "made all nations drink of the wine of the wrath of her fornication;" and to spiritual Israel is given the message, "Come out of her, My people, that ye be not partakers of her sins, and that ye receive not of her plagues." Verse 8; 18:4. As the captive exiles heeded the message, "Flee out of the midst of Babylon" (Jeremiah 51:6), and were restored to the Land of Promise, so those who fear God today are heeding the message to withdraw from spiritual Babylon, and soon they are to stand as trophies of divine grace in the earth made new, the heavenly Canaan.

In Malachi's day the mocking inquiry of the impenitent, "Where is the God of judgment?" met with the solemn response: "The Lord ... shall suddenly come to His temple, even the Messenger of the covenant.... But who may abide the day of His coming? and who shall stand when He appeareth? for He is like a refiner's fire, and like fullers' soap: and He shall sit as a refiner and purifier of silver: and He shall purify the sons of Levi, and purge them as gold and silver, that they may offer unto the Lord an offering in righteousness. Then shall the offering of Judah and Jerusalem be pleasant unto the Lord, as in the days of old, and as in former years." Malachi 2:17; 3:1-4.

When the promised Messiah was about to appear, the message of the forerunner of Christ was: Repent, publicans and sinners; repent, Pharisees and Sadducees; "for the kingdom of heaven is at hand." Matthew 3:2. [716]

Today, in the spirit and power of Elias and of John the Baptist, messengers of God's appointment are calling the attention of a judgment-bound world to the solemn events soon to take place in connection with the closing hours of probation and the appearance of Christ Jesus as King of kings and Lord of lords. Soon every man is to be judged for the deeds done in the body. The hour of God's judgment has come, and upon the members of His church on earth rests the solemn responsibility of giving warning to those who are standing as it were on the very brink of eternal ruin. To every human being in the wide world who will give heed must be made plain the principles at stake in the great controversy being waged, principles upon which hang the destinies of all mankind.

In these final hours of probation for the sons of men, when the fate of every soul is so soon to be decided forever, the Lord of heaven and earth expects His church to arouse to action as never before. Those who have been made free in Christ through a knowledge of precious truth, are regarded by the Lord Jesus as His chosen ones, favored above all other people on the face of the earth; and He is counting on them to show forth the praises of Him who hath called them out of darkness into marvelous light. The blessings which are so liberally bestowed are to be communicated to others. The good news of salvation is to go to every nation, kindred, tongue, and people.

In the visions of the prophets of old the Lord of glory was represented as bestowing special light upon His church [717] in the days of darkness and unbelief preceding His second coming. As the Sun of Righteousness, He was to arise upon His church, "with healing in

His wings." Malachi 4:2. And from every true disciple was to be diffused an influence for life, courage, helpfulness, and true healing.

The coming of Christ will take place in the darkest period of this earth's history. The days of Noah and of Lot picture the condition of the world just before the coming of the Son of man. The Scriptures, pointing forward to this time, declare that Satan will work with all power and "with all deceivableness of unrighteousness." 2 Thessalonians 2:9, 10. His working is plainly revealed by the rapidly increasing darkness, the multitudinous errors, heresies, and delusions of these last days. Not only is Satan leading the world captive, but his deceptions are leavening the professed churches of our Lord Jesus Christ. The great apostasy will develop into darkness deep as midnight. To God's people it will be a night of trial, a night of weeping, a night of persecution for the truth's sake. But out of that night of darkness God's light will shine.

He causes "the light to shine out of darkness." 2 Corinthians 4:6. When "the earth was without form, and void; and darkness was upon the face of the deep," "the Spirit of God moved upon the face of the waters. And God said, Let there be light: and there was light." Genesis 1:2, 3. So in the night of spiritual darkness, God's word goes forth, "Let there be light." To His people He says, "Arise, shine; for thy light is come, and the glory of the Lord is risen upon thee." Isaiah 60:1. [718]

"Behold," says the Scripture, "the darkness shall cover the earth, and gross darkness the people: but the Lord shall arise upon thee, and His glory shall be seen upon thee." Verse 2. Christ, the outshining of the Father's glory, came to the world as its light. He came to represent God to men, and of Him it is written that He was anointed "with the Holy Ghost and with power," and "went about doing good." Acts 10:38. In the synagogue at Nazareth He said, "The Spirit of the Lord is upon Me, because He hath anointed Me to preach the gospel to the poor; He hath sent Me to heal the brokenhearted, to preach deliverance to the captives, and recovering of sight to the blind, to set at liberty them that are bruised, to preach the acceptable year of the Lord." Luke 4:18, 19. This was the work He commissioned His disciples to do. "Ye are the light of the world," He said. "Let your light so shine before men, that they may see your good works, and glorify your Father which is in heaven." Matthew 5:14, 16.

This is the work which the prophet Isaiah describes when he says: "Is it not to deal thy bread to the hungry, and that thou bring the poor that are cast out to thy house? when thou seest the naked, that thou cover him; and that thou hide not thyself from thine own flesh? Then shall thy light break forth as the morning, and thine health shall spring forth speedily: and thy righteousness shall go before thee; the glory of the Lord shall be thy rearward." Isaiah 58:7, 8.

Thus in the night of spiritual darkness God's glory is to shine forth through His church in lifting up the bowed down and comforting those that mourn. [719]

All around us are heard the wails of a world's sorrow. On every hand are the needy and distressed. It is ours to aid in relieving and softening life's hardships and misery. The wants of the soul only the love of Christ can satisfy. If Christ is abiding in us, our hearts will be full of divine sympathy. The sealed fountains of earnest, Christlike love will be unsealed.

There are many from whom hope has departed. Bring back the sunshine to them. Many have lost their courage. Speak to them words of cheer. Pray for them. There are those who need the bread of life. Read to them from the word of God. Upon many is a soul sickness which no earthly balm can reach nor physician heal. Pray for these souls. Bring them to Jesus. Tell them that there is a balm in Gilead and a Physician there.

Light is a blessing, a universal blessing, pouring forth its treasures on a world unthankful, unholy, demoralized. So it is with the light of the Sun of Righteousness. The whole earth, wrapped as it is in the darkness of sin and sorrow and pain, is to be lighted with the knowledge of God's love. From no sect, rank, or class of people is the light shining from heaven's throne to be excluded.

The message of hope and mercy is to be carried to the ends of the earth. Whosoever will, may reach forth and take hold of God's strength and make peace with Him, and he shall make peace. No longer are the heathen to be wrapped in midnight darkness. The gloom is to disappear before the bright beams of the Sun of Righteousness. [720]

Christ has made every provision that His church shall be a transformed body, illumined with the Light of the world, possessing the glory of Immanuel. It is His purpose that every Christian shall be surrounded with a spiritual atmosphere of light and peace. He desires that we shall reveal His own joy in our lives.

"Arise, shine; for thy light is come, and the glory of the Lord is risen upon thee." Isaiah 60:1. Christ is coming with power and great glory. He is coming with His own glory and with the glory of the Father. And the holy angels will attend Him on His way. While all the world is plunged in darkness, there will be light in every dwelling of the saints. They will catch the first light of His second appearing. The unsullied light will shine from His splendor, and Christ the Redeemer will be admired by all who have served Him. While the wicked flee, Christ's followers will rejoice in His presence.

Then it is that the redeemed from among men will receive their promised inheritance. Thus God's purpose for Israel will meet with literal fulfillment. That which God purposes, man is powerless to disannul. Even amid the working of evil, God's purposes have been moving steadily forward to their accomplishment. It was thus with the house of Israel throughout the history of the divided monarchy; it is thus with spiritual Israel today.

The seer of Patmos, looking down through the ages to the time of this restoration of Israel in the earth made new, testified:

"I beheld, and lo, a great multitude, which no man could number, of all nations, and kindreds, and people, and [721] tongues, stood before the throne, and before the Lamb, clothed with white robes, and palms in their hands; and cried with a loud voice, saying, Salvation to our God which sitteth upon the throne, and unto the Lamb.

"And all the angels stood round about the throne, and about the elders and the four beasts ["living creatures," R.V.], and fell before the throne on their faces, and worshiped God, saying, Amen: Blessing, and glory, and wisdom, and thanksgiving, and honor, and power, and might, be unto our God forever and ever."

"And I heard as it were the voice of a great multitude, and as the voice of many waters, and as the voice of mighty thunderings, saying, Alleluia: for the Lord God omnipotent reigneth. Let us be glad and rejoice, and give honor to Him." "He is Lord of lords, and King of kings:

and they that are with Him are called, and chosen, and faithful." Revelation 7:9-12; 19:6, 7; Revelation 17:14. [722]

Chapter 60

Visions of Future Glory

In the darkest days of her long conflict with evil, the church of God has been given revelations of the eternal purpose of Jehovah. His people have been permitted to look beyond the trials of the present to the triumphs of the future, when, the warfare having been accomplished, the redeemed will enter into possession of the promised land. These visions of future glory, scenes pictured by the hand of God, should be dear to His church today, when the controversy of the ages is rapidly closing and the promised blessings are soon to be realized in all their fullness.

Many were the messages of comfort given the church by the prophets of old. "Comfort ye, comfort ye My people" (Isaiah 40:1), was Isaiah's commission from God; and with the commission were given wonderful visions that have been the believers' hope and joy through all the centuries that have followed. Despised of men, persecuted, forsaken, God's children in every age have nevertheless [723] been sustained by His sure promises. By faith they have looked forward to the time when He will fulfill to His church the assurance, "I will make thee an eternal excellency, a joy of many generations." Isaiah 60:15.

Often the church militant is called upon to suffer trial and affliction; for not without severe conflict is the church to triumph. "The bread of adversity," "the water of affliction" (Isaiah 30:20), these are the common lot of all; but none who put their trust in the One mighty to deliver will be utterly overwhelmed. "Thus saith the Lord that created thee, O Jacob, and He that formed thee, O Israel, Fear not: for I have redeemed thee, I have called thee by thy name, thou art Mine. When thou passest through the waters, I will be with thee; and through the rivers, they shall not overflow thee: when thou walkest through the fire, thou shalt not be burned; neither shall the flame kindle upon thee. For I am the Lord thy God, the Holy One of Israel, thy Saviour: I gave Egypt for thy ransom, Ethiopia and Seba for thee. Since thou wast precious in My sight, thou hast been honorable, and I have loved thee: therefore will I give men for thee, and people for thy life." Isaiah 43:1-4.

There is forgiveness with God; there is acceptance full and free through the merits of Jesus, our crucified and risen Lord. Isaiah heard the Lord declaring to His chosen ones: "I, even I, am He that blotteth out thy transgressions for Mine own sake, and will not remember thy sins. Put Me in remembrance: let us plead together: declare thou, that thou mayest be justified." "Thou shalt know that I the Lord [724] am thy Saviour and thy Redeemer, the Mighty One of Jacob." Verses 25, 26; 60:16.

"The rebuke of His people shall He take away," the prophet declared. "They shall call them, The holy people, The redeemed of the Lord." He hath appointed "to give unto them beauty for ashes, the oil of joy for mourning, the garment of praise for the spirit of heaviness; that they might be called trees of righteousness, the planting of the Lord, that He might be glorified."

"Awake, awake; put on thy strength, O Zion; Put on thy beautiful garments, O Jerusalem, the Holy City: For henceforth there shall no more come unto thee the uncircumcised and the unclean.

"Shake thyself from the dust; Arise, and sit down, O Jerusalem: Loose thyself from the bands of thy neck, O captive daughter of Zion."

"O thou afflicted, tossed with tempest, and not comforted, Behold, I will lay thy stones with fair colors, And lay thy foundations with sapphires.

"And I will make thy windows of agates. And thy gates of carbuncles, And all thy borders of pleasant stones.

"And all thy children shall be taught of the Lord; And great shall be the peace of thy children. In righteousness shalt thou be established:

"Thou shalt be far from oppression; for thou shalt not fear: And from terror; for it shall not come near thee. Behold, they shall surely gather together, but not by Me: Whosoever shall gather together against thee shall fall for thy sake.... [725]

"No weapon that is formed against thee shall prosper; And every tongue that shall rise against thee in judgment thou shalt condemn. This is the heritage of the servants of the Lord, And their righteousness is of Me, saith the Lord."

Isaiah 25:8; 62:12; Isaiah 61:3; 52:1, 2; Isaiah 54:11-17.

Clad in the armor of Christ's righteousness, the church is to enter upon her final conflict. "Fair as the moon, clear as the sun, and terrible as an army with banners" (Song of Solomon 6:10), she is to go forth into all the world, conquering and to conquer.

The darkest hour of the church's struggle with the powers of evil is that which immediately precedes the day of her final deliverance. But none who trust in God need fear; for "when the blast of the terrible ones is as a storm against the wall," God will be to His church "a refuge from the storm." Isaiah 25:4.

In that day only the righteous are promised deliverance. "The sinners in Zion are afraid; fearfulness hath surprised the hypocrites. Who among us shall dwell with the devouring fire? who among us shall dwell with everlasting burnings? He that walketh righteously, and speaketh uprightly; he that despiseth the gain of oppressions, that shaketh his hands from holding of bribes, that stoppeth his ears from hearing of blood, and shutteth his eyes from seeing evil; he shall dwell on high: his place of defense shall be the munitions of rocks: bread shall be given him; his waters shall be sure." Isaiah 33:14-16.

The word of the Lord to His faithful ones is: "Come, My people, enter thou into thy chambers, and shut thy [726] doors about thee: hide thyself as it were for a little moment, until the indignation be overpast. For, behold, the Lord cometh out of His place to punish the inhabitants of the earth for their iniquity." Isaiah 26:20, 21.

In visions of the great judgment day the inspired messengers of Jehovah were given glimpses of the consternation of those unprepared to meet their Lord in peace.

"Behold, the Lord maketh the earth empty, and maketh it waste, and turneth it upside down, and scattereth abroad the inhabitants thereof; ... because they have transgressed the laws, changed the ordinance, broken the everlasting covenant. Therefore hath the curse devoured the earth, and they that dwell therein are desolate.... The mirth of tabrets ceaseth, the noise of them that rejoice endeth, the joy of the harp ceaseth." Isaiah 24:1-8.

"Alas for the day! for the day of the Lord is at hand, and as a destruction from the Almighty shall it come.... The seed is rotten under their clods, the garners are laid desolate, the barns are broken down; for the corn is withered. How do the beasts groan! the herds of cattle are perplexed, because they have no pasture; yea, the flocks of sheep are made desolate." "The vine is dried up, and the fig tree languisheth; the pomegranate tree, the palm tree also, and the apple tree, even all the trees of the field, are withered: because joy is withered away from the sons of men." Joel 1:15-18, 12.

"I am pained at my very heart," Jeremiah exclaims as he beholds the desolations wrought during the closing scenes of earth's history. "I cannot hold my peace, because [727] thou hast heard, O my soul, the sound of the trumpet, the alarm of war. Destruction upon destruction is cried; for the whole land is spoiled." Jeremiah 4:19, 20.

"The loftiness of man shall be bowed down," declares Isaiah of the day of God's vengeance, "and the haughtiness of men shall be made low: and the Lord alone shall be exalted in that day. And the idols He shall utterly abolish.... In that day a man shall cast his idols of silver, and his idols of gold, which they made each one for himself to worship, to the moles and to the bats; to go into the clefts of the rocks, and into the tops of the ragged rocks, for fear of the Lord, and for the glory of His majesty, when He ariseth to shake terribly the earth." Isaiah 2:17-21.

Of those times of transition, when the pride of man shall be laid low, Jeremiah testifies: "I beheld the earth, and, lo, it was without form, and void; and the heavens, and they had no light. I beheld the mountains, and, lo, they trembled, and all the hills moved lightly. I beheld, and, lo, there was no man, and all the birds of the heavens were fled. I beheld, and, lo, the fruitful place was a wilderness, and all the cities thereof were broken down." "Alas! for that day is great, so that none is like it: it is even the time of Jacob's trouble; but he shall be saved out of it." Jeremiah 4:23-26; 30:7.

The day of wrath to the enemies of God is the day of final deliverance to His church. The prophet declares:

"Strengthen ye the weak hands, And confirm the feeble knees. [728]

Say to them that are of a fearful heart, Be strong, fear not: Behold, your God will come with vengeance, Even God with a recompense; He will come and save you."

"He will swallow up death in victory; and the Lord God will wipe away tears from off all faces; and the rebuke of His people shall He take away from off all the earth: for the Lord hath spoken it." Isaiah 35:3, 4; 25:8. And as the prophet beholds the Lord of glory descending from heaven with all the holy angels, to gather the remnant church from among the nations of earth, he hears the waiting ones unite in the exultant cry:

"Lo, this is our God; We have waited for Him, And He will save us: This is the Lord; We have waited for Him, We will be glad and rejoice in His salvation."

Isaiah 25:9.

The voice of the Son of God is heard calling forth the sleeping saints, and as the prophet beholds them coming from the prison house of death, he exclaims, "Thy dead men shall live, together with my dead body shall they arise. Awake and sing, ye that dwell in dust: for thy dew is as the dew of herbs, and the earth shall cast out the dead."

"Then the eyes of the blind shall be opened, And the ears of the deaf shall be unstopped. Then shall the lame man leap as an hart, And the tongue of the dumb sing."

Isaiah 26:19; 35:5, 6. [729]

In the visions of the prophet, those who have triumphed over sin and the grave are now seen happy in the presence of their Maker, talking freely with Him as man talked with God in the beginning. "Be ye glad," the Lord bids them, "and rejoice forever in that which I create: for, behold, I create Jerusalem a rejoicing, and her people a joy. And I will rejoice in Jerusalem, and joy in My people: and the voice of weeping shall be no more heard in her, nor the voice of crying." "The inhabitant shall not say, I am sick: the people that dwell therein shall be forgiven their iniquity."

"In the wilderness shall waters break out, And streams in the desert. And the parched ground shall become a pool, And the thirsty land springs of water."

"Instead of the thorn shall come up the fir tree, And instead of the brier shall come up the myrtle tree."

"And an highway shall be there, and a way, And it shall be called The way of holiness; The unclean shall not pass over it; But it shall be for those: The wayfaring men, though fools, shall not err therein."

"Speak ye comfortably to Jerusalem, and cry unto her, that her warfare is accomplished, that her iniquity is pardoned: for she hath received of the Lord's hand double for all her sins." Isaiah 65:18, 19; 33:24; 35:6, 7; 55:13; 35:8; 40:2.

As the prophet beholds the redeemed dwelling in the City of God, free from sin and from all marks of the curse, in rapture he exclaims, "Rejoice ye with Jerusalem, and be glad with her, all ye that love her: rejoice for joy with her." [730]

"Violence shall no more be heard in thy land, Wasting nor destruction within thy borders; But thou shalt call thy walls Salvation, And thy gates Praise.

"The sun shall be no more thy light by day; Neither for brightness shall the moon give light unto thee: But the Lord shall be unto thee an everlasting light, And thy God thy glory.

"Thy sun shall no more go down; Neither shall thy moon withdraw itself: For the Lord shall be thine everlasting light, And the days of thy mourning shall be ended.

"Thy people also shall be all righteous: They shall inherit the land forever, The branch of My planting, The work of My hands, That I may be glorified."

Isaiah 66:10; 60:18-21.

The prophet caught the sound of music there, and song, such music and song as, save in the visions of God, no mortal ear has heard or mind conceived. "The ransomed of the Lord shall return, and come to Zion with songs and everlasting joy upon their heads: they shall obtain joy and gladness, and sorrow and sighing shall flee away." "Joy and gladness shall be found therein, thanksgiving, and the voice of melody." "As well the singers as the players on instruments shall be there." "They shall lift up their voice, they shall sing for the majesty of the Lord." Isaiah 35:10; 51:3; Psalm 87:7; Isaiah 24:14.

In the earth made new, the redeemed will engage in the occupations and pleasures that brought happiness to Adam and Eve in the beginning. The Eden life will be [731] lived, the life in garden and field. "They shall build houses, and inhabit them; and they shall plant vineyards, and eat the fruit of them. They shall not build, and another inhabit; they shall not plant, and another eat: for as the days of a tree are the days of My people, and Mine elect shall long enjoy the work of their hands." Isaiah 65:21, 22.

There every power will be developed, every capability increased. The grandest enterprises will be carried forward, the loftiest aspirations will be reached, the highest ambitions realized. And still there will appear new heights to surmount, new wonders to admire, new truths to comprehend, fresh objects of study to call forth the powers of body and mind and soul.

The prophets to whom these great scenes were revealed longed to understand their full import. They "inquired and searched diligently: ... searching what, or what manner of time the Spirit of Christ which was in them did signify.... Unto whom it was revealed, that not unto themselves, but unto us they did minister the things, which are now reported unto you." 1 Peter 1:10-12.

To us who are standing on the very verge of their fulfillment, of what deep moment, what living interest, are these delineations of the things to come—events for which, since our first parents turned their steps from Eden, God's children have watched and waited, longed and prayed!

Fellow pilgrim, we are still amid the shadows and turmoil of earthly activities; but soon our Saviour is to appear to bring deliverance and rest. Let us by faith behold the blessed hereafter as pictured by the hand of God. He who [732] died for the sins of the world is opening wide the gates of Paradise to all who believe on Him. Soon the battle will have been fought, the victory won. Soon we shall see Him in whom our hopes of eternal life are centered. And in His presence the trials and sufferings of this life will seem as nothingness. The former things "shall not be remembered, nor come into mind." "Cast not away therefore your confidence, which hath great recompense of reward. For ye have need of patience, that, after ye have done the will of God, ye might receive the promise. For yet a little while, and He that shall come will come, and will not tarry." "Israel shall be saved ... with an everlasting salvation: ye shall not be ashamed nor confounded world without end." Isaiah 65:17; Hebrews 10:35-37; Isaiah 45:17.

Look up, look up, and let your faith continually increase. Let this faith guide you along the narrow path that leads through the gates of the city into the great beyond, the wide, unbounded future of glory that is for the redeemed. "Be patient therefore, brethren, unto the coming of the Lord. Behold, the husbandman waiteth for the precious fruit of the earth, and hath long patience for it, until he receive the early and latter rain. Be ye also patient; stablish your hearts: for the coming of the Lord draweth nigh." James 5:7, 8.

The nations of the saved will know no other law than the law of heaven. All will be a happy, united family, clothed with the garments of praise and thanksgiving. Over the scene the morning stars will sing together, and the sons [733] of God will shout for joy, while God and Christ will unite in proclaiming. "There shall be no more sin, neither shall there be any more death."

"And it shall come to pass, that from one new moon to another, and from one Sabbath to another, shall all flesh come to worship before Me, saith the Lord." "The glory of the Lord shall be revealed, and all flesh shall see it together." "The Lord God will cause righteousness and praise to spring forth before all the nations." "In that day shall the Lord of hosts be for a crown of glory, and for a diadem of beauty, unto the residue of His people."

"The Lord shall comfort Zion: He will comfort all her waste places; and He will make her wilderness like Eden, and her desert like the garden of the Lord." "The glory of Lebanon shall be given unto it, the excellency of Carmel and Sharon." "Thou shalt no more be termed Forsaken; neither shall thy land any more be termed Desolate: but thou shalt be called My Delight, and thy land Beulah.... As the bridegroom rejoiceth over the bride, so shall thy God rejoice over thee." Isaiah 66:23; 40:5; Isaiah 61:11; 28:5; Isaiah 51:3; 35:2; Isaiah 62:4, 5, margin.